Fit to Be Citizens?

AMERICAN CROSSROADS

Edited by Earl Lewis, George Lipsitz, Peggy Pascoe, George Sánchez, and Dana Takagi

Fit to Be Citizens?

*Public Health and Race in Los Angeles,
1879–1939*

Natalia Molina

UNIVERSITY OF CALIFORNIA PRESS
Berkeley · Los Angeles · London

University of California Press, one of the most
distinguished university presses in the United States,
enriches lives around the world by advancing
scholarship in the humanities, social sciences, and
natural sciences. Its activities are supported by the UC
Press Foundation and by philanthropic contributions
from individuals and institutions. For more
information, visit www.ucpress.edu.

University of California Press
Berkeley and Los Angeles, California

University of California Press, Ltd.
London, England

Library of Congress Cataloging-in-Publication Data

Molina, Natalia.
    Fit to be citizens? : public health and race in Los
Angeles, 1879–1939 / Natalia Molina.
        p.   cm. — (American crossroads ; 20)
    Includes bibliographical references and index.
    ISBN 0-520-24648-9 (cloth : alk. paper).
    ISBN 0-520-24649-7 (pbk. : alk. paper)
    1. Immigrants—Health and hygiene—California—
Los Angeles—History.   2. Asian Americans—Health
and hygiene—California—Los Angeles—History.
3. Mexican Americans—Health and hygiene—
California—Los Angeles—History.   4. Public health—
California—Los Angeles—History.   5. Los Angeles
(Calif.)—Race relations—History.   I. Title.   II. Series.

RA448.4.M65   2006
362.1'0979494—DC22   2005016385

Manufactured in the United States of America
15   14   13   12   11   10   09   08   07   06
10   9   8   7   6   5   4   3   2   1

This book is printed on New Leaf EcoBook 60,
containing 60% post-consumer waste, processed
chlorine free; 30% de-inked recycled fiber, elemental
chlorine free; and 10% FSC-certified virgin fiber, totally
chlorine free. EcoBook 60 is acid-free and meets the
minimum requirements of ANSI/ASTM D5634-01
(Permanence of Paper).

To my parents, Mary Molina and Héctor Molina

Contents

Illustrations

Acknowledgments

I have been blessed to work with many smart and generous people while writing this book. Like many historical monographs, this one started as a dissertation. I learned a great deal from my course work and conversations with professors and graduate students at the University of Michigan. I have to thank George Sánchez, who has been a good friend and mentor to me since I was an undergraduate at the University of California, Los Angeles. He has always helped me make more thoughtful connections in my work, through both our conversations and his scholarship. Maria Montoya served as my dissertation co-chair. Her intellectual insights, professional advice, and generous spirit have been invaluable. Conversations I had with Elsa Barkley-Brown, Carroll Smith-Rosenberg, and Roger Rouse still echo through my mind, adding unique perspectives to the work. Estévan Rael y Gálvez, John McKiernan-Gonzalez, Adrián Burgos, and Pablo Mitchell helped me through those years and remain my friends and colleagues today.

The Ethnic Studies Department at the University of California, San Diego (UCSD), the department I am privileged to call home, is as much an intellectual springboard as it is a workplace. I have learned greatly from each and every one of my colleagues in the department and am grateful to them all. The conversations we have during lectures, faculty meetings, and chance encounters in the hallways have clearly shaped this book. I would like to give a special thanks to Ramón Gutiérrez, who has served as my official mentor at UCSD. Ramón his given generously of his time, advice, and friendship to help me. He has helped me think more deeply about issues of race and ethnicity as well as adapt to academic life. Yen Le Espiritu and Ross Frank are my office "neighbors" and are always there for a friendly visit or to help in any way that they can. I would also like to thank Charles Briggs and George Lipsitz, now at the University of California, Berkeley, and the University of California, Santa Cruz, respectively, who were natural allies given our research and teaching interests and commitment to social justice. Charles read the entire dissertation at an important time, just as I began my revisions, and helped give me new direction. Charles was instrumental in bringing together a community interested in race, health, and inequality, with scholars from both on and off campus. Charles Briggs, Nayan Shah, and Steve Epstein each provided their support and comments in portions of the book through participation in our reading group. I have benefited tremendously from conversations with all of them over the years. This book would have taken a lot longer to write and it would not be as good without George Lipsitz's thought-provoking comments and careful line-by-line reading of the manuscript, not just once but twice. He urged me to make broader connections and to push my arguments, and he provided a road map. I am deeply grateful to him. I would also like to thank David Gutiérrez, who encouraged me to rewrite the epilogue and pointed me in the right direction.

During 2003–4, I received a Ford Post-Doctoral Fellowship. The fellowship gave me time away from my teaching responsibilities and allowed me to finish my revisions of the manuscript, for which I am very grateful. But you need much more than time to write a book. You need advice and direction. Even though I was already well prepared with the comments I had received from friends and colleagues, I was very fortunate that Vicki Ruiz agreed to be my mentor for the fellowship year, and I benefited from her advice tremendously. She helped me in ways I never imagined possible that far surpass the scope of this book.

I would also like to thank those whom I met along the way and who offered their help and support. David Sloane and Emily Abel generously offered to read the entire dissertation as I prepared to revise it into a book manuscript and offered their expertise in public health, Los Angeles, and crafting a compelling narrative. Kelly Lytle Hernández and I met and exchanged chapters; my work is better for knowing hers and for the insight she provided into her own writing process. I turned to Miroslava Chávez-García, Ernie Chávez, Jose Alamillo, Juan Mah y

Busch, and Danny Widener when I needed help with the writing process, and sometimes as well as when writing was the last thing I wanted to talk about. Clark Davis and Cheryl Koos shared their knowledge and experience with me, as well as a love for LA's culinary riches.

Many archivists and librarians helped me find proverbial needles in haystacks as I researched this project: Jill Cogen at the Huntington Library; Jay Jones and the former head archivist, Hynda Rudd, at the Los Angeles City Archives; Bruce Crouchet at the Records of the Los Angeles County Board of Supervisors; Dace Taube at the University of Southern California's Regional History Collection; Rod Ross at the National Archives in Washington, D.C.; and Vicki Williamson at UCSD.

There are no public health archives in Los Angeles, nor does Los Angeles County even have its own archive. This meant that research on one topic or event often required numerous research trips to several archives. This book, therefore, could not have been written without generous financial support. I received a Rockefeller Post-Doctoral Fellowship through the Center for the Study of Race and Ethnicity at the University of California, San Diego; a Haynes Foundation Research Fellowship at the Huntington Library; research money for trips to Mexico City, Washington, D.C., and Los Angeles from UCSD's Academic Senate; and summer support for research assistants through the Center for the Study of Race and Ethnicity at the University of California, San Diego. To this end, I would like to thank Tere Cesena, Faye Caronan, Blu Barnd, and Briseida Elenes, who not only helped with the research but ended up sharing my enthusiasm about it as well and offering many helpful suggestions. Of course, original research is only as good as the story you can tell about it, and I have Katherine Mooney and Ian Fusselman to thank for helping me to articulate my ideas and arguments as clearly as possible. I would also like to thank Neils Hooper, my editor, for making the publishing process just a little more pleasant.

My family—*las familias* Tavares, Pack, Porras, Diaz, Taylor, and Molina—and friends—the Montez-Chaidez-Berrones and Gutierrez-Reza-Martinez-Valdes families—make L.A. much more than a place of study. They make it my home. I am especially grateful to my parents, Mary Molina and Héctor Molina, and my brother, David Porras, who have always given me unconditional support. David also makes sure academic life never makes me "soft." When doing research in L.A., I stay with my mom. In the morning, before heading off to the archives, I go next door to my Tía Vicky's house for *café*. Often the neighbors and other family members come over as well. The stories told around my Tía Vicky's kitchen table were my introduction to, and remain my favorite part of, history and storytelling.

Ian Fusselman has supported me in so many ways in this project that he deserves an honorary PhD in ethnic studies at the very least. Michael Charles Molina did little to help me rethink the history of race and Los Angeles; instead, he helped this historian to look forward to the future.

Introduction

Health Officer Dr. Walter Lindley assured city residents in 1879 that Los Angeles had "everything that God could give" a city.[1] Among L.A.'s many virtues, the doctor emphasized "the health giving sun [present] almost every day in the year . . . the ocean breeze just properly tempered by hills and orange groves . . . pure water pouring down from a mountain stream [and] . . . the most equable temperature in the civilized world."[2] Such healthful abundance, however, did not lessen the need for the services of the city's chief health officer and his fledgling department. In stressing the importance of improving sanitary conditions in Los Angeles, he called for the construction of a municipal sewer system and appealed to the city council to eradicate Chinatown, "that rotten spot [that pollutes] the air we breathe and poisons the water we drink."[3]

And so began what became a long tradition among city health officials of tracing any blemish on the pristine image of Los Angeles— including all forms of disease and any manner of disorder—to the city's marginalized communities. As the chapters that follow will show, between 1879 and 1939, areas home to L.A.'s Chinese, Japanese, and Mexican populations were separately and serially targeted as "rotten spots." Armed with institutional power buttressed and legitimated by the language of "scientific objectivity," public health officials developed discourses that attributed the serious health problems confronting these minorities to purported deficiencies in the groups' biological capacities and cultural practices. Thus, from the start, Los Angeles health officials' efforts to promote the reputation of the city as modern and healthful were interwoven with their role as local arbiters of the meanings of race and racial identities.

Portraying people of Chinese, Mexican, and Japanese ancestry in Los Angeles as threats to public health and civic well-being obscured the real causes of communicable disease and illness—inadequate medical care, exposure to raw sewage, and malnutrition. Misled by their own racial assumptions, health officials betrayed their institution's mission. They devoted inordinate attention and disproportionate effort toward policing racial groups while neglecting the dangers posed by the incidence of communicable disease among the rest of the city's residents. Issues of race, class, and gender were considered in all aspects of health officials' work, from identifying and defining problems, to developing preventative health care programs, to handling disease outbreaks. Disease itself was defined as much by sociocultural beliefs in the inherent uncleanliness of immigrants and nonwhites as by biological explanations. Such definitions effectively stigmatized entire populations of already-marginalized groups in the city.

Perhaps most important in the long term was the public health department's gatekeeper role. Indeed, health and hygiene norms increasingly became standards for "Americanness," and health officers helped determine who was considered part of the body politic. They had the power to restrict people's sense of social membership and shape their relationship to the nation-state. As the historian Suellen Hoy argues, "[C]leanliness became something more than a way to prevent epidemics and make cities livable—it became a route to citizenship, to becoming American. It was, in fact, confrontation with racial and cultural outsiders that transformed cleanliness from a public health concern into a moral and patriotic one."[4] It was health officers, for example, who had responsibility for deciding who was healthy enough to work or attend public school. Public health ordinances dictated where Chinese fruit and vegetable vendors could establish businesses and even prescribed the architectural style of the produce markets. They determined when Mexican railroad laborers could leave their work camps and where Japanese residents could seek institutionalized health care. They approached these communities, which they considered a "menace,"[5] with the attitude that they needed to "safeguard the public" against them.[6]

City and county public health officials in Los Angeles consistently failed to distinguish between U.S.-born and foreign-born individuals in the Chinese, Japanese, and Mexican communities (even *Californios,* those Mexicans who had lived in California when it was still Mexico), thus marking all members of these groups as permanently "foreign."[7] Suspended indefinitely in this "not-yet-American" state, Japanese, Chinese, and Mexican residents of Los Angeles were excluded from the benefits of full social participation in the life of their city. Social membership is usually equated with citizenship status, but it is important also to investigate how those who are not citizens negotiate a sense of national identity, calibrating notions of citizenship and democracy in the process.[8] By shifting the focus to the local level, one can see the ways in which social membership is negotiated every day.[9] In this study, examining local institutions, particularly those whose mission was to promote public health, is crucial to demonstrating how institutional policies affected a sense of social membership. As an institution, the department of public health regulated immigrants' everyday life practices. Moreover, the city and county health departments' official standards, guidelines, and recommendations were routinely evoked by the city council and others to prevent Chinese, Japanese, and Mexican residents from bargaining freely over wages and working conditions; from owning land or accumulating other assets that might appreciate in value and be passed on to subsequent generations; and even from moving freely about the city in search of housing, employment, and business opportunities.[10]

The growth of Los Angeles and the increasing national recognition of public health as a prominent profession in the nation and important institution in the city were closely entwined. Just as demographic growth and increased immigration warranted the attention of government legislators and private investors, so too they demanded the attention of health officials. Sanitation and good health were central to the image of Los Angeles, and public health officials remained thoroughly committed to promoting the reputation of the burgeoning city. The many connections between the health departments and the broader municipal infrastructure challenge the idea of public health as being driven by pure principles of "scientific objectivity."[11] Overarching social and political issues of the time played essential roles in the development of the city and county health departments, determining where clinics were established and what types of programs were offered to whom.

Health officials not only incorporated their racially charged visions into policies and ordinances that targeted ethnic communities but also helped shape the ways mainstream populations perceived ethnic peoples. Moreover, people operating at various levels of power, in and out of government, routinely appropriated public health discourses to advance goals of their own, including the shaping of racial categories and meanings.[12] "Experts" from the fields of public health, public service, law, and social work reinforced each other's ideas, thereby increasing the legitimacy that the general public accorded to their claims. The process by which public health as an institution and a discourse evolved into a key site of racialization in late-nineteenth- through mid-twentieth-century Los Angeles—how it came to exert an influence that extended far beyond the realm of health—is the central question this book addresses.[13]

REFINING THE RACIAL HIERARCHY

In 1875, the Southern Pacific Railroad extended its line from San Francisco to Los Angeles. Additional connections to railroad lines during the 1880s made Los Angeles the terminus of two cross-continental railroads. Each new link precipitated another, larger jump in the size of the city. Census data place the total population of the city in 1880 at slightly over eleven thousand. By 1900, Los Angeles claimed a population of more than one hundred thousand within city limits and an additional seventy thousand residents in the county.[14] But in Los Angeles, unlike comparable cities in the Midwest and East, population density grew only modestly. As a result, the city and county developed into a sprawling metropolis with a much higher ratio of land per capita than was common elsewhere.[15]

If L.A.'s geographical limits seemed infinitely expandable, its social boundaries did not. The city and surrounding county were the site of persistent struggles between the white elite and the racially diverse remainder of the population.[16] Sparring matches over politics, civil rights, housing, employment, and the distribution of city and county services occurred regularly, increasing social polarization throughout the city. These conditions made having a stake in assigning L.A.'s ethnic groups their proper place in the city's racial order especially important. Public and private discussions of the need for maintaining a high standard of public health were laced with references to the perils presented by the city's immigrant minorities. Health officials recorded their racial concerns in quarterly and annual reports, in internal memos, in their correspondence with other health and government officials, and in the press. The multiethnic population of Los Angeles preoccupied public health officials because of a widespread perception that immigrants threatened the health of the nation in both a real and a metaphorical sense.

From the late nineteenth to the early twentieth century, Americans across the country struggled to adapt to the broad changes that accompanied industrialization. Large numbers of people moved from rural to urban areas, and major sites of labor shifted from the fields to the factories. The composition of immigration changed as well. In most cities, southern European newcomers replaced earlier Irish and German populations as the largest immigrant groups.[17] Public dissatisfaction and calls for reforms in various arenas, from business to social welfare programs, accompanied these sociopolitical and cultural transformations. As the country embarked on a "search for order" that would calm growing fears of chaos,[18] public health, which emerged as a field toward the end of the nineteenth century, seemed an ideal solution.[19] With its promise of "scientific objectivity" and its embodiment of many of the values championed by the Progressives, it was an institution well suited to the era.[20]

On the East Coast and in the Midwest, health workers and social reformers directed their efforts at the newly arriving white immigrants from southern Europe, whom they attempted to assimilate into American culture. In Los Angeles, the situation was more complicated. Los Angeles health officials dealt only infrequently with the city's ethnic white (southern and eastern European) immigrants. Their main concerns, instead, were the health issues posed by Chinese, Japanese, and Mexican residents. Asians and Mexicans were not easily classified into racial categories. They were neither white nor black. What position should they occupy in the racial order? The highest levels of government determined legal citizenship, but institutions, such as public health departments, determined who had access to social membership. Public health officials were able to inject new concepts and ideas into delineation processes that are usually informal and carried out at a much lower level (such as a city or even a neighborhood), marking some people as worthy, capable, and deserving members of society and others as correspondingly unworthy and incapable of participation. What degree of social membership and/or legal citizenship should be extended to which groups? Public health officials, with their standards and guidelines, programs and policies, helped answer and institutionalize responses to these questions. I argue that by examining public health as a site of racialization, we will see how public health workers at the local level contributed to the construction of racial categories. In Los Angeles County, the earliest interactions between public health officials and Mexican and Japanese immigrants reveal how race relations in this area differed from those in the rest of the nation.

DEVELOPING A REGIONAL RACIAL LEXICON

In the country as a whole, race was commonly perceived in dichotomous terms as the categories of "white" and "black." The general public identified other major "races" as Slavs, Hebrews, and Mediterraneans. Los Angeles had its share of these groups, but they were rarely mentioned as racially distinct. The black/white imagery that dominated conceptions of race elsewhere gave way in Los Angeles to a notion of race as a graded continuum shading from white, at the top, downward through various forms of "nonwhite," represented by the city's Chinese, Japanese, and Mexican populations. In Los Angeles, people "saw" race differently. The numerically small size of the African American population, combined with the fact that Asians and then, later, Mexicans were highly sought after as laborers, displaced the prejudices usually reserved for African Americans onto these three groups (table 1).[21]

The history of the development of the nonwhite category in contrast to the widely accepted black-white paradigm highlights the fluidity of racial understandings and the many ways in which racial categories evolved. In the wake of the major changes nationwide brought about by large-scale immigration and industrialization, the notion of "an unquestioned hegemony of a unified race of 'white persons' " broke down.[22] Poor and ethnic whites continually needed to define themselves against the "other," most often African Americans, in order to establish their racial privilege.[23] The fervor with which whites guarded their racial privilege is not surprising. Whites' position at the top of the racial order resulted in heightened access to institutionalized power.[24] By definition, racialized populations, since they were constructed in structural opposition to whites, had limited access to institutional power.

The ambiguity that resulted from retooling racial categories also meant that people who were neither white nor black had no clearly defined position in the racial hierarchy. The "nonwhite" category helped stabilize the new racial order. Like whiteness, nonwhiteness was neither a monolithic nor a static category; it incorporated degrees of access to privilege, and its composition changed in response to national factors (e.g., labor needs, immigration laws, and economic cycles) and more regional pressures (e.g., the presence or absence of other marginalized populations). The racial ordering within the category of "nonwhite" also was affected by the process of racialization itself. As Tomás Almaguer has shown, in nineteenth-century California, groups were racialized in relation to one another, falling into different places along a graded continuum that began with whites, who were followed by

TABLE I. POPULATION OF LOS ANGELES
BROKEN DOWN BY RACE, 1880–1940

Year	White		Negroes		Japanese		Chinese[a]		Mexicans[a]		Total Population (County)	Total Population (City)
	in County	in City	in County	in City	in County	in City	in County	in City	in County	in City		
1880	31,707	10,379	188	102	1	1	1,169	604	1,721 (FB)	N/A	33,381	11,183
1890	95,033	47,205	6,421[b]	1,258	36	26	4,424	1,871	1,293 (FB)	498 (FB)	101,454	50,395
1900	163,975	98,082	2,841	2,131	204	150	3,209	2,111	1,613 (FB)	817 (FB)	170,298	102,479
1910	483,478	305,307	9,424	5,101	8,461	4,238	2,602	1,954	11,793 (FB)	5,632 (FB)	504,131	319,198
1920	894,507	546,864	18,738	15,579	19,911	11,618	2,591	2,062	33,644	21,598 (FB)	936,455	576,673
1930	1,949,882	1,073,584	46,425	38,894	35,390	21,081	3,572	3,009	167,024	97,116	2,190,738	1,238,048
1940	2,660,042	1,406,430	75,209	63,774	36,866	23,321	997	4,736	59,260	36,840 (FB)	2,765,569	1,504,277

SOURCES: U.S. Census Office, Statistics of the Population of the United States at the Tenth Census (Washington, DC: Government Printing Office, 1883); Report on the Population of the United States at the Eleventh Census: 1890 (Washington, DC: Government Printing Office, 1895); Abstract of the Twelfth Census of the United States (Washington, DC: Government Printing Office, 1904); Thirteenth Census of the United States (Washington, DC: Government Printing Office, 1913); Fourteenth Census of the United States Taken in the Year 1920 (Washington, DC: Government Printing Office, 1923); Fifteenth Census of the United States: 1930 (Washington, DC: Government Printing Office, 1933); Sixteenth Census of the United States: 1940 (Washington, DC: Government Printing Office, 1943).

[a] From 1890–1920, Mexicans were legally considered white. The values entered for these years for Los Angeles City reflect the numbers of foreign-born (FB) Mexicans, not the native born of Mexican origin. In 1930, the census classified Mexicans for the first time as a nonwhite group; the figure represents all people of Mexican origin, foreign and native born. In 1940, the figure once again reflects only foreign-born Mexicans.

[b] In 1890, the census included Negro, Chinese, Japanese, and Indian in one category.

Mexicans, African Americans, Asians, and, finally, Native Americans.[25] As Claire Jean Kim has pointed out, the racial order is not a "single-scale hierarchy (A over B over C), but a field structured by at least two axes: that of superior/inferior and that of insider /foreigner. Blacks and whites constitute the major anchors (bottom and top respectively) of this order, and incoming immigrants and other groups get positioned relative to these two loci."[26] In Los Angeles, Mexicans were positioned above the city's Chinese and Japanese residents in many respects. For example, until the Depression, health officials extended Americaniza-tion programs to Mexicans.[27] Asians, meanwhile, remained labeled as outsiders, a threatening "yellow peril," simultaneously inferior and alien.

Mexicans' higher status relative to Asians, however, did not enhance their position vis-à-vis the city's white population. They continued to be regarded as subordinate, foreign, and disease ridden. This racialized view had significant and direct consequences for public health in Los Angeles and equally important indirect effects on the city's social struc-ture. During the 1916 typhus epidemic and the 1924 plague, for in-stance, public health officials focused on "reforming" Mexicans, whom they "knew" to be naturally dirty and inherently too ignorant to rectify their unsanitary living conditions. Because medical discourse had the power to naturalize racial categories, it also had the effect of naturaliz-ing societal inequalities. Rather than addressing the structural inequal-ity that produced the unhealthy environments that hosted virulent dis-eases, public health departments consistently identified the root problem as racialized people who were in need of reform. By shaping racial categories and infusing them with meaning, health officials helped define racialized people's place in society.

DEFINING THE MEANING OF MEXICAN

Throughout this book, I focus primarily on Mexicans because, by 1930, they were the largest immigrant group in Los Angeles. Beginning in the early 1900s and continuing through World War II, health officials in Los Angeles were more involved with Mexicans than with any other ethnic groups. Throughout the first half of the century, city and county health officials in Los Angeles tracked Mexican communities more consistently than they did the Chinese or Japanese populations (especially after a series of federal laws, culminating in the Immigration Act of 1924, severely restricted immigration from Asia).

Examining the connections between the experiences of the city's Chinese, Japanese, and Mexican residents demonstrates how immigrants were racialized in relation to one another, a process that often resulted in the institutionalization of a racial hierarchy. How the health officials came to view and treat Mexicans, however, was directly tied to their assumptions about and experiences with L.A.'s Asian residents. Indeed, from 1869 until 1920, the Los Angeles City Health Department used only two racial categories: "Chinese" and "the rest of the population."[28] As chapters 1 and 2 will make clear, in important ways, "Mexican" was a category constructed from what it was not: not white, not Chinese, not Japanese. Thus, in 1924, for example, what it meant to be "Mexican" in Los Angeles was determined in part by what it meant to be "Japanese." The relational nature of L.A.'s racial categories makes it imperative to include the public health experiences of the "Chinese" and "Japanese" in this study, even though the city and county health departments' policies and programs addressed these groups only intermittently.[29] A comparative examination of all three groups clarifies how racialization projects can differ in their intent, application, and impact, depending on the specific group targeted.[30]

Despite Mexicans' centuries-long history in the Southwest, L.A.'s city and county departments of health overlooked them until the early 1900s. Health officials subscribed to the then-popular belief that Mexicans, like Native Americans, were a race that eventually would fade away.[31] They essentially dismissed the city's Mexican residents as transients. By the early 1900s, however, officials realized that the number of Mexicans in Los Angeles was not diminishing but growing. Starting in the 1910s, Mexicans began to fill a manual labor void created by the exclusion of Asians. First, Chinese laborers were forced out, through the 1882 Chinese Exclusion Act (and repeated ten-year extensions of its provisions); later, Japanese workers faced a similar form of exclusion through the 1907–8 Gentlemen's Agreement and state laws passed in 1913 and 1920 restricting land ownership by "aliens."[32] As the number of Mexicans in Los Angeles increased, so too did concerns about how this group's presence might affect the economic, social, and physical landscape of the city.[33] Until the 1930s, labor shortages shielded Mexicans from some of the worst discriminatory practices leveled against the city's Asian communities.

City and county health departments' reports and policies indicate that Mexican women occupied a central place in public health officials' response to immigration. During the first decades of the twentieth century, L.A.'s resident Mexican population consisted mainly of single males. Mexican women immigrated in low numbers in the early twentieth century.[34] Nonetheless, an examination of institutional records and discourses reveals department-sponsored prenatal, birthing, and well-baby programs that targeted Mexican women and children. Public health officials viewed Mexicans and their "backward" culture as antithetical to their efforts to make Los Angeles a "modern" city. They launched Americanization programs in hopes that assimilation would eliminate Mexicans as an obstacle to progress. Mexican women and children may have seemed the best vehicles for achieving this goal. Officials considered Mexican women malleable and influential within their families, and they may have thought that infants, being too young to have absorbed their birth culture, stood a chance of being successfully Americanized.[35] In addition, they wished to stem the threat of unwanted births and alleged bad parenting.[36] Thus, although Mexican women were considered "*socially* peripheral" and represented only a small portion of the population, they were "*symbolically* central" because, unless they could be won over, Mexicans as a group would continue to threaten health officials' construction of Los Angeles as a bastion of health.[37]

In the early decades of the twentieth century, health officials' efforts to Americanize Mexicans sometimes consisted of little more than rhetoric. Still, even half-hearted assimilation programs indicated a possibility that this group, although not classified as white, might be capable of blending into American culture. No similar possibilities existed for Asians. Neither city nor county departments developed any significant health care programs for the Japanese and Chinese communities. Instead, members of these groups, recognizing that meeting institutionally defined standards for health and cleanliness was a precondition for social membership, often used their own funds to hire public health nurses to work with their communities.

When the U.S. economy collapsed and the Great Depression began, attitudes toward Mexicans shifted rapidly. In Los Angeles, with jobs scarce, white residents and government agencies increasingly regarded Mexicans as an economic burden, and the idea that Mexicans' social inferiority arose from their biological inferiority returned. Buttressed by ideologically defined medical standards, the inferiority of Mexicans soon became "indisputable." Assimilation programs were replaced with repatriation drives. Now public health discourses—especially the notions that Mexicans were disease carriers and an exceptionally fertile people—were mobilized to legitimize the removal of the same population that only a few years earlier had been deemed an essential source of cheap labor.

Beginning in 1930, many of the changes in health departments' programs and discourses with respect to Mexicans involved applying assumptions, terms, and actions once reserved for the city's Chinese and Japanese residents to this population. Now it was Mexicans who were deemed "aliens" and targeted for deportation. Thus, in the course of less than fifty years, three entirely different populations were assigned the lowest position in L.A.'s racial hierarchy: a powerful example of how rapidly racism can be repackaged, re-energized, and relegitimized.

CHALLENGING RACIALIZATION:
RESPONSES TO PUBLIC HEALTH DISCOURSES

Public health policies and discourse played an important role in shaping and promoting images of Asians and Mexicans as non-normative. Even today, stereotypes of the overly fertile Mexican woman, the unclean Mexican man, the wily Asian vendor, and the germ-spreading Chinese launderer persist.[38] Yet analyses of Chinese launderers' protests over restrictive ordinances and Mexicans' appeals to the Los Angeles City Council for public housing, for example, reveal that from the start these groups were not passive targets of discrimination. They appropriated legal and medical discourses to challenge dominant assumptions, made gains for their communities, and participated in defining the racial order.[39] As the chapters that follow will show, Chinese, Japanese, and Mexicans fought back in court, petitioned the city council, stalled the enforcement of city legislation, resisted through refusals to attend health clinics, utilized alternative health practices, refused to let housing inspectors into their homes, and wrote letters to state and national officials protesting unfair treatment. Sometimes they succeeded in having their demands met. Other times they did not. At the very least, they brought their concerns into the public forum.

CENTRAL THEMES AND ORGANIZATION OF THE BOOK

In the chapters that follow, I examine the role of public health as a key site of racialization by tracing several interrelated themes. Chapters 1, 2, and 3 highlight the importance of looking at racialization from a comparative perspective. The book as a whole is concerned primarily with Mexicans, but examining the experiences of nonwhite groups in

Los Angeles in relation to one another, as well as in relation to the dominant white population, reveals the ways in which racial logic assumed different forms during the same historical moment. The evidence these chapters provide regarding public health's role in the development of a regional racial lexicon also contributes to the main theme of chapter 4, namely, how powerful the idea of scientific objectivity became when it was harnessed to the institution of public health. Chapter 5 demonstrates how Mexican American activists appropriated the language of public health to make civil rights demands. Cumulatively, all five chapters confirm not only that race is best understood as a subjective, social construction but also that racialization is a dynamic, ongoing process.

In chapter 1, I argue that as a fledgling institution, public health in Los Angeles had a dual mission: promoting and preserving the biological health of the citizens *and* promoting and preserving the economic and cultural health of the city. Public health officials' commitment to making Los Angeles a "modern" (meaning sanitary and healthful) metropolis influenced the way they perceived and treated the city's nonwhite residents. The chapter assesses some of these booster narratives, focusing on public health departments' prominent role in projecting an image of Los Angeles as a healthy "Eden" where people lived carefree lives, surrounded by economic prosperity. Health officials often seemed just as concerned as the chamber of commerce that this idyllic image of Los Angeles reach its intended audience (white, financially secure Easterners and Midwesterners) without being marred by any reference to the presence of ethnic communities in the city.

Chapter 1 shows that public health discourses (often embedded in media narratives and newspaper photographs, as well as in policies and guidelines) characterized the Chinese in Los Angeles as dirty and unhygienic, disease carriers who, as launderers and produce vendors, threatened the health of citizens. City officials, including members of the city council, then used these stereotypes to justify developing legislation that undermined Chinese entrepreneurs' economic viability. By tracing the early interactions between Chinese communities and health officials, I demonstrate that health officials, far from embodying "scientific objectivity," had a history of racializing space and immigrant groups before Mexicans made their mark on the urban landscape beginning in the 1910s. The same public health discourses—and often the same public health officials as well—that racialized the Chinese later racialized Mexicans.

Chapter 2 focuses on the formative years of the Los Angeles County Health Department, when health officials nationwide first began to take stock of the country's large-scale health issues. I argue that as one of the early and primary contacts with Mexican and Japanese residents, public health officials helped establish a regional racial lexicon that categorized and ranked county residents as white, Mexican, Japanese, or other. The health department's records, including correspondence, testify to the far-reaching influence that county officials had in shaping what local, state, and national leaders, as well as the general public, knew about ethnic communities in Los Angeles.

Chapter 2's analysis of the county's response in 1916 to an outbreak of typhus fever in the Mexican labor camps run by the railroad companies reveals an important source of the stereotype of Mexicans as dirty and disease ridden. Under the guise of protecting the health of all residents, officials gained the authority to closely inspect the bodies as well as the living quarters of Mexican railroad workers and their families, force them to undergo delousing "baths," and quarantine anyone even *suspected* of being infected by typhus.

The 1920s were an important period of growth for the Los Angeles County Health Department. In chapter 3, I analyze the public health policies of the decade and trace the increase in services to Mexicans. The department introduced a system of health care centers, placing the largest center in Belvedere, a predominantly Mexican area. The chapter also examines county health programs directed at women and children (such as well-baby clinics) and these programs' underlying tenets. The department used well-baby clinics to intensify the programs it directed at Mexican mothers. Tropes of Americanization and citizenship permeated the program lessons directed at Mexican mothers. Health officials preached that embracing the benefits of a hygienic and healthy lifestyle was the first step on the road to assimilation—for Mexicans. No such possibility was extended to the Japanese, then the county's second-largest ethnic group. Because the racially coded language of public health constructed the Japanese as a threat to white Americans, this group was viewed as permanently ineligible for either legal or social participation in the community at large.

I contrast these proactive steps toward improving Mexican communities with the treatment of Japanese communities, showing how the Japanese continued to be marginalized. Local politicians, connecting Japanese birth rates to discussions of "yellow peril," fanned fears and resulted in calls from the general (white) public for increased immigration restrictions.

Chapter 4 examines city and county public health policies directed at Mexicans during the Depression. The health departments played a key role in the repatriation programs that gained popularity as the economy continued to worsen. Public health discourses appropriated by various government officials legitimated local efforts to force the city's Mexican residents to return to Mexico. The Americanization efforts of the 1920s were abandoned as health officials in the 1930s adopted racial assumptions emphasizing more immutable biological traits that rendered Mexicans unassimilable. Chapter 4 also assesses changes in attitudes and actions regarding the Chinese. Whereas in the 1910s zoning laws had circumscribed the location of Chinese laundries and produce markets, in the 1930s citizens used public health ordinances to drive Chinese launderers out of business.

Chapter 5 recounts Mexican Americans' demands in the late 1930s for better health and housing conditions in Los Angeles. Despite twenty years of county health programs and services, Mexicans' health and housing conditions languished in comparison to those of whites. In their appeals for change, Mexican Americans described the same dismal conditions in their neighborhoods that health inspectors had reported for decades. They, however, rejected inspectors' claims that they were to blame for their poor living conditions. Turning the tables, they indicted the city and county for perpetuating these conditions and for undercutting Mexican American communities' chances to thrive.

Encouraged by newly created New Deal programs, Mexican Americans, both as individuals and as members of labor and civil rights organizations, demanded that the city build public housing. This quest for better housing, which Mexican Americans saw as a way to improve overall health conditions in their communities, also signaled a major demographic shift. Mexican communities no longer consisted primarily of sojourners or seasonal laborers, typically single men who rented rooms while they were working in the area and who returned to Mexico for part of the year. In contrast to the 1910s, when the first waves of Mexican immigrants had arrived, the Mexican population in Los Angeles in the 1930s included a large proportion of family units and second-generation Mexican Americans.[40] Permanent housing, and single-family dwellings in particular, had become essential. Mexican Americans' demands for public housing marked their desire to be recognized as citizens, deserving of the same rights as all other Americans.

CHAPTER I

Interlopers in the Land of Sunshine

Chinese Disease Carriers, Launderers, and Vegetable Peddlers

When newly appointed Health Officer Walter Lindley first assessed the state of the city's public health in 1879, Los Angeles was a small town, overshadowed in both geographical size and population by San Francisco, the state's premier city.[1] For nearly three decades after its incorporation in 1850, Los Angeles relied on private enterprise to spur its growth. By the 1880s, however, city officials realized that government help in promotion of Los Angeles would be a wise investment. As the population increased, private entrepreneurs would be eager to further cultivate Los Angeles as a major West Coast city.

The public health department and Lindley, its chief spokesperson, readily embraced the booster role. Dr. Lindley made it clear that, like other branches of city government, the public health office would strive to promote the image of Los Angeles as a sunny, salubrious place. When he focused part of his inaugural report on Chinatown—"that rotten spot"—he exhorted the city council to take action. If allowed to fester further, the area could tarnish the image of Los Angeles as a health resort. In contrast, health department–sponsored projects, such as a municipal sewer line, would supply evidence that the city was modern and forward-looking. Public health officials would also help sustain the pristine image of Los Angeles by tracing the origin of all social problems to marginalized communities, beginning with the Chinese.

In calling Chinatown a "rotten spot," Lindley simultaneously established the space where the Chinese lived and the people themselves as antithetical to the "legitimate" residents of Los Angeles, namely, white Americans, many of whom (Dr. Lindley included) were themselves recent transplants. Prioritizing these white residents' needs over those of the Chinese community, Lindley cautioned that "for preservation of the lives of our own families [it behooves us] to put it [Chinatown] in the very best sanitary condition."[2] He estimated that in another year, the sewer system would be completed for the areas around the Old Plaza.[3] However, he offered no plan for accomplishing this goal. In the meantime, Chinese (and Mexican) residents who lived and worked in the Plaza area had to endure raw sewage spilling into their streets from the open end of the unfinished main line. This flagrant violation of health standards elicited no apparent concern from health officials or from any other representatives of city government. Dr. Lindley simply noted that "very soon it [would] be the city's imperative duty to either have the sewage disinfected or to extend the main sewer [line] farther from the city."[4] In fact, it took thirty years before the city's sewer system extended through Chinatown.[5]

The city council's simultaneous acceptance of Chinatown as L.A.'s "rotten spot" and long-term failure to implement a solution is not surprising. By the time Lindley was appointed health officer, rising anti-Chinese sentiment in the city appeared sufficient to support an "anti-coolie club" and a branch of the Workingman's Party (whose slogan was "The Chinese Must Go"). In California, dwindling numbers of railroad jobs and competition for agricultural work also heightened hostility toward the Chinese.

In 1879, the Los Angeles branch of the Workingman's Party backed a number of their members in the municipal election and won twelve out of fifteen council seats.[6] Once in office, they targeted Chinese entrepreneurs and the businesses that they were most likely to engage in, laundries and vegetable sales. The city council attempted to force Chinese entrepreneurs out of business by increasing their laundry taxes fivefold, from five dollars to twenty-five dollars per month, while raising the tax on vegetable peddlers from three dollars to twenty dollars per month. The potential loss of revenue expected as a result of driving these businesses from the city prevented the implementation of this plan.[7]

Economic pressure was only one of many elements that shaped these racist attitudes. Throughout the second half of the nineteenth century, fear of the "yellow peril" flourished across the country. Many Americans viewed Chinese immigrants as uniquely dangerous.[8] Their "heathen" beliefs, ancient culture, and impenetrable language marked them as permanent outsiders. Summing up the case against the Chinese in 1869, the *New York Times* damned the immigrants as "[a] population befouled with all the social vices, with no knowledge or appreciation of free institutions or constitutional liberty, with heathenish souls and heathenish propensities, whose character, and habits, and modes of thought are firmly fixed by the consolidating influence of ages upon ages."[9]

Forty years later, such attitudes had not let up. In a speech, W. Almont Gates, secretary of the State Board of Charities and Correction, stated that "[t]he white and yellow races flowing in opposite directions around the world have now met on the shores of the Pacific. . . . Talk of assimilation is nonsense. The white peoples coming to this country will unite into a homogenous race. . . . [S]ooner will the red and black race be assimilated with the future American, than will the yellow. More than sixty years of the yellow race in California has not brought that race nearer Caucasian civilization."[10] His observations revealed his own sense of the regional racial lexicon and the notion that the Chinese occupied the lowest position in the racial hierarchy.

This chapter examines some of the ways in which the interplay between social structure and ideology shaped the meaning of "Chinese" and "Chinatown" in late-nineteenth- and early-twentieth-century Los Angeles. The goals of the emerging profession of public health and those of the developers of Los Angeles were thoroughly intertwined. The tropes of health, hygiene, and modernization promoted by public health institutions proved equally powerful as tools for promoting the city. Vanquishing all disease, dirt, and contagion was not an achievable goal, of course, especially in the short term. But confining these problems to a single city space seemed both possible and rational. Thus, from the beginning, efforts to benefit "the public's" health legitimized and reinforced a racial order in which the Chinese occupied the lowest sector. Since the Chinese already bore the dual stigmas of difference and inferiority, they seemed especially vulnerable to the additional labels supplied by health-conscious city officials. The white population of Los Angeles did not need much convincing that the residents of Chinatown were carriers of dirt and disease and purveyors of vice.

These racial stigmas persisted, and in the early twentieth century many became codified in city legislation. The Cubic Air Ordinance required that all residents have at least five hundred cubic feet of space per person in their living quarters but was enforced only in Chinese communities. The Residence District Ordinance and other zoning regulations restricted where Chinese people could live and do business. Images in official reports and newspapers stereotyped Chinese, depicting them as peddlers of foul produce and as launderers who spread germs. Official views, regulations, and everyday practices such as these set the precedent for how mainstream Los Angeles would treat other communities (specifically Mexicans and Japanese) in the future.

INVENTING LOS ANGELES

After 1885, when both the Southern Pacific and Santa Fe transcontinental railroads were completed, the cost of rail travel decreased. Migration to Los Angeles from the East and Midwest surged, sparking a real estate boom from 1886 to 1887.[11] Efforts to promote the city as a center of commerce and tourism accelerated. Real estate agents, guidebook authors, novelists, and other boosters romanticized Los Angeles as a leisurely, inviting oasis.[12] Businesses, especially the citrus industry, also began disseminating popular images of the city in the 1880s. In 1902, for instance, Sunkist shipped its oranges in crates with vividly colored labels depicting a West Coast paradise. The California Fruit Growers' Exchange used the slogan "Oranges for Health—California for Wealth" to capitalize on images of the West in general and Los Angeles in particular as a land of opportunity.[13]

The invention of Los Angeles involved more than crafting a beguiling image. It involved more than building an infrastructure of roads and schools, hospitals and fire departments. And it involved more than spurring private investment in land, banks, and shops. The city was developed as a place for whites. A specific racial hierarchy informed the social and physical space of Los Angeles. By luring white Midwesterners and Easterners only and by racially segregating neighborhoods as they began to be settled by immigrants and migrants, the city fathers sent a clear message: social membership in the city would be reserved for whites only.

The creation of a "Spanish Fantasy Past" was a master narrative in the selling of Los Angeles. The noted historian, journalist, and activist Carey McWilliams coined the term to refer to the process by which Americans imagined California to have closer links to Spain than to Mexico.[14] It ascribed Spanish lineage to the ruling-class *Californios* who had settled the land and in the process made them more acceptable to the Euro-Americans, mainly men, who moved into the region after the Mexican-American War. The recasting of *California* women as Spanish instead of Mexican facilitated marriage between them and Euro-American men.[15]

The myth was reified in all aspects of local culture, from mission-style architecture to popular literature, most notably Helen Hunt Jackson's novel *Ramona* (1885).[16]

The notion of a racial hierarchy was at the center of this myth. It privileged the Spanish over the Mexican. Moreover, the myth revised history. It simultaneously recast the relationship between Spanish priests and Native Americans as paternalistic and benevolent, rather than filled with conflict and violence, and obscured the decline of the *Californios,* who had often lost everything after the American takeover.[17]

Many believed that the promotion of the white race in the West, California, and Los Angeles in particular was central to the city's development and success. The *Los Angeles Times* ran articles entitled "The Mighty West," "The Future of the Pacific," and the "Splendid Race Cradled Here," all of which extolled the virtues of the Aryan race. "The Aryan race is already on another great westward trek. It is digging a new foothold in our western country. Here is where the greatest centers of population will be a century hence," proclaimed one article.[18] With the "growth of all the other Aryan races," Los Angeles will "take its place among the great industrial and commercial communities in the coming years," stated another piece.[19] "Southern California has everything in environment to develop the finest race of people in the world. It has the outdoor life for children, the freedom from epidemic, the invigorating seashore and the equally invigorating mountain air. Beyond these things they say that 'blood will tell.' Then evidently right here in peaceful Southern California is to be found some of the best blood among all peoples," announced an additional column.[20] Regional identity was as rooted in whiteness as it was in geography.[21]

Some of the city's most prominent leaders were ardent believers in the supremacy of the white race. Charles Fletcher Lummis, editor of *Land of Sunshine,* a magazine central to the promotion of Los Angeles, and Abbot Kinney, a transplant from New Jersey and best known for his development of Venice Beach into a tourist attraction complete with gondola rides and an amusement park, were both strong believers in the supremacy of the Anglo-Saxon race. Both men also admired the native peoples in the region and fought to preserve their culture and history. Joseph Widney wrote books that espoused white supremacy, including *Race Life of the Aryan Peoples* and *The Three Americas: Their Racial Past and the Dominant Racial Factors of Their Future.*[22] These men stamped their vision of a racial order on everything they touched in every realm, from popular culture to scientific and educational institutions.[23]

Los Angeles residents were also well versed in white supremacy. In response to debates around the then-pending Chinese Exclusion Act in 1882, a transplant from Ohio wrote to the *Los Angeles Times* asking that, when debating the "Chinese question," the public consider not only the benefits of Chinese labor but the detrimental effects of this "foreign element." The writer posited that "we are endeavoring to work out in this land of ours, . . . a civilization which will develop in every point the highest characteristics, and at the same time advance the best interest of the human race. . . . [T]he civilization of the Anglo-Saxon . . . is that which is to-day *[sic]* bringing mankind up to the highest point of moral and civic improvement and well being."[24]

Preserving whiteness often involved creating mechanisms to separate the races. Some forms of racial restrictions were formalized, such as racial covenants that restricted selling property to racialized groups. Not only did various parts of Los Angeles County, like Glendale and South Gate, institute racial covenants, but real estate agents traded on them to make the areas seem more desirable. In her analysis of the Los Angeles suburb South Gate, the historian Becky Nicolaides writes that the South Gate Property Owners' Protective Association assured potential residents that they would not make the mistakes that other residential districts had made and would shore up racial restrictions for those living in the areas. Nicolaides also skillfully demonstrates how home ownership was pitched as a form of civic participation, a way to demonstrate one's citizenship.[25] In a society where citizenship was equated with whiteness, nonwhites could read between the sales pitch lines.

Boosters, such as real estate agents and land developers, obviously stood to gain personally from promoting the city. So too, though, did city officials, including public health staffs. In nineteenth-century Los Angeles, prominent residents dabbled in politics, real estate, and professions such as law, medicine, or banking simultaneously.[26] Walter Lindley proved no exception. An Indiana native, he migrated to California in 1875 and quickly established himself in the political and business realms of Los Angeles. Early in his career, Lindley, along with the California Progressive John Randolph Haynes and Haynes's brothers, Francis and Robert, opened a medical practice in the city, operating the Pacific Hospital out of a small adobe building.[27]

In 1887, Lindley founded the California Hospital. His position in the city was sufficiently prominent that he enlisted the city's best-known physicians as co-owners and staff.[28] He served as president of the Los Angeles Medical Association and superintendent of the State Reform

School in Whittier. He also coauthored with Joseph Widney an eight-volume guidebook, *California of the South,* that described and promoted the area.[29] His business connections included the Southern Pacific Railroad (through his brother Harvey, a prominent businessman) and the *Los Angeles Times* (through his own friendship with General Gray Otis, its owner and publisher).[30] Descriptions of Lindley characterize him as "an articulate spokesman for California of the South and the California way of life."[31] Like other private investors, Lindley realized that the growth of Los Angeles would increase the value of his own investments.

Many of the migrants who came to Los Angeles, like Dr. Lindley, brought along ideas of what Los Angeles should look like. These visions included single-family dwellings outside the developed city areas. The newcomers also envisioned these areas as settled by people who looked like themselves, thereby excluding ethnic populations. To ensure this vision, they developed housing restrictions to keep ethnic peoples out of their neighborhoods.[32] As this chapter explains, city ordinances helped sustain segregation in the business community as well by restricting the number and location of Chinese-owned laundries and the number and movements of Chinese fruit and vegetable peddlers.

SELLING PERSONAL HEALTH, PROMOTING PUBLIC HEALTH

Even before Lindley issued his call for a new sewage system that would mark the city as modern, businessmen had already identified and promoted Los Angeles as a health resort.[33] The Civil War had introduced thousands of Americans on and off the battlefields to the horrors of typhoid, diphtheria, measles, and scarlet fever. As war-related epidemics subsided, new diseases took their place. Increased industrialization made urban areas dirtier and more crowded, driving the incidence of communicable diseases upward. In particular, cases of tuberculosis (popularly known as "consumption") were on the rise.[34] The public's level of concern over disease was high nationwide. So when guidebook author Benjamin Cummings Truman insisted that "[t]he subject of healthfulness is the most important one in the world," few of his readers would have disagreed.[35] Truman, a fervent city booster (and then owner of the *Los Angeles Star*), followed this assertion with a description of the wide-ranging restorative effects of the Los Angeles environment: "There are a number of other diseases [besides consumption and asthma] for which the climate of Los Angeles offers superior advantages over those of any other countries in the world—such as diseases of the liver, spleen and general depression of the nervous system. In fact, the general climate of Semitropical California, and Los Angeles in particular, by its general invigorating influence, would be beneficial to an invalid in almost every case, on account of the remarkable tonic qualities of its atmosphere."[36]

By the middle of the nineteenth century, physicians had begun to advise their patients to move to locations with climates conducive to curing their ailments. Promotional literature that hailed L.A.'s warm, seasonable temperatures often explicitly compared the city's benign climate to the cold and fog that plagued its northern neighbor, San Francisco. Because city boosters sought to entice Easterners and Midwesterners, they also had to establish their area's advantages over Florida's. "Florida has a charming winter climate," an 1899 Los Angeles Chamber of Commerce article conceded, "but the summers in that state are intolerable. Depressing heat and insect pests drive visitors north as soon as the summer commences; as consumption cannot be cured in a single season, sufferers are forced to look elsewhere for a sanitarium."[37] "Sufferers" who chose Los Angeles, on the other hand, would need never again "look elsewhere," thanks to the city's year-round temperate weather.

Health seekers arrived in large numbers, especially in the 1870s–90s. Some, including Harry Chandler and Charles Fletcher Lummis, rose to positions of great prominence and are still celebrated and memorialized in histories of Southern California. Chandler, hoping to restore health to his weak lungs, migrated from New Hampshire to Los Angeles in 1883. Over time, he became a real estate magnate and then publisher of the *Los Angeles Times*.[38] Lummis, a New England native with tuberculosis who migrated to Los Angeles in 1885, literally walked from Cincinnati to Los Angeles. Along the way, he sent the *Los Angeles Times* weekly letters that chronicled his adventures.[39] Lummis eventually became editor of the *Los Angeles Times* and *Out West* magazine, and he wrote several books that contributed to the idyllic image of the West.[40] The successes of Chandler, Lummis, and other health seekers became a sort of Southern Californian version of a Horatio Alger story and helped sustain the notion of California as the promised land.

Not all who came seeking relief from their ailments were as warmly welcomed as Harry Chandler and Charles Fletcher Lummis. At the state level, officials rejected the idea of building health facilities because they believed that California might become a repository for invalids. Indeed, Lindley's 1879 health report claimed that the many invalids who settled in Los Angeles hoping to cure their ailments caused the city's high mortality rate.[41] Ultimately, selling health was a classed and raced issue. City boosters targeted middle-class Easterners and Midwesterners who would seek private medical care when they arrived in Southern California. Although their bodies were afflicted with disease, these newcomers' finances were robust. This group would not damage the image of Los Angeles.

Other settlers, by contrast, did seem threatening. The Chinese, especially, fell far short of Los Angeles boosters' class- and race-specific expectations. In sorting out how and where this group would fit in a space promoted to white Americans only, the racial category "Chinese" became a powerful organizing principle.[42]

PRODUCING DIFFERENCE

Many social, cultural, political, and economic forces combined to shape what *Chinese* meant in Los Angeles. Public health's contribution proved significant. Health experts' views gained even wider circulation toward the end of the century, when the city supplemented its department of health with a wholly independent Board of Health Commissioners. Originally a temporary assemblage of experts called into action when Los Angeles was struck by smallpox epidemics (in 1869 and again in 1873), the board became permanent in 1889.[43] The four commissioners, three of whom were medical doctors, and the mayor, who served as ex-officio president, were charged with appointing the city's health officer.[44] Though the city charter listed this act as their only official duty, from their very first meeting the board met to discuss the various aspects of city governance related to public health that they would oversee.[45]

Along with issues such as high rates of diphtheria and the underdeveloped sewer system, the board chose to focus on the area around the Plaza where the Chinese lived, referring to it as "that Chinatown nuisance."[46] In so doing, they reinforced the negative depictions regularly provided in the city health department's reports and confirmed popular stereotypes about the "heathen Chinaman." Although most health officials' views reflected the prejudices and cultural misunderstandings common among their fellow citizens, their pronouncements carried special weight with the public. Because they were doctors and health experts, and because they had the official approval of the mayor, the public believed in the scientific and objective nature of their findings. This section charts health officials' very subjective role in defining the area eventually known as Chinatown as a dirty, disease-filled, and immoral space.

CHINESE PRESENCE IN LOS ANGELES

More than twenty-two thousand Chinese came to California between 1848 and 1853, seeking jobs in agriculture, mining, and railroad building.[47] Only a tiny fraction of this first group settled in Los Angeles; those who did were employed as house servants or as laborers to clear a wagon route.[48] By 1870, a visible Chinese community had established itself just southwest of the city's Old Spanish Plaza, in an alley area referred to as Calle de los Negros (map 1).[49] In California and nationwide, these first Chinese immigrants were soon stigmatized as different from and inferior to white Americans. Yellow peril ideology portrayed them (and those who came later) as a perpetual threat. The Chinese were incapable of being assimilated; they would never become "real Americans." Their " 'pagan idolatry,' peculiar customs and attire, non-European features, and purported threat to white women"[50] proved insurmountable obstacles.

The line between being deemed incapable of assimilation and considered nonhuman was dangerously thin, as L.A.'s Chinatown residents discovered in 1871. After the accidental shooting and killing of a white man who was caught in the crossfire between two Chinese men, over five hundred men from other sections of the city mobbed Chinatown. Armed and angry, they were intent on revenge. In the many hours before city police re-established order, the mob killed nineteen Chinese males—chosen at random and dispatched mainly by lynching. They also looted several businesses.[51]

The Chinese were believed to imperil America's economy as well as its culture. The white working class saw Chinese laborers as a significant threat. Mainly Chinese men immigrated with the hopes of making enough money to send back home to their families and to return one day themselves. White working-class men characterized Chinese labor as undercutting the value of their own labor because they could be paid less.[52] By 1878, when California held its second Constitutional Convention, anti-Chinese sentiment was running high; the subject of Chinese labor was hotly debated.[53] One-third of the convention's 150 delegates represented the Workingman's Party. They drafted a list of restrictions they hoped to see adopted statewide, including banning further Chinese immigration, preventing employers from hiring Chinese workers, and curtailing the sale of Chinese-made goods. Party members took these demands to local, state, and national politicians, seeking new immigration legislation.[54]

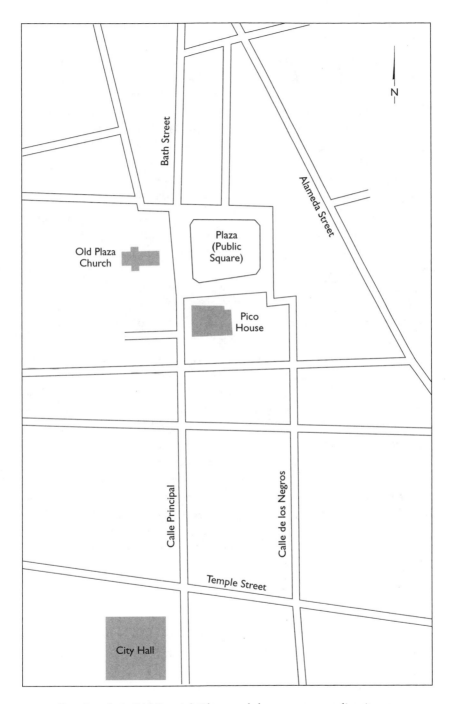

MAP 1. Los Angeles's Old Spanish Plaza and the area surrounding it.

Chinese immigrants threatened more than the economy and everyday cultural practices. They also endangered the nation's health—or so some experts believed. Increased immigration coincided with the development of public health as a prominent urban institution. Even as early as 1862, the impact of the Chinese population on public health was under study. Studies produced by doctors with titles such as "Chinese Immigration and the Physiological Causes of the Decay of the Nation"[55] and other similarly alarmist works reinforced health officials' suspicions that the Chinese were responsible for the spread of numerous diseases, including smallpox and leprosy.

In part because of the views of public health officials, whites across the country perceived the Chinese as carriers of diseases and pollutants. This "fact" only compounded public animosity. Official charges of poor hygiene and lack of proper sanitation confirmed the popular perception of the Chinese as a literal as well as metaphorical threat to the health of the body politic.[56]

In Los Angeles and San Francisco, Chinese settlers promptly came under health department scrutiny. By the 1870s, public health officials had sufficient credibility to construct what being "Chinese" meant—namely, dirty, depraved, and disease ridden.[57] These stereotypes in turn justified segregating Chinese people so that they would not taint white city residents.[58] Dr. Lindley carried this one step further. He worried that the Chinese would contaminate all the natural resources of Los Angeles. The air, water, climate, and soil could be marred by that "rotten spot," Chinatown. He emphasized the importance of protecting "the health of *our* beautiful city"[59] and suggested relocating the Chinese. He did not specify where.

Public health officials considered segregation or relocation viable solutions because they persistently traced the source of Chinese immigrants' deplorable living conditions to this group's personal habits and cultural proclivities. The lamentable truth, they concluded, was that Chinese people would always be disease carriers. They were dirty by nature, they preferred to live in crowded, ramshackle housing, and they seemed incapable of either learning or practicing good hygiene. In the short term, the best that could be hoped for was to limit their contact with other city residents. In the long term, tighter controls over immigration and stronger municipal codes might result in a satisfactory reduction in the population.

Health experts played an important role in the eventual ban on Chinese immigration in terms of the mounting public demands for congressional action. In 1875, Congress passed the Page Law, which limited the number of Chinese women granted entry to the United States. Pressured by the Workingman's Party, legislators drafted much more severe legislation seven years later. The Chinese Exclusion Act of 1882 curtailed all Chinese immigration, with the exception of students, travelers, merchants (not laborers), and the wives of merchants.[60]

At the municipal level, governments in California took action before Congress even considered the issue. In the early 1870s, San Francisco passed a series of blatantly discriminatory laws,[61] and officials in both Los Angeles and San Francisco drafted "Cubic Air Acts." The impetus for these legal stipulations was health officials' critique of the tight living arrangements of Chinese laborers, who mainly occupied crowded boardinghouses and apartments. The ordinances also reflected developments in understandings of public health. Contemporary medical wisdom held all "waste products of the body, particularly respired air and excrement, to be poisonous."[62] Logically, these new theories and the laws they helped generate should have applied to everyone. Officials targeted only the Chinese.

New understandings regarding the poisonous nature of bodily wastes spurred broader changes in urban infrastructure as well. Public health advocates in all major cities stressed the importance of "pure" water supplies and efficient garbage and sewage disposal. Thus, in his first report on the city's health, Dr. Lindley called for improving and extending the municipal sewer system and reminded his listeners of the importance of implementing improvements that would put Los Angeles on par with the country's older, more established cities. Safeguarding the city's image and protecting its citizens' health were two sides of a single coin. Just how badly the city still needed municipal improvements two years later is clear in an 1882 letter to the editor of the *Los Angeles Times* headlined "The Sewerage Question."[63] Using an argument strikingly similar to the health officer's, the author of the letter binds public health to tourism and city promotion. And, again like Lindley, the writer singles out "China town" as the source of especially noxious "filth and stench":

> To the Editor: The first thing a stranger does upon entering a town is to look into the health of its people. If a person is looking for a home he is more anxious to learn if there is a perfect system of drainage. He looks about to find the source of water, and if plentiful and pure. No town can be healthy with impure water. . . .
>
> How long can Los Angeles remain even as healthy as now, with China town with all its filth and stench under the nostrils. I've traveled much

and can safely say, Los Angeles has the dirtiest streets of any town of its size I have ever seen. I have noticed daily the water carts turning on the water onto the filth thus laying and packing it in, and in some localities the stench is intolerable as the sun pours its rays upon it. Let the "City Dads" bestir themselves. I predict that in three years Los Angeles will be a very unhealthy city.

   [signed] VISITOR.[64]

For some residents, Los Angeles already was "a very unhealthy city." From Lindley forward, health officials annually recorded the "deplorable sanitary condition(s) [and] the innumerable, intolerable nuisances existing [in Chinatown]."[65] And, year after year, they assigned responsibility for these conditions to the area's Chinese residents, even though these individuals owned none of the buildings they lived in or vended from and none of the land they farmed. Chinatown's absentee landlords, meanwhile, escaped both the stigma that attached to their Chinese leaseholders and the expense of maintaining even minimal levels of sanitation in their properties.[66] Chinatown may not have been the only area of Los Angeles afflicted by "filth and stench," but it was the only section whose inhabitants had almost no political recourse and even less social leverage with which to effect change. Structural improvements bypassed Chinatown.

Even when the area came under intense scrutiny, as happened, for example, during epidemics, the result was rarely positive. This is clear in the events surrounding an outbreak of bubonic plague in San Francisco in 1903. It is unclear from the sources whether there really was an epidemic or whether officials simply feared one.[67] Alexander Saxton observes that claims of the bubonic plague emerged amidst a political and labor maelstrom in San Francisco. Opponents of the mayor claimed that he and the Board of Health fabricated the plague and the ensuing quarantine to further the mayor's political agenda. Under political pressure, the mayor called off the quarantine for a short while and then renewed it when more bubonic cases were reported. The health department planned to quarantine Chinese in old warehouses, at which point the federal courts stepped in and declared these measures unconstitutional, thereby ending the quarantine. Yet the effects of the plague had already reverberated throughout the county as people worried how to avoid infection originating in San Francisco.[68]

Fearing that the disease would spread, San Francisco health officials contacted their counterparts in Los Angeles and advised them to investigate Chinese residents to detect any "Chinamen affected with contagious diseases."[69] "A general clean-up has been started, especially in Chinatown, where, if anywhere the plague might gain a foothold and the campaign will have a salutary effect, even if there is no danger of an introduction of the plague," stated one *Los Angeles Times* article.[70] Concurring, Los Angeles health officials began investigations of the recent deaths of both Chinese and non-Chinese city residents. Yet when Dr. S. P. Black, the lead investigator, presented the results to the Board of Health Commissioners, he discussed only the findings regarding Chinese deaths, reinforcing the stereotype that only Chinese people carried disease. A year later, fear of the epidemic had yet to be quelled. Stereotypes of Chinese as disease carriers guided the investigations rather than standard epidemiological practice. In 1904, complying with a California State Board of Health order to autopsy "all persons who died in Chinatown,"[71] Los Angeles officials found no evidence of the disease. The investigation ended, having brought neither medical nor sanitary improvements. Its chief result was to leave the Chinese and Chinatown even further stigmatized.

Despite being alternately harassed and ignored by city officials, and despite the sweeping provisions of the 1882 Exclusion Act, the Chinese community grew throughout the latter decades of the nineteenth and early twentieth centuries. By the late 1880s, L.A.'s Chinatown included restaurants, herbalists, washhouses, tenements, and a church, all serving the Chinese community. But the relative powerlessness of the residents, the disproportionate number of men without wives or families, and the comparatively cheap cost of property along Calle de los Negros and nearby streets also made the area vulnerable to vice-related businesses. Gambling halls, opium dens, and prostitution houses flourished, patronized by Chinese and by whites.[72] Only the Chinese, however—who had neither the capital nor the authority to control business transactions that occurred in Chinatown—were tainted by vice businesses.[73] Non-Chinese patrons and property owners were not stigmatized. "Respectable" people who came to Chinatown to gamble, take drugs, or visit brothels were understood to be victims, seduced by Chinatown itself.[74]

In 1887, a fire—rumored to have been set deliberately—destroyed much of Chinatown. The *Los Angeles Times* denounced "the lawlessness which sought to burn the [Chinese] out" but characterized the consequent relocation of Chinese residents as a "good result." Predicting that, with the Chinese gone, "the unsightly and noisome quarter of town [would] be revolutionized," the *Times* editor noted that it was a change that could not "come too quickly."[75] Chinese residents may have felt differently, but they had little choice. The fire necessitated finding a new location. The few Chinese residents that remained in the area were forced to move just three years later when the newly formed Board of Health Commissioners took steps to "clear that portion of the city of the objectionable element." City Health Officer MacGowan put up placards "ordering the heathens to remove."[76] Barred from owning property and faced with discrimination in both employment and housing, Chinatown residents simply moved a few blocks further south and then reestablished their homes and businesses. Over the next twenty years, the community grew in both numbers and the development of its built environment.

RACIALIZED MUNICIPAL REFORM

Anti-Chinese sentiment in Los Angeles was not linked directly to the number of Chinese present in the city. The infamous Chinatown massacre occurred in 1871, when the Chinese numbered less than two hundred. Still, hostility did intensify in the 1880s as Chinatown's population increased and the market for laborers contracted. Railroad companies, the largest single employer of Chinese labor in California, began laying off workers with the completion of the major intra- and interstate lines. The Chinese moved out of railroad construction and into more entrepreneurial work. Statewide, white working-class men were outraged. They believed Chinese laborers had usurped positions that should have been reserved for "real Americans." In 1897, the Los Angeles Trades Council issued the earliest recorded call for removing the city's Chinese.[77] At a public rally held in February and attended by an estimated 10 percent of the city's total population (approximately six thousand people), "a majority voted to impose a boycott, commencing May 1st, withdrawing their patronage from Chinese vegetable gardens and laundries and withholding patronage from all who employed Chinese or sold Chinese-made goods. Another resolution endorsed the use of all legal and peaceful means for 'ridding the city of Chinese.' "[78]

The crowd included some of the most influential leaders in the city—the mayor; current and former city councilmen; judges; and top newspapermen such as Colonel H. H. Boyce, co-proprietor of the *Los Angeles Times,* Joseph Lynch of the *Herald,* and Harry Osborne of the *Express*—and even "a considerable number of ladies."[79] Dr. Joseph P. Widney also attended and spoke at the rally. Widney was the brother of Judge Robert Maclay Widney, one of the founders of the University of

Southern California, and Widney himself was at the time serving as the
first dean of the University of Southern California's medical school.
Widney stressed to the crowd that the presence of Chinese "imperil[ed]
the whole experiment of our republic."[80]

Letters to the editor published in the *Los Angeles Times* indicate that
residents held a variety of opinions on the advisability of the boycott
(including concerns over who would do their housework if they had
to let go of their Chinese houseboys).[81] There was, however, agreement
regarding the main impetus for the boycott. The Chinese were charged
with taking jobs that rightfully belonged to whites. As one letter writer
explained, "The labor market in the United States is now overstocked,
and every Chinaman employed sends a male or female tramp upon
society. Sympathy for the Mongol is very cruelty and death to sons
and daughters of our own blood and nation. Away with this sickly
sympathy!"[82]

At the beginning of the twentieth century, similar sentiments prevailed in Los Angeles, but the city responded with neither "sickly sympathy" nor a boycott. As the next two sections will explain, local
lawmakers pressed public health discourse into service to justify cir-
cumscribing the entrepreneurial roles of the Chinese. Both city and
county officials used public health standards and imagery as the basis
for drafting legislation that limited the activities of Chinese fruit and
vegetable peddlers and launderers.[83] Reframing essentially economic
issues as public health concerns legitimated practices that otherwise
might have been challenged immediately as discriminatory.[84]

"Only the Beginning of the Crusade": Regulating the Sale of Fresh Produce

The 1910s were years of renewed municipal reform in Los Angeles, as
well as in other major urban areas throughout the country.[85] The city
health department's annual health reports recorded efforts to monitor
fruit and vegetable sales and restrict the movements of Chinese peddlers,
exposing the city's underlying racial tensions. There were no laws mandating racial segregation, but in practice Chinese and non-Chinese vendors occupied separate and unequal positions into a two-tiered system.
White and ethnic white vendors sold fruits and vegetables in the city's
two main marketplaces, both located downtown, approximately three
blocks from one another.[86] Combined, these two markets housed over
five hundred enclosed stalls and twenty wholesale commission houses.

Both benefited from city resources that made it easier for vendors to comply with health department standards. For example, in 1913 the city health department proudly reported to the Board of Health Commissioners that they had paved the street that ran parallel to the City Market of Los Angeles. This allowed the vendors to hose down the area whenever they deemed it necessary for keeping the marketplace clean.[87]

Chinese vendors, on the other hand, sold fruits and vegetables on the street and door to door, pulling wagons they piled with produce. At night, they stored their merchandise in wooden corrals, tall barnlike structures, where they also lived.[88] It is unclear whether white vendors or landlords barred Chinese from the two downtown markets or whether street vending was what the Chinese preferred.[89] There remains little doubt, however, that public health officials considered Chinese street vendors unsanitary and unscrupulous. They warned the public not to purchase any goods from them, describing vendors as "foreigners" who had "little regard for the State laws and City ordinances."[90]

Fruit and vegetable sales came under intense scrutiny for two reasons. The first was the symbolic association between fresh produce and the health and vitality of the city. Abundant fresh produce constituted an important aspect of the city's image that drew many visitors and new residents. (Ironically, since growers shipped the best fruit to Eastern markets, locals found it difficult to find high-quality produce.) The second reason for focusing attention on fresh produce was that the vast majority of door-to door fruit and vegetable peddlers were Chinese. One health inspector described almost 90 percent of the vendors, approximately five hundred vendors,[91] who sold outside the white-dominated central marketplaces as "foreign," by which he likely meant Chinese, as they were the only ethnic group ever referenced that way.[92] Chinatown could be segregated, isolated, and avoided, but Chinese produce vendors roamed freely throughout the city. If left unregulated, they could deliver disease literally to the doorsteps of the white community.[93] These peddlers also provided stiff competition for white produce vendors.

In 1912, the city health department hired its first fruit and vegetable inspector, Frank W. Mefford.[94] Mefford was assigned to regulate all fruit and vegetable sales in the city, including sales in both city markets, sales at street stands, and door-to-door vending. His written reports indicate the new inspector's frustration with the scale of his task and the challenges of dealing with the peddlers who bought and sold at the markets, a group not likely to have included Chinese, since they did not transact business at the markets.[95] Mefford noted the unsanitary condition of the marketplaces and described the "gutters [as] continuously filthy with mud and refuse from the market" before the city paved the street.[96] The majority of Mefford's reports, however, focused on Chinese vendors.

Photographs published in health department reports also contributed to the regional racial lexicon by providing visual representations that reinforced notions of Chinese peddlers as unsanitary.[97] The Chinese were so highly associated with street vending that their race often was not mentioned. One department report simply offers a close-up photo of a Chinese man's face to represent the job category of "vegetable peddler," using race metonymically for a form of vending (figure 1).[98] The text warned against unscrupulous dealers, without specifying their race, but then was accompanied by a picture of the corrals, demonstrating how the graphic added new, important information. The photographs also tended to be pejorative. One, for example, showed an inspector and a Chinese peddler standing outside the peddler's dilapidated shack. The state of the shack suggested that the produce kept inside would be of substandard quality. Nonetheless, the accompanying caption explicitly informed the reader that the shack lacked proper toilet facilities, that the peddler stored his merchandise where he lived and slept, and that he kept his horse in a room in the shack. The photograph clearly was meant to steer the "health-conscious" consumer away from all Chinese peddlers.[99]

In 1913, city officials approved an ordinance that created a municipal market department, run by a supervisor who would be appointed by the mayor, and authorized the construction of new buildings on city property, where vendors could sell fruit, vegetables, meats, and flowers.[100] Ostensibly to reduce the "high cost of living," the municipal market department regulated the prices charged by vendors at the public market.[101] Specifically, market vendors' rates were set to underbid street peddlers by at least 50 percent.[102] The Municipal Market Ordinance also extended the power of the health department's fruit and vegetable division, enhancing the section's ability to monitor Chinese vendors more closely. The fruit and vegetable inspector Mefford explained that the new ordinance "made it possible for the [health department] to enforce sanitation in a number of places which previous to its adoption [they] were unable to do, especially [in the] Chinese corrals."[103]

The fruit and vegetable division's newly expanded powers were gratifying, but Mefford still found his section seriously understaffed. He suggested that the city police might be able to "assist [them] in enforc-

FIGURE I. This photograph of an unidentified man was used to illustrate the Los Angeles City Health Department (LACHD/City) annual health report of 1913. The original caption reads, "Type of Vegetable Peddler." Source: LACHD/City, *Annual Report of Department of Health of the City of Los Angeles, California, for the Year Ended June 30, 1913, 75*, Southern Regional Library Facilities, UCLA Library.

ing the sanitary provisions of the ordinance." Such aid, if provided, would supplement the enforcement power of the city prosecutor, whose office prosecuted sanitation violations. The health department's ability to obtain assistance from these branches of law enforcement demonstrates how reforms initiated by the public health department were reinforced by other municipal institutions.[104]

In 1914, the police arrested eighteen Chinese produce peddlers for "carelessness in the handling of fruit." They were accused of storing their produce in the same areas of the corrals where they boarded their horses. The arrests spurred other Chinese peddlers to work directly with the representatives from the Board of Health Commissioners' office in order to satisfactorily demonstrate to Mefford that their corrals were sanitary and up to code. Mefford considered the state of the corrals as an extension of the unsanitary conditions in Chinatown and described the arrests as only the "beginning of the crusade" in regulating Chinatown.[105]

Increased surveillance of Chinese corrals did not prove a satisfactorily thorough reform. Health officials concluded that the corrals needed to be razed and rebuilt. The new structures were designed to comply with changes in public health guidelines that called for the separation of living quarters from businesses. The buildings consisted of two floors. On the bottom floor, Chinese vendors sold their produce and parked their wagons. Living quarters were on the second floor. The vendors' horses were housed in a separate building. Perhaps more significantly, health officials segregated Chinese vendors by selecting Chinatown as the location for the new corrals, rather than building them closer to the new municipal marketplace. Chinese vendors primarily sold door to door, however, so the relocation did not completely restrict them to Chinatown.[106]

The construction of the corrals may have satisfied concerns raised regarding Chinese peddlers because, in the years following, the fruit and vegetable inspector rarely mentioned them in his reports. Additionally, the municipal market department was abolished in 1920.[107] County health inspectors' increasing focus on Japanese farmers (as seen in chapter 2) may have also eclipsed the issues surrounding Chinese produce peddlers.[108] Nonetheless, the legacy of this official marking of the vendors as unscrupulous and unclean continued to stigmatize the Chinese for decades to come. Moreover, it demonstrated the ways in which public health, city, and law enforcement institutions worked together to racialize the wording and enforcement of local ordinances.

Zoning Out Chinese Laundries

One way city officials and real estate developers guarded the image of Los Angeles and protected development of housing in the city was through residential zoning ordinances.[109] In conjunction with private interests such as those represented by the Los Angeles Realty Board, the city drafted residential and business zoning laws that tailored the physical landscape to the cultural values of city promoters. This, in turn, guaranteed that communities of color would be marginalized.

For Chinese merchants, a zoning law passed in 1908 was especially important. The Residence District Ordinance designated three large sections of the city as residential areas. To preserve the residential character of these districts, the zoning ordinance prohibited the following businesses: "stone crusher, rolling mill, machine shop, planing mill, carpet beating establishment, public laundry or washhouse, fire works factory, soap factory or any other works or factory where power other than animal power is used to operate, or in the operation of same, or any hay barn, wood yard or lumber yard."[110] The ordinance changed to residential zones areas that previously had been classified as industrial. Moreover, the new law applied *retroactively*, without any grandfather clauses for existing businesses. So the city council not only had the power to dictate which businesses could and could not open in a given area but also could decide which of those already open could or could not continue to operate. The transformation of Chinese laundries into contested sites within the city reveals how space became racialized. The launderers' experiences testify to the central role of race in the politics of acquiring and using space, an aspect of the history of zoning in Los Angeles that is rarely acknowledged.[111]

Interestingly, neither market nor job competition seems to have played much of a role in prompting the redistricting ordinance. The subject of Chinese launderers and zoning comes up only once in the city's labor newspaper in the early 1910s. The single article in the *Labor Press* describes Chinese laundries as a "disgrace to the city and a positive menace to the health of the community" and asserts that Chinese launderers were the most likely source of an epidemic of infantile paralysis (health department reports do not substantiate this claim).[112] Furthermore, neither the city council members' arguments over zoning issues nor petitions from neighbors of Chinese launderers portray them as threats to white-owned businesses or to white laborers. The ordinance, instead, appears to have been an effort to give the council more control over land use within the city limits. Keeping ethnic and white communities separate and keeping residential areas free of loud, unsightly, or bad-smelling industries would allow developers to demand top dollar from newcomers seeking to make Los Angeles their home.

The Residence District Ordinance did provide owners of affected businesses with some recourse. Those whose businesses were already open and operating in an area that was newly zoned as residential could petition the city council for an exemption (which would allow the business to remain in its current location indefinitely) or for an extension (which would grant the business permission to remain in place for a specific number of years). Decisions in these matters were left to the council's discretion. By 1915, it had approved almost one hundred exemptions.[113]

Chinese launderers were among the petitioners who hoped to be allowed to continue operating their businesses in the redistricted residential zones. Chinese dominated the laundry business, constituting nearly 50 percent of the launderers in the city.[114] The Residence District Ordinance therefore posed a special burden for this group.[115] Given the U.S. Supreme Court's ruling in the 1886 case of *Yick Wo,* Los Angeles's zoning changes should have been unconstitutional.[116] In the *Yick Wo* ruling, the Supreme Court ruled that zoning regulations in San Francisco discriminated against Chinese launderers on the basis of race. But Los Angeles lawmakers argued that their zoning regulations did not take race into account but were meant to preserve the public's safety. The city's redistricting managed to slip through a legal loophole, however, partly because laundries were deemed a potential health hazard. While public health regulations were not specifically written into the residential ordinances, health issues, such as the spread of diseases and issues of cleanliness, often were cited in cases involving Chinese launderers.

For example, in April 1911, the police arrested the Chinese launderer Quong Wo for operating his laundry within a residential section of Los Angeles. Wo petitioned the California Supreme Court on the grounds that the residential ordinance violated his civil rights, as established in *Yick Wo.* For the six months before his case came to court, the police held Wo in jail. His attorney, George Hupp, argued that Wo should not be penalized under the residential ordinance. He buttressed his case with affidavits from Wo's neighbors, who asserted that the laundry was not a nuisance; Hupp also provided the court with evidence that the neighborhood in question was "sparsely built up" and therefore would not be harmed by the presence of a laundry. In addition, he presented evidence that several white-owned laundries in the area continued to operate.[117] The justices did not feel race was an issue in the case. They dismissed Hupp's charges that the ordinance was intended to unlawfully discriminate against a particular race. Consequently, the ruling in *Yick Wo* did not apply in the case. Instead, the California Supreme Court viewed this case as being about protecting the public's health, not about race. In the end, the court ruled against Quong Wo, holding that the Los Angeles ordinance was necessary "to protect the public health, morals, and safety, and comfort."[118]

In reaching its decision, the court relied heavily on a 1909 state appellate court case that highlighted public health issues. That case involved San Chung, a Chinese launderer in Sacramento, whose petition to the court for relief was similar to Quong Wo's petition and others brought by San Francisco Chinese launderers in the 1880s. Each was based on the Chinese launderers' individual rights. In the *San Chung* case, the appellate court focused, not on racial issues, but on the common good. The court maintained that the public needed to be protected from laundries because they were centers for "the propagation of disease [where] deleterious germs" could spread to the surrounding atmosphere, "giving rise to the danger of infection to persons coming into close proximity" with the laundries. The court's ruling cited "the progress of the medical profession, [and] the better understanding of the nature of disease and its transmission," as well as the municipal government's right and duty to protect and preserve the public's health. The *San Chung* decision attests to how widespread the acceptance of germ theory had become by the 1910s. Even during a period recognized for its progressive politics, germ theory was persuasive enough to sustain the restriction of individual rights, ostensibly for the greater good.[119]

Four months after the courts had ruled against Quong Wo, George Hupp brought eight more petitions on behalf of Chinese launderers before the city council. Each asked for an extension that would permit operation of his long-established business during the time it took to find a suitable place to relocate. The launderers argued that being forced to move their laundries immediately would cause them undue hardship. One Chinese launderer explained that he would be forced to "throw himself and all of his employees out of work" if an exemption was not granted.[120] All had signed leases that still had from two to four years remaining on them. Even if they were no longer allowed to occupy the buildings they had leased, each laundry owner still would be liable for the rent for the duration of his lease. Each would, in addition, need to spend a large amount of money to convert buildings in a new location into a laundry, assuming such buildings were available. The launderers surmised that the many expenses involved in moving would most likely force them to simply go out of business, causing financial hardship to both themselves and their employees. Furthermore, they pointed out that the council had granted other launderers in the same position extensions of as long as four years. The launderers reasoned that, given such a precedent, each should be granted at least two years to relocate.[121] Instead, the city council flatly denied the eight Chinese launderers' petitions. And, deviating from procedures that were followed with similar kinds of petitions, the council did not refer the launderers' requests to any other committees for consideration.[122] Council members maintained that before they could make a decision of their own they needed to know the outcome of a case involving a Chinese launderer that currently was making its way to court.[123] They could, of course, have granted the Chinese launderers an extension in the meantime, a step they had taken with other launderers, but they did not.

The Uneven Application of Law: Enforcement as Racialization

In their arbitrary and sometimes contradictory approach to petitions for exemptions and extensions, city council members demonstrated the new residential ordinance's implications for Chinese launderers. For Chinese launderers, securing an extension was a complex and arduous ordeal. For white launderers, the process was simple and relatively painless. For instance, not long after denying the eight Chinese launderers' petitions, the city council granted a three-year extension to Charles O. Humphrey to continue the operation of his laundry in a residential area. The success of Humphrey's one-sentence-long petition implied that white identity alone was sufficient to secure an exemption from the residential ordinance.[124] A second, similar appeal involved J. P. Hauret and J. P. Gacherieu, owners of the French Hand Laundry. The owners sought an exemption from the new zoning law on the ground that their business cleaned "fancy linens, silks, and woolens," all Eurocentric cultural symbols.[125] Hauret and Gacherieu's appeal emphasized their positionality as French foreigners and their consequent affiliation with haute couture, traditionally revered in the United States. This approach simultaneously allowed the French launderers to position themselves in opposition to the Chinese within the city's racial order. Chinese launderers, in contrast, could not afford to emphasize their difference. They were already considered "alien" and, by extension, inferior.[126] The French launderers also used testaments to cleanliness as a way to distinguish themselves from Chinese launderers. Hauret and Gacherieu's petition noted that they conducted their laundry "in a good sanitary manner and that there [was] no odor." The city council did not automatically grant the French launderers an exemption, but they did refer the matter to the Board of Health Commissioners, directing the board to assess the laundry facility.[127] Dr. Luther Milton Powers, the chief administrator of the board, concluded that he "[saw] no objection" to the laundry remaining in operation. The city council then granted the French launderers the exemption they sought.

The case that most incensed the Chinese launderers involved two laundries located within a block of one another. Nellie Snodgrass operated the Palm Hand Laundry, at 421 West Selma Avenue in Hollywood; Quong Long ran a self-named laundry on a small street behind Selma

Avenue. After the redistricting ordinance was issued, Snodgrass hired an attorney named Henderson to present her case to the city council. Henderson's brief discussed the merits of Snodgrass's business, including the "absolutely sanitary" condition of her establishment, and included a petition signed by her neighbors, supporting Snodgrass's efforts to remain in business at the Selma Avenue location.[128] Unlike the Chinese launderers, who had requested a two-year extension, Snodgrass felt entitled to ask for a three-year extension. The council granted her request.

Quong Long's appeal to the city council was very similar. Like Mrs. Snodgrass, he had supportive neighbors who signed a petition asking that he be allowed to continue to operate his laundry at its original location. The residential ordinance should not apply to Quong Long's business, the neighbors reasoned, because the district remained "industrial in its character," despite its new zoning as a residential area. Unlike Mrs. Snodgrass, whose neighbors' petition had appealed to the city council solely on the merits of her business, the petition Quong Long's neighbors signed mentioned his character. To counter prevailing stereotypes, the neighbors' petition referred to Quong Long as a man who was "industrious and unobtrusive [in] character."[129] Of the fifty-four neighbors who signed Quong Long's petition, most were white. Their class backgrounds varied, ranging from a bank teller to the bank president.

Despite the fact that so many of his white neighbors appealed on Quong Long's behalf, the city council denied his petition. In this case, it appears that the economic issues and racism that targeted the Chinese could be enforced by city government, in an effort to sustain the popular image of Los Angeles, even when many of his white neighbors demonstrated their opposition. Land use issues and racism took precedence over the expressed wishes of the people most directly affected by the Residence District Ordinance.

ORGANIZED RESISTANCE:
THE ROLE OF THE CHINESE SIX COMPANIES

When the city council denied the extension requests of the eight Chinese launderers, their attorney did not give up. Hupp petitioned the city council again, asking for a reconsideration of the initial decision.[130] The petitioners, meanwhile, took the additional step of seeking help from the Wing Hing Hong Company, a Los Angeles–based benevolent association for Chinese businesses. The association then contacted its parent organization, the Chinese Six Companies, the largest Chinese benevolent organization in the United States, and the consul general of China, both located in San Francisco.[131] They in turn wrote to George Alexander, the mayor of Los Angeles, asking him to intercede with the city council on behalf of the Chinese launderers. The secretary of the Chinese Six Companies, Wong Ngi Tong, explained that it was the Six Companies' duty as a benevolent society to intervene on behalf of their Chinese members when they "felt their rights or their property [were] imperiled."[132]

To establish its status, the Chinese Six Companies reminded the mayor of the power and size of its organization, noting in the letter that all Chinese in the United States belonged to and contributed to the organization. The Six Companies also emphasized the organization's legal connections. At two separate points, the letter encouraged the mayor, should he doubt any of the stated allegations, to verify their accuracy with the attorney George Hupp or with the Chinese Six Companies' general counsel in Los Angeles, the Honorable Carroll Cook.

The Chinese Six Companies' letter covered several points: it reminded the mayor of the debt the Chinese launderers would incur should they continue to be liable for rent until their leases expired; it emphasized that the launderers had spent a great deal of money converting their leased buildings into laundries; and it noted that the laundries were in compliance with city health codes. The launderers' original petitions to the city council did not mention health code standards, but perhaps having already dealt with government bureaucracy in San Francisco, the Chinese Six Companies felt it important to highlight sanitary conditions in order to counter stereotypes of the Chinese as unsanitary.

The letter further alleged that the city council had discriminated against Chinese launderers, denying them their rights, while simultaneously granting extensions to white launderers who also operated in residential districts (map 2). The letter explicitly mentioned a "white laundry" that had been permitted to continue to operate while a Chinese launderer located on the same block had been denied an extension.[133] Moreover, the letter stressed the city council had not stopped at this blatant discrimination; it had threatened the petitioners with arrest and prosecution if they failed to relocate by a specific deadline. The Chinese Six Companies' letter concluded that ultimately it was the mayor's responsibility to "persuade the city council to grant [the Chinese launderers] the same extensions that [had] been granted to people of [his] own race."[134]

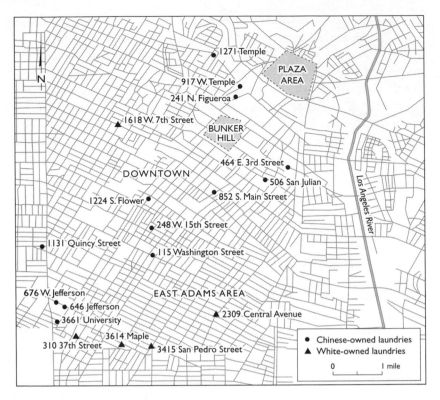

MAP 2. Chinese and white-owned laundries whose permitted locations were being disputed under the Residence District Ordinance in Los Angeles, 1913. Source: Los Angeles City Council Minutes, 1913, Los Angeles City Archives.

The Chinese consul general's letter echoed the concerns stated by the Chinese Six Companies and the eight petitioners. It also went beyond those issues to focus on the racial implications of the council's decision. The consul stated that he was confident the mayor would see that "all Nations and Races [were] treated alike" and prevent "unjust discrimination."[135] The consul general (and the Chinese Six Companies) recognized that the launderers' best chance for success lay in an appeal to the mayor's commitment to procedural rules. The consul, echoing the Six Companies, provided the mayor with a substitute ideology to legitimate action. The mayor could choose to recast the petitioners as innocent victims of discrimination in a country that prided itself on equality for all. Or the implied threat was that the consul could invoke the law, if need be. Five months after receiving the eight petitions from the launderers, two letters to the mayor, and one appeal requesting the city council to

reconsider their original ruling, the council granted the Chinese launderers a two-year extension.[136]

The denial of Chinese launderers' petitions to continue operating their
businesses can be viewed as an extension of nineteenth-century yellow
peril sentiment, which surfaced in different forms in later time periods.
Not only were these events a continuation of historical discrimination,
but they laid the foundation for future policy decisions that would affect
other communities of color in Los Angeles. As such, the history of the
Chinese laundries as contested sites within the city helps trace how space
became racialized within the cultural and political landscape. Further,
the appeals of Chinese launderers to maintain their businesses show their
agency in contesting against a range of institutions at the city, state, and
national levels, despite their being politically disenfranchised.

OVERLAPPING RACIAL DISCOURSES

At the national level, the nineteenth-century Exclusion Acts restricting
Chinese immigration paved the way for later laws that would limit or
exclude other groups. Similarly, city ordinances and laws established in
the early twentieth century had consequences that reverberated through
many decades to follow. In Los Angeles, Chinese residents were the nonwhite population most directly affected initially, but the treatment of the
Chinese also shaped the experiences of Mexicans, the other major ethnic group in California during this period.[137] Early relations between
city health officials and the Chinese established precedents for how officials in various branches of government would treat future residents
they designated as "foreigners."

The targeting of Chinese in Los Angeles was a local manifestation of
a contemporary national preoccupation with yellow peril–influenced
politics. Yellow peril discourse made the Chinese a hypervisible component of the nation's racial imagination. For Mexicans, the equivalent
racial discourse was that of Manifest Destiny. This ideology, which
gained popularity during the Mexican-American War and provided justification for U.S. expansionism, portrayed white Americans as superior
to Mexicans (and Native Americans). Its effect, however, was quite different from that of yellow peril ideology: Manifest Destiny rendered
Mexicans *less* visible in the public sphere. Expansionists argued that
after the U.S. takeover, Mexicans (and Native Americans) would eventually disappear in the Southwest because these peoples were not as biologically fit as Americans.[138] Travelers such as T. J. Farnham predicted

that Mexicans "must fade away" while the "old Saxon blood must stride the continent."[139] The depiction of Mexicans as likely to die out significantly lessened the threat they posed, especially as compared to the menace of the Chinese.

This uneven racialization reflects historically specific conditions. Since the mid-1800s, Chinese workers had been recruited by U.S. employers primarily to perform manual labor for the railroads and mines. In California, which was admitted as a free state, residents espoused a free labor ideology. The presence of the Chinese was antithetical to this ideology and represented a potential threat to white labor. Mexicans, by contrast, seemed harmless. Under the Treaty of Guadalupe-Hidalgo, which formally ended the Mexican-American War in 1848, Mexico had ceded a third of its land, including much of present-day California. Both the nation and its individual members seemed nonthreatening, even weak. Like most white Americans, Californians presumed that the Mexican presence in the United States would be completely erased in due time. Until 1908, the U.S. government did not even keep records of Mexicans as they entered the country.[140]

But descendants of the *Californios,* the Mexican ruling class before the 1848 Mexican-American War, and the children of immigrants who had come to the United States in the latter half of the nineteenth century did not disappear. In the sixty years between the United States' annexation of Mexican territory and increased Mexican immigration beginning in the early twentieth century, communities composed of these Mexican Americans had become well established. Historians of this period describe these communities as being bilingual, bicultural, and accustomed to American social mores. While overall such markers afforded them an edge in the job market over more recent Mexican immigrants, they were not necessarily better off than their more recently immigrated counterparts, and they often occupied the lowest jobs in the emerging industrial order alongside recent immigrants.[141] In addition, the majority lived in racially segregated neighborhoods known as *barrios.* Historian Albert Camarillo argues that the *barrioization* process did more than keep Mexicans spatially segregated. It also symbolized their social, economic, and political isolation from the greater American culture. Yet in many ways the barrios also provided a place to maintain and rejuvenate Mexican culture in a society where they faced marginalization and economic instability.[142]

In Los Angeles prior to the 1910s, Mexicans scarcely came under the purview of local officials. Few Los Angeles government sources even

mention the presence of Mexicans during this time period, in stark contrast to the attention focused on the Chinese. The city council records
show no evidence of complaints from or regarding Mexicans.[143] Records
of the Board of Health Commissioners from 1897 until 1911[144] yield one
mention of Mexicans, and that was by way of clarification. During a
presentation to the board, the city Housing Commission chairman Dr.
Titen Coffey used a city map to show where the Mexican population
lived.[145] The health commissioners apparently did not have firsthand
knowledge, attesting to the segregated nature of Los Angeles. As a spatially segregated population living and working in marginalized spaces in
the city, Mexicans did not readily come to the attention of public health
officials.

This attitude would change during the 1910s, when migration from
Mexico increased as a result of the Mexican Revolution. As we shall see
in the next chapter, public health officials would again play a major role
in informing the public about what they could expect from these newly
arrived immigrants and structuring how they would, or would not, be
incorporated into U.S. society. Along with Mexicans, Japanese immigrants, who replaced the Chinese in the labor force after the enactment
of the Chinese Exclusion Act, were judged by health and hygiene standards, the new yardsticks of Americanization.

CHAPTER 2

Caught between Discourses of Disease, Health, and Nation

*Public Health Attitudes toward Japanese
and Mexican Laborers in Progressive-Era
Los Angeles*

Not long after his appointment in 1915, Los Angeles County's new health officer, Dr. John Larabee Pomeroy, referring to Mexicans and Japanese, warned of the "influx of ignorant aliens into our county."[1] Sounding very much like Dr. Walter Lindley almost forty years earlier, Pomeroy implied that the county's only legitimate residents were whites.[2] All others, including Mexicans and Japanese, thus became "aliens," regardless of how long they had lived in Los Angeles.[3] Pomeroy's agitation over the burgeoning numbers of outsiders had its counterpart in cities and towns across the country. During the opening decades of the twentieth century, as Americans searched for ways to slow the pace of change within their communities,[4] an exponential increase in immigration, coupled with a change in the newcomers' countries of origin, seemed certain to undermine what remained of the nation's cultural, political, and economic stability.

In 1882, the 648,186 Europeans who emigrated to the United States came mainly from Great Britain, Ireland, France, Germany, the Netherlands, Scandinavia, and Switzerland. By comparison, in 1907, the vast majority (81 percent) of the 1,285,349 new arrivals were from such southern and eastern European countries as Greece, Italy, Poland, Spain, and Bulgaria. The magnitude of the influx prompted calls for restrictions, but it was more than the increased number of immigrants that caused alarm. Nativists and others charged that the "new immigrants" were socially and biologically inferior to the earlier cohort.

These alarmists insisted that the change in the composition of immigration would have disastrous consequences. In addition to an inevitable upsurge in disease, poverty, and crime, there would be a dangerous dilution of the pure Anglo-Saxon Protestant racial stock that had been responsible for safeguarding the republic's democratic institutions.[5]

In 1907, to counter growing fears, Congress turned to a favorite Progressive-Era remedy: the Senate and House of Representatives jointly appointed a panel of experts to study the problem.[6] The Dillingham Commission, named after the head of the task force, Republican Senator William Dillingham of Vermont, was charged with evaluating changes in immigration over the previous twenty-five years and with determining what effects these changes had had, and might continue to have, on U.S. society. Commission members operated under the assumption that the "old immigration" had been better than the "new immigration." Evoking the spirit of Manifest Destiny, they described the old immigrants as pioneers, "settlers who came from the most progressive sections of Europe for the purpose of making a home in the new world."[7] The new immigrants, by contrast, were "unskilled laboring men who have come, in large part temporarily, from the less progressive and advanced countries of Europe in response to the call for industrial workers in the eastern and middle western States."[8]

For nearly five years, the Dillingham Commission collected data, surveying people in the United States and abroad, in cities and in rural areas, questioning laymen and experts, employers and employees, old and young, rich and poor, ill and healthy—even the sane and insane. In 1910–11, when the forty-two volumes of information the commission had amassed were published, the findings held few surprises. Statistical analyses and expert opinion proved what the commission had assumed all along. The new arrivals from eastern and southern Europe were found to constitute a social and economic drain on the United States. Experts attributed to the presence of the newcomers such economic and social ills as high unemployment, growing labor unrest, political corruption, and increasing urban blight that had coincided with this most recent wave of immigration. The commission strongly recommended restrictive immigration standards to guard against any further influx of undesirable foreigners.

The legislation that followed (principally the 1917 Literacy Act) focused on the same group of immigrants who had so worried the Dillingham Commission. The intense concern over southern and eastern European immigrants highlights a very important connection between race and nation. Politicians and public figures positioned immigration policy as the first line of defense in keeping undesirables from entering the United States. Scientific reasoning was central in construing immigrants not only as detrimental to the nation's moral and social fabric but as a biological threat as well. Racial mixing would sully the country's otherwise pure stock.

But the history of immigration, race, and science in the early twentieth century involves more than the impact of hundreds of thousands of Europeans. There were other newcomers—men, women, and children who did not come across the Atlantic Ocean and did not enter the United States from an Eastern seaboard port. By repeatedly telling the story as if standing on Ellis Island, by always orienting ourselves toward Europe, as did the immigration policy makers at the turn of the last century, we miss how *regionally* constructed notions of race developed, circulated, and gradually percolated to the national level.

Racial categories in Los Angeles defied the black-white binary construction more typical of national race relations. By the mid-1800s, the Los Angeles racial lexicon included *white, Chinese* and *other*. As this chapter explains, in the opening decades of the twentieth century, this vocabulary expanded to include *Mexican* and *Japanese* as well. Public health officials, through everyday practices such as compiling statistics and reports, stemming epidemics, operating neighborhood health clinics, and visiting homes, helped shape the meaning of social membership at the local level. The understandings of race that prevailed in Los Angeles for the first twenty-five years of the twentieth century established a hierarchy that, like the racial categories it reflected, differed from the rankings common in other parts of the country. As elsewhere, whites occupied the highest position, but the places assigned to the city's Mexican and Asian residents were separate and unequal. How and why Mexicans came to occupy a higher position than Japanese during this period—and what role public health played in that outcome—are the main themes explored in this chapter. As seen in the next section, scientific reasoning played a pivotal role within the development of racial hierarchies.

STANCHING THE FLOW OF "BEATEN MEN
FROM BEATEN RACES"

When Americans groped for ways to respond to the surge of immigration that began in the 1890s and seemed only to increase over the next two decades, the influence of scientific reasoning became pivotal.[9] The successful construction of southern and eastern Europeans as undesirable depended in large part on the growing acceptance of race-based explanations of social inequality. Social Darwinism, an ideology first advanced by the Victorian sociologist and philosopher Herbert Spencer, asserted that a single natural law of progressive movement from the simple to the complex applied to all living things. This made it possible to rank all the races and cultures of the world on one linear scale. Spencer arbitrarily assigned the topmost rank to the English and then positioned other nations/races/cultures according to the degree to which they resembled the English. His ideas were enormously popular in the United States in the late nineteenth century and continued to hold sway in the early decades of the twentieth century. Spencer coupled his notion of progress with a concept of fitness that suggested that the most "fit" humans (defined as those who made the most money and thus lived the most comfortably) were the natural rulers of society. His followers argued that in human societies, as in nature, the least "fit" (defined as the poorest members of society) should be driven out (or, more passively, left to simply die out over time).[10]

Social Darwinism provided a pseudoscientific grounding for anti-immigrationists' argument that Anglo-Saxons were racially superior to southern and eastern Europeans. Charles Davenport, author of *Heredity in Relation to Eugenics* (1923), expressed his concern over the new face of immigration, arguing that southern and eastern Europeans would engender many social problems and ruin the nation's racial stock. Political economist Francis Walker expressed similar notions: "The entrance into our political, social, and industrial life of such vast masses of peasantry, degraded below our utmost conceptions, is a matter, which no intelligent patriot can look upon without the gravest apprehension and alarm. These people have no history behind them. . . . They are beaten men from beaten races; representing the worst failures in the struggle for existence."[11] Both Walker and Davenport unquestioningly accepted the premise that there existed a biologically based hierarchy of races.

Public health officials also helped bolster the case against the "new immigrants" by providing a scientific discourse and objective measurements that seemed to validate the culturally biased belief in the inferiority of southern and eastern Europeans. For example, standards developed by the U.S. Public Health Service (USPHS) legitimated more stringent U.S. entry requirements. Steamship companies required their passengers to undergo inspections before ships embarked to the United States, but as germ theory became better understood and more widely known, this existing precaution no longer seemed sufficient. Changes in the 1891 Immigration Law empowered the USPHS to conduct its own inspections of immigrants as soon as they arrived in the United States.[12] Officials hoped the second set of inspections would encourage steamship companies to look over their passengers more carefully in order to lessen the risk of having to transport them back to their port of origin.[13]

While USPHS staff concentrated on Europeans entering the United States through East Coast ports,[14] and the Dillingham Commission launched more and more investigations of southern and eastern European immigrants (only three of the commission's forty-two volumes focused on immigrants west of the Mississippi),[15] white residents and officials of Los Angeles County confronted a very different set of "undesirables."[16] There, the two largest racialized groups were Mexican and Japanese residents. In 1890, the Issei population (first-generation Japanese) in California numbered just over one thousand and was concentrated mainly in San Francisco and the San Joaquin Valley. When the 1882 Chinese Exclusion Act cut off West Coast employers' ready access to cheap labor,[17] many turned to the Japanese as replacements. In just ten years, the number of Japanese in the state grew to over ten thousand. Many Japanese settlers moved south to meet growing demands of Southern California's agricultural industry.[18]

The number of Mexicans in the Southwest also rose in the early twentieth century for several reasons. Under Mexican President Porfirio Díaz, Mexico began the momentous transformation to a capitalist economy fueled by foreign investment. The Mexican peasantry suffered tremendous losses in this process. Ninety-six percent of Mexican families were landless, and artisans and craftspeople lost their livelihoods. People who lived in small towns migrated to cities in search of employment opportunities. The Mexican Revolution, which began in 1910, encouraged further immigration to the United States. Finally, the establishment and connection of railroad lines in Mexico facilitated migration for residents of central Mexico who sought employment in the United States.[19]

Mexican immigrants' main port of entry was El Paso, Texas. Many moved further west after crossing the border, however, and settled in Los Angeles. The city's industrial growth and the expansion of large-scale farming in the county created a demand for low-wage laborers that fueled migration. In 1910, L.A.'s Mexican population numbered five thousand; in 1920, it was thirty thousand; and by 1930, it had more than tripled, reaching ninety-seven thousand. Before 1910, these newcomers often settled around the Plaza in an area near the original Chinese settlement. Increasing commercialization in that section of the city prompted resettlement of the Mexican population after 1910.[20] Many Mexicans moved outside the city limits, especially to rural and unincorporated East Los Angeles.[21] Japanese settlers, too, tended to congregate more outside than inside the city limits. Most had come to farm; land and jobs were both more plentiful in areas surrounding the city.

As political scientist Claire Jean Kim has pointed out, even though racial hierarchies in the United States consistently have placed whites at the top, rankings are rarely one-dimensional; a variety of factors shape relative positioning.[22] In Los Angeles at the beginning of the twentieth century, whether an immigrant group consisted mainly of employees or mainly of employers, and whether it consisted mainly of sojourners or mainly of settlers, served as important factors in determining the group's place on the racial spectrum. And, as I argue, the historical experiences of one nonwhite group could significantly affect the rankings of other nonwhite groups.

Once again, health officials helped mold public understandings of race and delineate the racial hierarchy. As suggested by Health Officer Pomeroy's complaint, quoted at the opening of this chapter, about the growing numbers of "aliens" in rural areas, county officials became aware of the increased numbers of Mexican and Japanese residents and were quick to blame these groups for unduly burdening the fledgling health department. The next section examines some of the ways the immigrant population shaped the county's new public health department, and vice versa.

BEYOND THE BLACK-WHITE BINARY: PUBLIC HEALTH OFFICIALS' EARLY ENCOUNTERS WITH MEXICAN AND JAPANESE COMMUNITIES

In April 1915, the Los Angeles County Health Department gained its first full-time health officer. The Los Angeles County Board of Supervisors appointed Dr. John Larabee Pomeroy to the post,[23] launching a new era in the department's history. In the first two years, Dr. Pomeroy hired six employees and several emergency employees as needed (such as quarantine guards, bacteriologists, and part-time nurses) and created an advisory council of fifty people in the county.[24] In 1917, Dr. Pomeroy assembled seven consultants, mainly doctors, in the areas of public welfare, school hygiene, and child hygiene, as well as one Japanese interpreter.[25] Previously, the health department's part-time and sole employee had concentrated on conducting inspections of rural hog farms and slaughterhouses. He turned his attention to the county's human residents only when epidemics threatened. County officials' decision to name a full-time department head signaled a recognition of the growing importance of public health as an institution. A department with full-time personnel would give health officials greater influence in urban forums and, as the department gained in reputation, would serve as officials' springboard to the national stage.

The man the board recruited, John Pomeroy, was already a seasoned professional. After receiving a medical degree in his home state of Kentucky, he had moved to New York City.[26] There, while working for the city health department, he trained under Dr. Herman Biggs, a national leader in public health.[27] Pomeroy served a few years in the U.S. Army as an assistant surgeon and then accepted a position as a resident physician in Monrovia, California (about fifteen miles northeast of Los Angeles). Soon after, he opened his own private practice. In 1912, he became Monrovia's health officer and remained in that position until 1915, when he accepted the Los Angeles County Health Department post.[28]

Dr. Pomeroy is a significant figure in the period's overlapping public health and racial politics. Under his leadership, the county department grew from a one-man operation to an agency staffed by six hundred employees responsible for overseeing thirty-six cities. During the twenty-six years he headed the Los Angeles County Health Department, Pomeroy directed the implementation of every program that targeted the county's racialized groups. Influential nationally as well, he addressed forums and conferences, published in professional journals and popular magazines, and wrote op-ed pieces. He taught at the College of Medical Evangelists (known today as Loma Linda University) and participated in meetings of the county Board of Supervisors. He also served as the director of the Los Angeles County Tuberculosis Association and the president of the western branch of the National Public Health Association.

As the newly appointed Los Angeles County health officer, Pomeroy faced nearly as many challenges as opportunities. His department had a very small budget and a very large domain. The health department served the county and all unincorporated areas outside the Los Angeles city limits (including East Los Angeles, which still remains unincorporated), amounting to 3,420 square miles of territory, over which

107,613 residents were dispersed, mainly in rural areas.[29] The health department had the authority to employ doctors and nurses on a case-by-case basis for those who could not afford medical care, but the great distances separating homesteads made it difficult for these professionals to visit all sick residents.[30] Without public clinics at this time, the county hospital, overseen by the Charities Department, provided the only options for those who could not afford private care.[31]

Even before Pomeroy's takeover in 1915, a key responsibility of the county health department had been stemming the spread of communicable diseases, such as diphtheria, scarlet fever, and typhoid fever.[32] To increase the efficiency of the department's response to emergencies, Pomeroy hired a stenographer, who started a card index and filing system. Organizing and storing information in an orderly fashion would help the health department contact physicians quickly, possibly saving lives during epidemics.[33] Like other public health experts nationwide, Pomeroy was familiar with the basic premises of germ theory and understood that diseases could not be contained within geographic boundaries. With the steady growth of the Los Angeles highway system, the county's once widely dispersed populations would come into much closer contact. Unless public health officials maintained their vigilance, there was a real possibility that illnesses carried by the county's growing Japanese and Mexican populations could be passed to whites. A 1917 department report noted that "the influx of ignorant aliens" had "greatly" increased the workload for health staff.[34] It also asserted that "the very large amount of work needed for preventing the spread of diseases, educating the ignorant classes, and reducing the death rate [placed] a constant burden on [the] present staff and budget."[35]

Although public health officials stigmatized Mexicans and Japanese as "ignorant classes"[36] whose unsanitary behaviors contributed to the spread of disease, they also recognized in these immigrant populations an opportunity for expanding the department's power and prestige. Surveying his jurisdiction, Pomeroy concluded that there existed a "grave necessity of constructive work among the alien population in the county."[37] County health officials repeatedly emphasized that the spread of disease could "cost the county thousands of dollars."[38] Noting that "sanitary education [was] less costly" than fighting epidemics, they pushed hard for funds and staff to cover the design and implementation of preventive programs.[39]

In drawing attention to how much the county as a whole needed their services, and to how efficiently they provided those services, health officials bolstered their institution. But men like John Pomeroy saw the mission of their institution as encompassing more than the preservation of local residents' physical well-being. They posited that living "under crowded conditions" and in unsanitary environments—the everyday reality of most immigrant populations—led to "immorality and vice."[40] Absent the efforts of public health officials, these kinds of social problems would flourish. Such destructive behavior would, in turn, lead to increased taxes to "support hospitals, jails, and police courts, and similar institutions."[41] Funding public health thus amounted to preserving an essential bulwark against social chaos and spiraling economic costs.

In turn-of-the-century Los Angeles, maintaining social order inevitably involved defining racial order. In gauging the desirability of the newcomers, elected officials often relied on public health standards. In the county, public health workers who, unlike most other officials, had frequent and direct contact with immigrants served as interlocutors. They defined the meaning of *Mexican* and *Japanese* for their fellow white Angelenos and established the position of each within the region's racial hierarchy. In all their official reports, correspondence, and presentations, health officials relied on the racial categories "white," "Mexican," "Japanese," and "other." The 1917–18 annual health report, for example, estimated the population of the entire county as 975,709 and the unincorporated population as 136,706. The report listed only two racial groups: Japanese and Mexicans, with populations of 7,500 and 10,000, respectively. The racial identity of the remaining 958,209 people was left unspecified.

The racial lexicon found in the earliest formal annual county health reports reflects their author's personal history as well as the county's demographics. John Pomeroy's upbringing in Kentucky and his training in New York City suggest that he would have understood race in terms of a black-white paradigm. But the county's African American population was very small, and local officials rarely mentioned these residents.[42] In the absence of a noticeable African American community, Mexican and Japanese residents occupied the position of the racialized other. The ways in which each group was racialized, however, differed.

The institutional practices that had promoted the perception of the Chinese as a racialized other who threatened to pollute the body politic tended to reify yellow peril discourse. As a result, all Asians came to be perceived as a dangerous threat. Specifically, the treatment of the Chinese population in and around Los Angeles paved the way for the racialization of groups that came after them, especially the Japanese. In Los

Angeles County, where few Chinese lived, most yellow peril–influenced policies were redirected toward the more numerous and visibly present Japanese.[43]

RACIALIZING THE JAPANESE:
MEDICALIZED YELLOW PERIL

Politicians and civic leaders popularized the belief that the Japanese represented a racial and economic threat to the United States by using tactics much the same as those directed against the Chinese in the nineteenth century. The twentieth-century version of the Chinese Exclusion Act was the 1907–8 Gentlemen's Agreement. This federal law curtailed immigration of Japanese laborers but left the door open to workers' wives and children.[44] When the number of Japanese residents in California continued to climb rapidly, state legislators passed the Alien Land Law Acts (one in 1913 and another in 1920), aimed at preventing immigrants from owning land or even leasing land for longer than three years. The Land Acts would, their supporters hoped, drive out the Japanese because farming was their chief source of livelihood. Particularly in the Los Angeles area, Japanese settlers were making rapid gains in agriculture. Between 1910 and 1920, the number of Japanese-owned farms tripled and the total acres they farmed increased more than seven times.[45] Undaunted by the physical challenges associated with working arid land, by 1920 Japanese farmers had tilled (mainly through lease agreements) an estimated 5 percent of the 440,000 acres of land under cultivation in Los Angeles County.[46] Their success with labor-intensive crops such as fresh berries and celery soon led to charges of monopoly and unfair competition. As with the Chinese, perceived economic threats were immediately wrapped in racist rhetoric. To rally support for the 1920 Land Act, for example, one slogan urged, "Keep California White."[47]

Again as had happened with the Chinese, a major mechanism for constructing the Japanese as a threat to white Americans was the racially coded language of public health. Through public speeches, municipal forums, and policy formation, public health officials clearly aligned themselves with those who opposed the presence of a Japanese community, adding medical authority to nativist campaigns. Moreover, since health officials were the only county employees who came into repeated contact with the Japanese, their statistics, reports, and interpretations became the official narrative on the Japanese. Dr. Pomeroy's contribu-

tions to newspapers and popular magazines further acquainted the average citizen with the county's "alien problem." His article "Japanese Evil
in California," which appeared in the California magazine the *Grizzly
Bear*, provides a good example of the power public health wielded in
legitimizing and perpetuating the threat of yellow peril.[48]

Pomeroy explained the economic threat posed by the Japanese in this
way. First, he claimed that their agricultural achievements could undermine (white) American farmers' prosperity. Second, he noted their
impact on wage labor. Employers supported the presence of Japanese
workers because they could pay them less than whites, but, Pomeroy
cautioned, hiring Japanese laborers actually was an economic liability
because the Japanese formed work cooperatives, thereby driving up low
wages.[49] He linked what he characterized as increasing Japanese birth
rates with the Japanese position in the agricultural industry, implying
that the Japanese economic stronghold would only grow over time, in
step with the population increase.

To strengthen his case, Pomeroy included a chart of total births in the
county from 1915 to 1919, broken down into the categories "white,"
"Japanese," "Mexican," and "other." In a separate chart, he tracked
births per district throughout the unincorporated areas of the county,
using a number sign to indicate where Japanese births outnumbered
white births. Pomeroy concluded that the Japanese, who accounted for
27 percent of births in the rural areas of the county, represented an esca-
lating racial threat. Citing birth rates as evidence of this looming menace also helped focus attention on Japanese women and the "double
threat" they constituted. Once in the United States, they could work in
the fields and give birth to Japanese Americans. Each carried its own
dangers. Pomeroy pointed out that the effects of Japanese women's fertility could be seen already in the "growth of a large American citizenship, yellow in color."[50] As American citizens, these children would
eventually have the right to purchase land, thereby undermining the
intent of the two Land Acts.

A second threat lay in the fact that as field workers the Japanese
women flaunted prescribed gender roles and deprived their children of
adequate mothering and a proper upbringing.[51] Underlying both cri-
tiques lay concerns that Japanese farmers had an added economic
advantage because they worked in family units in the fields. Interestingly, although Mexican women toiled with their families as hired hands
in the agricultural fields, no such criticisms were leveled at them. I suggest this is because Mexican women were much-needed cheap seasonal

laborers working land owned by whites, rather than family members working land they owned or leased cooperatively.

Negative depictions of Japanese women gained wide circulation in part because health officials and other professionals relayed their observations upward, to individuals in national institutions. Pomeroy suggested that the Board of Supervisors appeal to the Washington-based Children's Bureau to help with educating Japanese women regarding child care and to assist in enforcing birth registrations.[52] The casual nature of this suggestion implies that cross-institutional support for racially based agendas was not unprecedented. The request for help in compelling the registration of births seems also revealing: the politics of race influenced how and why statistics were gathered; attention to a public health issue such as fluctuations in birth rates could simultaneously engender yellow peril ideology and medicalize it.

Others in the medical community echoed Pomeroy's charges. Dr. W. O. Henry gave a talk at the Los Angeles County Obstetrical Society, which was later published prominently on the first page of the *Southern California Practitioner.* In the article, Henry advised women how to care for themselves in preparing themselves for pregnancy. Henry urged "well bred white women" to have four or five children because large families had made the United States great. He pointed out the decreasing birth rate in the country and warned them that if they did not "bear sufficient children, the Japanese and other foreign women [would] keep up the needful human production, just as the Japs and foreigners [would] meet the farming needs of the country when American men fail or refuse to do it." He thereby tied economic and racial fears together. Henry went on to ask, "Will it be the cultured, civilized, educated American women or must we depend upon the foreign, ignorant, uncultured, and half civilized?" He compared the urgency for white women to procreate to France's need to raise their birth rates after World War I. Racial fears also drove France's population campaign that labeled women midwives and abortionists as traitors to the state.[53]

In addition, Dr. Henry's comments mimicked the well-known rhetoric of former president Theodore Roosevelt, who had preached an eerily similar warning in 1901. In an effort to stir imperialist feelings among Americans, he argued that if Americans did not step in as an imperial power in the Philippines, "Some stronger, manlier power would have to step in and do the work, and we would have shown ourselves weaklings, unable to carry to successful completion the labors that great and high-spirited nations are eager to undertake."[54]

While there was much talk about the yellow peril, and while Pomeroy's figures for Japanese birth rates in the county were high enough to cause some readers alarm, their accuracy remains uncertain. In other contexts, health department officials, citing the challenges involved in obtaining exact birth counts in the rural communities, noted that actual numbers might be higher. Regardless of the uncertainty involved in their data collection methods, Pomeroy's (and other health officials') tracking and reporting of Japanese birth statistics added scientific legitimacy to otherwise unsubstantiated claims by politicians that Japanese immigrants were overtaking Los Angeles.[55]

Moreover, use of this sort of medicalized nativism was not limited to officials. As the general public became more familiar with public health discourse, they too resorted to medical discourse in framing their images of Japanese farmers as an economic threat. According to a popular line of reasoning, Japanese farmers were "manifestly more fitted for agriculture" because their body type allowed them to squat more easily. This difference in physiological makeup rendered the competitive-market playing field uneven.[56] Critics of Japanese farmers, including large agricultural employers, typically failed to mention their proimmigration stance when it came to Mexicans, whom they too believed were endowed with bodies biologically suited for work in agriculture. Mexicans, too, were known to be able to "stoop" more easily than whites. Agricultural employers may have found Mexicans' supposed "biological advantage" acceptable because they usually encountered Mexicans as dependent employees, not as independent competitors like the Japanese farmers.[57]

Other forms of medical discourse embedded in the speeches and reports of county officials also helped marginalize the Japanese. Notions of Japanese living conditions as unsanitary and of Japanese farmers as spreading disease through the produce they cultivated seemed particularly effective. Promoting the image of Japanese farmers as disease carriers brought every aspect of these people's lives, including their housing, under scrutiny. Most Japanese farmers lived on their farms, often in inexpensively constructed homes that housing and health officials portrayed as inferior to "typical" housing found in Los Angeles, such as California bungalow and craftsman-style homes.[58] Implicitly defining *inferior* as equivalent to *unsanitary,* officials reasoned that these assumed unsanitary conditions could spread to produce cultivated on the same land. They did not take into account the possibility that most Japanese farmers, regardless of the degree of their commitment to sanitary conditions, would have had little incentive to build permanent housing, given the provisions of the Alien Land Laws of 1913 and 1920. Since they could not own land, and could lease land for only three years at a time, inexpensive and quickly constructed housing might have seemed the only reasonable option. But more importantly, the Alien Land Law Acts produced disincentives for Japanese to invest in the land, which led to the very conditions health officials deemed they needed to monitor. In other words, dominant groups produced the non-normativity they purported to police.

Public health workers further contributed to the negative perception of the Japanese by explicitly raising the specter of food-borne disease, particularly intestinal diseases to which "the Japanese nation [was] subject."[59] The most common and worrisome form of food-borne illness at the time was typhoid fever.[60] Although reports of typhoid cases were few during this period, officials argued that the types of produce the Japanese farmed, such as berries and celery, were ideal carriers of typhoid, since people generally consumed them raw.[61] Dr. Pomeroy added to the climate of fear in his correspondence with the Board of Supervisors. In 1919, addressing concerns over the potential of Japanese-cultivated produce to spread typhoid, he urged the board to enact an ordinance that would "[prohibit] the sale of infected or unwholesome fruit and vegetables" and would be designed to directly target Japanese farmers and vendors.[62] He cited as a precedent the nineteenth-century law the city of Los Angeles had passed to limit the sale of fruits and vegetables by Chinese vendors, thus demonstrating how previous ordinances directed at immigrant groups paved the way for later racialized legislation. Furthermore, all fruit and vegetable stands would be subject to inspections by health officials, and vendors themselves would be subject to physical examination.[63] Mobilizing the specter of disease to increase the regulatory powers of the health department was a strategy Pomeroy relied on time and again. For example, in 1922, he proposed to expand the health department's still small staff, requesting funds to hire someone "who could devote his entire time" to monitoring Japanese-operated farms.[64]

The intensity of the Los Angeles County Health Department's interest in the area's Japanese population rose and fell over the first quarter of the twentieth century. By the early 1920s, the combination of the Gentlemen's Agreement, the two Alien Land Law Acts, and the Supreme Court's decision in *Ozawa v. United States* (1922), which reaffirmed that Japanese were ineligible for citizenship, had begun to slow the flow of settlers, although not enough to assuage the social and cultural anxieties of nativists or to calm completely the largely financial fears of those, especially in California, who felt themselves the victims of unfair competition for jobs. It took the draconian measures of the Immigration Act of 1924, which ended all Asian immigration to the United States, to satisfy those groups. Employers, meanwhile, faced increasingly severe labor shortages. The advent of World War I intensified the problem precipitated by the mounting restrictions on Asian laborers.[65] Employers in California and the Southwest turned to yet another non-native source of cheap labor: Mexicans.

LABOR NEEDS AND RACIAL DEFINITIONS

At the national level, widespread anxieties about foreigners, especially southern and eastern Europeans, continued throughout the first quarter of the twentieth century. The literacy requirement and head tax imposed by the Literacy Act of 1917 were aimed at restricting these groups' entry into the United States. In the Southwest, however, the Act had little effect. Mexicans crossing the border at El Paso, Texas, to look for work in the United States continued to pass through the border relatively freely. They did, however, face more obstacles. The head tax was a burden for some. The USPHS required that all second-class arrivals bathe and delouse their clothing and baggage in the interim. Anyone not already vaccinated was immunized at the border.[66] Employers, eager to protect and enhance the supply of cheap labor the incoming Mexicans represented, argued that these immigrants were neither a cultural nor an economic threat. What allowed potential employers the latitude to make such an argument was the relatively fluid position Mexicans occupied vis-à-vis immigration restrictions and laws. Federal authorities classified Mexicans as "white." Employers routinely depicted Mexicans as merely a temporary population, "birds of passage" who would eventually return to Mexico.[67] They countered stereotypes of Mexicans as lazy by recasting them as diligent employees. All in all, large employers assured the general public, this temporary workforce was an ideal solution—these laborers would ensure continued industrial and agricultural growth, thus bringing prosperity to all.

Public health officials in Los Angeles did not share big employers' enthusiasm. Still, they did not racialize Mexicans in the same way they did Asians. After 1910, when a steady flow of Mexicans began arriving in the county, officials realized that these newcomers would need to be accommodated in some way as a vitally important source of labor and characterized their work as part of the "regulation of the labor market."[68] As a state health bulletin put it, "The Mexican peons are said to be the only available labor for railroad construction."[69] Pomeroy had his department undertake what he described as the "very large amount of work" required to sufficiently educate this "ignorant" class in the basics of health and hygiene.[70]

These efforts took on a great urgency in the summer of 1916 with the arrival of typhus in the county. The outbreak, which spurred the creation of local policies based on the premise that all Mexicans spread disease, had far-reaching social and political effects in addition to its medical consequences. The next sections trace the connections between the public health response to typhus and the development of long-lasting cultural representations of Mexicans as disease carriers and the emergence of shriller calls for changes in national immigration policy.

"CONQUERING A FOREIGN FOE": TYPHUS IN MEXICAN RAILROAD CAMPS

Typhus is an infectious disease caused by rickettsia (a bacterialike microorganism) and transmitted to humans through lice and tick bites.[71] Although it is not contagious, given the right conditions (overcrowding, lack of facilities for bathing and washing clothes, poor sanitation), typhus can spread rapidly into epidemics.[72] Thus, when a Mexican laborer at a Southern Pacific Railroad camp near Palmdale (twenty miles north of Los Angeles) came down with typhus in June 1916, health officials were alarmed. Ultimately, the disease struck twenty-six persons (twenty-two of whom were Mexican railroad workers) over the four-month period from June to October 1916. There were five fatalities, all Mexican.[73]

The first case and subsequent ones in the railroad camp initially were referred to county officials because of the camp's location outside the Los Angeles city limits and because the county hospital treated many of the victims. Public health officials at the state and national level, however, also soon became involved. At the county level, measures to contain the outbreak involved hygiene, sanitation, and education campaigns, all of which were aimed exclusively at Mexicans. The stigma of the typhus outbreaks marked all the areas where Mexicans lived, whether railroad camps or "villages" (temporary housing for Mexicans, located near work sites), as locations in need of inspection (figure 2). Health officials characterized their efforts as a "campaign against filth

FIGURE 2. Health officials used this photograph to show the substandard housing available to Mexicans in labor camps. The original caption reads, "Typical row of dark and filthy Mexican dwellings in a southern California county." Source: *California State Board of Health Monthly Bulletin*, October 1916, 180.

and lack of personal hygiene."[74] Since the county health department did not have sufficient staff (or budget) to carry out all the necessary inspections, Pomeroy hired an emergency staff of twenty-six employees and sought additional sources of aid to "stamp out this dread disease."[75] The inspections covered more than one hundred railroad camps, some forty Mexican villages, and a large number of temporary sites where laborers camped briefly. In thirty railroad camps, health officials carried their campaign to an especially aggressive level, using cyanide gas to destroy lice, ticks, and other pests.[76] (Official reports make no mention of how the gas might have affected the Mexican residents of the camps.) A health department memo written in the aftermath of the typhus scare boasted that, "for the first time in the history of the county, every railroad camp and Mexican village has been thoroughly inspected."[77]

County officials were uneasy over the dispersed nature of the Mexican camps; they were distributed too widely throughout the rural areas of the county to allow effective oversight. They likened Mexican laborers to "nomad[s]" who wandered in and out of the camps, implying that the men were both aimless and primitive.[78] Even before the epidemic, some public health officials and doctors had objected to the "extensive

FIGURE 3. Through this photograph, health officials communicated to viewers the type of person likely to carry typhus. The original caption reads, "A gang of Mexican railroad section laborers in Los Angeles County. These men have but recently arrived from Mexico and are under the supervision of the railroad and health authorities." Source: *California State Board of Health Monthly Bulletin*, October 1916, 181.

migration of ignorant peon Mexicans who had been driven out of Mexico by the Revolution."[79] Dr. Howard D. King of New Orleans warned, "[E]very individual hailing from Mexico should be regarded as potentially pathogenic" (figure 3).[80]

Because public health officials fed concerns that Mexicans could at any time "slip through the border and get into the country without passing through the usual government quarantine stations," all Mexicans in the county came under suspicion. Health officials then used the typhus outbreak to justify intruding into the private lives of Mexican residents, regardless of their age, sex, or domicile location. For instance, the county department did not hesitate to investigate Mexican families who lived outside the railroad camps.[81] And they sent instructional flyers to the public schools, asking teachers to notify the department if they had Mexican children in their classes. Once so notified, health officers visited the schools to "enforce bodily cleanliness."[82] A headline on the cover of the *California State Board of Health Monthly Bulletin* in

November 1916 read, "typhus and the Mexican immigrant control of epidemics among school children," thus giving the impression that there was already an epidemic in place to be controlled when in fact there was none.[83] In the city of Los Angeles, the health department launched a delousing campaign that focused "particularly among the house court population."[84] There is no evidence that these efforts had any positive effect on the containment of typhus in Los Angeles County. They did, however, succeed in racializing private and public spaces, as well as stigmatizing the people within those spaces.

Officials at the state level too sought the kind of information they felt only a firsthand inspection of the railroad camps could provide. The California State Board of Health directed the Bureau of Communicable Disease to conduct a survey.[85] The bureau's assistant epidemiologist, the communicable disease specialist Dr. H. F. Senftner, visited over 150 of the Santa Fe Railroad's camps during the typhus epidemic. The camps were divided into two main groups, floating (14 sites) and stationary (137 sites).[86] Boxcars served as housing in all the floating camps as well as in some stationary camps. Other permanent camps provided houses constructed of concrete or ties. The tie houses (seventy-one in all) were built from "old, worm eaten, insect infected, white-washed railroad ties." Dr. Senftner quoted a high-ranking railroad official who declared that the tie houses "should have never been constructed in the first instance."[87] Dr. Senftner also reported on the camps' toilet facilities, which consisted of 43 flush toilets and 190 pit toilets. He judged the sanitary conditions of the toilets as poor. The facilities were shared by men, women, and children, but the children had to "[stand] on the seat of the toilet and [straddle] the seat opening, with a resultant unclean condition of the seat."[88]

The camp survey appeared to be a model of scientific inquiry. The sheer number of camps visited suggested thoroughness, and the quantitative analyses implied objectivity. When he interpreted his findings, however, Dr. Senftner allowed cultural conditioning to trump his scientific training. For example, despite the descriptions he provided of the substandard boxcar housing in the floating camps and the rotting tie houses in the permanent camps, he concluded that 21 camps were in good condition, 102 (67 percent) in fair condition, and only 23 camps (15 percent) in poor condition. There was a similar bifurcation between his qualitative description and quantitative analysis of camp toilet facilities. He characterized 90 percent of the toilet facilities he saw as "unclean," but in his quantitative assessment, Dr. Senftner listed 28 of the flush toilets as in good condition and 15 as fair. Of the 190 pit toilets, he tallied 134 (70 percent) as in fair condition, 36 in good condition, and only 21 (11 percent) as in poor or bad condition. The study's overall positive conclusion regarding camp conditions had significant consequences. Improving camps already classified as acceptable did not seem like a promising approach to stemming the typhus epidemic. Instead, health officials focused on changing the behavior of the Mexicans who lived in the camps, reforming their "unclean" and "ignorant" ways. Officials drafted regulations that implied that Mexicans needed to be taught hygiene practices and that they needed to be supervised in the process.

The California State Board of Health pressured railroad employers to play a role in containing the typhus outbreak. Officials drew up an eight-point list of regulations, printed in both English and Spanish, and labor recruiters distributed the list to the various railroad camps. The regulations applied to every man, woman, and child living in the camps, not just to laborers. They included instructions for sanitizing personal items, such as bedding and clothing, and living quarters. Bedding was to be boiled, then aired and shaken out; living quarters, including toilets, were to be washed down with equal parts coal oil and water. Clothing was to be boiled and shoes were to be submerged in gasoline and then left outside to air-dry.[89] All of the regulations focused on improving personal hygiene; not one addressed the inferior living conditions in the camps.

Compliance was mandatory. An order of the California State Board of Health criminalized a person with body lice as a public nuisance. The ordinance did not specifically mention race, but it was developed and enforced in response to the cases of typhus fever in the Mexican railroad camps.[90] It entitled railroad officials to require mandatory bathing with disinfectants on the part of those who lived in the railroad camps. The Southern Pacific Railroad and other (nonspecified) railroad companies agreed to implement weekly delousing procedures in their camps.

The delousing regulations required Mexicans to "bathe" in equal parts coal oil and warm water. The procedure for killing body lice involved rubbing the coal oil thoroughly into the skin, concentrating on any areas where body hair was present. The regulations suggested that Mexicans could remove the coal oil either by rubbing it off with a dry towel or by taking a shower. Neither approach was a practical possibility. Most camps lacked any bathing facilities, let alone showers.[91] Instead, the railroad companies provided the laborers with galvanized pails, cotton scraps for rubbing off the oil, and mops. Mexicans were required to endure such procedures once a week, under the supervision of health officials or railroad personnel.[92] The character of these weekly events is clear in the county health department's own accounts, where the delousing was described as "forced bathing" that "closely [resembled] a military procedure."[93]

In addition to complying with the state health mandates in the camps, three railroad companies established quarantine observation facilities in response to the typhus epidemic. These employers, aiming to prevent further outbreaks in the camps, required newly hired Mexican laborers to undergo a compulsory quarantine period of fifteen days before being released to work in the camps. Quarantine guards, invested with the same legal power as deputy sheriffs, policed the quarantine observation facilities to prevent anyone from leaving.[94] Once cleared to leave the quarantine areas, Mexican laborers could proceed to the camps, but the state Board of Health still required that railroad companies report the names of all new employees to the board. The increased level of scrutiny in the camps, the quarantine facilities, and the expanding information exchange between public agencies and private companies placed Mexicans under an unprecedented level of surveillance.

"WE ARE ALL HUMAN": MEXICAN LABORERS PROTEST THE RACIST ENFORCEMENT OF HEALTH REGULATIONS

When Dr. Senftner surveyed the Santa Fe Railroad camps, he had little direct contact with Mexican laborers, except during the delousing sessions.[95] In the internal department version of his report, Senftner reported that Mexicans "respectfully listened" to his detailing of the state's regulations (as relayed through his Mexican interpreter, Mr. E. Giron) and readily promised they would "carry out such regulations with precision and regularity" until informed otherwise.[96] But the published version of the report offered a revised assessment of how Mexicans perceived the regulations: there Senftner noted that Mexicans often expressed frustration with efforts to "maintain satisfactory hygienic and sanitary standards," given their inferior living conditions.[97]

This frustration is clear in a formal letter of complaint a group of Mexicans who lived in a desert camp about 140 miles east of the city of Los Angeles (near what is now Joshua Tree National Park) sent to the Mexican consul in Los Angeles. The men, angry over the crudeness and impracticality of the antityphus procedures and the overt racism of the regulations, submitted the following letter just two weeks after the state board issued the regulations:

> Dear Sir:
>
> Due to the difficult circumstances we find ourselves in this foreign country, we look to you asking for help in this case. We are enclosing a copy of the severe law that the railroad line has imposed on us Mexicans who work on the track, which we do not see as a just thing, but only offensive and humiliating. When we crossed the border into this country, the health inspector inspected us. If the railroad line needs or wants to take such precautions it is not necessary that they treat us in this manner. For this, they would need health inspectors who assisted every individual with medical care and give us two rooms to live, one to sleep in and one to cook in, and also to pay a fair wage in order to obtain a change of clothes and a bar of soap. This wage they set is not enough for the nourishment of one person. Health comes from this and these precautions are the basis for achieving sanitation. Health we have. What we need is liberty and the opportunity to achieve it. We need a bathroom in each section of camp and that the toilets that are now next to the sleeping quarters be moved. Many times their bad smell has prevented us from even eating our simple meal. Furthermore, we can disclose many other details which compromise our good health and personal hygiene.
>
> With no further ado, we remain yours, graciously and devotedly, your attentive and faithful servants. We thank you in advance for what you may be able to do for us.
>
> *Felipe Vaiz, José Martínez, Felipe Martínez, Adolfo Robles, Alejandro Gómez, Alberto Esquivel.*[98]

The letter writers enclosed a copy of the Spanish version of the eight-point list of antityphus regulations. Printed in capital letters, the last line of the regulations read, "NO TYPHUS—NO LICE." Next to this imperative, the men had written, "NO ES LA RAZA MEXICANA DIFERENTE DE LA AMERICANA PARA QUE SE CREA QUE SOLO EN NUESTRO CUERPO SE RECONCENTRAN LAS ENFERMEDADES. TODOS SOMOS HUMANOS Y NO DEBERÍAN APLICAR ESTE PROCEDIMIENTO ÚNICAMENTE A LOS MEXICANOS" ("The Mexican race is not different from the American race and one should not think that disease takes hold in only our bodies. We are all human and they should not apply this procedure only to Mexicans").[99]

Drawing on an alternative epistemology, the men explained their living conditions as resulting from systemic inequality, not from ingrained cultural habit. Unlike state and county officials, who crafted reports that avoided charging the railroad companies with any responsibility for the presence of disease and dirt in the camps, the workers did not hesitate to assign blame where it was due. While health officials focused their efforts to stem the typhus outbreaks on remedying Mexicans' "unclean habits," the letter writers pointed out the obvious: the unsanitary living conditions that so disturbed health officials when they visited the camps were provided by the railroad employers. Their Mexican employees liked them no better than anyone else. Throughout the letter, the men stressed that rather than their having created these unclean and unhealthy conditions, the camps' unsanitary environment had been imposed on them by their U.S. employer. They also emphasized that U.S. officials had declared them free of disease when they entered the country, implying that the typhus outbreak must have originated on American soil.

The men also appropriated the language of health and hygiene to assert their basic, universal right to better living conditions. In place of the officials' culturally based argument that Mexicans' hygiene standards were inferior, the workers observed that sanitary conditions had been denied them. In demanding improvements, they were also marking themselves as members of the body politic. Healthy work and living environments were basic human rights to which these laborers—and all others—were entitled.

RACE AS AN ORGANIZING PRINCIPLE IN THE CONTAINMENT OF TYPHUS

Although Mexican laborers knew that "the Mexican race is not different from the American race,"[100] the same could not be said for health officials. From the outset, race served as their interpretive framework for explaining the typhus outbreaks. Initial investigations revealed that 60 percent of the men in the railroad camps had body lice, a known carrier of rickettsia, the microorganism that caused typhus. This finding reinforced health officials' beliefs that all Mexicans were "naturally uncleanly" and "ignorant" and that they tended to live in overcrowded conditions.[101] Initial reporting of the typhus epidemics focused almost exclusively on the Mexican laborers. The health department issued no warnings to the general public on how to guard against transmission of the disease or how to recognize its symptoms. Very little attention seemed to be trained on the disease itself (epidemiological studies and lab reports were barely referenced), and no official seemed concerned with the living conditions the railroad companies provided in the work camps.

In part, this approach was a direct outcome of the health community's assumptions about the source of the typhus outbreaks. Having seen only infrequent evidence of bathing among the men in the work and railroad camps they visited, health officials assumed that Mexicans had an aversion to water and simply did not like to bathe. They concluded that Mexicans were a "class who habitually shunned water."[102] Other sources suggest a different genesis for the absence of bathing. Economist Paul Taylor, who conducted field research and oral interviews in the agricultural areas of California's Imperial Valley (east of Los Angeles) during the 1920s, reported that when employers made proper shower facilities readily available, Mexicans bathed daily. Moreover, health officials in the Imperial Valley determined that the water supplied by employers, not Mexicans' hygienic practices, could cause gastrointestinal disorders and even some cases of typhus, as the water was used for multiple purposes.[103]

These culturally induced misunderstandings had effects that reached well beyond the 1916 typhus scare. By not treating typhus as a threat to the public at large, officials constructed the disease as uniquely Mexican. This preference for using race as the organizing principle for understanding typhus also transformed Mexicans from unfortunate victims of a serious disease into active transmitters of deadly germs, thus adding a medicalized dimension to existing nativism. Backed by the notion of scientific objectivity, health officials gave wide circulation to constructed categories of Mexicans as unclean, ignorant of basic hygiene practices, and unwitting hosts for communicable diseases. These images were embedded in medical and media narratives and in public policy.

Visual depictions of Mexicans also were effective communicators, amplifying the meaning of politicians' and other commentators' casual references to the "typical Mexican." In October 1916, for example, the cover of the California State Board of Health's monthly bulletin was emblazoned with a photograph taken in the railroad camps (figure 4). The shot included two women, two men, and two children, all dressed in traditional but shabby Mexican clothes, including headscarves and sombreros. All the people in the picture had dark skin and indigenous features, and one woman held her child in a traditional sling, marking her as primitive. The scene as a whole resonated with then-current negative stereotypes of Mexicans as peons, and mainly of Indian stock. The presence of women and children implied that Mexican workers brought their families with them (or created new families once they arrived in the United States and found employment).[104]

This photograph and others like it not only provided a visual vocabulary that reinforced an already existing anti-immigration position but also implicitly and explicitly raised issues that eventually became key

FIGURE 4. This photograph of Mexican families appeared on the cover of the *California State Board of Health Monthly Bulletin*, October 1916, to illustrate the dangers of Mexican immigration.

reasons for including Mexicans in the immigration quotas that followed the 1924 Immigration Act. Even before the 1920s, concerns emerged about the greater fertility of Mexican women compared to their white American counterparts. Images of Mexican families implied that these immigrants would soon be a permanent population. In addition, captions such as "The type of people who are bringing typhus and other diseases into California from Mexico" made certain that not even the most naïve of readers could miss the point.[105] Used in this way, the word *type* reduced all Mexican immigrants to a static archetype. Race, not symptoms, became shorthand for "disease carrier."[106]

THE AFTERMATH

The typhus outbreak stigmatized Mexicans and Mexico alike. State Board of Health officials stated flatly that "(t)yphus fever [was] foreign to California."[107] Because the first reported case in Los Angeles County originated in a work camp where Mexicans lived, and because typhus had been reported in Mexico City[108] a few months prior to the Los

Angeles case, U.S. health officials felt justified in concluding that Mexicans had brought typhus fever to California.[109] They drew this conclusion without having conducted any sort of epidemiological investigation or even ascertaining whether any of the Mexican laborers in the county camps were from or had traveled through Mexico City. Nor were officials deterred by the fact that the incubation period for typhus ranges from two to fourteen days.[110] And, although most of the infected railroad Mexican laborers reportedly entered the United States through El Paso, no investigations were conducted to see whether the source of the typhus could have been in the United States. To be allowed to enter the United States, Mexican immigrants had to undergo intense health inspection procedures, including delousing and a visual inspection for the presence of rash and/or fever. Thus it was unlikely in the extreme that any immigrant who passed through the border at El Paso could have transmitted typhus. Finally, the very same officials who staunchly maintained that typhus could have originated only in Mexico and could have been transported to the United States only by Mexicans acknowledged the presence of cases identical to typhus on the East Coast (although there typhus was known as "Brill's disease")[111] and were aware that the first reported case of typhus in California involved an Italian who lived in the San Francisco Bay Area.[112] No amount of evidence to the contrary seemed able to shake their conviction that Mexicans were responsible for the typhus outbreak.

Health officials' response to typhus also changed border policies. Labor needs in the United States had kept border crossing relatively easy before the typhus scare. With the threat of an epidemic, however, general inspections increased, even for day laborers. The Los Angeles County Health Department received "assurances" that in the future, disinfections at the El Paso border would be performed by USPHS staff. Indeed, the USPHS planned to establish multiple inspection stations along the Texas border—in El Paso, Eagle Pass, Laredo, and Brownsville, a move county officials applauded.[113] Mandatory inspections continued into the late 1920s, further demonstrating the extent to which Mexican immigrants and disease had become conflated.[114]

During the typhus epidemic, health officials promoted ideas that constructed Mexicans as diseased and as inferior to white Americans, but they also posited that Mexicans could be trained in the areas of health and hygiene. After concern over the spread of typhus had subsided, county health staff began more systematic efforts at outreach. Dr. Pomeroy planned to improve Mexican camps by modeling them after "industrial villages."[115] The underlying philosophy of the villages was that by providing adequate living conditions employers could increase workers' productivity.

County health officials investigated health conditions in more urban areas, most prominently Belvedere, where Pacific Electric Corporation employees lived.[116] They kicked off the cleanup campaign in the Mexican sections of Belvedere with a three-day campaign in which they served five thousand notices, destroyed rubbish, and inspected water supplies.[117] County health officials pressured the owner of the land tract where Mexican families lived to improve the general living conditions of the land, as well as to provide better sanitary facilities for his tenants. The Pacific Electric Railway Company, which operated the interurban rail network and was owned by the Southern Pacific Railroad in whose camps the typhus outbreak had occurred, hired a nurse and sanitary inspector to help improve sanitation in the area.

Arguing that substandard conditions "could not be allowed to persist in Southern California," county health officials set forth a plan that called for rebuilding some of the homes and simply relocating others to clearly marked plots of land. All homes, old and new, would be whitewashed. Both sanitary facilities and water supplies would be improved. In an approach unlike the one they took with the Southern Pacific Railroad, county health officials strongly urged the landlord to be accountable to the people who lived on his land.[118] In their quarterly report, the county health department concluded that their cleanup campaign resulted in improved health in Belvedere.[119] The cleanup campaigns in Belvedere where railway workers lived paralleled health officials' efforts in the railroad camps, thus demonstrating how health officials initiated public health campaigns that would serve the needs of large employers in the city.

The tenets of the project provide insight into health officials' understandings of Mexicans as a racialized group. Like their peers nationwide, county health officials believed that the first step toward elevating Mexicans' living standards was to get this population to recognize the benefits of personal hygiene and sanitary conditions.[120] Then, health officials reasoned, with a "small outlay of capital" and "proper supervision" they would be able to improve Mexicans' overall well-being.[121] Health officials boasted that with some direction and supervision, "the Mexican [could become] a respectable citizen."[122]

To supervise the improvement project, Dr. Pomeroy assembled an advisory board including members of both private and public agencies, such as the El Monte Welfare Association and the County Welfare Association. The County Welfare Association raised money and provided "moral support." The California State Immigration and Housing Commission, an agency designed to study the working and living conditions of immigrants to California and to craft policies to Americanize this population,[123] assigned an employee to help supervise the project, and the county health department provided a deputy health officer to take a health census of the families and "organize the work." One of the commission's main duties was to enforce housing laws and support construction projects to improve immigrant housing.[124] In addition, county nurses made home visits to Mexican women to provide advice on matters of housekeeping and child rearing. The health department report noted that "the Mexican himself aided to reconstruct and render more livable his condition," but in reality, it was probably *only* "the Mexican" who rebuilt his/her own community, as everyone else involved was designated as a supervisor or an advisor.[125]

Despite their efforts to set up quarantine stations in the interior, and despite the increased number and complexity of physical exams conducted at the border, health officials readily acknowledged that "owing to the demand for labor, continuous shipments of Mexicans [would occur] through the regular ports of entry and through points along the border."[126] In Los Angeles City alone, the Mexican population increased more than sixfold, from five thousand to more than thirty thousand between 1910 and 1920.[127] With this sort of steady increase in the Mexican population, county health officials could never hope to accomplish all the revitalization efforts they believed necessary. Because they knew Mexican camps owed their existence largely to the fact that private companies actively recruited Mexican laborers, officials hoped these enterprises eventually would join in the effort to improve living conditions for their workers.[128] Such speculation indicates at least some degree of recognition on the part of health officials that the problems experienced by Mexican communities in Los Angeles were not solely the result of cultural pathologies but rather rooted in institutionalized inequalities.

CONCLUSION

Public health issues such as the spread of disease became a prominent way to gauge the social costs of immigration. Disease had long served as a trope to mark immigrants as outsiders. But in the 1910s, the link between disease and Mexican immigrants changed in two significant ways. First, the association broadened the issue of immigration from a labor question that affected employers to a social problem that could affect all citizens. Second, while warning the public about the dangers immigrants brought with them, public health officials also offered their services to work with these newcomers and transform them into an acceptable workforce. Mexican men and women were effectively robbed of their adult status. They were now viewed as and treated like stubborn children—a whole population who needed to be overseen, trained, controlled. Officials repeatedly stressed that Mexicans could be taught to adopt American practices. Just months after the typhus epidemic, Dr. Pomeroy reported to the county Board of Supervisors that "once the Mexican realizes hygiene and better sanitary conditions will prevent sickness, and his cooperation is secured, if proper supervision is given, we find rapid results can be obtained."[129] As a newly formed department and an emerging professional class, public health officials needed the Board of Supervisors to commit resources to their programs.

This racialized (re)construction of Mexicans had the full support of some employers as well. Complaining about the challenges they faced in keeping a close watch on their employees, these men asserted that Mexicans "required constant supervision." Yet others believed that Mexicans were an ideal labor force "once fixed," as if training Mexicans were akin to training animals.[130] Some employers assessed the "break-in period" as straightforward, arguing that Mexicans were "easily satisfied if [they had] sufficient clothes to keep [them] comfortable and enough to eat, together with a cigarette." One foreman for the Santa Fe railway, however, insisted that Mexicans became lazy once they were Americanized.[131] The overlapping agendas of health officials and employers with regard to monitoring the Mexican labor force and the negative perceptions of Mexicans as a group in need of surveillance would have lasting implications. The next chapter explores how such racial constructions became institutionalized as the Los Angeles County Health Department grew into one of the country's leading health departments. One could gauge where Mexicans and Japanese stood in the racial order both by the types of programs created for Mexicans that assumed they needed to be rehabilitated and by the lack of programs offered to Japanese.

CHAPTER 3

Institutionalizing Public Health in Ethnic Los Angeles in the 1920s

By the 1920s, Los Angeles County's white public officials and residents were considering the "Mexican situation" in a new light.[1] Conceiving of the area's thirty-thousand-member Mexican population as "birds of passage," unmarried male laborers who flocked to the United States for seasonal work and then returned to Mexico, was no longer tenable. In reality, women made up 43 percent of the Mexican-born population in the United States by 1920, according to the census.[2] And while most laborers did leave the farms once the picking season had ended, many relocated to nearby urban areas rather than returning home to Mexico. The early 1920s also brought a more widespread rural-to-urban shift in population as ever-greater numbers of nonseasonal agricultural workers (white and Mexican) headed for cities in search of higher-paying industrial jobs.[3] Reluctantly conceding that "[t]he Mexicans . . . are here to stay," white Angelenos hurried on to remind one another that they need not let this situation cause lasting harm: "[B]ut whether we are to let them live here in unhealthy conditions and ruin the appearance of our cities depends on [us]."[4]

Public health officials provided a first line of defense against the potentially ruinous effects of long-term Mexican residents. During the first two decades of the twentieth century, health officials' interactions with the county's Mexican population had been confined primarily to disease control efforts. As it became clear that Mexican immigrants in the Los Angeles area were permanent settlers, not itinerant seasonal laborers, public health workers, along with other professionals, such as social workers and the founders and staff of settlement houses, began establishing programs geared to this new reality.

The aims of these programs shifted over time. In 1917, elated over the success of his department's efforts to stem the spread of typhus, Los Angeles County Health Officer Pomeroy stressed that Mexicans could be educated to forgo their unsanitary ways and rise to more acceptable (i.e., American) standards of hygiene.[5] This training, of course, would be undertaken by Pomeroy's department; thus he requested a larger budget and more personnel. Pomeroy could expect to reap other advantages as well. Educating Mexicans about healthful living would help reduce the likelihood that in the future diseases like typhus could gain a footing among immigrant groups and then spread to the area's white population. The tone of Dr. Pomeroy's calls for rehabilitating the Mexican population began to change by the early 1920s. He grew more strident as the decade progressed, and the programs his department instituted for improving Mexicans' approach to sanitation and hygiene became correspondingly more coercive.

This chapter examines two important and interrelated public health initiatives the Los Angeles County Health Department championed: the development of preventative health care centers and the effort to monitor and modulate the infant mortality rate (IMR) in the area's various Mexican communities. The health centers offered various medical services in a central location, including well-baby clinics (WBCs) and prenatal care (both aimed at lowering IMRs) and diagnostic screening. The centers shaped the immigrant experience in Los Angeles. Indeed, as this chapter shows, the impact of the public health centers rivaled that of other, more commonly studied institutions such as schools and political parties. For Mexicans especially (Japanese residents had fewer direct contacts with public health programs and staff), encounters with health care professionals were problematic. The programs instituted by the Los Angeles city and county public health departments were deeply racialized. Based on unacknowledged racial norms, the programs resulted in unequal health care for groups at the lower end of the racial hierarchy. For example, the amount of money budgeted for the individual centers varied according to the specific population they were designed to serve. Similarly, there was no uniformity in the number or type of clinics offered at the centers. Finally, although most centers were segregated by default (most were localized by city or county area), those whose location was sufficiently central to serve a racially mixed clientele were explicitly designated either as "Mexican clinics" or as for "whites only."

Collecting and interpreting infant mortality data were tasks undertaken by all major municipal health departments in the United States by the mid-1920s. IMRs were important for several reasons. One was to provide a "scientific indicator" of a region's overall health. Equally important, however, was the role these rates played in reinforcing racial stereotypes and regional hierarchies. Los Angeles County officials separated the data by race and then relied on the differences across populations to further legitimize the existing regional racial order. By linking the high IMRs among Mexicans to the alleged ignorance and slovenly habits of Mexican women, officials branded these women as bad mothers. White women, on the other hand, emerged as especially good mothers, given their significantly lower IMRs.

Health officials chose to deal with high IMRs to the exclusion of other pressing health needs. The death rate from tuberculosis, for example, was twice as high in Mexican neighborhoods as in the rest of the city, prompting health officials to recommend the establishment of a tuberculosis clinic in Mexican neighborhoods like Belvedere.[6] Perhaps the single most objective factor contributing to high TB rates was the poor housing conditions in Mexican neighborhoods. Thus ameliorating tuberculosis rates would have required calling for comprehensive urban reform measures addressing such issues. "Better babies" required much less: home visits and cleanliness talks.[7] The disproportionate attention paid to high IMRs and, more specifically, Mexican women shifted the focus away from TB, thus sidestepping responsibility for improving overall housing conditions to help eradicate TB. The gendered approach toward addressing racialized health problems also helped avoid casting a shadow over another important issue at the heart of the Southern California economy, Mexican immigrant labor. By focusing attention on high IMRs and consequently on Mexican women, health officials marked Mexican women as engendering health problems, thus helping male Mexican laborers escape further stigmatization.[8]

Discussions of Mexican IMRs were always within the context of a general pathologizing of Mexican culture and Mexican spaces. Dr. Pomeroy described the Mexican communities where public health workers taught parenting skills as "crude and primitive."[9] The Los Angeles Times ran headlines such as "Shocking. Filth, Disease, and Poverty Rampant" in stories describing Mexican neighborhoods with high IMRs, which they labeled as "pest holes."[10] These accounts implied that if Mexican women chose to indiscriminately have children without proper parenting skills or under unsuitable conditions, surely they were to blame for the high IMRs (not to mention the cycle of poverty that would surely ensue from a high birth rate). Establishing the behavior and culture of mothers as the deciding factors in their infants' survival, therefore, directly affected the solution public health professionals proposed. High IMRs, they argued, could be lowered through education rather than structural change.

Finally, working with Mexican women would by extension help present Mexicans as a population that could conform to American standards and thus become an acceptable workforce. Disciplining bodies through health programs was the first step to creating a strong workforce. By focusing their public health efforts on women, health officials not only preserved the social and racial status quo but also helped prevent a public outcry against Mexicans that might have threatened the region's cheap labor supply.

As L.A.'s white officials and residents focused more and more attention on the "Mexican situation," worries over the area's Japanese residents diminished. A shift in the regional racial ordering was under way by the 1920s. Two significant structural changes contributed to this shift. Japanese immigration slowed following the passage of the 1907–8 Gentlemen's Agreement, and the California Alien Land Law Acts of 1913 and 1920 circumscribed the state's existing Japanese communities.[11] Nonetheless, negative depictions of Japanese continued. They are apparent in the medicalized rhetoric of nativist groups and in the public health departments' ongoing interest in birth rates among the Japanese living in Los Angeles City and County. Public health administrators also often compared the birth rates of Mexicans and Japanese, usually to direct attention to how the growth of racialized groups might affect the white population. In general, though, public health officials paid much less attention to Japanese residents than to Mexican settlers during the 1920s. (This was especially true after the passage of the 1924 Immigration Act, which ended the inflow of all Chinese and Japanese people.) The relatively low infant mortality rates in Japanese communities in and around Los Angeles meant that formal programs, such as the WBCs and prenatal care services, were not a priority. Perhaps most importantly, by 1920 the Japanese did not represent a ready pool of cheap labor for large employers. Most Japanese residents of Los Angeles City and County were farmers who worked land that they leased or owned cooperatively. The dominant discourse about the Japanese, unlike that about the Mexicans, held that they could never be assimilated no matter how much coaching health experts undertook. Accordingly, in allocating resources, officials invested much more heavily in the area's Mexican population than in its Japanese communities.

In contrast to the Japanese, Mexicans tended to concentrate in unskilled occupations. In Maravilla, regarded as a "typical" Mexican neighborhood, a labor survey described the majority of the workers as unskilled, mainly working as laborers. They brought home an average yearly income of $795, or $8,500 in 2004 dollars.[12] Mexicans were also the largest ethnic group represented in agriculture by 1920.[13] Mexicans also worked as laborers on Japanese-operated farms. One worker, Miguel Alonzo, described his experience working on a Japanese-operated farm. "They [the Americans] don't want us here, even the Japanese mistreat the Mexicans without any thought whatsoever, they think we are less than they are, as we allow ourselves to be exploited, they do what they want with our labor, and rob us with impunity in various ways," stated Alonzo.[14] Alonzo's description provides a sense of how, although Mexicans and Japanese may have both occupied a position lower than whites within the regional racial hierarchy, their occupational status also shaped their positions as racialized subjects.[15]

As in any other developing institution, the decisions of officials in the early years of the Los Angeles County Health Department had long-term effects. The choices Dr. Pomeroy and others made incorporated the period's prevailing social as well as medical views. These unexamined assumptions, along with the specific provisions of the programs and policies they informed, became part of the department's culture and daily operations.

RACIALIZING SPACE

One important way in which the expansion of the Los Angeles County Health Department in the 1920s directly affected immigrant groups was by defining the physical space in which they lived as disorderly and undesirable. Through their discourse, their initial decisions about which communities to target with health programs, and their handling of an outbreak of bubonic plague in 1924, Los Angeles health officials racialized the county as a chaotic and disease-prone place. They noted that with its size, and "especially with [its] two large foreign groups, the Mexicans and Japanese,"[16] the county sorely needed outreach programs. Public health workers lobbied for larger budgets and more personnel, but they also insisted that they could adequately address the welfare of county inhabitants even without major budgetary changes. This was possible because officials believed the source of problems among the county's poorest residents was these groups' ignorance and their wayward personal and cultural characteristics.

Concentrating on the supposed (negative) attributes of immigrant groups allowed officials to leave unexamined other, larger, structural factors as the cause of these residents' difficult circumstances. Chief among the systemic inequalities that plagued the county was its inadequate supply of basic resources, such as clean water and sanitary waste disposal. Moreover, access to these limited resources was skewed in favor of those who lived in the county's urban areas. What little services there were did not extend to rural residents, mainly Mexicans and Japanese. The lack of garbage collection or even accessible garbage dumps meant that those who lived in rural areas (whites included) disposed of their refuse indiscriminately.[17] Contaminated water was a recurring problem as well. In 1920, health officials traced an outbreak of typhoid fever to a polluted riverbank. Water that flowed through this area carried pollutants that sickened Mexicans who lived in work camps in El Monte, along with residents of Redondo (where many Japanese operated their own farms), Huntington Park, Whittier, and Santa Monica. And in Irwindale, another area where many Mexicans lived in work camps, a "faulty method of [water] distribution" caused outbreaks of typhoid annually, according to health officials.[18]

Both the problems and the opportunities facing county health officials were familiar to their counterparts nationwide. Urban and rural landscapes were undergoing major changes in the 1920s. Across the country, "farm boys"—year-round residents and nonseasonal agricultural workers—were moving to the cities in search of higher-paying industrial jobs. In Southern California, the population movement also included an outflow of poorer residents from the city of Los Angeles. Until 1920, the population of the city had been about twice as large as that of the surrounding area. In the 1920s, the county began to grow more rapidly, outpacing the city. Increasing industrialization in downtown areas raised property values; this in turn raised rents, making previously affordable housing out of reach for many people. Homes farther from the city center, in newly developing towns and unincorporated areas in the county, were considerably less expensive. Some cities in the county, such as Glendale and Huntington Park, ballooned in size; so, too, did enclaves on the margins of Los Angeles City, such as Belvedere (map 3).

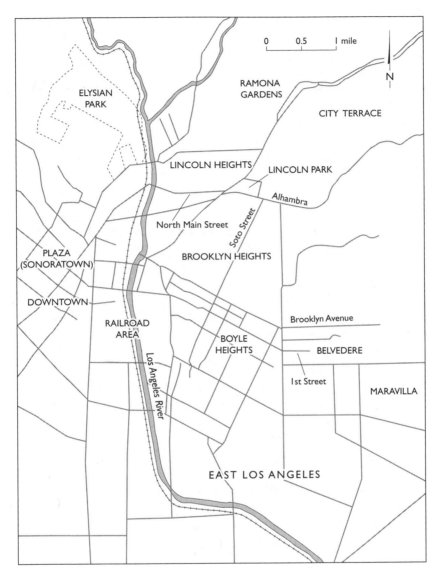

MAP 3. Neighborhoods in Los Angeles's Eastside.

When health officials began surveying Belvedere and a neighboring area they referred to as Laguna in 1915, they estimated that the region had a population of twelve thousand people.[19] Mexicans lived in camps in the area.[20] The area was subdivided in 1921 and quickly developed into a residential community. Belvedere was attractive to whites and to

Mexicans because of its affordability. Health officials distinguished between the "American sections" of Belvedere and the "Mexican sections," particularly "Maravilla," which was predominantly Mexican. Additionally, interurban railway systems made it possible for Mexicans to live in Belvedere but continue to work in the city.[21] As a result, Belvedere grew rapidly—reaching twenty-five thousand within the first three years of development and an estimated one hundred thousand by 1927. As the decade progressed, Belvedere became increasingly Mexican.[22] By 1930, Mexicans represented 95 percent of Belvedere's population; Belvedere was home to the fifth-largest Mexican urban community in the United States. To whites, it looked, as one writer lamented, "as if all Mexico were moving to Belvedere."[23] In the county as a whole, Mexicans constituted an estimated 11 percent of the population by 1928. One contemporary research report claimed that Los Angeles was home to more Mexicans than any other urban area except Mexico City.[24]

Population expansion continued throughout the 1920s; in 1927, the city and county populations were almost equal.[25] Geopolitical boundaries shifted with the redistribution of residents. Areas like Belvedere came to be defined as part of the county rather than the city. These kinds of changes left health officials feeling they were chasing an "ever receding horizon."[26] For its first five years, the county health department had been mainly reactive: staff surveyed the county, responded to epidemics, and tracked diseases. At the beginning of the 1920s, officials were moving toward a more proactive stance—hiring more staff, launching large-scale programs, and developing clinics. In attempting to position the department as one that would rival the nation's leading public health facilities, officials found themselves challenged by what they referred to as the "diffuseness" of their jurisdiction and its rapidly growing population.[27] Looking back on those formative years, Dr. Pomeroy characterized the changes at the health department as a movement from the "old shot-gun policy methods of enforcement of public health to education, more influence of the well trained intelligent official who is desirous of giving the public a health service rather than functioning as a police official."[28]

For the county's Mexican population, the health department's new service orientation may not have seemed significantly different from its policing function. The Mexican sections of Belvedere first drew the attention of health officials during the 1916 typhus epidemic.[29] Although there were no typhus cases reported in Belvedere, because many Mexican railroad and streetcar employees lived there, public health providers extended the parameters of their cleanup campaigns to include Belvedere, paying "particular attention . . . to the sections inhabited by Mexicans."[30] County health department officials continued to express concern over Belvedere throughout the 1920s, claiming that it represented a "public health and social problem without parallel in the entire United States"[31] and noting that the Mexican residents of Belvedere were of a "low type."[32] The characteristics of Belvedere's white population went unmentioned. The lack of infrastructure to support the area's rapid growth also was ignored. By the late 1920s, Belvedere had come to symbolize the "typical" (i.e., dirty and disorderly) Mexican neighborhood, so much so that it was referenced as an example of the "alarming" adverse effects of immigration during congressional debates regarding future immigration restrictions.[33] Similarly, the practice of linking Mexicans and their communities to disease has had a long and eventful history. An outbreak of plague in a Mexican neighborhood in 1924 helped make this casual linkage both more official and more commonplace.

MANAGING THE PUBLIC'S HEALTH: THE 1924 PLAGUE EPIDEMIC

In 1924, two forms of plague—bubonic and pneumonic—threatened a Mexican neighborhood on the eastern margins of downtown Los Angeles.[34] The first person infected, Jesús Lujón, reportedly had the telltale "buboes" (swollen lymph nodes in his armpits and groin), but no one suspected he had bubonic plague. Doctors later speculated that Lujón spread plague bacteria to Luciana Samarano, who contracted pneumonic plague. (Lujón and the Samarano family lived in the same neighborhood, and Lujón often visited the Samarano home.) The disease spread further at Luciana Samarano's funeral. Mourners who had had contact with Samarano before her death unknowingly infected other funeral service attendees.[35] By the end of October, nine people had died, all residents of the Mexican Clara Street neighborhood.[36]

The Los Angeles City Health Department did not become involved until October 29, when Dr. Elmer Anderson, a department physician, visited the Samarano home in response to a report that two more residents had become ill. Dr. Anderson sent these individuals, and six others in the neighborhood who also were ill, to the county hospital. There, all eight were diagnosed with plague and admitted for care. Public health officials declared Luciana Samarano, who had died a week earlier, the first victim of the plague and treated the Samarano residence on Clara Street as the locus of the outbreak. They quarantined a seven-block zone around the house, thereby restricting the movement of the neighborhood's 1,600 residents.[37] In addition, people who did not live in the neighborhood, but who happened to be present when the quarantine was instituted, were "caught in the net of the quarantine." They too could not leave until the restrictions were lifted, twelve days later.[38] Dr. Pomeroy characterized the quarantine as the "[s]upervision over certain Mexican areas where the disease may be hidden."[39]

The quarantine was implemented by staff from a network of municipal departments. Firefighters roped off the seven designated blocks. Health officials hired 450 guards (150 per eight-hour shift) to patrol the area twenty-four hours a day.[40] The police department provided an additional twenty-five officers for each shift to "assist the quarantine guards in handling the situation."[41] Later, with no further request from public health, this police presence was increased to seventy-five officers per shift, bringing the police presence in the seven-block Clara Street area to 225. Neither health nor police officials specified why they felt it necessary to triple the police presence.[42] The total number of guards grew to 675 (amounting to about one guard for every 2.5 residents), despite there having been no change in the size of the quarantined area.

Shortly after the Clara Street area was quarantined, two residents of the "Mexican quarter" in Belvedere also contracted pneumonic plague and died.[43] On November 5, a "corps of nurses" descended upon Belvedere to investigate. Although they found no new cases of plague, they recommended a quarantine.[44] Health officials designated a six-block area of Belvedere as closed to entry and exit and hired another 450 guards (150 per eight-hour shift) to police the perimeter twenty-four hours a day.[45] Although this area was just one block smaller than the one in the Clara Street neighborhood, the media paid relatively little attention to Belvedere.[46] In both neighborhoods, the guards were present, ostensibly, to ensure the public's safety. They were responsible for patrolling the border of the quarantined area to make certain that no one (other than crews who distributed rations) entered or left without authorization. Within days of the imposition of the quarantines, rumors circulated that guards had shot Mexicans who were attempting to leave. Health officials vehemently denied the rumors;[47] there are no extant sources of information to independently validate or invalidate these assertions. That such rumors circulated at all, however, speaks to the concerns Mexicans had over the extreme nature of the quarantine security measures.[48]

There was one glaring exception to the strict "no entry/no exit" regulation of the quarantined zone. Throughout the epidemic, one group was allowed to leave: laborers. Industrial employees were allowed to "pass out on permits and under observation."[49] The fact that the workers would be "observed" suggests that the workers would return to the quarantined area. Such an agreement raises questions regarding officials' commitment to public health versus corporate wealth. Longtime Mexican laborers who were working (or who once had worked) in agriculture or large industries (such as railroads) were likely to have found the quarantine regulations unpleasantly reminiscent of the lockdowns that occurred in work camps throughout the 1910s. Granting Mexican laborers permission to leave the quarantined area to go to work suggests an attempt to balance labor needs with public health standards. Indeed, during the 1916 typhus outbreaks, city and county health officials (including many of the same officials who now were involved in confronting the plague epidemic) argued for more stringent border-crossing policies, even while recognizing that employers' demands for cheap labor would ensure that immigration certainly would not cease and probably would not slow significantly. Thus officials tried to contain typhus-related threats to public health by urging railroad employers to hire private nurses for the camps, by overseeing delousing procedures, and by helping institute fourteen-day quarantine camps. During the plague epidemic, the compromise was similar: a stringent quarantine gave the appearance of increased public health precautions, but exemptions for laborers guaranteed the continued availability of a low-paid workforce.

In an effort to contain the plague, the city and county health departments initiated rat extermination campaigns. They concentrated their efforts on three sites: the two quarantined neighborhoods and the Los Angeles Harbor. The latter was targeted because public officials and business leaders feared that even in the absence of any evidence of infected rodents, the threat of plague would be enough to shut down the harbor, severely affecting trade in the region. "There is suspicion cast upon Los Angeles Harbor at the present time," warned Dr. Walter Dickie of the state Board of Health. He also noted that "[s]hips will not come into any harbor where any question of plague infection exists."[50] The *Los Angeles Times* described the harbor as receiving the most "con-

certed" efforts of the three-sited attack on rats. It was also the first area
to be scoured. Although they described these measures as simply preventative and confidently asserted that the harbor was sure to receive a
"clean bill of health,"[51] health officials nevertheless deployed the bulk
of their resources at this site. The extermination operation at the harbor
involved "twenty-five expert rat catchers" and an on-site laboratory
staffed by the "best bacteriological experts," who were prepared to test
"every rat" for evidence of plague bacteria. Health officials promised
that the testing would be followed by "extensive extermination campaigns."[52] At least one "campaigner" was certain he knew what the
hunting and testing would show. "[T]his plague is not unexpected," he
told a Los Angeles Times representative; "Los Angeles is exposed to
three lines of attack—from the ground squirrels in the north, from the
rats that may be imported from the Orient, and from the rats that may
be imported by train from Mexico. This epidemic is the first gun fired
by the enemy."[53] The idea that serious illness must have its origin outside the United States was a familiar one. During the 1916 typhus epidemic, health officials had claimed that typhus, too, was an "import."
For many readers, the reference to "Oriental rats" also must have
evoked memories of the 1900 bubonic plague epidemic in San Francisco's Chinatown.[54] Given this context, the assertion that Mexican and
"Oriental" rats were responsible for the plague was anything but comic.
By tapping into preexisting medicalized racial discourses, the extermi-
nator quoted in the Times reaffirmed the direct association between foreigners and disease.

In contrast to the description of the extermination efforts at the harbor, health officials reported the campaigns in the two quarantined residential areas merely as being "well under way." This suggests that the
procedures at these sites were not as extensive as those trained on the
harbor, where officials wished to avoid a port quarantine that would
interrupt commerce.[55] That the neighborhoods where plague had been
identified were given less attention than the harbor underscores the role
of competing interests in the management of public health.[56]

Newspaper accounts of the plague epidemic emphasized the outbreak as having occurred in the "Mexican section" or the "Mexican
quarter" of Los Angeles and specified that most of the victims were
Mexicans. The New York Times, for example, noted that the "disease
[was] confined to the residents of the foreign colony."[57] This and similar claims were reassuring to (white) readers because they suggested that

the contagion could be spatially segregated and that the plague was as foreign as its victims. In addition, the consistent marking of the diseased space as Mexican reminded the average reader that he or she was not merely physically separated from this dread illness but socially beyond its reach as well. Plague sufferers' addresses were published in the newspaper, along with their Spanish surnames. The list—Samarano, González, Puente, Herrera, and others—cemented the association between race and space. Furthermore, the highly segregated nature of L.A.'s residential neighborhoods makes it unlikely that the Clara Street area would have been familiar to many non-Mexicans. Instead, most newspaper readers would have associated the disease with Mexican neighborhoods generally. Even reporters seemed unable to correctly distinguish among the Mexican residential areas. The Los Angeles Times, for instance, despite having the address of plague victim Manuel Estrada and knowledge of the street where he lived as being in the quarantined area, still reported Estrada as a resident of Belvedere when he actually lived in the Clara Street enclave.[58]

The casual nature of the racism underpinning the public health response to the threat of plague was as evident at the state level as at the city and county levels. State Board of Health Secretary Dr. W. M. Dickie joined Los Angeles newspapers in depicting the quarantined zones as areas separate from the rest of the city. Six days after a quarantine had been imposed on the Clara Street neighborhood and two days after a similar quarantine had been established in Belvedere, a Los Angeles Times headline proclaimed, "no spread of disease." The title of the story in the column below, on the other hand, seemed to directly contradict the headline: "Four New Cases and Two Deaths of Pneumonic Plague in Infected Areas." Dickie had issued the statement on which the banner headline was based. The disease had spread, but its expansion had affected "only" Mexicans, living in Mexican neighborhoods. What the health secretary meant by his pronouncement was that no cases had developed outside the quarantine area. The grim facts that four more people had contracted the plague bacillus, likely guaranteeing their deaths, and that two residents had died were downplayed. The primary headline assumed that readers were not Mexican and did not live in the quarantined areas. In addition, although three of the four new cases involved residents of Belvedere, which was located more than three miles from the official locus of the plague (the Samarano home on Clara Street), health officials apparently did not consider the new outbreak a significant development in the plague epidemic. For as long as the disease's effects were limited to Mexicans, who lived on both the geographical and the social margins of Los Angeles, the plague would continue to be considered under control.

The last case of plague was reported on November 10. The quarantine was lifted three days later. In all, thirty-three of the thirty-eight people diagnosed with plague died. All but two (a priest who administered last rites and an ambulance driver who came into contact with one of the victims) of the deceased were Mexican. Officials reassured Angelenos that "[i]n all sections of the county, a very close watch is being kept among the Mexican population to prevent the recurrence of any epidemic disease."[59]

For L.A.'s Mexican community, the long-term implications of the epidemic were no less devastating than the sudden loss of friends and relatives. Newspaper accounts and health officials' reports reestablished the associations between disease and Mexicans that were forged during the typhus outbreak. In the months after the last reported plague case, health officials lauded the preventive measures put in place to safeguard the harbor.[60] The Mexican population was larger, more permanent, and more hopeful of gaining social membership than it had been in 1916. Being successfully labeled as carriers of the plague was a major setback.

THE DEVELOPMENT OF COUNTY HEALTH CENTERS

In the late 1910s, Health Officer Pomeroy divided the county health department's jurisdiction into twelve health "units" and designated a health officer for each. He stressed that this unit approach, with its emphasis on the individual and its adherence to principles of efficiency, would more closely align the Los Angeles department with the tenets of modern public health programs nationwide. It also would allow the county to "attack [health] problems in an intensive manner."[61]

A health center was established in each of the twelve units, beginning in 1919. Public health officials touted the centers as models of efficiency. Dr. Pomeroy boasted, "In an hour, the physician can take care of twenty patients in the clinics of a health care center . . . whereas if he were treating the poor patients in his own office, he would spend two or three times the amount of time."[62] The earliest centers were more rudimentary than officials' enthusiastic descriptions might suggest. More like what today are called "mobile clinics," they usually were held in business warehouses or settlement homes on certain weekday mornings or afternoons. The school board and employers of large numbers of Mexicans (e.g., the Citrus Association) sometimes loaned space in their buildings for the clinics.[63] The early health centers' staffs were limited, as were the services they offered. The local district health officer for Pomona, for example, divided his time between the two local health centers, in addition to his other duties.[64] In a one-year period, center staff would likely examine about 250 children and hold an average of three educational conferences to teach their parents the principles of sanitation and hygiene.[65]

In lauding the concept of the health center, officials emphasized that these centers provided a way for the health department to "meet the growing complexity of modern life."[66] One such "complexity" in the 1920s was the rapid increase in industrial accidents; many victims sought treatment at the new centers. The centers also served an important role in relieving the county hospital of some of its outpatient treatment services.[67] In the 1920s, the hospital began formally redirecting patients to the county health department's clinics.[68]

The vision of progress the health centers were said to embody was not so forward-looking as to see beyond the era's racial and ethnic boundaries. The next section examines the very different look and feel of the county's delivery of "modern" public health services in what were unabashedly labeled "Mexican clinics."

SEPARATE AND UNEQUAL CARE

Mexicans were considered antithetical to the vision of Los Angeles as a thriving, ultramodern city. The health care system that officials developed to serve this population's needs was both separate from and unequal to the system for whites. The county health department located its first neighborhood-specific basic health center in the "Mexican colony" in March 1919 at Simons Brick Yard, a company town of Simons Brick Company, a brick and roof tile manufacturer. Simons Brick Yard strove to attract Mexican workers by offering very low rents and encouraging them to live in the company town with their families. The Simons brothers even went so far as to offer a $5 gold piece to every baby born in the camp when it first opened in 1907.[69] The choice, however, was far from ideal. Residents considered Simons "a nuisance and menace to the health of the community" because the plant belched smoke.[70] Health department reports covering this center do not mention these hazardous conditions. A second neighborhood center, also for Mexicans, was opened in Los Nietos, near Whittier, two months later. In March 1920 the county established a clinic for both Mexicans and African Americans in the city of Duarte.[71]

Each of these facilities was referred to as a "Mexican clinic," and each was segregated intentionally, not merely as an accidental result of the county's demographics. The policy reflected the regional racial lexicon. Rather than separating whites from blacks, as Jim Crow laws in the South were designed to do, formal and informal procedures in Los Angeles County (as elsewhere in the Southwest) worked to "protect" whites from an array of nonwhites: blacks, Mexicans, and Asians (although the county did not regularly provide clinics for Japanese or Chinese residents).

The commitment to separate health care facilities for white and non-white populations is evident in the county health department's decision to open a clinic in Maravilla. This facility, located adjacent to the Belvedere Health Center, was specifically provided so that Belvedere's white public would not have to attend the same clinic as the area's Mexican residents.[72] In their directory of clinics, health officials classified Maravilla as for "Mexicans only." The neighboring Belvedere Health Center was for "Americans only." The Maravilla Health Clinic sign was written in Spanish, announcing its segregated status; the Belvedere Health Center's sign was written in English.[73] In San Fernando, the county's health center offered services for Mexicans in the morning and for whites in the afternoon.[74]

Dr. Pomeroy claimed it was "impossible to mix the Mexicans and the whites" in the same clinic because Mexicans' hygiene standards were so "appalling."[75] He argued that segregation was necessary because it was unfair to subject whites to an environment polluted by Mexicans' poor health. Pomeroy offered Mexicans' high IMRs to bolster his claim that segregated clinics were an essential public health measure. Segregating the health centers, much like zoning the residential areas, reinforced the existing racial hierarchy.

Not surprisingly, Mexican clinics proved to be not only separate but also unequal. For instance, although Pomeroy stressed the centers' role in providing health education, he advocated that staff restrict instruction for Mexicans to the "simpler laws of hygiene and sanitation."[76] Furthermore, instead of placing full-service health centers in Mexican areas, health officials set up "neighborhood centers," which they described as "health centers of the simplest form."[77] The allocation of resources for building centers also differed according to the population they were intended to serve. The Maravilla "Mexicans only" health center cost approximately $600 in 1920s dollars to construct. The department reused building materials, such as windows, doors, and plumbing fixtures, scavenged from razed county buildings.[78] The Belvedere "Americans only" health center, on the other hand, was both planned and executed as a far superior facility.[79] It cost $134,000 in 1920s dollars to construct,[80] and the opening was such a momentous event that leading public health and elected officials from all over the state attended—along with five thousand members of the general public.[81]

VITAL STATISTICS: MEASURING BIOLOGICAL HEALTH AND CULTURAL SUPERIORITY

In addition to its provision of a system of health centers, the county health department's commitment to compiling and analyzing vital statistics such as births and deaths marked it as forward-looking and sophisticated. Health officials routinely tracked birth and mortality rates for the key groups in the region's racial hierarchy: whites, Japanese, Mexicans, and "others." Every annual health department report included a chart that presented the birth and infant mortality rates in the county, broken down by race. No other statistics were as assiduously collected, analyzed by race, and published as these (table 2). In 1921, white infants constituted 60 percent of the births in the rural areas of the county, with Mexican and Japanese infants accounting for the remaining 40 percent in almost equal parts. Remarking on the latter, the 1921 report noted, "They constitute our principal foreign element and together are but two-thirds of the white births, so that 'yellow peril' has not grown in the rural districts here as in some parts of California."[82] Describing Mexican and Japanese birth rates in terms of "yellow peril" marked both groups as nonwhite and thus undesirable. It also reveals how the racialization of one group (here, Japanese) could pave the way for the racialization of another (Mexicans). When all Japanese immigration ceased after 1924 (the year Congress passed the Immigration Act), health officials and others seized on Mexican birth (and infant mortality) rates as a way to signal the dangerous aspects of Mexican immigration.

TABLE 2. BIRTHS BY NATIONALITY
IN THE UNINCORPORATED AREAS
OF LOS ANGELES COUNTY, 1915–26

	1915	1916	1917	1918	1919	1920	1921	1922	1923	1924	1925	1926	TOTAL
White	1484	843	830	828	776	1074	1372	1531	1999	2674	2461	2639	18511
Japanese	417	475	541	413	418	395	459	437	412	314	344	256	4881
Mexican	313	193	196	258	276	373	458	489	806	1189	1222	1340	7113
Black	0	0	0	0	0	0	9	9	8	13	13	15	67
Other	18	8	4	4	4	17	0	4	4	4	4	3	74
Totals	2232	1519	1571	1503	1474	1859	2298		3229	4194	4044	4253	

SOURCES: The figures for the years 1915–21 are from a chart in a Los Angeles County Health Department (LACHD/County) untitled report that begins with "I beg to submit herewith, annual report of the Health Department, Los Angeles County, for the year ending December 31, 1921," 16, DHS. There is no archived copy of the 1922 report. The 1923 report gives the totals of births by nationality for 1915–23. I subtracted the births by nationality in 1923 from the totals by nationality for 1915–23 in order to get the births by nationality for 1922. LACHD/County, "Annual Report of County Health Office to Board of Supervisors for Calendar Year 1923," 39, DHS. The figures for 1924 and 1925 are from LACHD/County, "Annual Report 1925 Los Angeles County Health Department," 52, DHS. The figures for 1926 are from LACHD/County, "Annual Report of Health Department Los Angeles County 1926," 20, DHS. There are no extant reports for 1927–29. The LACHD annual health reports for 1929–30 (the report runs from July 1, 1929, to June 30, 1930) and 1930–31 do not include a birth chart in their vital statistics reports. Sources for table 2 report births by "nationality" rather than "race."

Infant Mortality Rates

The practice of measuring a city's health using IMRs began in the early 1870s. Infants were believed to be more susceptible than adults to an unhealthy environment. Thus officials adopted these rates as a way of indexing an environment's overall health. The IMR's focus on young children, which gave it great emotional appeal with the general public, increased interest in and support of fledgling health departments across the country. The usefulness of IMRs, however, gradually went beyond the measure of a city's health that they provided. In the mid–nineteenth century, when the number of immigrants in the United States began to climb sharply, especially in cities along the Eastern seaboard, IMRs also increased sizably. Health officials promptly blamed this rise on immigrants and "their filthy immigrant slums."[83] By the early twentieth century, it was common practice to tie IMRs to specific groups and draw statistical comparisons between them. This in turn helped transform the significance of IMRs. They were no longer important only as a means of exposing environmental health problems; they became a key index of broad social concerns as well.

Los Angeles County health officials began tracking IMRs by race in 1915, the first year of John Pomeroy's tenure as the department's chief officer.[84] Health officials lamented, "Accurate statistics are not available, owing to the fact that the Mexican women are so ignorant that the births are not reported and consequently the ratio between births and deaths is not accurate."[85] As with number of births, infant mortality data were sorted into the categories "white," "Mexican," "Japanese," and "other." Mexicans living in rural areas suffered the highest IMRs among the county's ethnic and racial groups. In 1916, Mexicans lost an average of 285 children per 1,000 births. Four years later, the figure had dropped to 186 per 1,000 but then increased sharply in 1922 and 1923. And although IMRs subsequently decreased up to 1927, they remained consistently almost triple those of whites and higher than Japanese IMRs (table 3).[86]

Gastrointestinal problems such as diarrhea and enteritis (inflammation of the bowels) and communicable diseases caused by viral and bacterial infections were major contributors to infant deaths.[87] The effects of an epidemic of infant diarrhea in 1920 in some of the Mexican camps, for example, are apparent in the increased IMRs for that year.[88] Mexican children were ten times more likely to die from gastrointestinal problems than were white children.[89] IMRs were especially high among the Mexi-

TABLE 3. INFANT MORTALITY RATES BY
NATIONALITY IN UNINCORPORATED SECTIONS
OF LOS ANGELES COUNTY, 1916–27

	White	Japanese	Mexican	Negro	Total
1916	69.98	56.84	284.97	—	92.88
1917	67.47	79.48	255.10	500	92.99
1918	71.29	111.38	348.06	333.33	134.39[a]
1919	61.85	64.59	170.02	500	83.44
1920	60.24	50.25	186.66	125	84.62
1921	57.58	74.07	179.04	111.11	85.29
1922	78.38	91.53	243.35	142.85	113.45
1923	80.54	53.39	250.62	250.00	120.16
1924	61.33	50.95	163.16	—	89.17
1925	58.51	66.86	168.12	153.84	91.98
1926	41.91	42.96	124.62	266	67.81[b]
	44.04	47	130.87	266	71.38[c]
1927	45.36	41.86	96.92	—	61.57[b]
	47.75	42.10	100.99	—	64.49[c]

SOURCE: Ira V. Hiscock, *A Survey of Public Health Activities in Los Angeles County, California* (Los Angeles: Los Angeles County Bureau of Efficiency, 1928), 43. Hiscock reports IMRs by "nationality" rather than by "race."

[a] Dr. Pomeroy claimed that the rise in IMRs for Mexicans in 1918 was due to the 1918 influenza epidemic. John Pomeroy to Los Angeles County Board of Supervisors, November 6, 1919, Los Angeles County Board of Supervisors, Records.

[b] County births recorded in Los Angeles City included in this rate.

[c] County births recorded in Los Angeles City not included in this rate.

can agricultural workers who lived in the San Gabriel Valley. There the rates climbed to as many as 300 deaths per 1,000 live births.[90]

Although county officials made frequent use of IMRs, they rarely cited rates for the overall population. Instead, they drew comparisons—typically between whites and Mexicans.[91] One health report, describing Mexican IMRs as four times whites' rates, noted that high IMRs "among the Mexicans [are] a problem upon which we have already put much work."[92] The implication here, and in other reports, was that while whites had no trouble maintaining low IMRs, Mexicans, even with assistance from public health professionals, seemed incapable of taking proper care of their infants. The contrast sent the not-too-subtle message that whites were better parents. Finally, separating Mexican IMRs from those of whites and then using only whites' IMRs to represent the county as a whole marked Mexicans as outside the social membership of Los Angeles.[93]

Perhaps the most important reason for health officials' reluctance to report IMRs for the county as a whole was that aggregate rates were high and thus damaging to Los Angeles's image as a modern, healthful, pristine destination for tourists and other visitors. Segregating IMRs by race allowed officials to focus on the relatively low rates among whites and to develop explanations for the high rates among nonwhites that reinforced the racial order and directed attention away from the inadequacies of the area's infrastructure.

Accounting for the County's High IMRs

Since health officials relied on IMRs to assess and advertise the health of the county, the explanations they provided for high mortality rates usually avoided discussing the region's strained resources. When inadequacies in the infrastructure were mentioned, the most frequently cited culprits were the lack of a clean water supply in some areas and the lack of proper garbage collection and waste disposal.[94] Department reports sometimes mentioned Mexican camps where polluted water sources were common, such as those in El Monte and Irwindale, noting that in these areas epidemics were a constant threat.[95] Unlike the 1916 typhus epidemic, however, which prompted officials to call for a major expansion in public health efforts, potential health hazards in Mexican communities did not become catalysts for change. Mexicans' high IMRs concerned health experts, but they never served as a rallying cry for better county resources.

Health providers consistently failed to link the county's limited resources and underdeveloped infrastructure to infant mortality in Mexican communities. Instead, the preferred way of accounting for the high IMRs was to blame the parents' cultural habits and overall ignorance. For example, in the 1920 infantile diarrhea epidemic, a county health department report cited "the ignorance of the parents handling food" as a source of the problem.[96] Dr. Pomeroy characterized Mexicans as "absolutely ignorant of the fundamentals of hygiene" and traced the high IMRs to this failing.[97] He argued that adopting an "intelligent type of living habits and precautionary measures" could control infant deaths that were due to gastrointestinal problems and communicable diseases.[98] IMRs became emblematic of all that was wrong with the behavior and culture of the area's Mexican population.

In pathologizing Mexican culture, health officials focused on Mexican women as primarily responsible for high IMRs. So, for example,

one report pointed out that "the foreign mothers permit through ignorance many serious conditions to obtain a foothold in their families.
This relates not only to medical treatment but also the sanitation of the
household."[99] The same report also noted, "There are no free hospitals,
dispensaries or clinics in the rural districts," but it drew no connection
between this lack and high IMRs. Similarly, a different report, in referring to Mexican communities, pointed to two quite different sources for
high IMRs: "There is no question but what lack of proper sewage disposal in the rural districts and improper feeding influences the infant
mortality a great deal."[100]

Because they held Mexican mothers responsible for many of the conditions related to high IMRs, the county health department officials recommended the "training of foreign mothers, especially the Mexican
group[,] in modern preventive medicine."[101] Mexican women's "improper feeding" techniques and "unkempt" homes marked them as bad
mothers. These programs were based on dominant stereotypes of the
"dirty Mexican" that conflated health and hygiene with morality and
poverty.[102] More importantly, successfully establishing Mexican women
as the primary cause of high IMRs freed public health officials from the
need to look any further for precipitating factors. It also positioned education campaigns—rather than structural change—as an effective
response. Diarrhea, a leading cause in infant mortality, could be attributed to viruses and bacteria found in the polluted water sources in Mexican camps. Nevertheless, health officials stressed the need to teach
Mexican women how to clean their homes to help fight high IMRs. Creating an image of Mexican women as bad mothers had two important
results: It diverted attention from the county's lack of resources, and it
bolstered health officials' position as professionals who could identify
and rectify threats to community health.[103]

The use of IMRs as the basis for characterizing Mexican women as
bad mothers had a significant consequence of its own. Since IMRs for
the county's white residents were much lower than the Mexican communities' rates, comparing IMRs confirmed white women as *good*
mothers. This in turn reinforced the validity of the two groups' relative
positions in the regional racial hierarchy. Moreover, the concept of
motherhood itself was charged with meanings that extended well
beyond biological capabilities. Most Americans in the early twentieth
century would have understood the concept of a good mother to include
a specifically civic component. White women had pointed to their moral
authority as mothers and homemakers as the basis for a public voice

long before they won the right to vote. In the eighteenth century, middle- and upper-class white women argued that as good mothers they had something valuable to contribute to public life, a concept later referred to as Republican Motherhood. Being a good mother was tantamount to being a patriot.[104] During the Progressive Era, when a wide array of groups sought reform for a host of issues, white middle-class women again traded on their roles as mothers and wives. They argued that the skills they had honed in the private sphere, caring for their families and homes, were transferable to the public realm. They were municipal housekeepers who could improve society.[105] To the degree that motherhood was key in legitimizing women's relationship to the state,[106] marking Mexican women as bad mothers simultaneously confirmed their inferiority to whites and firmly placed them outside the bounds of social membership in the United States.

WELL-BABY CLINICS: "SCIENTIFIC SUPERVISION OF THE HEALTH OF THE COUNTY"

In his first years as health officer, Dr. Pomeroy had stressed the "need for constructive movement for conservation of child life among the Mexicans and Japanese."[107] One form this "constructive movement" eventually took, particularly for Mexican communities, was the WBC.[108] WBCs provided prenatal care to pregnant women and offered preventive medical care to babies and children under six years of age. The clinics were part of a national movement to improve children's health and thus significantly lower IMRs. Initially, public health departments had tried to combat early deaths through the establishment of pure-milk stations.[109] Follow-up studies showed, however, that because of contamination and lack of bottle sterilization, bottle-fed babies had mortality rates six to ten times higher than breastfed babies. Most departments with existing pure-milk stations responded by converting these facilities into WBCs, which emphasized educating mothers.[110]

Structurally, the county health department's WBCs were similar to those nationwide. Doctors and nurses staffed the clinics. They measured, weighed, bathed, and observed babies; they also charted children's physical development. Staff members presented lectures that instructed mothers in the proper care and feeding of infants and emphasized the need to maintain high standards of sanitation and hygiene; some clinics offered cooking classes as well. Clinics targeting Mexican communities usually included a Spanish interpreter on the staff.[111] Occasionally, mothers were treated to a show of "moving pictures on health problems." In aims, the county WBCs and those in other regions of the country were somewhat less similar. A key goal of all the clinics was to assimilate immigrants—WBCs were one aspect of what typically were multipronged efforts to Americanize newcomers. Los Angeles health officials certainly embraced this aim. But there were limits as well. Health officials' characterization of the WBCs as a way to "save the State a great loss of prospective citizens" served as a reminder that Mexican Americans remained suspended in a "not-yet-American" state, regardless of where they were born. The comment also echoed the rhetoric they used when promoting their department's potential for regulating and sanitizing the Mexican workforce.[112] Moreover, the county worked directly with both industrial and agricultural employers in implementing and running the WBCs,[113] much as it had done when instigating other large-scale health projects (e.g., cleanup campaigns in Mexican work camps during the 1916 typhus epidemic).

But the development of WBCs in Los Angeles also incorporated a pernicious racism. The main mission of these clinics was to combat high IMRs. As previously noted, Los Angeles health professionals understood these rates as reflecting the culture and behavior of mothers. As one report explained, "In 1916 we found that the Mexican women were losing about one in three of their babies during the first year of life. Analysis of the causes showed that most of these deaths occurred through ignorance of child hygiene."[114] County health officials contended that "the real solution to the problem of the conservation of children [lay] in the field of education of future mothers."[115]

One obstacle health officials faced as they labored to "train" the aliens in their midst was a language barrier. Dr. Pomeroy considered Mexicans a high-risk group because they "spoke not one word of English."[116] He surmised that an inability to communicate in English would prevent this group from following quarantine regulations and from properly caring for their children when they became ill. Pomeroy's first concern seems unwarranted: the city and county health departments had already demonstrated, during the 1916 typhus epidemic, for instance, a willingness to post important health notices in Spanish as well as English. The second charge, that not knowing English compromised an adult's caretaking skills, makes sense only if what Pomeroy meant was that Mexican parents who spoke only Spanish would be ignorant of American (i.e., superior) standards of health and hygiene. His casual conflation of knowledge, culture, and language shows how easily language can be used as a marker. Lacking fluency in English rendered Mexicans inferior, uncivilized. Since Mexicans were lower than whites in the racial hierarchy, this kind of reasoning worked in one direction only: health officials never questioned whether their own lack of Spanish-language skills might have hampered their understanding of Mexican culture.[117] In sum, the underlying impetus for the WBCs was the belief that Mexicans were inferior to whites and the associated fear that this population's alleged ignorance and primitive habits would open the door to disease and disorder.

During the period in which WBCs were first established, all aspects of Mexican culture were pathologized.[118] Pomeroy argued, for example, that educational outreach programs were essential because Mexicans were a "menace to their neighbors."[119] Mexicans, Pomeroy elaborated, had "little or no knowledge of sanitation and tend[ed] to bad housing, over-crowding, and conceal[ed] contagious diseases."[120] The implication was that disease in the Mexican home could spread and thus was everyone's problem. Schoolchildren seemed especially likely to carry germs from the private to the public sphere. Pomeroy reminded the Board of Supervisors that there were over 130 schools in the county with more than twenty thousand students, including many "Mexicans, Japanese, and other alien people" who came from "deplorable" homes. Once at school, children from these groups could easily transmit contagious diseases, including diphtheria, "skin diseases and eye troubles."[121]

Pomeroy's condemnation also implied that Mexicans deliberately concealed the diseases they bred despite the fact that no mention of any person in any Mexican neighborhood attempting to hide illness ever appeared in the department's official reports.[122] Mary Coman, vice-president of the Public Welfare Commission of Los Angeles County, reinforced Pomeroy's message in a letter she sent to the Board of Supervisors. Stemming disease before it ever left the home was crucial. Coman supported the use of public funds to hire a public health nurse to work with Mexicans "not as relief merely but for safety to the general public." "They need teaching, if the general public health is to be conserved," she argued.[123]

By June 1918, two years after Pomeroy and Coman had urged the Board of Supervisors to approve more outreach programs, the Los Angeles County Health Department established a Division of Child Hygiene.[124] Its staff included full-time director Dr. Margaret Furr, her assistant, one Spanish-speaking nurse, and eight other nurses whose services were contracted to incorporated cities and school districts. Nurses developed traveling exhibits and educational outreach programs that included child-rearing classes for mothers. These programs, which fused the tenets of health reform with the goals of Americanization, advocated gender-specific roles.[125] For instance, Dr. Pomeroy designed a twelve-part lecture series on hygiene, entitled "Little Mothers," to be taught to female students in the public elementary schools. Health officials hoped to influence immigrant mothers via their daughters, who would share at home what they had learned in school.[126] In the best-case scenario, a wholesale transformation of the Mexican home and family would result from the combined effects of outreach programs, WBCs, and in-home visits from public health nurses.[127] Once these programs were under way, health officials extended their efforts to changing attitudes and behaviors in another area connected to IMRs—birthing practices.

BIRTHING OPTIONS

Scholars interested in immigrant groups' adaptation to life in the United States often focus on the degree to which members of these groups take part in the country's social and political institutions.[128] Key measures used in these kinds of studies include naturalizing, voting, and joining unions. Examining the decisions Mexican women made around child-birth offers a similar opportunity for assessment. Very few county records regarding birthing options during this period still exist. The few that are available suggest that the regional racial lexicon shaped decisions regarding which birthing services would be extended to whom. The options available to Mexican women and which of these they chose to use give a sense of these women's place vis-à-vis the social member-ship of Los Angeles. The choices Mexican women employed shed light on how they navigated the cultural terrain of their new environment.

By 1927, physicians attended 95 percent of births overall in Los Angeles County; 38 percent of these physician-attended births took place in hospitals.[129] Women who could not afford a private physician had three main options: use the county health department's birthing services, give birth in the county hospital, or use the services of a midwife.

County Clinic Programs

The Los Angeles County Health Department offered obstetrical home delivery services and prenatal care programs. Public health nurses (also referred to as visiting nurses) made house calls to new mothers in the days following their delivery. Staff from the White Memorial Hospital, which was affiliated with the Medical College of Evangelists, the Seventh Day Adventists' medical institution, worked in conjunction with the health department's home nursing program. The hospital's obstetrical department provided home delivery services through the Mexican WBC in Maravilla, and staff also visited women ten days following delivery.[130] Obstetrical services were provided for free or for a fee of $10.[131] It is unclear whether the services were provided by doctors or by medical students; the reports refer to work done by staff members from the college rather than from White Memorial Hospital, which suggests that they were associated with the affiliated college, not the hospital. If those helping at the clinics were not doctors, the quality of care offered to Mexicans may have been substandard and may have prompted some Mexicans to boycott the clinics.[132]

Other county health department programs directly contradicted medical trends and legislation that directed women to give birth only at the hands of a physician. Health providers trained Mexican women to give birth without assistance from a doctor. The county health department offered its first childbirth class to female employees of the Orange Packers Association.[133] Dr. Charles Bennett, a physician who had moved to Los Angeles in 1910 after practicing in Mexico for fifteen years, was in charge of the clinic.[134] He served on various medical boards throughout his career in Los Angeles, most notably as president of the Southern California Medical Association.[135] Though surely aware of medical trends that advised women against giving birth without formal medical care, he sanctioned these childbirth classes. Instruction took place in one of the two-room cement houses that the Orange Packers Association originally had built as housing for their Mexican employees. A WBC was held in one room. County health workers used the other room as a model delivery room to teach women how to replicate a sterile environment in their own homes. Mexican women were encouraged to have their babies here, in the showcase delivery room, and then stay for a twenty-four-hour period following delivery, "thus assuring the mother the usual aseptic precautions needed."[136]

No records survive to indicate how well these services were received or the degree to which they were used. County health department reports do, however, provide insights suggesting fundamental problems that may have undermined the programs. Women were allowed to stay at the clinic only twenty-four hours after giving birth. The average hospital maternity stay, in contrast, was ten to fourteen days. There is no indication why county health department policy differed so vastly. What appeal the clinic might have had for women is equally uncertain. Even for those who could not afford hospital care or who had no access to a hospital, delivering at the clinic had no obvious advantage over delivering at home. There was no doctor or full-time nurse on duty, and the facility itself was a replica of the structures in which they lived. Furthermore, a Mexican cultural norm, *la dieta,* dictated that women and their newborns stay indoors for a full forty days after the birth of a child. It would not be surprising for Mexican women to prefer not to leave their homes in the first place, given that they would just have to return when their allotted twenty-four hours at the clinic had elapsed.

County Hospital Services

Women residents of Los Angeles County who could not afford a private hospital could give birth at the county hospital, a charity facility. The hospital was built in 1878 and became affiliated with the University of Southern California School of Medicine in 1885.[137] Although the hospital was located near many Mexican neighborhoods, including Maravilla and Belvedere, how much use Mexican women made of the hospital's maternity services is open to debate. My examination of Los Angeles County Hospital birth records (i.e., births entered in the hospital's birth register) for a six-month period between October 1921 and March 1922 indicates that many babies were brought to the hospital *after* they were born.[138] During this period, Mexican births made up about 15 percent of the births at the hospital, while half the cases of newborns brought into the hospital involved Mexican infants. Penciled next to one entry is the notation "born twenty minutes before entering." Three other records for Mexican infants are marked "born outside." Only the entries for Mexican infants include notations such as these. Bringing newborns to the hospital may be an indication that Mexican women were fusing the use of midwives (discussed below) with institutionalized medical practices.

Mexican women may have hesitated to give birth at the county hospital for fear of being labeled undeserving charity seekers. Reports published by the county Charities Department, which oversaw the county hospital, claimed that Mexicans overburdened the hospital services.[139] A 1925 report maintained that although Mexicans constituted an estimated 10 percent of the county's population, they made up 40 percent of the hospital's caseload.[140] The hospital's 1925 maternity service report estimated that Mexicans composed 62 percent of its cases. In contrast, my research of individual birth records and surgical records reveals that Mexican women constituted an average of 25 percent of the hospital's maternity cases during this time.[141] This striking discrepancy may represent a reaction to the fact that the recently passed 1924 Immigration Act did not include Mexicans in its quota restrictions. The figures the hospital included in its annual report may have been an attempt to remind the public of the drawbacks associated with allowing Mexican immigration to continue. A final reason Mexican women may have preferred not to use the county hospital delivery services is that at least some of those who attempted to do so seem to have been shunted into the surgery ward. Women ready to give birth were supposed to be processed through the maternity ward, not through general surgery. During a six-month period in 1924, the hospital's records show that eight women gave birth in the surgery ward. Of those eight cases, four were Mexican. The records do not indicate why the women were not registered according to standard procedure.[142]

Midwifery Practices

Mexican immigration coincided with major shifts in attitudes toward childbirth in the United States. Increasingly, childbirth was characterized as a medical procedure that required a doctor in attendance, rather than as a natural process at which a midwife would preside. Doctors' tendency to blame midwives for the high mortality rates of infants and mothers fueled existing tensions between the two groups. The professionalization of medicine that had begun in the United States in the nineteenth century gave doctors' opinions a legitimacy that midwives could not successfully challenge. By 1930, the number of practicing midwives had fallen by 80 percent.[143]

The historical literature on midwifery provides little information about the women who continued practicing their skills. Black, ethnic, and poor midwives typically did not leave any records behind.[144] What little we do know comes mainly from a few community studies and oral histories that specifically focused on these midwives.[145] Works in Chicano/a history often acknowledge the importance of *parteras* (Mexican midwives) both in providing medical services and in strengthening social networks.[146]

National data indicate that midwifery practices were being phased out by the 1920s, but there was significant variation by region and ethnic group. The approach health officials took to the "midwife problem" in immigrant communities often differed from their approach in white communities. Frequently, immigrant and African American midwives were allowed to practice in their own communities.[147] In Texas, for example, health officials permitted unlicensed *parteras* to practice in Mexican immigrant and *Tejana* communities. The director of the Texas State Department of Health admitted that midwives had always been perceived as a "necessary evil." According to the director, the state intervened only to eliminate the most "undesirable ones."[148] High-ranking national officials commented that these types of "situations [had] been allowed to drift along without regard for consequences," but they took no actions to remedy the problem in marginalized communities in the Southwest.[149]

In the Los Angeles area, unlike some other regions of the country with sizable immigrant populations, midwifery was not a highly charged issue.[150] Even during the Progressive Era, when reforms were undertaken on almost every front, the possibility of revising the laws governing midwifery arose only once, and on that occasion the goal was simply to ensure that city and state laws did not conflict.[151] Appointed in 1918, Dr. Margaret Furr, the director of the county's Division of Child Hygiene, supervised and regulated midwives. Yet aside from recording how many midwives were registered in the county, Furr's division seems to have done little else. Los Angeles officials' laissez-faire approach continued throughout the 1920s, even as many other cities cracked down on midwives.[152] The granting of midwifery licenses in and around Los Angeles also was uneventful.[153] A majority of the women whose applications for licenses came before the Board of Health Commissioners had surnames that suggest the applicants were white. Occasionally, though, women with Latina/o or Japanese last names applied for licenses. The board approved the majority of applications without any delay.[154]

County health officials surmised that the practice of midwifery was common among—and limited to—the area's Mexican and Japanese populations. In 1925, health providers kept track of who attended births in the Belvedere district. Of 1,264 births, 70 percent were attended by physicians, 17 percent by midwives, and 3 percent by "others" (this last category typically included fathers and neighbors). When broken down by race, 29 percent of the 709 Mexican births were attended by midwives (12 percent higher than for the district overall).

Among the twenty-six Japanese births, midwives attended three.[155] At the Mexican clinic at Simons Brick Yard, physicians attended twenty-eight of forty-four births, or 63 percent. Of the remaining sixteen births, midwives attended eight and neighbors or relatives attended eight.[156] Data from a 1923 California State Health Department report support county officials' supposition that midwifery was common in Mexican and Japanese communities. But the report also suggests that midwifery may have been common across many immigrant communities in the rural areas of Los Angeles County. It states that a majority of the midwives practicing in the county were Japanese and the remainder Russian, English, Italian, Sicilian, German, Greek, Spanish, Hungarian, Slovenian, and African American.[157] Los Angeles health officials, in contrast, mention Mexican and Japanese midwives only.

Health officials who publicly censured Mexicans' health practices and their failure to utilize public health services casually accepted the extralegal practice of midwifery in Mexican communities.[158] On the basis of their initial tracking of birth attendants, health officials surmised that the home delivery services they offered through the White Memorial Hospital did little to curb the practice of midwifery.[159] Their findings, however, did not prompt them to draft an alternative means for lowering Mexicans' IMRs. Nor did Dr. Anna Rude, who was in charge of the campaign to lower IMRs in Belvedere,[160] develop any comprehensive programs to curb midwifery in the county, although she was on record as opposing the practice. In a presentation to the American Medical Association in 1923, Dr. Rude assessed the "midwife problem" in the United States and specifically in the Southwest.[161] She discussed the "large [numbers]" of Japanese midwives who practiced in the Pacific states. In addition, she claimed that in the Southwest, "practically every [Spanish-speaking] married woman in rural areas [was] a potential midwife," a situation she believed posed distinct problems. Moreover, Dr. Rude continued, "with the exception of an exceedingly few of the larger urban localities, no successful control or supervision of the midwife [has] been effected. Failure to enforce laws [has] in many instances been due not only to a lack of recognition of the gravity and enormity of the problem, but also to the lack of funds with which to operate successfully."[162] Despite the "gravity and enormity of the problem," Dr. Rude offered no remedy—not even a suggestion that prompt change was needed. When it came to monitoring Japanese births, however, the county health department used a completely different approach.

THE JAPANESE IN LOS ANGELES COUNTY:
A "SILENT INVASION"

During the 1920s, the Japanese continued to be the second-largest racialized group in Los Angeles County.[163] They settled in areas such as Gar-
dena, Carson, Compton, Hawthorne, Lawndale, Dominguez Hills, and
Redondo Beach and established their own churches and schools in each
of these communities. Many Japanese residents were farmers, growing
flowers, vegetables, and fruits (especially strawberries). By 1930, their
farms produced 90 percent of the produce consumed locally.[164]

Despite the anti-immigration provisions of the 1907–8 Gentlemen's
Agreement, the Japanese population in the state and in the Los Angeles
region continued to grow. By 1920, California claimed the nation's
largest population of Japanese.[165] More than twenty thousand of the
state's Japanese residents had been born in California. The ongoing
presence of Japanese "aliens" rekindled interest in and activity by
nativist groups such as the Asiatic Exclusion League and the Los Angeles County Anti-Asiatic Association. What especially worried white Californians was that all children born to Japanese residents of the state
were U.S. citizens by law. Moreover, members of this second generation
("Nisei") were entitled to own (and/or lease) land, thus undermining the
intent of the Alien Land Law of 1913. California's U.S. Senator James
Phelan and state legislator J. M. Inman championed new bills in 1920
to strengthen the 1913 act so that Japanese farmers could no longer buy
or lease land in the name of sympathetic whites and/or in the name of
their own American-born children. California Governor William Steph-
ens also urged stricter laws to combat the Japanese "menace." The Japanese were depicted as an unassimilable threat—a population who
refused to toil for the white man and who, in working only for themselves, took more from the soil than they contributed. (The advocates of
restrictive legislation did not address how these laws might discourage
Japanese from cultivating the land for long-term use, given that they
would have to move on after three years.) There was so much anxiety
about Japanese immigration that in 1920 Congress formed a special
committee to investigate the "Japanese question."

Public health discourse offered a legitimate way for whites to express
their fears concerning nonwhite foreigners. In the late 1910s, nativists
focused attention specifically on birth rates as the new manifestation of
yellow peril. The birth rates of Japanese living in California were as-

sailed in many forums, including newspaper articles, public speeches, and radio addresses. Articles such as one entitled "Yellow Race Overrunning the State" linked Japanese women's "amazing fecundity" with an imminent economic and geographical takeover of California by the Japanese. Writers warned the public of the "almond eyed stork" who brought as many Japanese babies into the United States as ships transported Japanese immigrants.[166]

The concerns regarding Japanese immigrants differed starkly from those about Mexican immigrants. Accordingly, public health approaches to the two populations diverged as well. Since few employers depended on Japanese labor, there appeared to be no need to sanitize this immigrant group, as was the case with Mexicans. Thus, instead of developing regular clinics and other forms of health outreach for the Japanese, county health officials focused on gathering birth and mortality data. The next section examines how these figures became the starting point for a constructed "knowledge" regarding Japanese birth rates that health experts and others made ready use of to portray Japanese residents as a threat.

Counting Heads

The statistic that most interested health officials with regard to Japanese communities was the number, not of infant deaths, but of births. They viewed birth rates as a sort of early warning indicator of yellow peril. Health officials had little firsthand knowledge of the area's Japanese communities, particularly those in the county's rural sections. According to the 1920 census, there were 19,911 Japanese living in Los Angeles County, amounting to 5 percent of the total population.[167] Census takers did not, however, distinguish between those who lived in the county's rural areas and those who lived in its urban centers. Officials hoped to get a better sense of the growth rate of the rural Japanese population by actively enforcing the birth registration laws.[168] Collecting Japanese birth data became a priority. Dr. Pomeroy contracted Dr. James Hatsuji Hara, who served as a consulting physician at White Memorial Hospital and also ran his own practice, to investigate Japanese births in the county. Dr. Pomeroy also assigned Dr. Margaret Furr, head of the Division of Child Hygiene, to assist Dr. Hara. (Dr. Pomeroy later discovered that Dr. Furr and Dr. Hara had fallen in love during the course of their work. Dr. Pomeroy promptly fired Dr. Furr on the grounds that by marrying a Japanese man, a person ineligible for citizenship, she too lost her citizenship and therefore could not be employed by the county.)[169]

On the basis of birth rates, Dr. Pomeroy speculated there were six thousand to eight thousand Japanese living in the rural areas of the county.[170] But in the same report he also provided an entirely different figure. He calculated this second, much larger number by starting with the 2,659 Japanese births officially recorded by the county and then hypothesizing the presence of five adults for each birth. This creative mathematics produced an estimate of 13,295 Japanese living in the county.[171]

During the county health department's first five years (1915–20), officials noted the importance of establishing connections with both Mexican and Japanese communities. Taking steps to "reach the Japanese problem"[172] was a sensible precaution. As one report explained, "The recommendation relative to the Japanese is not as particularly for the benefit of the Japanese race itself so much as for the protection of our own people."[173] The health of L.A.'s white residents would be safeguarded by "educating the Japanese in sanitation."[174] As with Mexicans, health professionals concentrated their efforts on child hygiene. And, again as with Mexicans, officials felt they would have more success with the Japanese community if they hired a nurse who was Japanese or who at least spoke Japanese.[175]

Unlike the approach taken with Mexican communities, however, the programs the county health department made available to Japanese residents were limited and intermittent. As noted earlier, county officials began introducing WBCs in Mexican neighborhoods in 1919 as a way of reducing high IMRs. In Japanese communities, where IMRs were much lower (in fact, they were only slightly higher than those of whites), WBCs were begun a year earlier—but were then discontinued.[176] Department records do not indicate why the clinics started, or why they were suspended for five years and then reinstituted in 1923. One possible explanation is that county officials used WBCs as a way to learn about the Japanese community. The 1918 "special conferences" might have provided a benchmark for rural birth rates. The next clinic, not offered until 1923, was held in the "Jap colony" in Belvedere, at a kindergarten for Japanese children.[177] By that time, the boundaries of Belvedere had expanded to include a few Japanese ranches.[178] This may have prompted officials to feel that they needed a better sense of "the Japanese situation." In addition, yellow peril fears were again on the

rise. Congress at that time was considering legislation that would completely halt Asian immigration (the 1924 Immigration Act). The attention trained on Asians at the national level may have promoted more
scrutiny at the local level as well.

Health officials consistently placed more emphasis on Japanese birth
rates than on those of any other racialized group. Birth charts broken
down in accordance to the regional racial lexicon—*white, Mexican,
Japanese,* and *other*—were always included in the department's annual
health report. In addition, these reports provided separate charts with
birth rates for the Japanese *only,* broken down by individual county district, and including both incorporated and unincorporated areas.[179]
From 1919 to 1925, every annual health department report included
such a chart. These tables also supplied a running tally of the number of
Japanese births to date in each district. The overall effect was to make
the number of Japanese births appear larger than it really was. This was
likely intentional. Tracking Japanese births by district added to a heightened sense of yellow peril. For example, although Japanese infants
accounted for 20 percent of the county's births in 1919, that year's
annual health report created a different impression: "Japanese have
averaged twenty-seven percent of the total births in certain districts of
the county—noticeable in the vicinity of Covina, El Monte, Compton,
Long Beach, Redondo, San Gabriel, and Santa Monica." Focusing on
specific districts made Japanese birth rates appear to be 27, not 20, percent. These tabulations, moreover, had much wider circulation than the
annual reports in which they regularly appeared. The health department
shared their statistics with the general public. In 1917, for instance, a
county health department memo issued to the *Los Angeles Tribune*
stated, "Of 1,725 births last year, 25 percent were Japanese, 12 percent
Mexicans, and only 62.5 percent white. . . . The Japanese are rapidly
increasing throughout the rural districts."[180] This preoccupation with
the size of Japanese communities reflected practical considerations as
well as general yellow peril fears. Japanese birth rates translated into citizenship rights and, by extension, into property rights as well. Health
officials made this connection explicit, observing that "registration of
[Japanese] births [is] important relative to the problem of ownership of
land."[181]

As the memo to the *Tribune* suggests, health officials also used Japanese birth rates for comparative purposes, juxtaposing white birth rates
with Japanese ones. "The Japanese births increased somewhat in Huntington Park, Belvedere, and San Gabriel. There was again an excess of

42 Japanese births over the white births in Redondo district, an excess of 26 births over the white births in El Monte district, an excess of 5 in San Gabriel district," stated the 1919 annual health report.[182] For good measure, the same report also included a chart of Japanese births in the unincorporated areas for the previous five years. A plus sign indicated that Japanese births outnumbered white births in a specific district. The notation system is significant because it mimics annotations Pomeroy made earlier in personal notes he drafted for a public speech.[183] This overlap between personal and public arenas shows how individual biases can become embedded in institutional practice. Pomeroy's notation scheme may have begun as personal prejudice, but its appearance in a formal year-end report indicates that it soon evolved into standard department policy.

"The End of the White Race in California"

The emphasis county health officials put on Japanese births also spoke to broader social trends, including eugenics and a fear of (white) "race suicide."[184] In the early 1900s, eugenics gained prominence as a practice and a discourse aimed at improving society. Eugenicists embraced hereditarian beliefs that advocated limiting reproduction to a select segment of society. In the conceptual framework of eugenics, the interdependent theories of race suicide and race betterment posited that as white women's birth rates dropped, those of immigrant women rose. Proponents of race betterment urged white women to reproduce frequently, thus strengthening the racial stock of the nation through white births. President Theodore Roosevelt himself appealed to white women to reproduce in order to help ensure that the United States would continue to reign supreme over other nations.[185] In his annual message to Congress in 1906, President Theodore Roosevelt chastised middle-class, white American women for their "willful sterility . . . the one sin for which the penalty is national death, race death."[186] Conversely, adherents of race suicide beliefs promoted negative eugenics: that is, they called for decreasing the birth rates of immigrants and African Americans. By shaping ideas about what size the normative family should be, race suicide and race betterment discourses influenced everyday public health programs.

Current scholarship indicates that the eugenics movement had many more adherents than previously thought and that the movement was influential in the American West.[187] Earlier work had focused on African

Americans and poor whites on the East Coast and in the South.[188] More recent works by Wendy Kline and by Alexandra Stern show that California Progressives also promoted eugenics programs, advocating procedures such as forced sterilization for the "mentally inferior." Some embraced positive eugenics, imploring white women to procreate so that other races would not overpopulate. Nationwide, the majority of public health officials distanced themselves from extreme eugenicist policies. But many public health programs shared with the eugenics movement a belief in the existence of a racial hierarchy in which whites occupied the topmost position.[189] In the early twentieth century, public health professionals viewed some ethnic groups as in need of greater uplift than others (e.g., Mexicans required more "training" than southern Europeans). In Los Angeles, health officials' persistent portrayal of Japanese birth rates as a threat to U.S. cultural homogeneity reinforced the very low position that the Japanese occupied in the regional racial hierarchy.

ENCOUNTERING RESISTANCE

The clinics and other outreach programs that Los Angeles County Health Department officials launched in the 1920s were met with a range of responses from Mexican and Japanese residents. Not surprisingly, given the public health department's tendency to direct the bulk of its efforts toward Mexican rather than Japanese residents, the two groups reacted differently to the programs. Japanese communities tended to organize their own health services, but when approached by county officials, they were more likely to utilize these services. An example from 1918 is illustrative. The county health department received funds to hire a Japanese physician.[190] Health officials then asked the Japanese Association of Los Angeles County to provide a nurse for one year to "reach the Japanese problem."[191] The association complied and also raised money to employ a Japanese worker to assist the health officer on sanitation issues.[192] The historian John Modell characterizes the Japanese Association as an organization that embraced Americanization and sought social acceptance through accommodation, not resistance.[193] Given this characterization, the case can be read as an indication that the Japanese Association had internalized U.S. medical hegemony and thus sought U.S. public health care over community medical care. Japanese Association members may have viewed working with the health department as a means of gaining more acceptance from dominant society. In funding health care themselves, they may have stripped the county's programs of some of their clout.[194]

In Mexican communities, the dynamics of public health care were almost the exact opposite of those in Japanese communities. Public health officials were prepared to go to great lengths to recruit clients from Mexican neighborhoods. Doctors and nurses who staffed the WBCs, for instance, reported having to "wage a determined campaign to sell themselves and their services to mothers suspicious of these strange, new-fangled notions about bringing up children. Foreign women, especially Mexicans, needed much coaxing."[195] Dr. Pomeroy claimed that he and his staff "did not wait for clients to come to them: they went out to hunt for clients."[196] Public health nurses used birth registrations to obtain names and addresses of women who had recently given birth. The nurses would then visit the new mothers, give them informational litera-ture, and tell them about the WBCs.[197] The department hired Spanish-speaking staff in hopes of increasing the programs' effectiveness. "[I]t is almost a necessity to have a Spanish-speaking nurse or assistant in order to win the confidence of the Mexican population," one county health department report acknowledged.[198] Mexican women may have re-sented the implications of segregated clinics. Thus, although having staff who spoke Spanish was important, it was not, seemingly, sufficient. Establishing a connection, such as through a common nationality, was essential. "We have found," health officials claimed, "that it would be impossible to do any public health work among this class of people with-out a native born assistant who speaks the language."[199]

As with the Americanization programs of the time, health reforms were directed at mothers because mothers could bring about change in the family.[200] Health officials therefore offered classes on cooking and nutrition to immigrant women.[201] They taught Mexican mothers how to prepare American meals, on the grounds that these foods were more nutritious than traditional Mexican fare. The county health department reported that before long Mexicans mothers realized that "beans and fri-joles were not the proper food for [their babies]." This claim reveals health providers' lack of even the most basic knowledge of their clients' culture: in the Spanish language, frijoles are beans.[202] If the staff were unable to translate correctly a word this common among the population they served, it seems nearly certain that their efforts to establish mean-ingful connections would end in failure. Such negligence may well have contributed to the resentment and/or resistance within Mexican immi-grant populations to the changes the county health department was determined to impose on them. One nurse reported that Mexican women showed indifference to advice from clinic staff because "they had their own way of doing things," but the women brought their children to the clinics if the babies were sick.[203] According to Dr. Rude (director of Child and Maternal Services), younger women were more willing to listen to a doctor's advice than were older women who had already had children.[204] Perhaps this was because experienced Mexican mothers found the "simpler" education Pomeroy advocated imparting to immigrants too rudimentary or were more fearful, given their life experiences.

WBC staff used incentives to persuade women to attend the clinics. A woman received a "gay button decorated with a ribbon, to be displayed before her envious friends."[205] At some WBCs, the staff put on parties periodically, serving cake and lemonade to clients. Reportedly, "the Mexicans particularly couldn't resist the parties. They had such a good time, they came again and again. And before they quite realized it, they were learning the importance of fresh air and sunshine in raising a healthy baby."[206]

Mexican women had many factors to consider in deciding whether to attend a WBC, as the following case shows. In November 1920, the Los Angeles County Health Department established a WBC in Pomona. A Mexican Protestant church donated the use of some rooms in the parsonage. Health officials described the clinic as having been "fairly well attended for two or three weeks, when the attendance dropped. Upon investigation it was discovered that this was caused because of our connection with the Protestant Church. Most of the Mexicans here are of Catholic denomination."[207] If the officials' assessment was correct, this case implies that the department learned that in addition to addressing language and cultural issues it needed to take its clients' religion into account when making programming decisions. On the other hand, it is not clear why Mexicans would have attended the clinic in the first place if they objected to its connection with a Protestant church. After all, that association was transparent—each clinic was held in the pastor's home. In a similar case in Texas, Mexicans in El Paso came to programs hosted by a Methodist community center and church. The historian Vicki Ruiz has argued that the attendees accepted the services and programs this Methodist church had to offer while resisting its religious message and practices.[208] Mexicans in Pomona may have been prepared to take a similar approach. If so, the drop in attendance would suggest that what was being opposed was not the religious affiliation of the host facility but the clinics themselves.

Some procedures at the clinics were controversial. At the Simons Brick Yard WBC, health staff tested Mexican women for syphilis. It is unclear why. Before this testing was initiated at Simons, few cases of syphilis had been reported at WBCs attended by Mexicans. There is no mention of syphilis testing in any other racialized group. In 1924, the year the testing began, 6 of the 270 women screened, 2 percent, tested positive for syphilis. This result did not dissuade officials from conducting further testing. They contended that although the numbers were very small, they were significant. There had occurred five abnormal events among the six syphilis carriers: two miscarriages, one stillbirth, one infant death, and one premature delivery. "Although Simons is a small district and the figures are too small to be of much value, yet they are representative of the Mexican families throughout the County. It would seem that if routine Wassermann could be taken of all pregnant Mexican women in the County, with consequent *required* adequate treatment, that a dedicated reduction in the infant mortality rate from prenatal causes would take place," concluded a report on the syphilis testing.[209] This statement is a reminder that even strictly quantitative evidence is open to interpretation. Rather than consider 2 percent too small a figure to support any conclusions, LACHD officials saw it as justifying a continuation of syphilis testing. Moreover, they attached the negative stigma of venereal disease to all Mexicans—first to the women, who all were subject to testing, but also, by extension, to their families as well.

The next year, two other clinics, Belvedere and Maravilla, had also begun syphilis testing. Within three years, they examined 1,505 women, both white and Mexican; 135 women, 9 percent, tested positive. The difference in results for Mexicans and "Americans" was described as "slight."[210]

The majority of Mexican women also resisted using the county hospital's maternity services. As already noted, they may have wished to avoid being perceived as burdening the system. Other possible factors that may have dampened interest include language barriers and fear of discrimination. A 1920s interview with María and Wenceslao Orozco, a Mexican immigrant couple who lived in Belvedere, provides insight into such concerns. When María Orozco became pregnant, her husband refused to allow her to give birth at the county hospital. He had heard rumors that doctors might mistreat his wife because she did not speak English. The interviewer noted María's "distinctly Indian" looks, a comment that raises the possibility that some Mexican women faced discrimination based on their appearance and skin color.[211]

CONCLUSION

The programs the Los Angeles County Health Department offered during the 1920s demonstrate the complicated and sometimes contradictory elements of racializing discourses. The services that department staff directed at Mexicans often contradicted the prevailing racial discourses that at least some health officials themselves espoused. For instance, they offered WBCs but worried about race suicide. They associated high IMRs with Mexicans and Japanese but allowed both groups to continue the services of midwives, even as health experts across the country tied high IMRs to midwifery.

Their perceptions of Mexicans as backward and provincial led Los Angeles health officials to view Mexican culture as antithetical to the department's goals in the 1920s. The county health department's attempts to provide health care to Mexicans were based on officials' belief that Mexicans, unlike the Japanese, could be Americanized. But because the department's health center programs were based on cultural, racial, class, and gender misperceptions, the programs often fell short. Mexican communities continued to suffer high disease rates. Health officials compounded their errors by disseminating to state and national experts data about the area's Mexican and Japanese populations that had been gathered through surveys and health center programs and then analyzed and interpreted in terms of the regional racial lexicon. This furthered cultural misconstructions of Mexicans and the Japanese as disease carriers who threatened the nation.

Over time, the county health department's racialized policies institutionalized segregation. The department's programs and health centers did not even attempt to meet the health needs of all immigrants. The Japanese, in particular, were frequently excluded from public services and thus relied on alternative health care practices within their communities. Overall, public health programs directed toward the Japanese were not about extending social membership but about policing boundaries. The county health department's approach to the Japanese community also confirmed the group's low position in the regional racial hierarchy. Mexican immigrants had access to more programs, but they sometimes shunned these options. Many were reluctant to use public health services because they loathed being castigated by health officials for allegedly overusing public services and for their alleged ignorance and cultural pathology. As we shall see in chapter 4, such stigmatization only increased as resources became scarcer during the Depression.

"We Can No Longer Ignore the Problem of the Mexican"

*Depression-Era Public Health Policies
in Los Angeles*

Traditionally, Los Angeles mayors composed annual messages that were published in pamphlet form and distributed to city residents.[1] The 1930 annual address by then-mayor John Porter included a health report that singled out the "high death rate among Mexican babies," which it characterized as a "stumbling [block] in the way of reducing infant mortality rates in Los Angeles."[2] Another source of concern was Mexicans' high death rates from tuberculosis,[3] which rendered the group a "menace to the community at large."[4] Mayor Porter promised to take steps to contain the spread of tuberculosis by "concentrat[ing] on the control of TB among the Mexicans, where poverty, illiteracy, and low standard of living and poor housing exist."[5]

Mayor Porter's annual message differed greatly from that of his predecessor, George Cryer. Mayor Cryer's message to city residents, issued just one year earlier, had made no mention of Mexicans. The shift in focus can be attributed to the onset of the Depression, which had begun to take its toll on Los Angeles. Politicians and citizens alike were eager to find easy solutions to complicated issues. The Depression marked a major turning point in the treatment accorded to Mexicans living in the United States. The marginal acceptance that stemmed from being a source of cheap labor disappeared as rapidly as the jobs Mexican laborers had been hired to fill. As jobs ceased to exist, so also did the justification for allowing an open immigration policy with Mexico. Opponents of unrestricted immigration began insisting that Mexicans return home and followed up those demands with political pressure at the local, state, and national levels. In the words of the historian Vicki Ruiz, "rhetoric exploded into action" during the Depression.[6]

Public health standards provided a ready justification for restricting Mexican immigration. Public health officials, policy makers, and ordinary citizens increasingly relied on medical reasons as the basis for their objections to immigrant populations. Faced with budget cuts and a volatile political atmosphere, Los Angeles public health officials reversed their assimilation policies during the Depression and argued that Mexicans' biological inferiority precluded any possibility of rehabilitation. For example, health officials previously had interpreted high infant mortality rates (IMRs) as evidence of Mexicans' ignorance and thus had argued for publicly funded public heath education programs to ameliorate the problem. In the cost-conscious 1930s, health officials pointed to these same statistics as evidence that Mexicans were genetically flawed—a problem that no amount of education could erase. Public health officials who not many years earlier had lured Mexican women to clinics and well-baby clinics now objected to "diseased" Mexicans overburdening health and charity facilities. Thus, while cultural inferiority arguments about Mexicans dominated public health discourse in the 1920s, the Depression brought a return to biological determinism, often linked to eugenicist arguments.

This chapter describes two significant shifts that took place during the Depression. First, public health policies toward Mexicans changed dramatically, often resulting in the suspension of services. Second, the new policies were based on a construction of Mexicans as a biologically, not just culturally, inferior racialized group. Public health as an institution played an important part in the development of these new racialized understandings of Mexicans.

DISRUPTING THE RACIAL ORDER

The virulent policies and heightened racialization of Mexicans during the Depression represented the outcome of shifts that had begun in the mid-1920s. The concentrated focus on Mexicans that characterized the 1930s gained momentum during the five-year period between the passage of the 1924 Immigration Act and the onset of the Depression. The 1924 legislation established a national origins quota for southern and eastern Europeans but placed no such restrictions on immigrants from countries in the Western Hemisphere.[7] Mexicans could continue immigrating with few limitations. Many supporters of the 1924 Immigration Act were outraged by this imbalance. Continued immigration of Mexicans to the exclusion of southern and eastern Europeans was an affront to the logic of racial ordering. Mexicans were seen as inferior to Europeans; logically, then, they should have been barred from immigrating. This seemed so patently obvious that the lack of provisions for curtailing immigration from Mexico caught many Americans by surprise. Restrictionists worked feverishly to extend the quotas. Congressman John C. Box of Texas first proposed such legislation in 1926.[8] Box attempted to show that these "birds of passage" created various social problems while in the United States. Citing institutional reports in Los Angeles, he depicted Mexicans as overburdening charity departments and hospital services, particularly maternity wards, and accused Mexican children of overstraining the services of the children's hospital. Another committee member, Riley Wilson from Louisiana, pointed out that even if Mexicans returned to their home country, "they have children, and a child born in California is an American citizen."[9] Not surprisingly, agricultural employers and others who relied on large numbers of Mexican workers fought the Box proposal.

Pro- and antirestrictionists' views were not as divergent as their opposing positions might indicate. Both sides mainly viewed Mexicans in terms of their place in the American capitalist and racial order. Both groups supported and opposed Mexican immigrants for the same reason: they represented low-wage exploitable labor. Neither group was arguing for their inclusion on the basis of Mexicans' right to full social membership.[10]

The entire debate was so heated that the House Immigration and Naturalization Committee chose not to act on the Box bill.[11] This decision preserved the status quo, an outcome that left restrictionists deeply dissatisfied. They renewed their efforts, and in 1928 Congressman John Box and Senator William Harris of Georgia introduced new legislation to impose a quota on all Western Hemisphere countries. The bill proposed following the same sort of national-origins quota principle established in the 1921 and 1924 federal immigration legislation. Each nation in the Western Hemisphere would be allotted 2 percent of the total number of their citizens who were residing in the United States as of the 1890 census.[12] This formula would have allowed Mexico 1,500 slots. This time around, Box spoke of not only the social problems Mexicans engendered but also their bad genetic stock. He quoted a 1926 report by the California State Commission of Immigration and Housing that stated, "For the most part Mexicans are Indians, and very seldom become naturalized. They know little of sanitation, are very low mentally, and are generally unhealthy."[13] The bill did not pass in the end because of the lobbying power of southwestern agriculturists and the intervention on behalf of the State Department, who wished to maintain diplomatic relations with Mexico to resolve disputes over oil properties owned by Americans in Mexico.[14]

From the mid-1920s on, opposition to unrestricted Mexican immigration was vented in a variety of popular forums. The *Grizzly Bear,* published in California by the Native Sons and Daughters of the Golden West, repeatedly aired restrictionist sentiment toward Mexican (and Japanese) immigration.[15] Clarence Hunt,[16] the magazine's general manager, editor, and regular contributor, characterized the publication as a way to "keep the spirit of '49 alive." The slogan appeared to refer to the gold rush of 1849 (gold seekers were referred to as forty-niners), as well as to be an oblique reference to white numerical and political dominance in the aftermath of the 1848 Mexican-American War. The magazine's statement of purpose praised the racist Alien Land Laws of the 1910s and encouraged increasing California's white population. In the late 1920s, articles in the *Grizzly Bear* claimed that the 1924 Immigration Act had not adequately restricted immigration from Mexico. The following quote is representative:

> [The United States] cut down immigration from across the oceans, but lets in people who are more alien and less-easily assimilated than the poorest of European [immigrants]. [The United States lets in] people whose threat to the American standard of living and the organization of civic life is greater than any emanating from Europe. To reject the Italian, for instance, and take the Mexican is an important conclusion with no profit to the country and with benefit for but a minority of "interests" who know what they want: cheap peon labor that taxpayers are compelled to help support through charity.[17]

With the cessation of the flow of southern and eastern European immigrants, brownness came to signify the most important new threat to racial hegemony as anti-immigrationists set out to prove that Mexican immigrants were a menace. They did so by promoting an image of the racially inferior and diseased Mexican. After 1924, medical discourse and public health standards became a dominant way of expressing concern over and opposition to the threat to racial order that Mexican immigration seemed to pose. It is important to note that constructions of Mexicans first as culturally and then as genetically inferior preceded the economic downturn marked by the Depression, thus challenging assumptions by some academics that racial constructions flow strictly from structural influences.[18]

RALLYING AROUND IMAGES OF THE DISEASED MEXICAN

To ensure that Mexicans would be included in quota-based immigration legislation, it was imperative to depict them as dangerous. Medicalized nativism was central to this effort. Biologically based negative representations that intensified during the mid-to-late 1920s and during the Depression served as a key justification for the deportation of Mexicans. Health officials made unprecedented contributions to the new view of Mexicans as an undesirable immigrant group.

Public health as a race-making institution did not function in isolation. In the years leading up to the 1924 Immigration Act, Congress launched various investigations of the effects of immigrant populations. Politicians typically depicted Mexicans as peons whose Indian racial stock was inferior—but these claims appeared largely rhetorical. No supporting studies were cited, no experts were called to testify to this inferiority, and no scientifically generated statistics were quoted.[19] Instead, the majority of the hearings centered on immigrants from eastern and southern Europe and the countries bordering the Mediterranean. These groups constituted the racial "others" considered inferior to Anglo Saxons. In the years following the 1924 Immigration Act, the tenor of the claims regarding Mexicans changed. Politicians and others began to rely on public health discourse that specifically addressed how continued, unrestricted Mexican immigration might affect the country's health standards. Public health as a racializing discourse worked in tandem with other institutions to both racialize and criminalize Mexicans. The fortification of the border and the development of the Border Patrol were among the most significant racializing processes and institutions that developed at this same time.[20]

Edythe Tate-Thompson, director of California's Bureau of Tuberculosis (a division of the state Board of Health), wrote a forceful response to the open immigration policy. In "A Statistical Study of Sickness among the Mexicans in the Los Angeles County Hospital," she presented results of a study of Mexican TB rates and argued that Mexicans were a drain on municipal governments' budgets.[21] An important aim of the report's attention to the social costs of Mexican immigration was to prove false arguments by agricultural and business leaders that Mexican labor was an asset to the country. Tate-Thompson based her contention that Mexican immigration should be limited on both biological and cultural grounds. She argued that Mexicans were inherently less able-bodied and thus more prone to be infected by and be spreaders of tuberculosis. Mexicans' biological makeup, she asserted, rendered them less able to fight off the progression of TB once infected. Her culture-based reasoning completed the picture: Mexicans ate poorly, lived in deplorable conditions, and, due to language barriers, were less likely to follow health codes. Combining these scientific and cultural arguments, Tate-Thompson arrived at a representation of Mexicans as irresponsible and diseased. This image also conveniently masked systematic inequalities (such as segregation and dual labor market segmentation) that were the actual basis for the conditions Tate-Thompson observed and criticized.

The report's findings could not have come as a surprise to Los Angeles County Health Department officials. They had been aware of TB cases among Mexican residents since at least 1920 and would have been well aware of this population's high rates of tuberculosis.[22] In 1920, Mexicans in Los Angeles County died of tuberculosis at a rate two times higher than the rest of the population.[23] TB hit poor Mexican neighborhoods hard. These areas were so commonly known as areas affected by tuberculosis that students in the University of Southern California's Social Work Program studied the health and social effects in these neighborhoods, including the Macy Street district (just southeast of downtown in the same area as where the 1924 plague occurred) and Elysian Park (where Dodger Stadium now stands).[24]

County officials chose to define the high rate of TB among Mexican residents as a condition that did not threaten the general public. The county health department did not produce the same types of charts or statistics around TB as they did for birth rates, and they did not compare TB rates by race as they systematically did for birth and IMRs. Nor did they set up TB clinics; instead, they concentrated on well-baby clinics. The department, then, concentrated its outreach efforts on Americanization programs rather than on tuberculosis treatment and prevention.[25] As a consequence, during the 1920s, TB in Mexican communities generally did not serve as an impetus for reform, nor did it prompt warnings against open immigration. So, for instance, in 1917, when Dr. William Sawyer of the state Board of Health testified before Congress on tuberculosis cases in California, he made no reference to Mexicans.[26] At the time, health officials took the position that tuberculosis was a disease Mexicans contracted *after* they arrived in the United States.

Tate-Thompson pursued her agenda of identifying Mexicans as health burdens in the years following the publication of her study. Two years after Tate-Thompson issued her study, she wrote to the Los Angeles County Board of Supervisors asking them to create stricter admissions policies for the Olive View Sanitarium. In the letter, she maintained that during 1925 and 1926 alone, the Olive View Sanitarium, the county's tuberculosis facility, had housed 374 tubercular Mexicans, at a cost of $300,000.[27] Official policy at Olive View was to admit Mexicans who had established residency in California. The supervisor of the sanatorium, W. H. Holland, reported that contrary to Tate-Thompson's estimates, only 139 (23 percent) of the facility's patients were Mexican.[28] The discrepancy between the two sets of figures (374 versus 139) may reflect an error in tabulation on Tate-Thompson's part. It was common for patients with TB to be interned for several months. Thus Olive View patients who were counted as in residence in 1925 may have been counted again in the 1926 tally. In addition, Holland noted that sixty-seven of those the report counted as "Mexican" were in fact U.S. citizens.

Just one year after the formation of the Border Patrol in 1924, Tate-Thompson called for immigration policy reform in her study of tuberculosis, calling on the U.S. government to fortify its borders by placing physicians at U.S.-Mexico ports of entry.[29] Health officials in El Paso, site of the busiest of these entry points, had made similar requests during other disease outbreaks.[30] Tate-Thompson's position was different. She argued for these reforms as a California health official, working out of Sacramento, 1,200 miles from this main port of entry in Texas.[31]

In the California State Department of Public Health's biennial report, Tate-Thompson also used public health issues explicitly as a springboard to influence immigration policy. Tate-Thompson specifically called for "shutting off the tide of [Mexican] immigration" in order to reduce California's tuberculosis mortality rates and to lower the economic costs associated with the disease. She based her policy recommendation on the assumption that diseased Mexicans immigrated when their TB was in a latent stage; the infection moved into its more active and severe stages only after the carriers had settled in the United States.[32] Tate-Thompson refers in passing to "activities" that had begun "toward the restriction of migration of tubercular Mexicans into the United States," but she does not describe any programs.[33] She also notes that health authorities attempted to deport sick Mexican immigrants. When these attempts were unsuccessful, health departments would "care for [the ill] until the immigration authorities could deport them."[34]

Tate-Thompson's writings are especially important because they were widely used by those who supported restrictions on immigration from Mexico. The editors of the *Grizzly Bear* quoted her argument that Los Angeles County had become a dumping ground for poverty-stricken Mexicans. This development, the editors maintained, was part of a "carefully laid scheme to make the taxpayers of the county pay for the support and care of indigent foreigners."[35] Similarly, politicians who supported the 1928 Box-Harris bill's quotas for Mexico rallied behind images of Mexicans as disease carriers whose cheap labor was outweighed by the high cost to taxpayers in terms of public health and social services. "Not only do these people cause the county to spend thousands of dollars for relief, but they are compelling the expenditure of a great deal more public money in treating them for contagious diseases, including tuberculosis," Senator Box charged during hearings on his bill. He, like the *Grizzly Bear* editors, quoted Tate-Thompson's assessment of Los Angeles County as a "dumping ground."[36]

Other California public health officials were also on record as endorsing the claim that Mexicans imported TB and other diseases. In a weekly bulletin issued in February 1928, the state health department published an article that asserted just such a link. The article ran alongside another piece that described immigration legislation under consideration that would decrease or eliminate immigration from Mexico, including the Box bill.[37] In the bulletin, state health officials implored border officials to ensure that physical examinations at the U.S.-Mexico border were comparable to those conducted at stations with longer histories, such as the ones at Ellis Island and Angel Island.[38] They also urged the U.S. Public Health Service staff to equip border stations with all of the necessary "machinery" (most likely a reference to x-ray machines to test for TB) to adequately examine Mexicans crossing the border. California state health officials expressed concern that even if Mexicans passed the inspections, they would manifest signs of a chronic disease that was in an inactive stage after living in the United States for a period of time. These health officials called for the deportation of Mexicans who showed any "evidence of chronic infectious diseases" within a year of being admitted to the United States. This, officials hoped, would eliminate the possibility that these immigrants would seek state-funded charity services. Since 1882, federal immigration laws had prohibited the entry of individuals deemed unable or unlikely to be able to care for themselves due to illness (and thus likely to become public charges).[39] In the Southwest, these laws were racialized upon enforcement, and Mexicans were the only immigrant group mentioned in reference to them.

Just as lawmakers relied on the racialized knowledge produced by health officials, well-known eugenicists began to use medical and public health standards as a gauge for determining the deleterious effects of immigration. They still relied on the tried and true racial tropes they had used against southern and eastern Europeans, confidently declaring, in the words of one female writer in California, that "Mexican peons can never be assimilated with white Americans."[40] Others spoke of Mexicans as peons and charged that their "Indian stock" would result in national decay.[41] But they also began to rely on data that public health officials had been amassing for over a decade. Birth and disease rates became fundamental building blocks in efforts to construct Mexicans as dangerous.

Opponents of open Mexican immigration, including self-described eugenicists like Madison Grant, wrote numerous articles in support of the passage of the Box and Box-Harris bills. Medicalized constructions of Mexicans were a common theme across these publications. With titles such as "The Menace of Mexican Immigration," "The Influx of Mexican Amerinds," and "Mexicans or Ruin," authors showcased their beliefs in the inferiority of Mexicans.[42] Some articles were published in such extremist journals as *Eugenics: A Journal of Race Betterment,* but others made their way into more popular and mainstream publications, including the *Saturday Evening Post,* which claimed a circulation of over two million, revealing the degree to which eugenics-based notions of a racial hierarchy were accepted into mainstream culture before and during the Depression. The use of public health information to advance eugenicist arguments also casts doubt on the success of any effort to separate neatly eugenics projects from public health programs.

The image of the racially inferior, tubercular Mexican often was used to rally support for the restriction of immigration. For example, Samuel Holmes, the Berkeley zoology professor and eugenicist, although preoccupied with birth rates as evidence of race suicide, also publicly advocated immigration limits. Holmes used tuberculosis statistics from the Los Angeles County Health Department to support his position. He also quoted John Pomeroy as stating that the health department had "found 4,000 [Mexicans] to have been infected before they crossed the border."[43] (There is no indication of any such finding in health department records.)

Authors of anti-immigration articles reported that a "growing dread of the Mexican invasion" was seeping into the hearts and minds of the

American public.[44] Until the mid-1920s, the growth of the Mexican population in the United States had been attributed mainly to immigration. But with the increased arrival of Mexican women, the Mexican family (as opposed to the single, sojourning Mexican male) became the favorite target of those who advocated immigration reform.[45] "They bring their women, their children," warned C. M. Goethe, a California philanthropist, conservationist, and eugenics advocate, adding that Mexicans were "a group that is most fecund."[46] Samuel Holmes echoed Goethe's contentions in a separate article. Holmes cited a survey from San Bernardino, California, that found that "three out of every eight babies born were Mexican."[47] "The menial laborers of today produce the citizens of tomorrow," he warned in another article.[48] The shift in focus from immigration flows to birth rates confirms the role that fears about race suicide played in fueling immigration reform efforts. Many of the examples emphasized not just that Mexicans reproduced in high numbers but that they would soon outnumber white Americans. Goethe, for instance, offered as an instructive case the apocryphal tale of a charity-seeking Mexican man in Los Angeles who had thirty-six children. "By the fourth generation, however, he would at the same rate, become the progenitor of 1,185,921 descendents. In other words, it would take 14,641 American fathers to produce as many children, at a three-child family rate, to equal the descendents of this one Mexican father four generations hence," claimed Goethe.[49] Though both extreme and implausible, this example reveals the pliability of racial tactics. Advocates had no qualms about applying the same arguments to successive waves of immigrants, whether they were southern and eastern Europeans, Japanese, or Mexicans.

With the expansion of the Mexican population through immigration and natural growth, the image of the diseased Mexican who infected his or her family and larger social networks began to supplant the image of the inassimilable Mexican. Notions of Mexicans as vectors of infection were not new. As discussed in previous chapters, these ideas had been aired during the 1916 typhus epidemic and again during the 1924 plague. In the latter part of the 1920s, however, restrictionists began to emphasize that because Mexicans came from large families, they had more opportunities to infect a larger number of people. Goethe, in the same article that featured the prodigiously prolific Mexican father, provided readers with a second example, the case of the Espinoza family. Two of the Espinoza children had contracted smallpox. The local health authorities had done their part to stem the disease by quarantining the home. But the children's father, unable to curb his "passion for gambling," slipped out of the house to appease his craving. Mingling with others, he infected two men, who spread smallpox to ten more individuals. Five of the fifteen people infected died.[50] In another case, also involving smallpox, the author Remsen Crawford quoted an El Paso official as saying that epidemics "spread among [Mexicans] to a great extent before the health authorities could stop it."[51] These medicalized stereotypes and the reactions they provoked intensified during the Depression. The next sections trace the ways in which the economic downturn contributed to further racialization and provided additional justifications for new legislation against Mexicans.

THE IMPACT OF THE DEPRESSION

The Great Depression pummeled Los Angeles.[52] During much of the 1920s, the city had experienced tremendous growth and prosperity. By 1930, the city and county encompassed more than 1,400 square miles, surpassing the physical size of such prominent cities as Chicago and Boston. In addition, city and county populations increased by 115 percent and 136 percent, respectively, by the end of the decade.[53] The industrial sector also expanded. Low-paid Mexican laborers often filled the newly created blue-collar jobs. For Mexicans living in Los Angeles and, in particular, for first-generation immigrants, the changing economic conditions that accompanied the Depression were devastating. Workers from these groups typically were the first to be fired during industrial downsizing. Mexicans endured unemployment rates that were consistently higher than those of all other ethnic groups in the city[54] due to a "hire Americans first" approach by employers who often presumed that all Mexicans were foreign born.[55] In 1932, the *New York Times* estimated that out of the 2.5 million Mexicans in the United States, 2 million were unemployed.[56]

As the economic situation worsened, both officials and citizen groups began taking overt action. The Los Angeles City Council passed a resolution in 1931 calling for the suspension of immigration. They sent copies of this resolution to various government officials, including California's state and national senators and representatives, the chairmen of the Senate and House of Representatives' immigration committees, and the president of the United States. The council maintained that immigration had to be halted because "the large influx of aliens into California [accentuated] the problem of unemployment [which resulted] in the displacement of native-born Americans and citizens including veterans of World War [I]." Further, council members asked state and federal officials to establish "rigid and effective patrolling of our borders to prevent the illegal entry of aliens." They also demanded, for immigrants already residing in Los Angeles, "registration and finger printing of aliens ... in order that identification [could] be established at any time."[57] The resolution did not specify particular groups of "aliens," but, as the remainder of this chapter will make clear, the term *aliens* generally was used to refer to Mexicans, a major shift from fifty years earlier, when the term usually singled out Chinese residents.

Private citizens weighed in as well. Nativists sought scapegoats for their economic hardships during the Depression. Mexicans, who by 1930 were the third-largest (numbering 1,422,533) racial group in the country after whites and African Americans, were a highly visible target.[58] Nativists blamed Mexicans for the economic downturn, once again claiming that these workers stole jobs from American citizens and burdened the government's charity system. Los Angeles Representative Joe Crail (R) claimed that 75 percent of public charity funds in Los Angeles went to Mexicans.[59] Recent scholarship shows otherwise. In their re-examination of the statistics government officials used to justify deportation drives, historians Francisco Balderrama and Raymond Rodríguez exposed assertions such as Crail's as self- and race-serving fabrications. Despite media reports to the contrary in the 1930s, Mexican immigrants constituted 20 percent of the city's population but accounted for less than 10 percent of its welfare recipients.[60]

Over the first few years of the 1930s, a consensus that Mexicans were undeserving immigrants who disproportionately took more than they gave to U.S. society began to form. In addition to the characterizations of Mexicans as interlopers who were stealing the jobs of "real Americans" and/or as undeserving drains on municipal charity, a new social construction emerged to spur immigration reform during the Depression. As the next section explains, with the explicit assistance of L.A.'s public health officials, the image of the diseased Mexican and the Mexican who was too sick to work took root.

THE POLITICS OF BLAME: REINFORCING THE RACIAL ORDER FROM THE TOP DOWN

Los Angeles health officials who in the 1910s and 1920s had encouraged Mexicans to attend clinics now argued that Mexicans overburdened the public health system. The image of the charity-seeking Mexican expanded to include the sickly Mexican in need of public medical care. Earlier definitions of Mexicans as an important source of labor that could be Americanized, given the proper education by health experts, gave way as the economy collapsed.

Health officials worried that the economic downturn would negatively affect public health, so they monitored disease levels in the region, hoping to gauge where best to concentrate their efforts. Monitoring showed that cases of measles, mumps, and chickenpox all were on the rise. On the other hand, communicable diseases such as influenza, diphtheria, scarlet fever, whooping cough, and typhoid fever had decreased.[61] These conflicting results suggested that no obvious correlation existed between the economic slump and disease rates. Still, clinic attendance rose markedly. So, despite the lack of evidence of an increase in the rate of any specific disease, officials remained concerned that they could not meet the public's needs.[62] This was not an unfounded worry, given the health profiles of many area residents. Since the late nineteenth century, Angeleno boosters had promoted the city's salubrious climate to attract health seekers. Now, health workers began to speculate about the negative impact these individuals might have on the area's public health system. Zdenka Buben, a county medical social worker, claimed that Southern California was "an attraction to the chronic sick from all the states in the Union," who needed immediate medical attention once they arrived.[63] Concerns over how resources would be allocated shifted much more attention to both which and how many people made use of public health services.

Determining who was entitled to public health services brought to the fore questions about social membership. It was within this highly charged climate that public health reporting began to shift. In general, after 1930, public health reports no longer provided separate statistics for Mexican, Japanese, and Chinese residents. Instead, studies presented data on Mexicans only and increasingly highlighted Mexican immigration and its cumulative impact. For instance, the Los Angeles County Health Department's annual health report for 1932 reviewed all cases of communicable disease reported since 1920 and stated that of those 83,140 cases, 13,697, or 16.5 percent, could be attributed to Mexicans.[64] The few reports that mentioned the area's Japanese or Chinese communities usually cast these groups in a favorable light. So, for example, the 1932 report noted that Japanese residents accounted for only 2.3 percent of communicable diseases. This unfavorable comparison with the Japanese reflected Mexicans' new position at the bottom of the racial hierarchy. Thanks to the provisions of the 1921 and 1924 Immigration Acts and California Alien Land Law Acts, the Japanese population in and around Los Angeles was no longer a visible threat. Fears of the Chinese had begun to recede with passage of the 1882 Exclusion Act, and the 1924 legislation provided L.A.'s white residents with an additional measure of security.

Brown peril came into stark relief, coexisting with yellow peril. Depression-era public health reports narrowed the reported data on disease and vital statistics to two racial categories, "white" and "Mexican."[65] In addition, the Department of Charities (operators of the county's general hospital) began to use the category "alien" in their hospital records.[66] *Race* and *alien* both came to be synonymous with *Mexican,* to the exclusion of all other racialized groups. As these examples indicate, the regional racial lexicon collapsed into a brown-white binary.

Public health reports depicted Mexicans as a dual threat—a population at once large and unhealthy. Los Angeles health officials contended that Mexican families were more likely to attend public clinics because they could not afford private medical care.[67] A county social worker cautioned that if left unchecked, the "large, socially under-privileged Mexican population . . . would unquestionably become a public health problem."[68] A health department report was more explicit about the expected effects of this "large population": "There is no question that the Mexican race throws a great burden out of proportion to its percentage of population on both the Health Department and Charities Department."[69] These and similar comments had the cumulative effect of portraying the Mexican community in Los Angeles as excessively large and undeserving of public health services.

The image of the undeserving Mexican had significant ramifications that extended beyond the public health system. City health officials used the threat of Mexican immigrants as disease carriers to advance agendas of their own. In the 1930s, Christine Sterling, a developer of Olvera Street, sought to purchase the property on which the city's quarantine hospital was located. She hoped to raze the building and develop a tourist zone. Los Angeles Health Officer Dr. Charles Decker (1931–34) objected, even though the hospital had been closed for several years. Playing on fears that germs brought from Mexico might at any time erupt into an epidemic, Decker advised against the sale in an address that he presented to the Los Angeles City Council. To bolster his argument, he pointed to a current smallpox epidemic in El Paso, which presumably had spread through contact with residents of its sister city, Juárez, just across the Mexican border. Decker claimed he could trace at least two cases of smallpox in Los Angeles to the outbreak in El Paso. His discussion of these smallpox cases must have evoked memories of L.A.'s own smallpox epidemic in 1928. During that outbreak, 3,442 cases had been reported.[70] Controlling the epidemic had cost the city thousands of dollars.[71] Attributing the origin of the two smallpox cases in L.A. to El Paso (where there was a large Mexican population) gave more credibility to Decker's cause. The link tapped the power of an already accepted association between Mexicans and disease.[72]

Decker reminded council members that "[a] new generation of children is growing up unprotected by vaccination. This city is now ripe for another major outbreak of smallpox." Specifically, "If the seeds of smallpox from Juárez and El Paso are sowed among the unprotected unvaccinated people of this city, we might easily have a major epidemic to contend with. Without adequate isolation quarantine hospital facilities [sic], Los Angeles would be subject to all the adverse publicity that such a condition would occasion, with resultant loss of millions in hotel and tourist trade and curtailment of general business activities."[73] In the end, the city demolished the quarantine hospital, citing the inadequacy—not the irrelevancy—of the facilities.

County Health Officer Dr. John Pomeroy also had occasion to invoke the specter of Mexicans (and Japanese) as disease carriers. In 1934, private physician groups challenged Dr. Pomeroy's right to provide county health services to unincorporated cities in Los Angeles County.[74] The physicians alleged that the county health department overcharged the unincorporated cities for these services and that the department's arrangement with unincorporated cities siphoned paying patients from doctors in private practice. Rather than responding to these specific concerns, Dr. Pomeroy recast the debate. He warned Angelenos of the dangers the county faced because of L.A.'s "large, foreign born population, particularly [of] Mexicans and Japanese," many of whom lived in the surrounding unincorporated cities. "The reputation of Los Angeles County is seriously endangered as a tourist center," he continued, "and next year we are expecting visitors in great numbers to see the Olympic Games. We are certainly courting danger in lowering our standards of public health in any respect." Maintaining public health standards, Pomeroy asserted, "is certainly insurance against disaster at this time." Perhaps to make absolutely certain his audience appreciated the gravity of the scenario he was sketching, Pomeroy also reminded city officials and boosters that should an epidemic break out, the "news [would travel] rapidly in the day of the radio and airplane."[75] By linking the potential for widespread disease to the city's tourists and by focusing on Mexican and Japanese residents, Pomeroy left no doubt that L.A.'s image and prosperity were at stake.

THE POLITICS OF BLAME: REINFORCING THE RACIAL ORDER FROM THE BOTTOM UP

Depictions of Mexicans as a threat to the body politic also affected the ways in which everyday white Americans thought of Mexicans and related to them. During the Depression, many Angelenos absorbed and (re)produced rhetoric attacking the Mexican population, often incorporating public health arguments into their anti-immigrant agendas. When common citizens appealed to public health institutions or appropriated public health discourse to voice their concerns over immigrants, they demonstrated the power of medicalized reasoning. This process can be traced in the case of the city resident Mrs. Nellie Duncan and her Mexican neighbors, the Martínez family. In 1938, Mrs. Duncan complained to the city health department's Bureau of Sanitation and Housing about what she termed the Martínez children's "unruly behavior." She claimed that the children used her sidewalk for "unsanitary purposes and other immoral conduct." The family's most unforgivable offense, however, was their failure to corral their goat securely. The animal had escaped and trampled Mrs. Duncan's flower garden, the ultimate symbol of domestic order. Mrs. Duncan turned to the Bureau of Sanitation and Housing under the pretext that her neighbors were a health menace. Her complaint, however, conflated sanitary concerns with moral and racial anxieties: "Now that the city health department [is] quarantining the dogs, why not the goats and tar babies?" she asked in her letter.[76]

While the children's behavior and the goat's rampage obviously irritated Mrs. Duncan, the larger—and more intractable—source of her woes was the Southern Pacific Railroad. The company had purchased the property across the street from her, had it condemned for railroad purposes, and then used the land as a site for housing for railroad laborers and their families. Mrs. Duncan felt that the presence of these "peons" (the term she used for describing the Martínez family) would lower her property values. Moreover, she believed that this depreciation of land value in the area was precisely what the Southern Pacific Railroad had in mind. She charged that the company hoped to undermine property values so that they could "buy out [the neighborhood property owners] for a song."

The Bureau of Sanitation concluded that it had no jurisdiction over the Martínez family, as an inspection showed their toilet facilities and running water were in order. "Considering the class of occupancy, there seems to be no unreasonable sanitary condition," an inspector wrote. On the subject of property values, however, the bureau was more sympathetic, readily concurring that the presence of Mexican residents would lower values. For help with the "immoral conduct" of the Martínez children, Mrs. Duncan was directed to approach the Juvenile or Mother's Bureau of the police department.[77] This referral to another policing agency legitimized her prejudicial views of her neighbors. With the Bureau of Sanitation's encouragement, Mrs. Duncan carried her battle to yet another branch of government, the city council. "When we consider that under our State law Negroes, Mexicans, and others all attend school with our children, the lack of physical inspection is little less than criminal," she declared, and then continued, "Under such conditions our public schools become actual centers for the dissemination of disease."[78] (In actuality, California public schools were segregated until 1947, when the trial court ruled in Méndez v. Westminster that school segregation violated Mexican students' Fourteenth Amendment rights, which in turn spurred state legislation repealing school segregation regulations.)[79] Ultimately, it was the Board of Health Commissioners who heard Mrs. Duncan's complaint. The board assured her that a housing inspector would keep a "constant check on this matter."[80]

Mrs. Duncan's use of we and our leaves no doubt about whom she deemed acceptable insiders and whom criminal outsiders. Her call for physical inspection shows that these insider/outsider categories were more than tacit understandings at the individual level; they were indicative of an implied racial order incumbent on the state to preserve. Segregation was not legally sanctioned in Los Angeles at this time, but the power of the state (as wielded by an agency such as the city's health department) could be marshaled to reinforce citizens' personal visions of an ideal racial order.[81] Mrs. Duncan's conflation of race with disease, an overlap commonly found in medical discourse, is also noteworthy as an indication of how widespread these ideas had become outside public health arenas.

An important function of the trend begun in the 1920s of using medicalized cultural representations of Mexicans was to buttress calls for immigration reform. One common approach during the Depression, foreshadowed by Edythe Tate-Thompson, was to link Mexican immigrants and tuberculosis. The image of the tubercular Mexican became key in portraying the dangers of an open immigration policy with Mexico.

"THE MEXICAN IS COMING IN THOUSANDS": THE NEW IMMIGRATION THREAT

In 1929, in an article in the prestigious *American Journal of Public Health*, Dr. Benjamin Goldberg, a prominent physician, professor of medicine, and author of several articles on tuberculosis, raised a cry of alarm over the rising danger of tubercular Mexicans, individuals who would be an inevitable component of the "thousands" of immigrants pouring across the border.[82] At about the same time, the California State Department of Public Health noted that the state's tuberculosis mortality rate was higher than that of other states. The department attributed this to the presence of migrant workers and immigrants from Mexico who arrived in California already in the advanced stages of tuberculosis.[83] For their part, Los Angeles county health officials reported (in the annual health report for 1932) the "noteworthy" statistic that Mexicans had contributed 2,795 cases of tuberculosis over the previous twelve years.[84] As these three sources indicate, images of the sick Mexican were invoked repeatedly and across multiple arenas.

Tuberculosis was not the only disease to be linked to Mexicans, but it was the one most frequently attributed to this group. The association was not groundless: by 1930, Mexicans accounted for 20 percent of all tuberculosis deaths in California. Edythe Tate-Thompson had speculated at the end of the 1920s that tuberculosis was the chief cause of death among Mexicans in the country as a whole.[85] Before the 1930s, high tuberculosis rates in California typically were attributed to migrants from the northeastern parts of the United States who came westward hoping to find a cure for their respiratory ailments. Often arriving in advanced stages of the disease, these newcomers were apt to die within a year of moving to California.[86] Even into the 1930s, health officials continued to recognize that such health seekers contributed to the state's tuberculosis mortality rate. Tate-Thompson, for example, acknowledged the detrimental contribution of newly arrived migratory workers from the Midwest. "[T]he tuberculosis situation is far more serious among the native poor whites than it is among any foreign group including Mexicans," stated Tate-Thompson.[87] But neither awareness of the health seekers' effects nor the fact that *white* Americans constituted 66 percent of all deaths from tuberculosis in California in 1930 deterred her or other officials and commentators from assigning blame for the spread of TB to Mexicans only.[88] "We have and will continue our agitation for an adequate physical examination of Mexican laborers and their families before entry into this country," she insisted. "We have and continue to urge deportation of all aliens who have entered this country and are spreading disease wherever they go. Our compulsory education law means that children of these families must be in school many hours in close contact with other children, frequently wearing clothes that may have been placed on the bed of some sick person all night, spreading communicable disease."[89] According to this reasoning, even healthy Mexican children were suspect as potential carriers of disease.

The 1930s interpretation of Mexicans' comparatively high TB rates placed the blame for the disease squarely and exclusively on immigrants. Tuberculosis came to be understood as a dangerous disease with two important characteristics: it was imported from Mexico, and its treatment and prevention placed unacceptably high financial burdens on state and local governments already strapped for funds. Given the context of the Depression, financial considerations were a very high priority for Los Angeles officials. On the other hand, new cases of TB seemed to be occurring at a frightening rate. Los Angeles County health officials characterized TB as "by far the most important and most expensive of all the communicable diseases."[90] In a single year, from the summer of 1931 to the summer of 1932, TB cases in Los Angeles increased 38 percent. The rise in cases translated into increased costs to both the city and county health departments. In an attempt to meet the higher demand for care, the county health department operated tuberculosis clinics in which physicians diagnosed TB and nurses provided educational services. Those who needed institutionalized care but could not afford private medical facilities were directed to seek treatment at the county's facility, the Olive View Sanatorium.

Doctors and health officials used Darwinian language in their explanations for the disproportionate presence of TB among Mexicans. They traced the high rates to Mexicans' genetic inferiority. Other factors— living conditions, work environment, class—were not taken into consideration. Mexicans' resistance, the experts asserted, was "lower than that of the white races, but on the other hand they were more docile and obedient."[91] Casting Mexicans' allegedly inferior disease resistance as a byproduct of their biology made it unnecessary, and certainly impractical, to expend funds on TB prevention and treatment among this population. Not surprisingly, then, biologically based arguments for deportation of the sick as well as for a curtailment of immigration regardless of the health of the border crossers gained a wider audience in the 1930s.

Dr. Goldberg, in the same article in which he warned that the "Mexican is coming in thousands," demonstrated the logic of the genetic argument. He first established (by assertion) that "all men were not created equal" and then argued that "health heredity was a part of biological heredity."[92] Goldberg provided a history of tuberculosis in two non-Mexican racialized groups—Indians and African Americans—to show that the effects of disease on biologically inferior types had been seen previously. Indians, he contended, had died off because they were unsuited for urban life. African Americans had lived healthy lives on plantations during slavery; they suffered high rates of tuberculosis in urban centers because they could not adapt to life off the plantation.[93] By extrapolation, Goldberg maintained that as a similarly inferior race, Mexicans also posed a serious health threat. Accordingly, he called for stricter immigration laws.

The article's conclusions relied heavily on two of Edythe Tate-Thompson's reports and on the series of inflammatory anti-immigration articles originally published in the *Saturday Evening Post*. Goldberg's article, which, as noted earlier, had been published in the widely respected *American Journal of Public Health*, illustrates how arguments people may initially have dismissed as extremist, such as those in the three *Saturday Evening Post* articles, could find their way into scientific publications. The boundaries between popular culture and scientific arenas were permeable. Ideas from one realm could and did flow freely to another.

A physician at the Olive View Sanatorium, Dr. Emil Bogen, publicly responded to Goldberg's assertions. In an article published in the *American Review of Tuberculosis* in 1931, Bogen maintained that Mexicans did not have a higher susceptibility to tuberculosis because of their race. On the basis of findings from autopsies of Mexican patients who had died at Olive View, he argued that Mexicans often were misdiagnosed as tubercular. In addition, Bogen stressed the need for taking into account the effects of housing and economic conditions, along with race. Moreover, Bogen argued that Goldberg's sample size was too small to draw any significant conclusions.[94]

As the Depression ground on through the 1930s, the image of the tubercular Mexican gained additional force through merger with a second powerful stereotype, that of the hyperfertile Mexican woman. An example of this conflation appears in a Department of Charities study. The department (which oversaw the operation of Olive View Sanatorium) conducted surveys of families afflicted with tuberculosis. One of the reports featured the story of a Mexican immigrant couple with tuberculosis. The pair was alleged to have infected at total of eighty-three people, all (supposedly) members of the couple's own family network.[95]

The ways in which public health officials chose to deal with tubercular Mexicans demonstrate how the lines between public health as a science and as a public service could blur and how science could bleed into public policy considerations. During the Depression, severe financial constraints and widely accepted constructions of Mexicans as a large, diseased, charity-seeking population combined to make deportations and so-called voluntary repatriations a cornerstone of immigration policy.

DEPORTING THE DISEASED

The depiction of Mexicans as a diseased, charity-seeking group did more than place them outside the bounds of social membership of the United States. These negative cultural constructions prevented some Mexicans from remaining in the country at all. In the early 1930s, the Los Angeles County Department of Charities developed a "Transportation Section" or "Deportation Section" (the names were used interchangeably). This new division's charge was to identify and then deport any undocumented Mexican receiving county-sponsored medical aid.[96] Because the Department of Charities oversaw the county hospital, they located the deportation section there. The county hospital was a key site for finding deportation candidates because it provided medical care to indigent persons only if they were "acutely ill," or "suffering from contagious diseases," or victims of "emergencies, such as accident cases."[97] The Department of Charities justified deporting hospital patients by interpreting the use of medical services as a form of charity seeking. In a two-year period between 1931 and 1933, the department deported "to their former homes" over thirteen thousand Mexicans deemed guilty of receiving county medical or financial aid.[98]

Deportation programs were of course not limited to the expulsion of sick Mexicans.[99] In fact, Depression-era programs began under the direction of Secretary of Labor William Doak as a federal initiative to deport *all* illegal immigrants.[100] The profile of the illegal quickly narrowed. It was mainly Mexicans who were singled out to be labeled as burdens on the community's charity system and feared as competition for the white workforce. The deportation campaign gained momentum once municipal governments became involved. Los Angeles was the first city to initiate a deportation program. A newly formed Citizens Committee on Coordination of Unemployment Relief, under the direction of Charles Visel, undertook efforts to deport "illegals."[101] Within this climate, the Department of Charities also looked for ways to relieve their charity rolls by deporting and encouraging the return of Mexican nationals.[102]

Government-backed deportation programs created a climate of intense fear and uncertainty that prompted many Mexicans and Mexican Americans to return to Mexico "voluntarily," often with the aid of the Mexican consulate.[103] Officials such as Doak deliberately created this hostile environment by making certain that immigrants knew that regardless of where they were, "dances, homes, missions, and hospitals," they could be rounded up for deportation.[104] Only undocumented Mexicans were supposed to be deported, but records show that the U.S. government mainly deported American citizens of Mexican descent.[105] The peripheral position Mexicans had been occupying in Los Angeles for decades proved no shield against the excessive fears of the city's white majority. Calls for the "removal" of Mexicans mounted.

As work by pioneering scholars in Chicano history has shown, L.A.'s officials perceived Mexicans as overburdening city resources by relying too much on relief programs. Abraham Hoffman's *Unwanted Americans* describes the role Los Angeles County officials played in the Mexican repatriations from Southern California. Francisco Balderrama's *In Defense of La Raza* examines how the Mexican government cultivated national loyalty in Mexicans residing in the United States in order to encourage and facilitate their return to Mexico. *Decade of Betrayal* by Francisco Balderrama and Raymond Rodríguez reveals different layers of repatriation policies. The authors examine official government policies held by both the United States and Mexico, noting how these policies were interpreted and implemented at the state level and how they were received by the citizenry of each country.[106] These early studies all focus on how deportations pivoted on the image of the Mexican as a charity seeker. I argue that the image of the sick and diseased Mexican also provided a strong justification for deporting Mexicans and for constructing them as outside U.S. social membership.

The protocol for deporting Mexicans was quite straightforward. The Department of Charities identified patients they considered candidates for deportation.[107] A department representative then went before the Board of Supervisors and requested authorization, not for the deportation itself, but for the necessary funds and staff for travel to various parts of Mexico. In addition to taking this step, the Department of Charities had to comply with other guidelines. Mexico's Customs and Immigration Services regulations called for examining disabled persons who intended to enter the country.[108] Furthermore, both U.S. and Mexican railroads required that a highly contagious passenger be isolated and have adequate medical supervision.[109] A patient with a communicable disease was to be accompanied by a trained medical official. A patient with a serious illness would travel with a doctor or nurse.[110] If the individual's condition was less serious, he or she might be escorted by a Transportation Section staff person. Joseph Vargas, the section's repatriation investigator, often performed this function. Staff members also drove patients back to Mexico. Mexican officials sometimes met deported patients as they entered the country.[111]

The Department of Charities deported Mexicans to various parts of Mexico, including Aguascalientes, Colima, Chihuahua, Coahuilla, Jalisco, Mexico City, Querétaro, Michoacán, Guanajuato, Sinaloa, and Zacatecas (misspelled as Zacaticos in the department's records). The Department of Charities also listed one patient as having been deported to Calexico, which is actually in California. It appears the department attempted to return Mexicans to their region of origin. Though the records do not explicitly say so, they do discuss returning patients to their relatives in Mexico, and they often list the deportees' city of origin.[112] There is not enough information in the records, however, to determine which deportations were lawful and which were not. There is no indication of the deportees' status, nor of how long they had resided in the United States. Presumably, the patients were legal residents; otherwise, they should have been handed over to and deported by U.S. Immigration Services.

Immigrants who had entered the country illegally could be deported only after a formal federal hearing. The deported patients from Los Angeles were sent back to Mexico, not after legal hearings, but following approval of a one-page memo.[113] Immigrants might also face deportation if, owing to any preexisting conditions, they became a public charge within five years of their entrance into the United States.[114] Immigrants who had entered the country legally would have passed a health inspection at the border. Disease, then, was used not just to marginalize Mexicans but also to criminalize them. Despite having provided the proper identification to border officials, paid the head tax, and passed the physical examination, a Mexican who became sick or injured in the United States within five years after crossing the border might face deportation. Illness and illegality could be merged into a single condition: disease marked Mexicans as illegal.

Extant records of Depression-era deportations from Los Angeles are few. The ones that do exist give some sense of who was deported and under what conditions. For the period 1932–42, I have located deportation requests for 145 Mexicans, mainly those identified as deportable while in the county hospital. Even these lists, though, do not give a complete picture of those actually deported. The approval left the authorization open in order to include "any additional patients" if the need arose.[115] Men and women, young and old, contagious, injured, and healthy—are all represented in the sample. Patients with communicable diseases make up the minority. Tuberculosis was the most common reason to deport Mexicans, though out of the 145 cases, only 16 had tuberculosis. Given that TB was such a lightning rod for discussing the perils associated with Mexican immigration, the singling out of tubercular Mexicans was not surprising. Three other patients had leprosy. (The county's general hospital had a leprosy ward.) Three of four patients with venereal diseases were diagnosed as having syphilis (and were referred to as *luetic*). Before the Depression, Mexicans typically were not labeled as VD carriers, tracked for VD rates, or even regularly treated for VD. This changed significantly in the 1930s. Contracting a venereal disease could result in deportation. The Los Angeles Clinic and Hospital Association began sending out notices to their Mexican patients who were already undergoing treatment for syphilis to let them know that if they stopped these treatments, they would be subject to deportation. Mexican Consul F. A. Pesquería notified the Los Angeles branch of the U.S. Immigration Service of this questionable practice.[116]

The remainder of the Mexican deportees had various other, noncommunicable ailments (e.g., clogged arteries, arthritis, chest pains, hypertension, stomach and leg ulcers). Some individuals were deported because they had been diagnosed as having a specific mental illness, such as paranoia; others were simply grouped under the general category "mental." One patient was deported for being mentally deficient, others for being old or senile or for showing signs of dementia. Three deportees were blind, one had glaucoma, two had broken bones, three had paralyzed limbs (including a seven-year-old with infantile paralysis), and one was a postoperative patient (the records do not provide any details regarding the operation or the length of the patient's recovery before deportation). In addition to these patients from the general hospital, and the patients' children, the Department of Charities' Transportation Section returned to Mexico some TB patients from Olive View. Finally, agents of other institutions, including the probation office, the Child Welfare Department, and the Whittier Reform School, also selected certain Mexicans for deportation.

The memo-style deportation requests provide little information about the individuals being deported. They list the deportee's name (e.g., Ricardo Guttierez [sic]), the requesting institution (e.g., county general hospital) and the reason for deportation (e.g., tubercular).[117] The brevity of the descriptions raises several questions. What happened to Mexicans who were injured on the job and used the general hospital's services because they lacked insurance? This had been an accepted, routine practice since at least the 1920s.[118] When a parent was deported due to illness, what became of the children? In the case of Altagracia Oliva and her children, the outcome was bleak. After being labeled as "mental," she and her seven children, ranging in age from one to fourteen, were deported to Mexico City.[119] The records do not indicate the citizenship of anyone in the family. In other cases, children were deported without their parents. In 1938, the Arias girls (ages four, five, and seven), the Miranda boys (ages six and nine), and the Robledo children (ages three, eight, ten, twelve, and fifteen) were deported, along with patients from the general hospital, after being identified by the Child Welfare Department as good candidates for deportation. Since all were minors, the Department of Charities assigned a "matron" to travel with the children.[120] Emilia Mesa and her newborn (the baby was described as being in an incubator) were deported in 1939. This might indicate that a mother risked deportation should her child need additional medical aid or perhaps that the mother and child were deported for using the general hospital's maternity services.[121]

The Transportation Section carried out investigations and deportations even though officials readily admitted that undocumented Mexicans were not overburdening medical or charity services. A Department of Charities report submitted to the Board of Supervisors admitted, "Less than 6 percent of all cases receiving medical and material relief from the Department of Charities are aliens. Mexican aliens constitute only 3.3 per cent of the total caseload. There is frequently considerable confusion resulting from the popular belief that the majority of our so-called Mexican cases receiving relief represent alien persons. In truth, only 38 per cent of those so-called Mexican cases afforded medical or material aid by this Department of Charities are aliens, the balance being of Mexican descent who are American citizens and long time residents."[122]

Despite this acknowledgment, County Supervisor Leland Ford expanded his deportation staff to "add impetus to the steady reduction in Mexican alien cases receiving aid."[123] In a single month, the newly enlarged staff interviewed seven hundred Mexicans receiving aid and closed 16 percent of the cases.[124] Considering that county officials readily recognized that departments commonly conflated *Mexican* and *alien,* it seems likely that undocumented Mexicans, legal residents, and Mexican Americans all would have been included in these roundups.

Historians mark the most intensive phase of deportation as ending in 1931 or 1932 and describe almost all deportations, forced and voluntary, as ending by 1935.[125] Camille Guerin-Gonzales argues that the intervention of agricultural employers, who saw the deportations as depriving them of their workforce, also helped temper deportation campaigns.[126] But even this minimal protection did not extend to Mexicans who were sick or who had been injured on the job. These groups remained utterly vulnerable. As late as 1942, Mexicans who sought medical care at public institutions ran the risk of deportation.

In 1942, the U.S. government, although still deporting Mexicans, entered into an agreement with the Mexican government to launch the Bracero Program. This guest worker program (which lasted from 1942 to 1964) brought approximately five million Mexicans to the United States to work in agriculture throughout the Southwest.[127] The Bracero Program clearly proved false the racial logic on which deportation programs were based: that Mexicans' rank within the American racial hierarchy was so low as to warrant this group's wholesale removal. The fact that the deportations and guest worker solicitations coexisted also speaks to the pliability of racial logic.

GENDERING ANTI-IMMIGRANT NARRATIVES DURING THE DEPRESSION

Throughout the late 1920s, Mexican women became more central to depicting what was wrong with an open immigration policy with Mexico. Immigration restrictionists intensified their campaigns, identifying Mexican women's reproductive capacity as another reason to end immigration. They argued not only that Mexican women had too many children but also that both mothers and their offspring were likely to end up needing charity. Mexican women were seen as dependent on free birthing and medical services and reliant on charity to support their newly expanded families. The belief that Mexican women were unusually "fecund" and anxieties over the potential for race suicide helped focus attention on birth rates during the 1930s.

Birth Rates

Mexican immigration increased throughout the 1920s, and, with the arrival of more women and families during this period, the demographics of Mexican communities in the United States also changed. Birth rates rose steadily (see table 2). In 1915, Mexicans accounted for 14 percent of the births in the county overall. Fifteen years later, they accounted for 14 percent of the births in incorporated cities in the county and 27 percent in the rural areas of the county.[128]

County health department reports commonly included information on Mexicans' increasing birth rates. Health officials first commented on this trend in the late 1920s. In a report to the Board of Supervisors, Dr. Pomeroy stated, "The Mexicans are increasing at an alarming rate in the rural districts of the county."[129] Similar kinds of statements (e.g., "The Mexican births have shown a most tremendous increase")[130] persisted into the early 1930s. The reports also connected these high birth rates to specific geographic areas, thus racializing the spaces in the process. "Belvedere District showed the greatest number of births with 1,756. In this area, however, over half the births were Mexican," is a typical formulation.[131] Again focusing on Belvedere, another report led with the headline, "mexican exceed white births." The accompanying text noted, "Over 160 more Mexican babies were born in Belvedere district in 1930 than in 1929 and the Mexican births were 54% of the total as against 45% for the whites. Also, while the white births declined 8%, the Mexican births increased 3.5% for the two years."[132] The annual health report stated, "Going back to 1916 there were 160 white births; in 1930 there were 777,—an increase of nearly 500%; in 1916 there were 43 Mexican births, in 1930 there were 930,—an increase of 2,163%! In other words while the white births in 1930 were only 5 times as many as [in] 1916, the Mexicans had 216 times as many births as [in] 1916."[133] By failing to highlight or contextualize their unit of analysis, the reports often left the reader with the erroneous impression that the Mexican population would soon eclipse the white population. Yes, there were more Mexican births than white births in Belvedere, but that was because Belvedere was composed increasingly of Mexicans. Yes, Mexican births had increased greatly from 1916 to 1930, but so had white births, both in proportion to the growing population. White births in the incorporated areas of Los Angeles increased from 843 in 1916 to 2,639 in 1926, representing an increase of 3,130 percent (see table 2).

The high number of Mexican births in rural areas was a stark contrast from just ten years earlier when Japanese had totaled one-third of the births in these areas of the county. The public understood rising Mexican birth rates within the context of decreasing Japanese birth rates. The *Los Angeles Times* reported, "The Mexican birth rate also has increased heavily, almost in direct proportion to the decline in the Japanese birth rate. Mexican birth rates represent 30 per cent of total births in 1926 as compared with 12 per cent of the total in 1917. On the other hand, Japanese births have declined from the high peak of 34 per cent of the total in 1917 to 5 percent of the total in 1926. However, the report shows that the Japanese children have more than twice the chance for life of the Mexican infants."[134] The concerns over Mexican birth rates echo worries aired in the 1910s, when fears of yellow peril accompanied the publication of Japanese birth rates.

Concerns over rising Mexican birth rates were expressed in other forums besides those related to public health. An article in the *Grizzly Bear* discussed birth rates in the unincorporated areas of Los Angeles County and claimed that in the previous seven years white births numbered 241, as compared to 4,070 for Mexicans.[135] The *Grizzly Bear's* figures are highly questionable and do not seem to have been based on any specific reports. The Los Angeles County Health Department, the main producer of such statistics, showed that whites composed the largest majority of births in both incorporated cities and rural areas (table 4). The health department reports and the *Grizzly Bear* coverage, however, share an important trait: both consistently depicted Mexican birth rates as eclipsing white birth rates.

The economic ramifications of Mexican birth rates were an overriding concern among Los Angeles officials across several institutions. In an expenditure report submitted to the Los Angeles County Board of Supervisors, welfare officials accused Mexican families of abusing the county welfare system's resources. "Of all the manifestations of pauperism that [come] to our attention, nothing [is] more insidious than the

TABLE 4. PERCENTAGE OF BIRTHS
BY NATIONALITY IN LOS ANGELES COUNTY,
1930 (TOTAL POPULATION = 705,846;
BIRTHS = 11,292)

Nationality	Incorporated Cities	Rural Areas
White	83	66
Mexican	14	31
Japanese	1.2	2.4
Other	1.8	0.6
Total	100	100

SOURCE: Los Angeles County Health Department, "Health Department of Los Angeles County Annual Report Year Ended June 30, 1931," 26, DHS. Births are reported by "nationality" rather than by "race" in this source.

birth rate among the indigent," they claimed.[136] Highlighting examples of Mexican women who gave birth to up to five children while on welfare, the report described Mexican families that had exhausted their welfare resources and then found fraudulent ways to continue collecting money. The report also noted that many members of these families suffered from diseases such as tuberculosis and thus were a burden on the county's general hospital as well.[137]

The increasing Mexican birth rates of the 1920s began to drop in the early 1930s, reacting quickly to deportations and repatriations. Even as early as 1932, Mexican births in the rural areas of the county had decreased by 22 percent. "This is the greatest decline of Mexican births in the history of this county, and undoubtedly reflects the large exodus of Mexicans from this district," Pomeroy boasted in a health department publication.[138] As Mexican births declined, white births rose. Dr. Giles Porter of the California State Department of Public Health wrote an article entitled "Mexicans Gone, Disease and Birth Rates Down." "The exodus of Mexicans to their native land has been productive to a certain extent of better public health records, particularly in southern California," he argued in the article.[139] The Los Angeles Times featured a story with the subtitle "Percentage of Whites Rises and Mexicans Down" and included the column head "More White Children."[140] The preoccupation with birth rates during the Depression demonstrates how concerns over Mexicans in the United States were about much more than competition over scarce jobs. The overarching worry was what

Mexicans' position in the United States would be if they continued to grow as a Mexican *American* population.

Reinterpreting Infant Mortality Rates

The stereotype of the fecund Mexican woman who relied on charity to support her growing family had an even darker implication. A common argument was that Mexican women were likely to have unhealthy children who died at birth or within the first year of life, thus increasing the area's IMRs.[141] A renewed focus on IMRs cast both Mexican women and their children as racially inferior.

By the early 1930s, the county health department had established a national reputation as a leading public health department, especially in the area of children's health. President Herbert Hoover's interest in child welfare drew attention to Dr. Pomeroy's activities in Los Angeles, and Pomeroy participated in child welfare conferences convened by the president. Thus Pomeroy was in contact with leading members of the national child welfare movement.[142] Leaders in prestigious and powerful medical organizations, including the American Medical Association, discussed emulating the Los Angeles County Health Department's health centers.[143] The health department received accolades at the regional and national level for the success of its well-baby clinics (WBCs) in particular. The national average for infant deaths was 58 per 1,000. In Los Angeles, there were 38 deaths per 1,000 births.

Health department officials were proud of their reputation and chagrined by the impact of Mexicans' IMRs on the region's overall rate. City officials asserted that the Mexicans' IMR was higher than whites' IMR because "where ignorance prevails, the infant death rate rises."[144] When the *Los Angeles Times* ran an article entitled "Babies Are Safe in Los Angeles," featuring the county health department's WBC programs, it described the challenges to child health posed by the large Mexican population. The article disaggregated Mexican IMRs from those of the rest of the county to highlight an IMR of 26 per 1,000 versus 38 per 1,000 when Mexican IMRs were included.[145] A 1930 city health department report was even more direct. "White babies of American parentage have the best chance to live" in Los Angeles.[146]

By the early 1930s, national health officials had begun to look closely at Mexican IMRs. Officials gathered at the 1934 convention of the American Public Health Association (held in Pasadena, California) discussed Mexican IMRs. They concluded that the high Mexican IMRs in

California stemmed from the "natural law of survival of the fittest."[147] Such reasoning reprised eugenicists' arguments equating IMRs with national deterioration, depopulation, and race suicide.[148]

In the mid-1930s, Los Angeles city health officials declared that they "could [no longer] ignore the Mexican problem as a contributing factor in increasing our infant mortality rates."[149] They highlighted this connection by reorganizing how they gathered their data. They began reporting IMRs by the mother's residence, using the categories "Los Angeles County," "elsewhere in California," "Mexico," and "other foreign."[150] This tracking system lent itself readily to isolating and scapegoating first-generation Mexican immigrant women and their higher IMRs in particular.[151]

The focus on Mexican women's birth rates and the practice of attributing the region's elevated IMRs to these women became yet another way to mark Mexicans as inferior. These discussions also paved the way for future cultural constructions of Mexican women as overly fertile and as content to rely on the state to support their children.[152] Such depictions are the precursors of stereotypes such as the "welfare queen" and the notion that Mexicans are resigned to live in a "culture of poverty." They are pernicious and to this day have serious policy implications.[153] During the Depression, they may have also led to sterilization policies.

Sterilizations

Rising birth rates increasingly became equated with the threat of permanent settlers, not just sojourner immigrants. Many interpreted the large numbers of Mexicans as evidence that the immigration threat was now an internal one, evoking social, cultural and even psychological concerns. Within this xenophobic climate, more overtly discriminatory policies and procedures evolved. Intensified surveillance policies at the "border" were not limited to a physical site such as the geographic border between Mexico and the United States. During the Depression, and particularly at heightened times of racial scapegoating, "the border" expanded to include large geographic expanses.

Sterilization in the 1930s provides another example of the flexibility of the era's race politics and illustrates how bodies were regulated through state policy. California was a hotbed of eugenicist thought and sterilization in the early to mid–twentieth century. Eugenicists and advocates of sterilization for the unfit were not considered extremists. In California, they often were well-respected leaders, such as Harry Chandler, publisher of the *Los Angeles Times;* David Starr Jordan, president of Stanford University; and Joseph Widney, president of the University of Southern California. California also was home to a group of eugenics organizations, including the Eugenics Section of the Commonwealth Club of California, the Eugenics Society of Northern California, the Human Betterment Foundation, and the Institute of Family Relations.[154]

California hosted the largest sterilization movement in the country. The state had adopted a sterilization law in 1909 (after Indiana, the first in the nation to do so) with the express intent of improving society by keeping the "feeble-minded" from reproducing. Generally, sterilizations were performed in the state's six mental institutions and in the Sonoma State Home for the Feeble-Minded. By 1930, approximately seven thousand men and women in California had been sterilized, more than in any other state and more than in all other Southwest states combined. From 1909 through the 1960s, an estimated twenty thousand people in California were sterilized, as compared to an estimated sixty-three thousand nationwide.[155]

Labels such as *feeble-minded, idiot,* and *moron* reflected the common belief that people with mental illnesses were intellectually inferior and therefore unfit to reproduce. Other labels, such as *immoral* and *degenerate,* were also applied.[156] All of these terms addressed the issue of who was fit to be a citizen. Connecting state-initiated reproductive decisions to the social value assigned to a group would likely have had serious ramifications for Mexicans, whose position in the racial hierarchy plummeted during the Depression. Little is known for certain about how racial politics and sterilization procedures collided in early-twentieth-century California. But data from a study by Paul Popenoe, a leading eugenicist of the time, on the sterilization of the insane in California from 1909 to 1926, which encompassed 3,666 cases, indicate that both immigrant men and women were sterilized and then deported.[157]

After the onset of the Depression, the Mexican consul in Los Angeles began receiving letters from Mexicans living in all parts of the United States, asking for help in avoiding forced sterilization.[158] Tomás Sánchez, for example, sought assistance in getting his sixteen-year-old son Félix discharged from the Pacific Colony State Home for the Feeble-Minded, located in east Los Angeles County, when he learned his son would likely be sterilized. The home's medical superintendent had recommended this action after the boy scored 50 points on an IQ test, putting him firmly within the category of feeble-minded.[159] Vice-consul

Enrique Bravo appealed directly to the medical superintendent of the hospital, Thomas Leonard, to release Félix at his father's request.[160] Leonard responded. In his opinion, the best course of action would be to deport Félix Sánchez. First, though, "For [Félix's] own interest and for the welfare of the public," Leonard explained, "regardless of what country he should reside in the future," Félix should be sterilized. This kind of recommendation was in keeping with sterilization procedures practiced even before the onset of the Depression.

Because Félix Sánchez faced the strong possibility of being sterilized against his will, Vice-Consul Joel Quiñones appealed the case to California Superior Court Judge F. A. Leonard, who had originally sentenced Félix to the Pacific Colony Home.[161] Vice-Consul Quiñones did not challenge the merits of the procedure or the validity of the tests. Instead, he informed the judge that if the hospital would release the boy, father and son would immediately and permanently return to Mexico. The records do not indicate how the case was resolved; in general, such cases were characterized as "voluntary repatriations."

The case of Félix Sánchez highlights an important additional aspect of public health. Besides being a powerful institution that shaped social membership, public health policy and its implementation affected the rights associated with formal, juridical citizenship. None of the correspondence in the Sánchez case specifies whether Félix was a U.S. citizen. Since Vice-Consul Quiñones did not appeal for the boy's release as a Mexican citizen—which was standard practice—it seems likely that his father Tomás was a Mexican citizen but that Félix was Mexican American. If he was, medical reasoning did more than mark the boy as a foreigner and thus an outsider. The threat of sterilization forced Félix's father to consider making his son an expatriate rather than risk sterilization.

Though there are few extant records pertaining to forced sterilization of Mexicans, investigations initiated by Mexican Consul Rafael de la Colina indicate that his office expressed concern over links between the scapegoating of Mexicans during the Depression and decisions to sterilize them. In 1930, only a few months after the Sánchez case, Consul de la Colina requested a complete list (starting in 1929) of sterilizations performed on Mexican citizens at the behest of the Los Angeles County Juvenile Department.[162] Requesting the Juvenile Department's statistics was appropriate because most sterilizations were performed on fifteen- to twenty-four-year-olds. The consul's focus on 1929 reflected a concern over the increased attention Mexicans had received with the onset of the Depression. Finally, his request indicates an awareness of the ways in which Mexican youth began to be criminalized during this period.[163] The line between deviant and feeble-minded behavior was vague. For Mexican youth, entanglements of any kind with the state's juvenile system could have unforeseen consequences. For Félix Sánchez, sterilization was recommended for behavior that initially had provoked only a simple sentence to a boys' home.

De la Colina decided to bring public attention to the problem of forced sterilization after being alerted to two more cases, these involving Mexican women. Fermina Villanueva sought legal counsel after her daughter Margarita narrowly escaped a forcible sterilization. The other case involved Concepción Ruiz, a young unmarried *third-generation* Mexican American woman. According to Consul de la Colina, Ms. Ruiz had filed a complaint at the Mexican consulate in San Francisco, saying she had been sterilized against her will.[164] This case is particularly interesting because Concepción Ruiz, although an American citizen, sought intercession from the Mexican consul. It is unknown whether she also sought or gained redress from any U.S. institutions.

Consul de la Colina shared the details of these cases with the editor of the binationally distributed newspaper *El Heraldo de México*, with the express desire that the paper run stories on them. During the Depression, Colina regularly communicated with the Mexican community through the Spanish-language press. He was critical of the English-language press's lack of coverage on the impact of the Depression on Mexicans in the United States.[165] There is no record of what eventually happened with Consul de la Colina's investigations or what response *El Heraldo de México* made to the consul's request. In the months following de la Colina's initial contact with the paper, *El Heraldo* published various stories on how the Depression was affecting Mexicans, including stories about the many Mexicans who were forcibly repatriated (seven thousand deportations daily from June to December 1930), but there were no articles that focused on sterilization.

The justifications offered for sterilizing young Mexican men and women were a bold indication of just how far outside the bounds of social membership in the United States Mexicans were positioned. Mexicans living in the United States, especially those who had made California their home, were a highly vulnerable population during the Depression. They were not, however, the only racialized group to find themselves scapegoats for the difficult times most U.S. citizens faced. In Los Angeles, the 1930s brought a resurgence of animosity toward an old target, Chinese launderers.

CHINESE LAUNDERERS UNDER SIEGE (AGAIN)

Following passage of the Chinese Exclusion Act in 1882,[166] the Chinese population in Los Angeles steadily diminished and remained relatively small. The 3,009 Chinese in Los Angeles composed 0.2 percent of the population of the city in 1930.[167] Most Chinese residents nevertheless continued to be spatially segregated from white Angelenos, living in only a few areas of the city (mainly Chinatown and two neighborhoods south of downtown).[168] In 1933, Old Chinatown was demolished, and many residents relocated to New Chinatown in the following years (map 4).

Contacts between the races typically were limited to commerce and tended to occur in locations such as Chinatown that, according to newspaper coverage of the period, were "unchanging" and dominated by "an older civilization in which custom outweighs sanitation."[169] In short, whites, on those limited occasions in which they paid any attention, viewed the city's Chinese as quaint—a small, isolated, nonthreatening population. The arrival of the Depression dramatically altered that image.

With the economic downturn, concern over the presence of Chinese laundries promptly resurfaced.[170] Once again, white launderers' profit margins were the underlying issue—Chinese launderers were blamed for taking business away from whites. While Mexicans were depicted as sickly and dependent on charity, the Chinese were believed to be wily competitors. They were guilty, not of overreliance on the state's largesse, but of just the opposite: the Chinese were too successful as entrepreneurs.[171] Once again, city legislation made it virtually impossible for Chinese launderers to operate their businesses. The new ordinances, both in specific provisions and in selective enforcement, disproportionately affected the Chinese. And once again, the commonly held belief that the Chinese practiced lower standards of cleanliness held sway.

The impetus for revising city ordinances at the start of the Depression came from public health officials, who cited concerns about the spread of disease. In August 1931, the Los Angeles City Board of Health Commissioners proposed to the city council a series of amendments to the health codes that regulated public laundries.[172] The proposed amendments encompassed three areas. The commissioners recommended a provision prohibiting people with infectious or communicable diseases from lodging or sleeping in any building that housed a laundry. Most launderers did not have diseases, so to the healthy majority this pro-

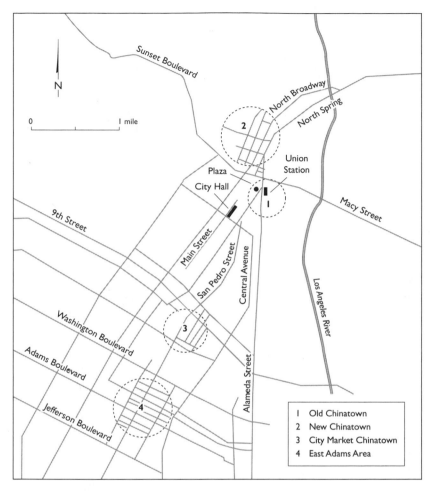

MAP 4. Los Angeles's Chinese neighborhoods before 1950.

posed amendment was not of much concern, though it could serve to reinforce late-nineteenth- and early-twentieth-century stereotypes of the dirty Chinese launderer. The commissioners also urged that commercial launderers be prohibited from spraying water from their mouths onto customers' laundry.[173] This recommendation was an attempt to curb a local myth attributed to the Chinese—that of deliberately spraying spittle on the clothes they laundered, again reinforcing another stereotype.[174]

The third recommendation, the "Laundry and Living Quarters" section, prohibited launderers from living in the same building they used for their laundry business. The ordinance stated that there could be no opening (window or door) between a public laundry and any area used for living or sleeping purposes because it might "affect the sanitation of any public laundry or any articles laundered therein."[175] This ordinance particularly concerned the Chinese who lived at their business sites because they could not afford to live elsewhere. The launderers were in compliance with prior health codes that required living quarters and business areas to be separated by a wall or partition, but the new ordinance would put them in violation of sanitary health codes.

Chinese launderers operated over half of the 450 laundry establishments in Los Angeles in the early 1930s. Because of earlier experience with municipal legislation that had restricted their ability to operate businesses, Chinese launderers felt this latest code was yet another example of an ordinance "disguised as a health measure . . . intended to make it impossible for the small independent [Chinese] laundry to operate."[176] They were right. Once the revised ordinances had been passed by the city council in April 1932, the primary recipients of health code violation citations and of punitive actions taken by the city attorney were Chinese launderers.[177]

The cited launderers pleaded their cases before the Board of Health Commissioners, with no success.[178] They also appealed to the city council through ethnic organizations, including the Chinese Consolidated Benevolent Association (CCBA) and the Chinese American Citizens Alliance, a Chinese civil rights group.[179] The CCBA had fought for Chinese launderers in the 1910s, and they once again stepped in to represent the defendants.[180] The Chinese American Citizens Alliance, based in L.A., was composed of Chinese American citizens.[181] The CCBA reminded the city council that if the city enforced the citations ordering them to vacate their businesses, this would amount to forced closure. The launderers would then have no other recourse than to rely on charity for their subsistence, which they proudly stated that they had never done before. The CCBA noted that other cities, such as Oakland, had "listened with sympathetic ears" and granted similar requests made by launderers in their municipalities. Finally, it behooved Los Angeles to repeal the amendments because the launderers paid "no small amount in taxes." The enforcement of the ordinance would "ultimately result in more unemployment and detriment to the fair city." As entrepreneurs who paid taxes and citizens (suggested by the affiliation of many of the launderers to the Chinese American Citizens Alliance), Chinese might have felt a certain entitled relationship to the city.[182]

When they brought the issue before the city council, Chinese launderers sought support from their landlords. If the laundries went out of business, landlords would lose good tenants. Unlike in the 1910s (the last time the Chinese had been the targets of new city legislation), this time white real estate owners also saw themselves as affected by the ordinance changes. Accordingly, landlords petitioned the Los Angeles City Council both individually and through their professional associations. Property owners supported their Chinese tenants because the proposed ordinance would "take bread and butter away from the small business people." The East Side Taxpayers Association, the East-Side Taxpayers' Protective League, and the Business Men's Association all protested the proposed ordinance as "too drastic," noting that it "would add an additional burden to many property owners at this unfortunate time."[183] Property owners also were concerned that they could be held liable for health code violations involving the properties they rented to launderers.[184] They thus urged the city council not to enforce the "Laundry and Living Quarters" provision.[185] Eighty-one white property owners signed a petition in support of the CCBA's appeal. The petitioners did not mention the race of the launderers, nor did they allude to any sense of discriminatory intent in the legislation. Instead, they framed the issue in terms of the survival of small, independent businesses and of their own economic well-being.

The proposed amendments passed despite the protests. Chinese launderers immediately began lobbying for repeal. The Chinese American Citizens Alliance joined in echoing many of the concerns raised by the CCBA and the white petitioners. The alliance labeled the ordinance a restrictive piece of class-based legislation and called for its repeal to safeguard the survival of small independent laundries. Additionally, however, the alliance focused attention on the racist intent of the legislation, pointing out that *all* 250 launderers affected by recent rulings of the city attorney were Chinese. The alliance again reminded the city council that closing Chinese laundries also would have significant adverse effects on white property owners.[186] Here, in petitioning as citizens and/or taxpayers, Chinese launderers evoked a language of entitlement.

In response, Councilman George Baker introduced a resolution to repeal the "Laundry and Living Quarters" measure in October 1932. Although Chinese launderers had been at the center of council meeting debates over the repeal of the ordinance for over a year, Councilman

Baker did not allude to them once in his arguments. Baker's comments referred to the expansion of the definition of a laundry that accompanied the "Laundry and Living Quarters" measure from a "building, room, or place, or portion thereof, used for laundering, washing, and/or ironing for compensation," to include the phrase "or for public use."[187] He asserted that the city should not encroach on the rights of families with washing machines who might want to take in laundry to make some extra money during the Depression, or penalize small launderers who were "compelled" to sleep in their businesses during the economic crisis. Baker received considerable support, mainly from landlords and prominent Los Angeles businessmen, who saw the repeal as a way to protect their tenants and hence their own incomes.[188]

The Board of Health Commissioners and Los Angeles Health Officer Decker voiced strenuous opposition to the ordinance's repeal. The commissioners maintained that the ordinance addressed important sanitary concerns. In stating their opposition, however, they revealed other motivations as well. They refuted the allegation that health inspectors issued citations to Chinese launderers unfairly. Health inspectors, the commissioners argued, uniformly enforced the ordinance in both steam and hand laundries.[189] The board reasoned that hand laundries operated by whites did not receive as many citations as those operated by Chinese because "Caucasians rarely, if ever, [seek] to evade the provisions of the sanitary ordinance." Furthermore, "The experience of this Health Department with all Orientals or native American citizens of Oriental parentage, is that they do not have the same standards of living that we are accustomed to refer to as standards of the American family, neither do they yet have the American family's ideals of sanitary conditions. Because of these racial differences of understandings the Health Department is constantly confronted with grave violation of both statute laws and City Ordinance."[190] Clearly, race had been a consideration in designing the legislation in the first place. The board's motivations rested upon their ethnocentric notion that cultural norms of sanitation needed to be legislated. The board left little doubt of its position that regardless of citizenship status and generation, Chinese launderers would never Americanize.[191]

According to the Board of Health Commissioners, failure to enforce the laundry ordinance could be seen as "an assault upon the standards of living of the American family" because "[u]nless the American family lowers its standard of living to an Oriental basis they cannot compete economically with hand laundries operated by Orientals who work their employees 14 hours a day or more and constantly seek to evade the expense of required standards of housing and sanitation."[192] The claim implied that white-owned laundries financially supported their families. Conversely, the accusation suggested that the Chinese launderers did not have traditional nuclear families to support, which somehow made their businesses less worthy. This contention was a reference to the fact that, owing to the combined effects of the 1882 Chinese Exclusion Act and the 1924 Immigration Act, many Chinese launderers were not married or did not have their families living with them in the United States.[193] As a result, Chinese launderers tended not to live in traditional nuclear families. The commissioners chose to interpret this necessity as a free choice and then labeled the launderers as deviant. In shaping legislation around this misperception, the board extended the purview of public health beyond the public sphere and into the private. Chinese launderers thus were dealt a doubly discriminatory blow. U.S. exclusion laws prevented family reunification, and local municipal ordinances punished single male entrepreneurs for not having families to support.[194]

More interestingly, and perhaps more importantly, the commissioners also explicitly acknowledged that economic "fairness" was at stake in upholding the ordinance. They reasoned that Chinese launderers had an economic advantage over white launderers because the former worked longer hours and often lived in their places of business. So "not [enforcing] the law impartially where Orientals are concerned is not only a health menace but an economic menace to white men and women engaged in the laundry business." If the board failed to enforce this ordinance, they would "become the agency that [would] drive American citizens, both men and women, out of employment."[195]

Dr. Decker claimed that the repeal of the laundry ordinance would "leave the City without any legal machinery to control unsanitary practices of hand laundries." Addressing larger economic and racial issues, he maintained that "such repeal would be an encouragement to Chinese, Japanese, Filipinos, and other Orientals to enter into hand laundry business in competition with *our* native American labor. . . . To repeal section 311 is to give preference to Oriental labor and to discriminate against American citizens."[196] Decker failed to recognize, or even to acknowledge, that some Chinese launderers *were* American citizens. Like the Board of Health Commissioners, he believed that repealing the ordinance was akin to "breaking down American standards of labor."[197]

The editors of and contributors to the *Grizzly Bear* also supported the ordinances targeting Chinese launderers. In an article entitled "Cooperation Asked That Deserving Unemployed Whites May Have Work," the magazine included a letter from the Laundry Workers Union in San Francisco, stating that laundry plants had laid off many of the union's members. The letter writer suggested that if whites patronized "white plants" instead of "Oriental" laundries, more white citizens would likely be employed.[198] Like the Board of Health Commissioners and Dr. Decker, the author posited that Chinese launderers would always underbid white launderers because the former were content with a lower standard of living.

Various municipal government agencies worked in tandem to uphold the "Laundry and Living Quarters" ordinance. While the Board of Health Commissioners originally drafted the laundry sanitation codes, the city attorney rewrote them and continued to prosecute Chinese launderers.[199] The city council's Health and Sanitation Committee regularly referred these matters to the board. The board and Dr. Decker also worked jointly to prosecute Chinese launderers. In its appeals to the city council to uphold the ordinance, the board hoped it could "count upon the sympathetic understanding and cordial support of the Council in [their] efforts to uphold the law and to protect and safeguard the standards and ideals of the American family."[200] Indeed they could. The day after receiving the appeal from the Board of Health Commissioners, the city council asked the city attorney to draft an ordinance regulating laundries.[201] For their part, the city's health inspectors made certain that the intent of the ordinance was realized: in issuing citations for health violations, they concentrated mainly on the city's Chinese launderers.

Ultimately, in an October 1932 decision involving some thirty companion cases, the Los Angeles Municipal Courts declared the "Laundry and Living Quarters" ordinance unconstitutional.[202] The court's broad ruling did not bring immediate relief, however. Various fragmented interests in city management either were unaware of or willfully disregarded the ruling and continued to enforce the ordinance for at least another few months.[203]

CONCLUSION

Public health discourse produced widely accepted narratives that reified Mexicans and Asians as carriers of disease in 1930s Los Angeles. When such discourse was used to create and enforce ordinances that severely restricted Chinese launderers' livelihoods, it went beyond public health concerns. Medicalized constructions of Mexicans had existed since the

Mexican-American War in the mid–nineteenth century. The discourse of the 1930s, backed by the legitimacy of science, reinforced these preexisting stereotypes of Mexicans as disease carriers and breeders. This reinscription of medicalized racializations occurred as Mexicans were becoming a more permanent population in the United States and as second-generation Mexican American citizens in Los Angeles were coming of age. These constructions led to "public fictions" regarding each group that shaped the members' life chances.[204] Moreover, such public fictions were quickly absorbed into the American social consciousness and racial imagination. As we shall see in the next chapter, Mexican Americans also learned to appropriate public health discourse and put it to use in their fight for civil rights and access to public resources.

CHAPTER 5

The Fight for "Health, Morality, and Decent Living Standards"

Mexican Americans and the Struggle for Public Housing in 1930s Los Angeles

Since the mid-1910s, when the Los Angeles County Health Department began providing services to Mexicans, their health conditions improved little compared to those of whites. What did change was the stance Mexicans and Mexican Americans in Los Angeles began to take concerning their life conditions.[1] From the 1910s and continuing into the 1930s, Mexicans had tended to turn to the Mexican consulate with their problems and complaints, such as during the typhus epidemic and in response to forced sterilizations. But as the population began shifting toward the second generation as a result of deportation and repatriation, Mexican Americans with U.S. citizenship made increasing demands on U.S. institutions.[2] Dissatisfaction with the state of public health services, concern over the lack of decent housing, and a growing anger over issues such as institutionalized racism and discrimination contributed to the development of "oppositional political and cultural strategies" that rejected the tenets of Americanization and mobilized efforts toward improving Mexican communities.[3] Most importantly, Mexicans increasingly directed their appeals beyond local government. In the late 1930s, they enlisted the help of federal agencies and New Deal programs in their quest for better housing, which many saw as key to the overall improvement of public health conditions.

This chapter begins with an examination of the dismal health conditions and unequal access to resources Mexicans faced during the Depression and then discusses the controversial role of newly developed publicly funded housing programs. The remainder of the chapter explores the efforts of organized groups, especially the National Congress of Spanish Speaking Peoples (El Congreso), to articulate the links among housing, health, civic responsibility, and social membership. As Mexicans and Mexican Americans came to see decent housing and good health as basic civil rights that should be extended equally to all members of society, they grew more overtly political and activist.

THE DEPRESSION AND THE HEALTH OF L.A.'S MEXICAN COMMUNITIES

Examining health conditions among Mexicans in Los Angeles during the Depression and public health officials' response to these conditions makes clear the increasingly precarious position of these Mexican communities. It also provides insight into Mexican Americans' motivations for change. According to the historian George Sánchez, during the late 1930s Mexican Americans had to remake their communities; one-third of Mexicans living in Los Angeles had been repatriated by 1935 (see chapter 4 for a discussion of repatriation/deportation), leaving a population of about two hundred thousand Mexicans and Mexican Americans in the county.[4] In general, this remnant was more isolated and had lost ground in terms of both health and housing. Public health officials continued to rely on allegations of cultural inferiority and the principles of Social Darwinism to explain the state of public health within Mexican areas, thus effectively divorcing their findings from socioeconomic conditions.

Children's health, especially, worsened under the harsh circumstances created by the Depression. In East Los Angeles, the decline was dramatic. When the Los Angeles County Health Department hosted a regional meeting of the White House Conferences for Child Health and Protection[5] in 1933, concerns focused on the health of children living in East L.A. Health officials concluded that half of the children attending the county's elementary schools, many of whom were Mexican, were "starving." In part, the children simply were not getting enough food, but officials also contended that the children suffered because their parents "unnecessarily omit[ted] one or two of the three diet essentials."[6] As with typhoid and tuberculosis (see chapters 2 and 4), the root cause of the crisis was traced to ignorance rather than to economic conditions. The health department was well aware of the Mexican community's desperate poverty. In reporting the jump in pellagra cases between 1934 and

1935, the agency characterized this population as "generally very poor and unable to procure food."[7]

In contrast to the rest of Los Angeles, birth rates in the Mexican community decreased dramatically during the 1930s, falling from 20 percent in 1930 to 14 percent in 1936. A 1936 county health department report stated simply, "[T]he decline in Mexican births continues every year" and commented that, "[with] respect to race, it is significant that the number of white children born continues to rise while the number of Mexican births continues to decrease."[8] The report failed to specify any possible causes or remedies for the drop in births,[9] and although later reports continued to note a decrease, the department apparently did not interpret these changes as calling for remedial action. Following on the heels of the race suicide discourse (see chapter 4), it is not surprising that the large decrease in the Mexican birth rate seemed neither to alarm nor to seriously concern health officials.

Mexican tuberculosis rates also were particularly high during this period. After a sharp increase in tuberculosis cases in the early years of the Depression, national rates began to decrease in the late 1930s, although TB still ranked as a leading cause of death in the United States.[10] In Los Angeles County, Mexicans continued to be disproportionately afflicted with the disease.[11] In the late 1930s, Mexicans, who represented 10 percent of the county's population, composed approximately 22.5 percent of its reported tuberculosis cases.[12] Studies of various neighborhoods by the county health department's Division of Tuberculosis reported that Mexican neighborhoods were particularly hard hit by tuberculosis.[13]

Health officials continually stressed the exorbitant expense of treating tuberculosis. Each advanced tuberculosis case cost the county an average of $4,000 to treat; testing and early detection, in contrast, averaged about $600 per patient.[14] "It is clearly a matter of common sense," health officials argued, "that more money should be spent by the county to prevent tuberculosis for economic reasons, if for no other purpose."[15] Yet strategies to reduce tuberculosis routinely excluded the Mexican community. For example, when the county Board of Health Commissioners requested funding for tuberculosis prevention, it specified that this aid be for citizens, a provision that symbolically excluded Mexicans, regardless of their citizenship.[16] Given that the county's own reports identified Mexicans as a group with disproportionately high rates of tuberculosis, the inequity embedded in this and similar directives is especially significant.

One result of the county's stated preference for helping "citizens" was that Mexican, Asian, and African American children received only a fraction of the resources allocated for tuberculosis detection, as compared to white children.[17] During the 1931–32 and 1932–33 school years, the county health department tested students ages five to nineteen for tuberculosis as a way to detect tuberculosis cases in its early stages.[18] If a child tested positive, a public health worker informed the family and a department physician and nutritionist provided advice. The health department stressed the cost efficiency of early intervention, without which "the thousands of children infected with tuberculosis . . . subsequently [would need to] be cared for in Olive View Sanatorium."[19] White children composed 93 percent of the 6,805 children tested; Mexican, Asian, and African American children trailed, representing 6, 0.8, and 0.2 percent, respectively.[20] Since Mexicans were disproportionately affected by tuberculosis, the health department's testing of this group was clearly inadequate.[21] Extrapolating from the data reported in such studies, there is little room to wonder why Mexican and white children's health statistics diverged so sharply.

On the east side of the county, where most Mexicans lived, those seeking care for tuberculosis had few options available other than the county health department's underfunded and understaffed health centers and clinics. The county hospital offered tubercular care, but, as explained in chapter 4, Mexicans may have hesitated to obtain treatment there. The Department of Charities' Transportation Division used the hospital as a deportation site; in addition, the hospital's reputation suffered during the late 1930s, after a grand jury investigation found that "patients suffered delay and humiliation in obtaining admission."[22] In addition, although Olive View Sanatorium did admit Mexicans, this public tuberculosis facility was constantly overcrowded and had a waiting list throughout the 1930s. Even the patients that the county hospital transferred to the sanatorium were turned away because Olive View was consistently filled to capacity.

Efforts to control and prevent tuberculosis generated numerous studies, some of which focused on nutrition. The county health department's analysis of family nutrition during the Depression resulted in a list of explanations accounting for residents' inadequate diets. Racial customs emerged as a negative factor, which prompted the agency to develop nutrition classes and a program of home visits designed to teach tuberculosis patients American ways of cooking. Across the twelve county health department districts, the largest percentage of nutritional classes

(21 percent) and home visits (20 percent) took place in Belvedere's pre-dominantly Mexican communities.[23] Citing culture and customs as the source of an improper diet ascribed blame for high TB rates to the Mexican community itself.[24] Moreover, the nutrition and home visit program proved an ineffective means of combating the disease: There were no significant changes in the rate of TB cases.

Findings reported by the medical social worker Eva Neal offered a different perspective from the one popular with many of the area's public health officials. Neal's study focused on Mexicans afflicted with pulmonary tuberculosis, a disease that can be exacerbated by poor housing conditions. She described housing in the area as inadequate, poorly constructed, and not weatherproof.[25] In her follow-up commentary, Neal mentioned that the county's Bureau of Indigent Relief had both the resources and the authority to supplement the support offered to families afflicted with tuberculosis or any other major illness.[26] At a time when Mexicans still faced the possibility of deportation if they received charity, Neal's recommendations were radical. Although they failed to generate any significant debate or change, her suggestions did signal an increasing awareness of the relationship among poor housing, economic strife, and public health. As the next section makes clear, health officials showed an increasing awareness of these connections and, when confronted with what they considered a more deserving population, proved ready and willing to develop ameliorative health programs. White midwesterners fleeing drought-devastated farms for a new life in California faced circumstances similar to those confronting L.A.'s Mexican population. Unlike their Mexican counterparts, however, these displaced midwesterners evoked a generally sympathetic institutional response to their plight.

EXTENDING PUBLIC HEALTH BENEFITS
TO DUST BOWL MIGRANTS

Although public health officials discouraged Mexicans from seeking help through medical institutions during the Depression, they readily looked for ways to help other newcomers to Los Angeles, especially the white migrant laborers from Oklahoma, Texas, Arkansas, and Missouri who came to California in search of employment and to escape the Dust Bowl. Among those who migrated westward between 1935 and 1940, ninety-six thousand (38 percent) settled in Los Angeles. The often destitute newly arriving midwestern migrants made their homes in makeshift camps throughout the county.[27] It was the opinion of the chief public health officer, Dr. John Pomeroy, that these newcomers contributed to the sharp increase in tuberculosis and venereal disease in the county. He attributed one-third of the increase to this population and, on that basis, characterized the camps as health hazards.

Breaking from past policies relating to immigrants, Dr. Pomeroy attempted to meet the camp dwellers' needs by offering them medical help rather than educational hygiene programs designed to change their behavior. Unlike Mexican laborers, white migrant laborers were deemed deserving of "the benefits of modern medical science." Health officials hoped to bring smallpox vaccine to the people who lived in the camps, but it is unclear whether they acquired the funds to do so.[28] Funding problems also limited care for newcomers with tuberculosis. The Los Angeles County Health Department reported regretfully that, except in emergency cases, it lacked the money necessary to treat tuberculosis among white migrant families.[29] The agency argued that if only the federal government would provide the necessary funds, simple surgical procedures and the provision of nursing care in the home could help reduce tuberculosis.

Health officials appealed to the federal government to help them supplement their inadequate city and county budgets. Roosevelt's New Deal programs, which began in 1933, initiated substantial changes in the area of public aid.[30] The Works Progress Administration (WPA), the Public Works Administration (PWA), and the Federal Emergency Relief Act (FERA) provided nursing services, funding, and other public health services to state and city health departments. FERA also allocated $1 million to the U.S. Public Health Service to fund public health in rural areas. In 1935, under the Second New Deal, further funding in the areas of child health, maternal health, and general public health was provided through Title VI of the Social Security Act.[31] These monies were much needed in California, where budget cuts had further reduced the state and county's ability to provide medical care for transients. In 1935, Dr. Pomeroy requested and received permission from the Board of Supervisors to apply to the U.S. Public Health Service for a $100,000 grant to be used for public health nurses to help with the tuberculosis problem.[32] Once it received the award, the county health department intended to apply the federal money toward helping recently arrived midwestern migrant laborers.

State health officials also displayed a more sympathetic tone when discussing white migrants' (as opposed to Mexican migrants') tuberculosis rates. Edythe Tate-Thompson, chief of the Bureau of Tuberculosis for the state Board of Health, assessed migrant laborers' intentions in the late 1930s.[33] In a 1941 report to the L.A. Board of Supervisors, she posited that midwestern migrant laborers had moved to Los Angeles in order to pursue economic prospects. Once there, though, they fell victim to disease and often ended up as public charges. Tate-Thompson stressed that these migrants had not *planned* to burden society; on the contrary, they had no "desire . . . to secure care at public expense."[34] Such characterizations contrasted markedly with L.A. officials' charges that tubercular Mexicans immigrated in order to seek medical aid. Similarly, Los Angeles County Health Department officials seemed determined to distinguish Mexicans' health needs from those of midwestern newcomers. The department's reports failed to note that these two migrant laborer groups' needs overlapped. Nor did officials advocate equal levels of assistance for the two groups. Instead, they attempted to justify the disparity by implying that midwestern migrant laborers were a more salvageable population in terms of health. They viewed midwestern migrants' health conditions as more easily treated, and they viewed the laborers themselves as more unambiguously "American," in contrast to the "foreign" Mexican laborers.

Despite public health officials' willingness to direct resources toward midwestern migrants, many of these newcomers had not met the residency requirement of one year and thus were not legally eligible for aid from the Charities Department.[35] Moreover, some city officials took a much less welcoming stance toward midwestern migrants than did public health personnel. "[S]tay away from California," H. A. Carleton, director of the Federal Transient Service, warned migrants from the Midwest. California's shelters were full, and newcomers were not eligible for WPA jobs.[36] For those who did not heed Carleton's warning, Los Angeles Police Chief James E. Davis sent "136 of his 'coppers' to the State line 'trenches'" to bar indigents' entry into California.[37] Further reinforcing this reluctance to embrace new migrants, then-mayor Frank Shaw declared that Los Angeles would not be "the dumping ground of charity-seekers, fleeing from the more rigorous winters in practically every other State in the Union."[38]

The Los Angeles County Health Department believed that the federal government had an obligation to provide aid to the states because migrant families were "necessary to the prosperity of the State." According to the department, since California relied on migrant laborers from other states, the state was compelled to "work out a plan on a statewide basis to assure these non-residents some degree of health and social security commensurate with [an] American standard of living."[39] Thus health officials' new programs and rhetoric excluded the transnational Mexican labor pool on which California had been relying so heavily since the early 1900s. The fact that this long-established group of laborers had similar or, in some cases, more severe health-related concerns than the new immigrants from the Midwest was left unacknowledged. Denied access to institutional support, Mexicans took it upon themselves to fight for a healthier environment and way of life.

ERADICATING "THE STAIN OF THE SLUM": THE ACTIVIST
STATE AND ITS EFFECTS ON PUBLIC HEALTH AND HOUSING

In the latter half of the 1930s, Mexicans sought to attain a paramount symbol of social mobility—home ownership.[40] The desire for permanent housing signaled a major demographic shift. Mexican communities were no longer composed primarily of sojourners or seasonal migratory laborers who returned home to Mexico regularly and thus could tolerate renting single rooms in the Plaza area of Los Angeles or living in the field camps managed by railroad and agricultural employers. As permanent residents who were establishing new families and who were unlikely to return to Mexico, Mexicans in Los Angeles needed stable homes. Single male laborers were being replaced by family units, a trend that also increased both the need and the desire for permanent single-family dwellings.[41] A combination of factors, including segregation and dual labor market segmentation, precluded home ownership for most Mexicans, however. According to the 1930 census, just over 18 percent of Mexicans in Los Angeles owned their homes.[42] The remainder lived in house courts, shantytowns, and railroad and agricultural work camps.[43]

The link between poor housing conditions and poor health conditions had been known for many years. Tuberculosis was by now correctly understood to be caused by a type of bacteria, but public health officials also recognized that factors such·as overcrowding could increase the chances of contracting and spreading the disease. A study by the President's Conference on Home Building and Home Ownership in 1932 concluded that, "although no direct relationship between housing and tuberculosis has been shown, nevertheless the house is an important factor in this disease [and] may be of some importance both in [its] prevention and in its cure."[44] Thus positive health outcomes could be achieved, not just through medical outreach, but also through improvements in the built environment.

There was also an awareness of effects of physical living conditions on social behavior. During the 1910s and 1920s, the Los Angeles City Housing Commission conducted surveys that noted the condition of homes, how many people lived in each residence, and the density of the neighborhood.[45] The surveys also took into account social conditions. "The housing problem must be considered from three points of view—the sanitary, structural, and social," read one early report.[46] A later report, written by social worker Elizabeth Fuller, observed that "[c]rowded quarters, strangers living together in one house of two rooms, lack of sanitary arrangements—these produced moral degeneracy."[47] Such surveys mentioned various nationalities, including Italians, Spaniards, and Russians, but they focused mainly on Mexicans and suggested that it was cultural preferences that led Mexicans to live in inferior housing. "Accustomed to very little in Mexico, the Mexican accepts the very worst in the way of a home that Los Angeles has to offer him," Fuller explained.[48] Similarly, a report by the California State Commission of Immigration and Housing suggested that disease was to be expected among Mexicans.[49] These early conversations linking race and space in the area of housing served as the foundation for assessing slums in the 1930s.

An opportunity for improved housing conditions arose as a result of Roosevelt's New Deal programs. In 1937, Congress passed the U.S. Housing Act, which created new possibilities for the use of public money to build low-rent housing projects.[50] The act required that public housing built with federal money include accommodations for those in the lowest income groups.[51] Los Angeles was an early target for housing assistance; the federal government earmarked $25 million for public housing in the city. In return, Los Angeles needed to fund $25,000 to establish a housing authority and would eventually need to furnish matching funds of $2,500,000 (10 percent of the amount committed by the federal government).[52] The housing authority would survey the city to identify areas as "slums," raze those areas, and build in their place affordable public housing.[53]

The new public housing programs were controversial both nationally and locally. Many organizations, including the U.S. Chamber of Commerce, the National Association of Real Estate Boards, and the U.S. Building and Loan League, opposed the federal housing act on the grounds that "public housing was a dangerous socialistic experiment which threatened free enterprise and the traditional American principles of government."[54] The California Real Estate Association went far beyond this opposition, declaring itself "unalterably opposed to public housing on several grounds."[55] The association feared that public projects would discourage private investment in housing and would negatively affect property owners and taxpayers because the projects would be tax exempt. Locally, officials were divided. Frank Shaw, who served as mayor from 1933 to 1938, supported public housing measures; his proposal that the city council adopt a resolution to form a housing authority provoked conflict, but the council approved the measure in June 1938. The Municipal Housing Commission was composed of five members appointed by the mayor. Shaw was removed from office in September 1938 amid corruption allegations unrelated to housing. His elected replacement, Fletcher Bowron, a self-declared "New Deal Republican," also supported public housing.[56] Despite the new mayor's declared stance, opposition at other levels of city government impeded city council support of public housing. Many Los Angeles City Council members wanted some basic questions answered—such as "How much is it going to cost, and where is the money coming from?"—before they allocated any funds to public housing projects.[57]

This initial opposition to public housing stalled construction. According to the city's agreement with the Federal Housing Authority (FHA), housing funds could not be disbursed until the city council authorized a survey of possible low-cost housing sites. The council delayed performing this task, despite prodding from other quarters. Mayor Bowron reminded the city council that he could not move forward on the matter until council members reached consensus regarding an approved plan of action.[58] In addition, council members received irate letters from citizens, pushing them to take the necessary steps to establish L.A.'s eligibility for federal money. One constituent warned that if city council members lost the federal contract, they would "find themselves losing their jobs at the next election."[59]

Perhaps the first hurdle city officials needed to clear in order to launch a public housing program was their own disinclination to halt, even temporarily, polishing and bolstering the city's image. Depictions of Los Angeles as a near-paradise had to give way if the city was to succeed in tapping into federal housing funds. Bending to the task, the city health department produced a survey that calculated that a third of the population was "living in unsanitary and unsafe quarters."[60] Not to be outdone, Robert H. Parker, the Board of Supervisors' advisor on tax-delinquent lands, estimated that 20 percent of the houses in L.A. were "unfit for human habitation" and that an additional 30 percent were in serious need of repair and rehabilitation.[61] Nonresidents had no trouble spotting the city's underside. On a visit to Los Angeles in 1939, U.S. Housing Authority Director C. A. Shire declared that some neighborhoods "on the east side make the New York slums look like Buckingham palace."[62] Shire's comment echoed a declaration that the social reformer Jacob Riis had made decades earlier. During his stay in Los Angeles at the end of the nineteenth century, he remarked that he "had seen larger slums, but never any worse."[63]

Riis's observations probably did not convince many local residents. Most would likely have thought like the members of the Los Angeles City Housing Commission. In the 1910s, the commissioners regularly identified Mexican housing as dilapidated or uninhabitable, but in their view, such conditions were confined to Mexican communities and thus were of minimal importance. The commission emphasized the city's *lack* of slums and contrasted L.A.'s housing with the crowded tenements prevalent in East Coast cities.[64] In the late 1930s, when the city began documenting housing conditions in anticipation of public assistance programs, some commentators took a similarly protective position. They claimed that mentioning the city's poor housing conditions put Los Angeles in an "undeservedly bad light."[65] The *Los Angeles Times*, irritated by the city health department's survey calculations, declared that "overzealous seekers of Federal slum clearance funds" tended to "recklessly" exaggerate local housing conditions.[66]

Public health professionals, regardless of the actual level of their zeal, provided Los Angeles officials with essential information.[67] Los Angeles ranked as the nation's fifth-largest city, but municipal leaders had very little knowledge of the conditions that characterized low-income housing.[68] At officials' request, health department staff helped define which areas of the city should be deemed "slums."[69] In surveying prospective public housing sites, health officials used standards developed several years earlier to define a residence as a slum. These included "poor lighting, no ventilation, dampness, insufficient drainage and bad plumbing, fire hazards, vermin, disease dangers, poor water supply, and toilet accommodations, overcrowded conditions and cellar tenements."[70]

In their reports, health officials often commented not only on the residences but also on the people who lived in them. In 1937, the county health department completed a health survey that demonstrated a direct relationship between overcrowded housing and high tuberculosis rates. The report asserted that poor housing posed a threat to the inhabitants and to the entire district, in addition to "[placing] a great hardship on the Health Department in carrying out its preventive work under most trying conditions."[71] A separate housing survey of Belvedere conducted a few years earlier contained photographs of area residents—mainly poor whites and Mexicans.[72] The picture captions listed diseases affecting the residents; tuberculosis was the most frequently noted ailment. Studies such as these increased housing inspectors' conviction that overcrowded conditions could lead to the spread of tuberculosis.[73]

Both the city and county health departments shared their reports on tuberculosis with the city and county's housing authorities in order to help identify geographic areas that would benefit most from low-income housing. Health officials called attention to areas such as Belvedere and Maravilla as locations with "a most serious need [for] proper slum clearance through a government project."[74] Dr. Pomeroy stated unequivocally that "poor housing and overcrowded conditions among Mexican residents of Los Angeles result in a high rate of tuberculosis."[75] In an abrupt break with both past and more recent county health department reports citing Mexicans' inferior genetic makeup as responsible for their high rates of TB, Pomeroy proclaimed that "[t]he incidence of tuberculosis among Mexicans is in no way a reflection upon the character and make-up of the Mexican as a citizen." Pomeroy's input was instrumental in the county housing authority's decision to select Maravilla as a site for a large public housing project.[76]

The connection between poor housing and disease was not the only link discussed in the conversation regarding public housing. The association between poor housing and immorality drawn by Elizabeth Fuller and others twenty years earlier was again frequently noted as well. Newspaper stories framed public housing as a "defense measure" because it would reduce juvenile delinquency.[77] In a panel discussion on public housing, Los Angeles officials argued that better housing could decrease the incidence of social as well as physical ills. The speaker asked the audience to balance "the relations of disease and delinquency to bad housing and the comparative costs for eliminating these conditions once they [were] in existence [versus preventing] them by better housing."[78] If social ills were inextricably linked to poor housing, then it followed, according to some proponents, that public housing would eliminate the city's social problems.[79]

The conflation of morality and space was also evident in the stereotypes associated with rundown and overcrowded neighborhoods. At the
request of the city council, M. S. Siegel, director of the Bureau of Housing and Sanitation, surveyed eighteen homes in an area just east of
downtown Los Angeles. Siegel aimed to give the council a better sense
of the housing conditions in the city. The survey was designed to rate all
factors that defined a home as a "slum dwelling"—poor construction,
inferior building maintenance, inadequate plumbing, and overcrowded
conditions. Many of the residences examined were house courts where
Mexican laborers lived. Siegel, after concluding that the residences were
slums, offered his personal evaluation of the occupants' moral character. In the qualitative section of his report, he noted that he took into
consideration "vice, crime, immorality, truancy, drunkenness, and other
consequences that inevitably complete the picture of bad housing," even
though no questions on the survey rated such conditions.[80] Nor were
there any notes or discussions that revealed what, if any, criminal acts
Siegel had witnessed while performing his investigations. Still, he judged
vice and treacherous morals as so closely related to poor housing that
he never questioned his assumptions. He simply passed them along as
empirical truths when he made his policy recommendations.

With public health surveys and recommendations in hand, the housing authority focused on identifying areas for slum clearance. Residents
in the targeted areas petitioned both for and against the proposed raz-
ings. In particular, Mexicans fought the city health department's selection of Maravilla, the Mexican section of Belvedere. When the city
scheduled a public meeting to discuss the proposed slum clearance project, those opposed paraded along Whittier Boulevard before the meeting. Five hundred residents, mainly Mexicans, showed up at the meeting. Further, of the 177 landowners in the area, 140 refused to accept
government offers to buy their land. "We won't let them make refugees
out of us. We love our homes and will fight for them," they vowed.[81] In
contrast, in a neighborhood immediately east of Boyle Heights, residents petitioned the city council to take the necessary steps to procure
federal housing money. One cross-cultural neighborhood coalition of
twenty-five residents, a group which included whites, Jews, African
Americans, Mexicans, and others, formally petitioned the city council to
initiate legislation that would facilitate tapping into federal funds.[82] The
Bureau of Housing and Sanitation described the residents in this geographic area as "souls who dwell under conditions which are detrimental to human health and welfare."[83] The various ethnic backgrounds of

the petitioners are a valuable reminder of the diversity of those who lived in slum housing.

A LOUDER VOICE FOR CHANGE: THE ROLE OF UNIONS IN HOUSING AND HEALTH IMPROVEMENTS

Several groups and organizations petitioned the city council to hasten the initiation of public housing projects. Most advanced the time-tested argument that slum housing does not foster a healthy lifestyle and can lead to the inception and perpetuation of immorality among residents and in larger communities. Among the petitioners on behalf of the slum clearance program was the International Workers Order (IWO), an ethnically organized fraternal order with several chapters and strong ties to the Communist Party. The organization, composed of workers, felt that issues of class, access to adequate medical care, and decent housing were interrelated.[84] The IWO argued that rents in Los Angeles were excessively high and placed an unfair burden on the working class, whose members often spent one-third to one-half (or more) of their income on rent. Rent payments came at the expense of "health, morality, and decent living standards," as workers were "forced to deny themselves and [their] families proper nourishment in order to pay these excessively high rentals." Furthermore, the city and county health departments had declared many of these rentals "unfit for human habitation."[85] Other unions joined in championing the construction of public housing in Los Angeles. The United Fishermen's Union of the Pacific, the Los Angeles Industrial Union Council, and the International Council of United Electrical and Machine Workers and Utility Work Organizing Committee advocated low-cost housing because their members would reap the benefits offered by the projects. Union members also appealed to the city council on the grounds that the new projects would create jobs and reduce unemployment in the city.[86]

The involvement of these unions in the push for public housing brought racial as well as economic politics to the foreground. Certain unions, such as the IWO, represented a broad-based coalition of whites, Jews, African Americans, and Mexicans.[87] Bert Corona, for example, a prominent Mexican American labor and community activist, began his career as a member of the International Longshore Workers Union (ILWU), an organization known for its leftist politics and opposition to racial discrimination.[88] With the increased participation of ethnic whites and people of color during the late 1930s, unions provided recent and established immigrants with a vehicle to voice their concerns about their civil rights.[89] This was an important role, for example, of the National Congress of Spanish Speaking Peoples, also known as El Congreso de Pueblos que Hablan Español (El Congreso). As a civil rights organization, El Congreso dealt with issues its members felt were important to those living in the United States, regardless of citizenship status or generation.[90] The group claimed that compared to native whites, Mexicans, whether citizens or immigrants, often disproportionately suffered the ills associated with poor health and housing.[91] Instead of grounding their call for change in a concept of citizenship that rested on national origin, El Congreso referenced shared social membership, which included both Mexican immigrants and Mexican Americans.

While historians remember El Congreso for its commitment to workers' rights and to the organization of Latinas/os as a political force, it is also important to recognize El Congreso's contributions toward improving health and housing. The organization formally called attention to the poor state of health among Mexicans in the United States and urged the government to take a leadership role in remedying the problem. The issue was of such importance that El Congreso, although still in the process of forming itself as an organization, submitted a petition to the Los Angeles City Council.[92] Invoking the power of their membership base of fifty thousand, El Congreso urged the city council to use the federal government monies earmarked for public housing to maintain quality living standards within Mexican communities.[93] The organization's concentration on everyday issues such as health and housing, and its contributions toward improving these areas, broadened the rights to which Mexicans in this country felt they were entitled. El Congreso's petition demanded the "promotion and extension of government subsidized health projects, and slum clearance projects, to protect the health of the people."[94] In addition, signaling a growing sense of entitlement, El Congreso argued that Mexicans deserved federal aid as residents of the United States, regardless of their citizenship status. The organization asked city council members to build decent and affordable housing in the city. They also specifically appealed on behalf of younger Mexican Americans, "the future citizens of [the] city."[95]

El Congreso premised their petition to the city council on the relationship of proper housing to health and the body politic. Bringing their concerns to the forefront in appeals for better housing, El Congreso described the same dismal conditions in Mexican enclaves that health inspectors had reported for decades, but the group challenged inspectors' claims that Mexicans were to blame for their poor living conditions. Instead, El Congreso turned the tables, blaming the city for perpetuating these conditions. The petition reviewed the facts, noting that "many thousands of people inhabit crowded quarters, lacking the most elementary sanitary facilities—conditions which invited the spread of infectious diseases. . . . Streets are unpaved, unlit, and without sidewalks or drainage in many sections, particularly in Watts, Central Avenue district, and Belvedere Gardens." Putting the city council's own statistics to better service, El Congreso charged that tuberculosis affected areas where Mexicans lived at a rate of eight to twelve times higher than in other areas of the city. In another twist, El Congreso suggested housing projects as a way to remedy the high infant mortality rates in the Mexican community, a subject of long-standing complaint among city health officials. The petition pointed out that the money spent on affordable, decent housing would help lower infant mortality. In sum, El Congreso made effective use of the city's own discriminatory rhetoric, reshaping it into a solid basis for actions that would help remedy decades-old problems within the Mexican community in Los Angeles.[96]

Similarly, El Congreso's appeal echoed many of the same sociological arguments public health workers, sociologists, and social workers had raised previously in their reports about the Mexican community in Los Angeles. But again, El Congreso turned the tables on the city. For example, the petition connected the need for better housing to social issues, such as crime and juvenile delinquency, to reduce rather than increase the gap between citizens and immigrants. El Congreso argued that it was in the city's best interest to provide decent, affordable housing, as this would foster "the development of healthy, competent, civic minded citizens from the young people of these sections."[97] Whereas city and health officials had defined Mexicans as blemishes on the image of Los Angeles, El Congreso now held the city accountable for allowing slum conditions, hazards that were a "real menace to the welfare of the community as a whole, and a discredit to the city of Los Angeles."[98] After going through various city council committees, the petition finally reached the Finance Committee. There, committee members advised that El Congreso's appeal be filed away, a recommendation that ensured that the complaint would receive no further consideration.[99]

Despite these setbacks, El Congreso continued to include public health as an important issue.[100] Its April 1939 meeting (held in Los Angeles) brought together a broad-based coalition of 1,000 to 1,500 delegates from all over the nation, including prominent activists such as

Luisa Moreno, Josefina Fierro de Bright, Bert Corona, and Eduardo Quevedo.[101] Among its list of concerns, the assembly included the advancement of cultural unity, protection from deportation, elimination of discrimination, protection for workers to organize, and promotion of health issues. With regard to public health, members addressed conditions in Mexican neighborhoods, describing them as generally unhealthy, unhygienic, and conducive to the spread of disease. They called for paved streets and lines to deliver electricity to homes and businesses.[102] El Congreso contended that the problems in Mexican neighborhoods were not the unavoidable result of inevitable cultural differences and that resolving these issues was a municipal responsibility. They suggested that city government officials should seek funding for improvements in these neighborhoods through federal monies made available by New Deal administration programs such as the WPA and the PWA. In addition, El Congreso campaigned to secure both the passage of a national health bill, proposed by President Roosevelt's Inter-Departmental Committee, and a state health insurance bill, introduced by the California State Legislature. The organization also demanded that the municipal government provide public health services for all with medical needs and that public health facilities be developed in rural and urban areas and be open to all patients, regardless of their "race, religion, color, or political affiliation."[103]

Moreover, El Congreso blazed new trails in securing a foothold in the social membership of the United States by expressing its concern over the potential impact of racial discrimination in the development and implementation of local programs for public health and public housing. All of the organization's demands for improved public health care were followed by a clause that called for the needs of the Mexican American community to be met without "discrimination of any kind." They also asked that government clinics and hospitals hire more Mexican doctors. Moreover, in the interest of fair housing, El Congreso demanded the construction of public housing projects wherever there was the greatest need, regardless of the racial composition of the area.[104] This demand may reflect members' awareness of reports, such as the report by the Home Owners Loan Corporation, that labeled the racial diversity of Mexican communities, such as Boyle Heights in East Los Angeles, as a negative selling point because they were perceived as "hopelessly heterogeneous."[105]

Six months after their first convention El Congreso held a second one, during which they continued to push for better housing and public health conditions. They repeated their concerns over the "deplorable unsanitary conditions [that existed] in the Mexican districts, caused by the run-down and overcrowded state of a great number of the houses, the lack of adequate [sanitation] facilities, and the high percentage of persons afflicted with all kinds of diseases." The organization expanded its demands to add that Mexican workers be employed for the construction of the new publicly funded houses. In addition, they asked that the federal government utilize funds for housing and sanitation projects instead of allocating the monies to prepare for possible involvement in World War II.[106] El Congreso's efforts called widespread attention to public housing issues. Not all of the this attention was positive, however.

BACKLASH: CASTING SLUM CLEARANCE PROPONENTS AS SUBVERSIVES

Within days of El Congreso's presentation of their concerns, City Councilman Vernon Bennett (D), one of the original supporters of public housing, asked the council to endorse Senate Bill 470, introduced by Senator Ralph Swing (R) of Inyo and San Bernardino Counties. The bill sought State Relief Administration funds for the "purpose of returning indigent or dependent aliens to the country of which they [were] citizens."[107] Deportation programs created during the first years of the Depression had peaked by 1935; the proposed bill was an effort to revive such programs. This revival seemed to be, at least in part, a response to Mexicans' growing demands for social membership.[108]

Councilman Bennett reasoned that Mexicans should be repatriated because "many substandard slum habitations in the city [were] occupied by Mexican families who because of poverty would suffer extreme hardships if their dwellings were demolished by the city under agreement with the Municipal Housing Authority."[109] Bennett's motion failed to address advocacy groups' arguments that public housing projects would adequately replace the demolished homes. Instead, Councilman Bennett tried to mitigate the harshness of the proposed legislation by reminding the city council of previous meetings with Mexican government officials who had promised they would financially assist repatriated Mexican families once they settled in Mexico.

Siegfried Goetze, a private citizen and building planner, volunteered to help realize Bennett's plan. He joined members of the Los Angeles City Housing Commission on a trip to Mexico for the International Housing and Town Planning Conference.[110] The Board of Supervisors presented Goetze with a letter of support for his initial meeting with the chief planning architect of Mexico, a personal friend of Goetze. The letter expressed the supervisors' opinion that L.A.'s Mexican families "would be better off and happier in their native lands."[111] Reporting to the city council on these meetings, Goetze suggested more concrete steps for repatriating Mexicans. He outlined his "Plan of Belvedere." This was a "seven point program for the re-housing and rehabilitation of Mexican families in Belvedere township ... and the resettlement of Mexican relief clients." Under the proposal, repatriated Mexicans would work in Mexican government–sponsored agrarian colonization programs. Goetze characterized the repatriated Mexicans' potential participation in these programs as a "great incentive" to return to Mexico. He surmised that relief clients would not be able to afford the public housing rents and so would have to return to Mexico anyway. Goetze's plan would thus have two main results: "clearance of the slums and a permanent reduction of relief loads by resettlement."[112] The Board of Supervisors weighed the merits of the Plan of Belvedere, but Superintendent of Charities Rex Thompson rejected it. Thompson argued that the plan hinged on deported Mexicans' working in Mexico's agrarian colonization program. This was not feasible, however, because Los Angeles had only "below par" Mexicans on their rolls, those who, because of age, or mental or physical barriers resulting from accidents or disease, could not perform such duties.[113]

Councilman Steven Cunningham's proposal went even further than Bennett's had. He urged that the council support both Senate Bill 470 and an amendment to the bill. Cunningham proposed using the monies to "repatriate persons who, *whether aliens or not,* [were] active in subversive activities or [belonged] to groups or organizations which [subscribed] to plans to change [our] form of government."[114] The legislative committee eventually shelved the amendment motion, but it took them six months to do so.[115] The council's stance against Mexicans drew support from many citizen groups. Some pushed for additional restrictions on Mexicans' participation in American society, particularly in the workplace. The San Diego–based National Club of America for Americans, for instance, petitioned the Los Angeles City Council to pass an ordinance barring non-naturalized aliens from working in the Los Angeles area "unless no American citizen [was] available for the job." Further, this organization petitioned the council to prohibit any labor organization from electing or appointing any non-naturalized alien to represent them in any labor dispute in L.A., revealing anxieties over the increased participation of immigrants in labor unions.[116]

While other works have examined Mexican Americans' increasing demands for civil rights, few theories have been developed to explain why city officials again began to see Mexicans as threatening enough to warrant deportation.[117] Some Chicana/o history scholars have argued that city and state officials viewed Mexicans' participation in labor unions and civil rights organizations as potentially undermining the status quo.[118] City officials also may have been concerned about the rising political strength within the Mexican community. Earlier deportation programs had led to a community with many fewer immigrants and many more second- and third-generation families with American citizenship. Many of these Mexican Americans (along with Mexicans who were long-term residents but not necessarily citizens) assumed roles as activists and became involved in various organizations, from youth groups to unions. As citizens they had the right to vote, and, considering their increased involvement in unions and civil rights organizations, they were potentially a powerful new force in city politics.

Another impetus for the renewed interest in deportation legislation may have been officials' belief that Mexican union members were involved in communist organizations. Historian David Gutiérrez points out that the question of communist, socialist, and anarcho-syndicalist influences among Mexican workers in the United States remains a contentious subject. Consequently, historians continue to examine and evaluate evidence that Mexican American strike activities were affected by labor organizers associated with communist organizations.[119] City council members may have had similar concerns regarding El Congreso's ties to communism. Historians have debated the extent of the communist influence within the organization; it seems clear, though, that El Congreso did not actively exclude communists from their ranks.[120] Potential affiliation with communist groups added to an already politically charged subject.

But it was deplorable housing conditions and poor health that helped mobilize labor unions and civil rights groups.[121] El Congreso explicitly incorporated the right to decent housing and health care into its demands for Mexican civil rights. Unions representing Mexicans were similarly clear in this regard. The IWO flexed its political muscle by warning the city council that union members would work "actively for the defeat of any and all reactionary candidates who opposed a comprehensive slum clearance program in defiance of the people's wishes."[122] Ironically, it was the city's own failure to respond to the needs of its residents that fueled the calls for change officials now found so worrisome. Despite decades of appropriating public health discourses, first to support Americanization programs and then to justify deportation agendas, the city had never addressed a root cause of poor health in Mexican communities: deplorable housing conditions. Had government officials attended to this fundamental problem instead of busying themselves ascribing blame, there would have been significantly less impetus for Mexican organizations to challenge the city government on this issue.

In the early 1940s, attention shifted from public housing to home-front housing needs created by the United States' impending entry into World War II. Los Angeles geared up for industry during this period and converted housing projects built as part of slum clearance programs to wartime public housing for war production workers.[123] But the absence of controversy over public housing would be temporary. Mexicans faced another round of confrontations in the 1950s: two projects, a public housing site planned for Chavez Ravine and the construction of the East Los Angeles Freeway interchange, displaced hundreds of Mexican residents.[124]

CONCLUSION

The struggles over public health and housing reveal the multilayered ways in which Mexicans and Mexican Americans fought for their civil rights during the late 1930s. Mexicans had become a resident population, intent on making their homes in the United States. They fought for basic rights that affected their daily lives. Along with civil rights and workers' rights, they focused on health and housing, two critical components of everyday life. They asserted their citizenship rights by asking local and federal officials to fulfill the government's responsibilities toward constituents. They demonstrated that tangible quality-of-life issues were inseparable from more abstract notions of democracy and citizenship. These demands provided evidence that Mexicans were long-term residents of the Los Angeles community. So began Mexican families' struggle to find a permanent place within American society.

Epilogue

*Genealogies of Racial Discourses
and Practices*

The history of public health in Los Angeles demonstrates how race demarcates the boundaries of social membership. By systematically associating dirt, disease, and disorder with immigrant status, late-nineteenth- and early-twentieth-century city and county public health officials redefined citizenship in racialized and medicalized terms. The boundary-setting role of public health discourse is significant for more than historical reasons. Health officials left lasting ideological footprints in the institutions they worked in through their writings, the policies they developed, and the people they trained. Health departments, boards of health, and municipal, state, and federal governments were deeply implicated in generating practices that embedded racial logic in their institutional culture. Their influence on L.A.'s regional racial lexicon was far-reaching, informing national political and legislative agendas. Such policies became the standard operating procedure for decades to come.

Scientific discourses and public health practices played key roles in adding new ideas and theories to an existing arsenal of racial knowledge. They also helped set the stage for new ways of gauging and understanding race. The racial logic evidenced in government policy and embedded in cultural representations in the early decades of the twentieth century has persisted, but it has assumed new forms. Other institutions have borrowed, built on, and recalibrated racial discourses and practices first used in public health departments. This continuity is especially clear with regard to the racialization of space.

Housing policies set in place in Los Angeles in the late 1930s—and left essentially unmodified until the 1970s—echoed the racial logic of the early public health policies that characterized certain areas of the city, such as diverse neighborhoods in East Los Angeles, as substandard. Contemporary analyses of the role of race in urban renewal focus attention on the federal government's sponsorship of home loans during the late 1930s.[1] Federally backed private loans offered low to no downpayments. To determine which areas were appropriate for investment, the government relied on appraisals, in the form of City Surveys, carried out by the Home Owners Loan Corporation (HOLC). In general, the HOLC surveys resulted in the awarding of federal mortgage assistance loans to whites seeking to buy homes in areas deemed worthy of investment, particularly the suburbs. By contrast, racialized groups who lived in urban areas were routinely denied the federal loans. Rather than promoting individual investment in private homes in urban areas, the federal government built public housing, which was then offered to racialized groups. Tom Sugrue's study of postwar Detroit, for example, demonstrates how urban areas became increasingly populated by African Americans who rented or lived in public housing as whites relocated from these urban areas into suburban homes, thus creating a spatial binary.

An area's racial makeup was (and continues to be) a primary factor in assessing its value. HOLC standards, evident in the City Survey questions, reflect a racial logic much the same as that which informed health and housing reports from previous decades. In a section at the very beginning of the survey, survey takers entered the percentage of foreign families, including their nationalities, and the percentage of "negro" families in each area. The next section of the survey covered the "shifting and infiltration" factor of the neighborhood, meaning the degree to which the neighborhood was "infiltrated" by "foreigners" or "negroes."[2] The survey wording and the data requested are eerily reminiscent of John Pomeroy's lament, twenty-four years prior, regarding the "influx of ignorant aliens into our county."[3] The surveys also demonstrate how Mexicans, after generations in the United States, continued to be suspended in the process of becoming American. A City Survey of San Gabriel Valley described that area's Mexican American population as "hybrid Mexicans," who, "while American-born, [were] still peon Mexicans."[4]

Thus, just like public health officials, who for decades had used an area's racial diversity as a shorthand index of the residents' health practices and moral standards, HOLC bureaucrats used an area's racial diversity as a ready gauge of its desirability. Survey takers jotted down the percentage of Mexicans versus whites as unreflectively as they noted the percentage of homeowners versus renters in an area. The impact of the City Surveys, however, was more immediate than that of the housing reports prepared by the health department. The message underlying the City Survey data was that nonwhites were not only illegitimate residents but also liabilities to their white American neighbors. The urban land-scape and patterns of home ownership were redrawn accordingly.

HOLC surveyors, like public health officials before them, routinely conflated the condition of a house with the worthiness of its occupant. One evaluation used the presence of makeshift houses as evidence that their inhabitants, Mexican laborers, had no "pride of occupancy," even as the surveyor referenced the occupants' socioeconomic positions as agriculture and railroad workers. Another, first noting that an area's population was "extremely heterogeneous," a reference to the Mexican, Japanese, and black residents, went on to describe the area as a land-scape of "shacks." By the late 1930s and early 1940s, decades of health and housing reports had so thoroughly cemented the connection between dilapidated structures and the city's racialized populations, that simply using the word *shack* would be sufficient to make clear the racial makeup of an area. These examples demonstrate how cultural reason-ing that influenced local policy (such as determining which neighbor-hoods to quarantine during the 1924 plague), when adopted and insti-tutionalized by federal agencies, both recast and extended the longevity of such racial logic. Racial and class segregation would continue, only now the key vehicle would be housing policy.

The ways in which the housing surveys began to standardize and quantify racial knowledge lent the appearance of scientific objectivity. Policy decisions seemed color-blind because geographical areas were targeted, not people. The two-pronged process of funneling federally backed mortgages into the suburbs while denying the same loans to racialized groups in urban areas went largely unnoticed. Indeed, histo-rian George Lipsitz reminds us that many still fail to recognize the ways in which such programs institutionalized inequality and "widened the gap between the resources available to whites and those available to aggrieved racial communities," an illustration of a broader process that he terms "the possessive investment in whiteness."[5] The historian Robin D. G. Kelley has examined the legacies of these programs and argues that "cultural and ideological constructions of ghetto life have irrevo-cably shaped public policy, scholarship, and social movements."[6]

A second major factor in the ongoing racialization of space in Los Angeles was the growth of freeway systems. The movement to build major highways to facilitate the commute into and out of urban centers developed in tandem with postwar urbanization. The creation of the East Los Angeles interchange in the Boyle Heights area divided neighborhoods, displaced ten thousand people, and destroyed twenty-nine thousand homes.[7] Community members protested—they wrote letters to their councilman (Edward Roybal), attended California State Highway Commission meetings, formed committees, and demonstrated in the streets. The project went forward. While I was going through Roybal's archived papers, I came across a petition the neighbors had circulated to protest the freeway system. I decided to look for the people who had signed, hoping to interview them. I walked down streets, reading the house numbers as I went. Just as I would near the address I was looking for, the street would end, bumping up against the freeway. The homes of all the petitioners had been razed to build the freeway.

The Urban Land Institute, the research arm of the National Association of Real Estate Boards, became a leading voice in decisions regarding suburban expansion and urban renewal in the nation. Representing real estate developers' interests, the institute recommended that freeways be built through areas the HOLC had already declared as slums during their housing assessments.[8] Relying on the City Surveys for guidance in siting the growing freeway system seemed perfectly reasonable. Why spend time and money to find appropriate sites (i.e., neighborhoods where land values were low) when that work had already been done? The fact that the surveys incorporated racial biases, and that such a possibility apparently was never even considered, demonstrates precisely how invidious institutionalized racism can be.

A final aspect of the racialization of space in and around Los Angeles involved the area's Japanese residents. Two months after the bombing of Pearl Harbor in 1941, President Roosevelt signed Executive Order 9066, which declared all Japanese enemy aliens. The U.S. government forcibly relocated Japanese and Japanese Americans, regardless of citizenship, to internment camps in the U.S. interior.[9] Eastside Los Angeles communities like Boyle Heights were torn apart as many of their residents were interned. The Boyle Heights high school lost one-third of its student body to the Japanese internment.[10] The message that Japanese continued to be seen as foreign and outside social membership was unmistakable.

All of these processes—health inspections, urban renewal, freeway construction, and the internment of Japanese who lived in these areas—

were ideologically linked. All served to exclude the racialized communities in these areas from social membership. These processes were also institutionally linked. Once one institution, such as the public health department, had declared an area substandard, it was that much easier for another institution, such as the HOLC, to produce the same evaluation in the future. These strata of racialized practices became normalized, transforming hegemony into common knowledge.

INSTITUTIONALIZED RACISM TODAY

The notion that certain immigrant groups are outsiders remains with us, and vividly so in California. During the 1990s, voters passed three propositions that marked racialized groups as outside the bounds of social membership. The first in the series, Proposition 187, sought to deny public services to undocumented immigrants. It passed by an overwhelming majority in 1994. The court, however, immediately barred implementation of the law, pending settlement of the legal challenges lodged against it. Ostensibly, Proposition 187 was directed at all undocumented immigrants, but within California's political and cultural climate it was understood that the proposition's primary target was Mexicans.[11] The two public services most discussed were education and nonemergency medical care, specifically infant and maternal care.[12] Thus Mexican women and children would have been disproportionately affected by the proposition.[13] Proposition 187 demonstrates how gender plays a key role in shaping the contours of anti-immigrant discourse.

The authors and supporters of the proposition failed to recognize that denying health care to any group would necessarily undermine the health of the broader community. The nativism and racism directed at immigrants, especially Latinas/os and Latin Americans, during and after the Proposition 187 campaign resulted in immigrants' reluctance and even refusal to use public health services and government insurance, such as the Children's Health Insurance Program; even documented residents and citizens feared deportation.[14] In East Los Angeles, for example, the Edward R. Roybal Comprehensive Health Center reported a noticeable drop in prenatal appointments in the wake of the passage of Proposition 187.[15]

Even if, as is likely, Proposition 187 does not survive its many legal challenges, its initial passage is still significant in that it starkly demonstrates how solidified the boundaries of social membership have become and how important race remains in setting those boundaries. Proposition 187 mandated that public service employees report anyone *suspected* of being an illegal immigrant. This meant that regardless of citizenship status, merely having dark skin or an accent or living in a certain part of town could mark one as suspect. In the early 1900s, sources ranging from public health reports to mainstream media informed Angelenos, and the rest of the country, of the meaning of *Mexican*. One hundred years later, the cultural signifiers that marked Mexicans as outsiders have become so fully ingrained in the popular imagination that Proposition 187 did not even need to specify the grounds for viewing people as likely "illegals."

The racial logic that propelled the passage of Proposition 187 parallels the implementation of maternity and infant programs of the early twentieth century. In both cases, Mexican women and children were seen as the source of serious problems. In the early twentieth century, public health officials offered well-baby clinics in the hope that cultural retraining would mitigate the dirt and disease associated with these groups, while circumventing debates over much-needed male Mexican laborers. In the 1990s, Proposition 187 identified immigrants and their alleged overuse of public services as a cause of the state's economic crisis, ignoring the impact of defense industry cutbacks and military base closures on California's economy. In both cases, scapegoating Mexican women and children made it possible to sidestep discussions of larger causes.

Following on the heels of Proposition 187, in 1996 California voters passed Proposition 209, which was aimed at eliminating government-sponsored affirmative action programs in public-sector jobs and in higher education. Proposition 209 rested on the logic that in a post–civil rights society there is no legal basis for racial inequality. Thus any racial disparities that still seem to exist are the fault of individuals rather than evidence of any sort of structural inequality.

Completing the triumvirate of California nativist legislation in the mid-1990s was Proposition 227. This was primarily an anti–bilingual education measure that championed a legal definition of English as the official state language. Yet linguistic theories, such as the merits of additive versus subtractive bilingualism, were rarely part of the debates over the proposition. Instead, many focused on the need to reassert the primacy of English as the nation's language lest we face the "disuniting of America."[16] The very first article in Proposition 227 called for teaching English to schoolchildren because the "English language is the national public language of the United States of America and of the state of California, is spoken by the vast majority of California residents, and is also the leading world language for science, technology, and international business, thereby being the language of economic opportunity." In addition, by mandating English as California's official language, Proposition 227 would have implicitly criminalized the use of other languages.

In all three cases, the primary goal of the proposition was to demarcate who had access to social membership and who did not. Propositions 187 and 209 were framed as economic issues, protecting dwindling state resources for utilization by deserving citizens. This message resonated loudly in a state in the midst of its deepest recession since the 1930s. The image that certain groups were outside social membership was so widely accepted that when Proposition 227 was introduced there was no pretense of it being about economic issues. Indeed, supporters' rhetoric as well as the language of the proposition itself blatantly asserted that the proposition was aimed at defining and protecting what was "American."

GENDERING RACIALIZATION DISCOURSES

In the early decades of the twentieth century, public health programs frequently targeted Mexican and Japanese women because their combined attributes of color and fecundity constituted a dual threat. Such concerns continue to manifest themselves in different forms through the present day. Women of color often are cast as sexually and intellectually aberrant and therefore in need of being taught normative behavior or controlled.

In U.S. culture, with its enduring emphasis on the black-white paradigm, social representations of women as deviant are most often associated with black women. These women are connected to their historical Mexican and Japanese counterparts through ideological forces that construct all women of color as sexually and morally aberrant. Nonetheless, they have their own historical specificity. Dorothy Roberts argues that cultural constructions of black women as unfit mothers can be grouped into three categories: the careless mother, the matriarchal black unwed mother, and the welfare queen.[17] The image of the careless black mother emerged during slavery when black women who were assigned as mammies to white children were expected to put their white charges' needs over those of their own children.[18] This stereotype was revamped after emancipation when black women who sought paid employment were viewed as neglecting their children, a construction that did not take into account their socioeconomic status. The most recent incarnation is that of the crack-addict mother who places her desire for drugs over the welfare of her children. In the 1990s, this image was so commonplace that it propelled the plot of the movie *Losing Isaiah* (1995).[19]

The remaining two cultural constructions, the matriarchal black unwed mother and the welfare queen, are closely connected. Welfare queens are poor women of color assumed to be sexually irresponsible and morally questionable and suspected of deliberately bearing children in order to increase their welfare payments. The welfare queen stereotype is a feminized version of the "culture of poverty" argument. As originally formulated by the anthropologist Oscar Lewis, this theory purported to explain Puerto Ricans' poverty as arising from their own bad choices, which in turn were conditioned by a deficit culture that encouraged pleasure-seeking and bad behavior.

The welfare queen is a public identity, and one that is commonly assigned across the full range of the racial spectrum, implicating various groups of women of color. The African American version that took shape in the 1960s was informed by social science studies on the disintegration of the black family and the rise of the matriarchal black mother and by political findings, in particular Senator Daniel Patrick Moynihan's report (now commonly referred to as "the Moynihan Report"), which discussed the disintegration of the black family. African Americans, like their Mexican counterparts during Proposition 187 debates, were and continue to be characterized as living off white taxpayers' money.[20] Because the behavior of women of color is defined as the problem, policy decisions often place the reproductive choices and lifestyles of poor women under scrutiny and once again ignore structural issues. Foster care policy decisions provide an example. In her analysis of black children in the foster care system, Roberts argues that "race influences decision making through strong and deeply embedded stereotypes about Black family dysfunction."[21] If the black family is widely understood to be dysfunctional and black mothers are seen as bad parents, the decision to place black children in the foster care system is seen as a step in the right direction. Thus cultural reasoning continues to trump examinations of structural inequalities.

The formulation of racialized groups as non-normative and therefore needing to be controlled serves a dual purpose. It excuses inequality by attributing it to the non-normative behavior of racialized groups. It also legitimizes intrusive measures of social control under the guise of civilizing projects. It is this line of racial logic that underpins policies that restrict or deny the rights of women of color, even if they are citizens, to reproduce. One notable example is forced sterilizations. The same argument that sustained the sterilizations projects of the 1920s and 1930s (see chapter 4) was transformed and presented as a defense strategy in *Madrigal v. Quilligan*. In 1975, eleven Chicanas filed suit against the Los Angeles County Medical Center, seeking damages for having been forcibly sterilized at that facility between 1971 and 1974. In this post–civil rights–era case, the judge ruled in favor of the medical center. He reasoned that there had been a "communication breakdown" because the doctors and their patients came from two different social worlds. He also argued that it was unreasonable for the physicians to have been expected to understand Mexican culture well enough to have assessed the effects of the sterilizations on the women's physical and emotional well-being. The judge's cultural reasoning argument assumed that there is a hierarchy of cultures and that the plaintiffs' culture had conditioned them to be unable to act and think rationally. Cultural reasoning replaced biological explanations, but the end result was the same: institutionally affirmed race-based injustice. The recurring nature of projects such as these makes clear that dangerous politics are by no means confined to a less-enlightened, bygone era.[22]

POINTS OF SOLIDARITY AND MOBILIZATION

If the past repeatedly intrudes on the present, will the racialized other in our society always be suspended in the process of becoming American? Is real change possible? Definitive answers, of course, are unknowable. Postwar experiences of Mexican Americans in Los Angeles offer some hopeful signs, however. The very health injuries and social indignities that most seriously threatened Mexicans' well-being became focal points for organization that helped build a positive Mexican American identity. The career of Edward Roybal provides a good example. As a social worker for the California Tuberculosis Association, Roybal had firsthand experience with the disparate municipal services and inferior housing conditions in which Mexicans lived and many opportunities to see how this affected their health. He turned to politics, in part, as a way to advance his public health agenda.[23]

Roybal ran for city councilman in the city's ninth district in 1947. He lost—but quickly regrouped and set his sights on winning the same seat in the 1949 election. He and volunteers from his campaign formed the Community Service Organization (CSO), a nonpartisan group whose mission was to involve the community more directly in electoral politics.

The CSO focused on voter registration drives and on helping residents organize to get their community's needs met. While campaigning, Roybal focused on the structural inequalities he had witnessed in his years as a social worker. Mexicans took his message to heart, and Roybal became the first Mexican elected to the city council in nearly one hundred years. In voting overwhelmingly for him, Mexicans and others in the ninth district demonstrated how health and housing issues could serve as an impetus for organization among a diverse group of poor and working-class voters.

Such community building continued. In East Los Angeles, grassroots activists formed groups such as the Mothers of East L.A. (MELA) to advocate for their community. MELA's efforts were so successful that they halted the construction of a prison and a toxic waste incinerator. MELA also fought for other issues that affected East L.A. residents, such as stopping lead poisoning, increasing awareness around immunizations, removing graffiti, and raising funds for higher education.[24] The sociologist Mary Pardo argues that these women activists also had to combat negative cultural constructions of their neighborhoods. The same depictions that rationalized the quarantining of neighborhoods during the 1924 plague while leaving the harbor untouched, that allowed some areas to receive the lowest housing grade and thus lose out on federally backed mortgages, and that justified the bulldozing of homes to make way for freeways had culminated in making East Los Angeles a dumping ground for everything from prisons to oil pipelines.

Health injuries and environmental injustices have served as the rallying point for Mexicans at other times and in many other communities as well. The United Farm Workers Organizing Committee, demonstrating how social and environmental struggles come together, fought to ban the use of pesticides. The Young Lords started in New York by protesting against the city's failure to pick up garbage in Puerto Rican neighborhoods. Establishing sickle cell anemia research foundations and implementing free breakfasts for schoolchildren were both central to the Black Panthers' agenda. Stopping toxic and nuclear dumping on or near tribal lands and reforming national environmental, economic, and energy policies that are genocidal to indigenous people are central to the agendas of some American Indian groups.[25] Thus, although a critical historical perspective teaches us to be wary, it also offers some cause to hope. The very forms of racialization that have harmed and excluded communities of color have also, eventually, become focal points for solidarity and collective mobilizations aimed at turning negative ascription and exclusion into positive affirmation and empowerment.

Notes

ABBREVIATIONS

BHC	Los Angeles City Board of Health Commissioners
BHC/M	Los Angeles City Board of Health Commissioners, Minutes (in LACA)
B of S	Los Angeles County Board of Supervisors
B of S/R	Los Angeles County Board of Supervisors, Records
CP	Council Petition
CSBHMB	*California State Board of Health Monthly Bulletin*
DHS	Los Angeles County Department of Health Services Library
DIHR	California Department of Industrial Relations, Division of Immigration and Housing Records, Bancroft Library, University of California, Berkeley
HEH	Henry E. Huntington Library
JAF	John Anson Ford Collection (Huntington Library)
LACA	Los Angeles City Archives
LACC	Los Angeles City Council
LACC/M	Los Angeles City Council, Minutes (in LACA)

LACHD/City   Los Angeles City Health Department
LACHD/County   Los Angeles County Health Department
MAM   Mayor's Annual Message (in LACA)
SRE   Secretaría de Relaciones Exteriores
SRE/A   Secretaría de Relaciones Exteriores, Archives
SRLF   Southern Regional Library Facilities (in UCLA
                   Library)

INTRODUCTION

1. Lindley was the first head of the city's public health department. He delivered the inaugural "Los Angeles City Annual Health Officer's Report, November 13, 1879" (not the same as the Annual Health Reports, which started in 1889), Los Angeles City Archives (Untitled) Records, LACA; quote from 14:997.

2. Ibid., p. 3.

3. Ibid.

4. Suellen Hoy, *Chasing Dirt: The American Pursuit of Cleanliness* (New York: Oxford University Press, 1995), 87.

5. John Pomeroy to B of S, February 17, 1916, B of S/R.

6. John Pomeroy to B of S, December 17, 1918, B of S/R.

7. Health department reports confirm that health officials overwhelmingly regarded all Asians and Mexicans as foreigners and immigrants, no matter how long they or their families had lived in the United States.

8. The anthropologist Renato Rosaldo introduced the concept of "cultural citizenship" to refer to the practices immigrants engage in to claim space in society that leads to forms of empowerment through cultural representations or political involvement. Renato Rosaldo, *Culture and Truth: The Remaking of Social Analysis* (Boston: Beacon Press, 1989). Others, such as Aihwa Ong, have built on Rosaldo's definition but also shown the limits of this interpretation. Ong argues that by focusing only on the agency of the individual one neglects how the political economy constrains actors. Aihwa Ong, "Cultural Citizenship as Subject-Making: Immigrants Negotiate Racial and Cultural Boundaries in the United States," *Current Anthropology* 37, no. 5 (1996): 737–63, and *Flexible Citizenship: The Cultural Logics of Transnationality* (Durham, NC: Duke University Press, 1999).

9. James Holston, ed., *Cities and Citizenship* (Durham, NC: Duke University Press, 1999).

10. Such practices led to an ideological control of space that resulted in de facto racial segregation in certain parts of the city. For an insightful analysis of the uses of social control of space in Los Angeles, see Raúl Villa, *Barrio-Logos: Space and Place in Urban Chicano Literature and Culture* (Austin: University of Texas Press, 2000).

11. For studies that examine race and municipal politics in the United States, see Nayan Shah, *Contagious Divides: Epidemics and Race in San Francisco's Chinatown* (Berkeley: University of California Press, 2001); William Deverell,

Whitewashed Adobe: The Rise of Los Angeles and the Remaking of Its Mexican Past (Berkeley: University of California Press, 2004), ch. 5; Tera Hunter, *To 'Joy My Freedom: Southern Black Women's Lives and Labors after the Civil War* (Cambridge, MA: Harvard University Press, 1997); Keith Wailoo, *Dying in the City of the Blues: Sickle Cell Anemia and the Politics of Race and Health* (Chapel Hill: University of North Carolina Press, 2001).

12. Michel Foucault's work has been instrumental in examinations of the role institutions play in "the subjugation of bodies and control of populations." As he pointed out, power is a dispersed and decentered force that is difficult to grasp and possess fully. Michel Foucault, *The History of Sexuality,* vol. 1, *An Introduction,* trans. Robert Hurley (New York: Random House, 1976), 137–40.

13. The following works also examine medicine within a U.S. paradigm during this same period and have furthered my understanding of the racialization process: Alexandra Stern, *Eugenic Nation: Faults and Frontiers of Better Breeding in Modern America* (Berkeley: University of California Press, 2005); Charles L. Briggs and Clara Mantini-Briggs, *Stories in the Time of Cholera: Racial Profiling during a Medical Nightmare* (Berkeley: University of California Press, 2003); Laura Briggs, *Reproducing Empire: Race, Sex, Science, and U.S. Imperialism in Puerto Rico* (Berkeley: University of California Press, 2002); Shah, *Contagious Divides;* Alan Kraut, *Silent Travelers: Germs, Genes, and the "Immigrant Menace"* (New York: Basic Books, 1994). These works have been very helpful to my understanding of the development of public health in the United States: John Duffy, *The Sanitarians: A History of American Public Health* (Urbana: University of Illinois Press, 1990); Judith Walzer Leavitt and Ronald L. Numbers, *Sickness and Health in America: Readings in the History of Medicine and Public Health* (Madison: University of Wisconsin Press, 1978); Judith Walzer Leavitt, *The Healthiest City: Milwaukee and the Politics of Health Reform* (Princeton, NJ: Princeton University Press, 1982); Charles Rosenberg, *The Cholera Years: The United States in 1832, 1849, and 1866* (Chicago: University of Chicago Press, 1962); Nancy Tomes, *The Gospel of Germs: Men, Women, and the Microbe in American Life* (Cambridge, MA: Harvard University Press, 1998).

14. In 1900, L.A.'s total population was 102,479. See U.S. Census Office, *United States Census of Population, 1900* (Washington, DC: Government Printing Office, 1901–3), 1:796–803. The same year, Los Angeles eclipsed Chicago as the nation's fastest-growing city. Just ten years later, L.A.'s population increased by another 211 percent. See Janet Abu-Lughod, *New York, Chicago, Los Angeles: America's Global Cities* (Minneapolis: University of Minnesota Press, 1999), 5–15.

15. By 1930, New York reported a central city population per square mile of 23,179; Chicago, 16,723; and Boston, 17,795. Los Angeles, in comparison, had a central city population per square mile of only 2,812 in 1930. Robert M. Fogelson, *The Fragmented Metropolis: Los Angeles, 1850–1930* (Berkeley: University of California Press, 1967), 143.

16. I use the term *white* because health officials consistently used "white" as a racial category. In 1900, foreign-born residents totaled 19,964, compared to 82,515 native born. Forty-one percent, or 8,266, of the foreign born were En-

glish speaking, including immigrants from England, Canada, Ireland, Wales, and Australia. The non-English-speaking foreign born were German, Chinese, French, Italian, Mexican, Slavic, and Japanese (in descending order from highest to lowest percentage). U.S. Census Office, *United States Census of Population, 1900,* 1:796–803. For histories of Los Angeles that trace the city's socioeconomic development, see Fogelson, *Fragmented Metropolis;* Abu-Lughod, *New York, Chicago.*

17. Oscar Handlin, *The Uprooted: The Epic Story of the Great Migrations That Made the American People* (Boston: Little, Brown, 1973); John Higham, *Strangers in the Land: Patterns of American Nativism, 1860–1925* (New Brunswick, NJ: Rutgers University Press, 1955).

18. Robert Wiebe identified the search for order as a goal unifying various reform initiatives. See Robert Wiebe, *The Search for Order, 1877–1920* (New York: Hill and Wang, 1967). For alternative interpretations of the Progressive Era, see Gabriel Kolko, *The Triumph of Conservatism: A Re-Interpretation of American History, 1900–1916* (New York: Free Press of Glencoe, 1963); Richard Hofstadter, *The Age of Reform: From Bryan to F.D.R.* (New York: Knopf, 1955); Samuel P. Hays, *The Response to Industrialism, 1885–1914* (Chicago: University of Chicago Press, 1995). Daniel Rodgers's classic essay challenges using the term *Progressivism* as a central organizing principle in American history. Daniel Rodgers, "In Search of Progressivism," *Reviews in American History* 10, no. 4 (1982): 113–32.

19. Breakthroughs in bacteriology at the end of the nineteenth century drastically changed the development of the field. New discoveries in microbiology provided scientific explanations about how infectious and contagious diseases spread. This new information helped launch campaigns to battle disease and promote public health. Tomes, *Gospel of Germs;* Duffy, *Sanitarians;* Hoy, *Chasing Dirt.*

20. According to James Whorton, "Progressivism combined confidence in science with an expansive social optimism and sense of progress." James C. Whorton, *Crusaders for Fitness: The History of the American Health Reformers* (Princeton, NJ: Princeton University Press, 1982), 140.

21. In 1910, the city's African American population was 7,599 (2 percent of the total) and was confined mainly to the segregated areas of Central Avenue. See U.S. Census Office, *Thirteenth Census of the United States Taken in the Year 1910* (Washington, DC: Government Printing Office, 1913), 180. African Americans did not, of course, escape racism on the West Coast. My point here is simply that in the presence of other racialized groups, discrimination against African Americans took different forms than those prevalent in the South. For a history of African Americans in early-twentieth-century Los Angeles, see Josh Sides, *L.A. City Limits: African American in Los Angeles from the Great Depression to the Present* (Berkeley: University of California Press, 2003); Lawrence B. de Graaf, "Recognition, Racism, and Reflections on the Writing of Western Black History," *Pacific Historical Review* 44 (1975): 22–47.

22. Matthew Frye Jacobson, *Whiteness of a Different Color: European Immigrants and the Alchemy of Race* (Cambridge, MA: Harvard University Press, 1998), 42.

23. David Roediger, *The Wages of Whiteness: Race and the Making of the American Working Class* (London: Verso Press, 1991).

24. George Lipsitz, *The Possessive Investment in Whiteness: How White People Profit from Identity Politics* (Philadelphia: Temple University Press, 1998). For studies of whiteness, see Eric Avila, *Popular Culture in the Age of White Flight: Fear and Fantasy in Suburban Los Angeles* (Berkeley: University of California Press, 2004); Deverell, *Whitewashed Adobe;* Neil Foley, *The White Scourge: Mexicans, Blacks and Poor Whites in Texas Cotton Culture* (Berkeley: University of California Press, 1997); Thomas A. Guglielmo, *White on Arrival: Italians, Race, Color, and Power in Chicago, 1890–1945* (New York: Oxford University Press, 2003); Ian Haney-Lopez, *White by Law: The Legal Construction of Race* (New York: New York University Press, 1996); Jacobson, *Whiteness.*

25. Almaguer emphasizes the importance of region and historical period in understanding how we think of bodies as racialized. He argues that the small population of African Americans in California, coupled with the diverse populations of natives and immigrants, resulted in a racially stratified hierarchy among Mexicans, Asians, Native Americans, and whites that defied binary racialization. My study demonstrates how these categories continued to be negotiated in the twentieth century, as the Native American population was drastically reduced, as Asians faced severe immigration restrictions, and as the perception of Mexicans as *Californios* gave way to the view that Mexicans were immigrants. Tomás Almaguer, *Racial Fault Lines: The Historical Origins of White Supremacy* (Berkeley: University of California Press, 1994).

26. Claire Jean Kim, *Bitter Fruit: The Politics of Black-Korean Conflict in New York City* (New Haven, CT: Yale University Press, 2000), 10.

27. I do not mean to suggest that health officials extended the notion of Americanization to Mexicans as easily or comprehensively as they did to European immigrants. Health officials publicly chastised Mexicans for their "unclean living habits" even while engaging in rhetoric that advocated Americanization. At various historical moments, health officials also suggested limiting immigration from Mexico, thereby completely denying Mexicans the opportunity to become Americans.

28. After 1920, the city health department expanded its categories to include "Mexican," "Japanese," and "Negro"; the county department used "white," "Mexican," "Japanese," and "other" to keep track of the populations under its jurisdiction.

29. Since public health departments at the city, county, state, and national levels focused on Japanese and Chinese communities inconsistently, there are few records available. The limited source material makes it difficult to analyze these groups' experiences in any depth. There are, however, ample primary sources that show how racialization projects *differed* for Mexican, Chinese, and Japanese communities.

30. In their highly influential study, Omi and Winant define racialization as a "sociohistorical process by which racial categories are created, inhabited, transformed, and destroyed." Michael Omi and Howard Winant, *Racial Formation in the United States from the 1960s to the 1980s* (New York: Routledge,

1986), 56. They emphasize the historically specific and socially constructed nature of racial categories by drawing attention to "*projects* in which human bodies and social structures are represented and organized" (55–56, emphasis in the original).

31. For a history of Manifest Destiny, see Reginald Horsman, *Race and Manifest Destiny: The Origins of American Racial Anglo-Saxonism* (Cambridge, MA: Harvard University Press, 1981). Martha Menchaca has examined legal discrimination against Mexicans from 1848 through 1947. She argues that Mexicans often were considered akin to Indians. U.S. officials classified lighter-skinned Mexicans as white and darker-skinned Mexicans as Indian. See Martha Menchaca, "Chicano Indianism: A Historical Account of Racial Repression in the United States," *American Ethnologist* 20, no. 3 (1993): 583–603.

32. The Chinese Exclusion Act provided for an absolute moratorium on the immigration of Chinese workers (a category defined so broadly that it included nearly anyone who attempted to emigrate from China) for a ten-year period (a provision that was renewed in 1892, made permanent in 1902, and not re-scinded until 1943). The 1882 act also denied the possibility of U.S. citizenship to resident Chinese aliens. The Gentlemen's Agreement was a treaty forged between the United States and Japan in 1907 (with an additional provision appended in 1908 to strengthen the agreement) to quell increasing tensions, especially in San Francisco, over the immigration of Japanese workers. The Japanese government agreed to deny passports to laborers bound for the United States, and President Theodore Roosevelt promised to persuade San Francisco city officials to rescind a blatantly discriminatory law aimed at Asian school-children in the city. Chapters 1 and 2 provide further information about the early-twentieth-century legal and social experiences of the Chinese and Japanese in the United States.

33. For many Mexicans it was the lure of employment that spurred migration (Los Angeles employers in the early twentieth century sought laborers to build railroad lines, plant and harvest agricultural crops, and work in low-wage jobs in the city's newly developing industries), but for others it was the start of the Mexican Revolution in 1910 that prompted emigration. Devra Weber examines Mexico's transformation to a capitalist society that left over 96 percent of Mexican families landless and thus forced to seek a new life in the United States. Devra Weber, *Dark Sweat, White Gold: California Farm Workers, Cotton, and the New Deal* (Berkeley: University of California Press, 1994), 48–53.

34. George Sánchez, *Becoming Mexican American: Ethnicity, Culture, and Identity in Chicano Los Angeles, 1900–1945* (New York: Oxford University Press, 1993), 41. For studies of Mexican women in the early twentieth century, see Vicki Ruiz, *Cannery Women, Cannery Lives: Mexican Women, Unionization, and the California Food Processing Industry, 1930–1950* (Albuquerque: University of New Mexico Press, 1987), and *From out of the Shadows: Mexican Women in Twentieth-Century America* (New York: Oxford University Press, 1998); George Sánchez, " 'Go after the Women': Americanization and the Mexican Immigrant Woman, 1915–1929," in *A Multi-Cultural Reader in U.S. Women's History*, ed. Ellen DuBois and Vicki Ruiz (New York: Routledge, 1990), 284–97. Histories of Mexican women in the nineteenth century are

scarce. Notable exceptions are Miroslava Chávez-García, *Negotiating Conquest: Gender and Power in California, 1770s to 1880s* (Tucson: University of Arizona Press, 2004); Antonia Castañeda, "Engendering the History of Alta California, 1769–1848: Gender, Sexuality, and the Family," in *Contested Eden: California before the Gold Rush,* ed. Ramón Gutiérrez and Roberto Orsi (Berkeley: University of California Press, 1998), 230–59; Deena J. González, *Refusing the Favor: The Spanish-Mexican Women of Santa Fe, 1820–1880* (New York: Oxford University Press, 1999).

35. Ruiz, *From out of the Shadows,* ch. 3, "Confronting America"; George Sánchez, " 'Go after the Women.' "

36. On the pervasiveness of the eugenics movement in California, see Stern, *Eugenic Nation.*

37. I am drawing on the terminology used by Peter Stallybrass and Allon White in *The Politics and Poetics of Transgression* (Ithaca, NY: Cornell University Press, 1986), 23.

38. Roderick Ferguson's unique study of how racial and sexual difference is produced and how these standards in turn serve as the justification for marginalizing nonheteronormative black bodies is very insightful. Ferguson argues that much of the work of professional sociology in the twentieth century revolved around this discourse of normativity. Roderick Ferguson, *Aberrations in Black: Toward a Queer of Color Critique* (Minneapolis: University of Minnesota Press, 2004).

39. The historian Alan Kraut argues that public health historians usually write history as if power flowed in one direction with only immigrants being affected, "medicine and hygiene being merely aspects of newcomers' acculturation." Kraut, *Silent Travelers,* 278 n. 5. The following works examine how racialized groups protested medical discourses and processes that constructed them as nonnormative: Paul Farmer, *AIDS and Accusation: Haiti and the Geography of Blame* (Berkeley: University of California Press, 1992); Shah, *Contagious Divides;* Briggs and Mantini-Briggs, *Stories;* John McKiernan-Gonzalez, "Fevered Measures: Race, Contagious Disease and Community Formation on the Texas-Mexico Border, 1880–1923" (PhD diss., University of Michigan, 2002); Alexandra Stern, "Buildings, Boundaries, and Blood: Medicalization and Nation-Building on the U.S.-Mexican Border, 1910–1930," *Hispanic American Historical Review* 79, no. 1 (1999): 41–81.

40. George Sánchez, *Becoming Mexican American,* 224–25.

1. INTERLOPERS IN THE LAND OF SUNSHINE

1. The population of Los Angeles barely approached 11,000 in 1879, compared with 233,959 in 1880 in San Francisco. Moreover, the developed portions of the city "did not extend more than two miles from the town's center." Fogelson, *Fragmented Metropolis,* 137; Douglas Monroy, *Rebirth: Mexican Los Angeles from the Great Migration to the Great Depression* (Berkeley: University of California Press, 1999), 137; Abu-Lughod, *New York, Chicago,* 11.

2. "Los Angeles City Annual Health Officer's Report, November 13, 1879," in Los Angeles City Archives (Untitled) Records, 14:1000, LACA.

3. The city relocated Chinatown in 1933 in order to construct the railroad station. Roberta S. Greenwood, *Down by the Station: Los Angeles Chinatown, 1880–1933* (Los Angeles: Institute of Archaeology, University of California, Los Angeles, 1996).

4. "Los Angeles City Annual Health Officer's Report, November 13, 1879," 14:998.

5. The BHC passed a motion to implement sewers in Chinatown in 1909. BHC/M, April 28, 1909, 2:242.

6. See Ralph E. Shaffer's introduction to the "Anti-Chinese" section of his online anthology "Letters from the People: *Los Angeles Times*, 1881–1889," 1999, retrieved May 3, 2005, from www.intranet.csupomona.edu/~reshaffer/contents.htm.

7. William Locklear, "The Celestials and the Angels: A Study of the Anti-Chinese Movement in Los Angeles to 1882," *Southern California Quarterly* 42, no. 3 (1960): 248–50; Greenwood, *Down by the Station*, 11.

8. The historian Alan Kraut writes that some immigrants were "repelled because their very appearance suggested to their hosts' gazes a physical inferiority or vulnerability that the native born feared might be contagious. . . . The Chinese, especially produced such visceral reaction in native-born Caucasian Americans." Kraut, *Silent Travelers*, 78–79.

9. Quoted in U.S. Commission on Civil Rights, ed., *Civil Rights Issues Facing Asian Americans in the 1990s* (Washington, DC: U.S. Commission on Civil Rights, 1992), no page cited. Two years later, in 1871, mob violence in Los Angeles resulted in the deaths of nineteen Chinese males. And in 1879, California's Second Constitution made it illegal for corporations to hire Chinese, forbade Chinese from working on public projects, and awarded the state legislature the authority to "remove" foreigners who were not within the limits of a given city.

10. W. Almont Gates, *Oriental Immigration on the Pacific Coast* (San Francisco: 1909), 11–12. Gates's comments also tapped into the unified notion of whiteness that would solidify after the passage of the 1924 Immigration Act drastically reduced immigration from southern and eastern Europe. See Jacobson, *Whiteness*, 88.

11. Abu-Lughod, *New York, Chicago,* 5–15. The Southern Pacific line to the East was completed in 1883. When the Santa Fe transcontinental line opened n 1885, competition between the two railroads resulted in a ticket price war. See Shaffer's preface to the "Real Estate Boom" section of his "Letters from the People."

12. On Los Angeles boosterism, see Mike Davis, *City of Quartz: Excavating the Future in Los Angeles* (London: Verso Press, 1990), ch. 1, "Sunshine or Noir?"; Clark Davis, "From Oasis to Metropolis: Southern California and the Changing Context of American Leisure," *Pacific Historical Review* 61, no. 3 (1992): 357–86; Kevin Starr, *Americans and the California Dream, 1850–1915* (New York: Oxford University Press, 1973), and *Inventing the Dream: California through the Progressive Era* (New York: Oxford University Press, 1985).

13. Josephine Kingsbury Jacobs, "Sunkist Advertising: The Iowa Campaign," in *Los Angeles: Biography of a City,* ed. John Caughey and LaRee Caughey (Berkeley: University of California Press, 1977), 216.

14. Carey McWilliams, *Southern California: An Island on the Land* (Salt Lake City, UT: Gibbs Smith, 1946).

15. For an analysis of the role of gender, class, and race in the aftermath of the annexation of Mexico, see Rosaura Sánchez, *Telling Identities: The Californio Testimonios* (Minneapolis: University of Minnesota Press, 1995). For an examination of how Mexican and Native women challenged patriarchy by filing for divorce, suing for their property, and asserting their rights in the home, see Chávez-García, *Negotiating Conquest.*

16. For more on the construction on the Spanish Fantasy Past narrative, see William Deverell, *Whitewashed Adobe;* Phoebe Kropp, " 'All Our Yesterdays': The Spanish Fantasy Past and the Politics of Public Memory in Southern California, 1884–1939" (PhD diss., University of California, San Diego, 1999); Starr, *Americans,* 365–414.

17. Mike Davis, *City of Quartz,* 365–414.

18. "The Mighty West," *Los Angeles Times,* August 4, 1909, II4.

19. "The Future of the Pacific," *Los Angeles Times,* April 24, 1909, II4.

20. "Splendid Race Cradled Here," *Los Angeles Times,* January 9, 1916, III4.

21. Women also played a role in maintaining a vision of a racial hierarchy. While the women's movement in California envisioned radical change in demanding the vote, they refused to disrupt the racial order and form any cross-racial alliances. Gayle Gullett, *Becoming Citizens: The Emergence and Development of the California Women's Movement, 1880–1911* (Urbana: University of Illinois Press, 2000).

22. Joseph Widney, *Race Life of the Aryan Peoples,* 2 vols. (New York: Funk and Wagnalls, 1907), and *The Three Americas: Their Racial Past and the Dominant Racial Factors of Their Future* (Los Angeles: Pacific Publishing, 1935). His writings are still quoted today by white supremacist groups like the National Vanguard. See "The White Race's Place in the Universe," retrieved May 26, 2005, from the National Vanguard's Web site: www.nationalvanguard.org/story.php?id=317.

23. Starr, *Inventing the Dream,* 89–93; Mike Davis, *City of Quartz,* 27–28.

24. Letters to the editor, "An Ohio Republican," *Los Angeles Times,* May 11, 1882, 3, in the "Anti-Chinese" section of Shaffer, "Letters from the People."

25. Becky M. Nicolaides, *My Blue Heaven: Life and Politics in the Working-Class Suburbs of Los Angeles, 1920–1965* (Chicago: University of Chicago Press, 2002), 16–17, 19. Thomas Sugrue also discusses how working-class whites in Detroit's suburbs mobilized to prevent African Americans from moving into their neighborhoods. Thomas Sugrue, *The Origins of the Urban Crisis: Race and Inequality in Postwar Detroit* (Princeton, NJ: Princeton University Press, 1996). For more on racial covenants in real estate, see Fogelson, *Fragmented Metropolis.* William Deverell discusses cases in which Mexicans, though not barred by racial covenants, may have chosen not to live in certain areas in order to avoid hostile climates. William Deverell, "Privileging the Mission over the Mexican," in *Many Wests: Place, Culture, and Regional Identity,* ed. David Wrobel and Michael Steiner (Lawrence: University Press of Kansas, 1997), 247–48. For housing discrimination toward African Americans in Los Angeles in the post–World War period, see Sides, *L.A. City Limits.*

26. Describing Los Angeles boosters, Abraham Hoffman notes, "Ambitious entrepreneurs looked to the future and the potential opportunities Los Angeles could offer them. Looking at their careers, it is difficult to pin them down to one particular business activity. Businessmen were involved in several ventures at once, from banking to merchandising to real estate development." See Abraham Hoffman, "Needs and Opportunities in Los Angeles Biography. Part One: The 18th and 19th Centuries," 2001, retrieved May 4, 2005, from the Historical Society of Southern California Web site: www.socalhistory.org/pages/ LABioah.htm.

27. Lindley married the Haynes brothers' sister, Florence, in 1893. In the late 1910s and early 1920s, John Randolph Haynes sought to maintain the vision of Los Angeles as an urban utopia by, among other things, advocating state-administered sterilization. See Alexandra Stern, "Eugenics Beyond Borders: Science and Medicalization in Mexico and the U.S. West, 1900–1950" (PhD diss., University of Chicago, 1999).

28. Initially, the California Hospital, a three-story wood-frame building, was known as Dr. Lindley's Private Hospital. Lindley paid $1,825 for the building and property in 1887. The facility, which was the city's first physician-owned and operated hospital, was renamed, relocated, and expanded (under Lindley's supervision) several years later. See "History," retrieved May 11, 2005, from the California Hospital Medical Center Web site, www.chmcla.org/index.asp?catID =au&pg=au_History, for further details about Lindley's role as founder and director of the hospital, as well as the Dr. Walter Lindley Papers, Claremont College, Special Collections.

29. Walter Lindley and Joseph Pomeroy Widney, *California of the South* (New York: D. Appleton, 1896).

30. His friendship with Otis enabled Lindley to publish the *Southern Californian Practitioner,* a monthly medical journal that he both edited and contributed to frequently.

31. Edward E. Harnagel, "The Life and Times of Walter Lindley, M.D., 1852–1922, and the Founding of the California Hospital," *Southern California Quarterly* 53, no. 4 (1971): 303. I thank Tom Sitton for referring this article to me and for sharing his insights on Dr. Walter Lindley.

32. Fogelson, *Fragmented Metropolis,* 145. Fogelson argues that "exploited economically, separated residentially, isolated socially, and ignored politically, [people of color] remained entirely outside the Los Angeles community" (xviii).

33. According to John Baur, "the health quest was more significant for southern California's development than the great gold rush had been." John Baur, *The Health Seekers of Southern California, 1870–1900* (San Marino, CA: Huntington Library, 1959), xi. See also Starr, *Inventing the Dream,* 54–55.

34. Tuberculosis was one of the most common ailments people sought to cure by moving to Los Angeles. See Baur, *Health Seekers,* xii.

35. Benjamin Cummings Truman, *Semi-tropical California: Its Climate, Healthfulness, Productiveness, and Scenery* (San Francisco: A. L. Bancroft, 1874), 34. Truman arrived in California from Rhode Island in 1866. He worked for a while as the Washington correspondent for the *New York Times* and the *San Francisco Bulletin,* but by the early 1870s he had become editor of the *Los*

Angeles Evening Express and then owner of the *Los Angeles Star.* Truman wrote *Semi-tropical California* as a guidebook.

36. Ibid.

37. Los Angeles Chamber of Commerce, "Climate and Health in Los Angeles County and Southern California," January 1899, 1, HEH.

38. Chandler married Marion Otis, the daughter of Harrison Gray Otis, the original owner and publisher of the *Times.*

39. Dudley Gordon, "Charles F. Lummis and Jack London: An Evaluation," *Southern California Quarterly* 46 (March 1964): 83–88.

40. He also founded the Southwest Chapter of the American Institute of Archaeology.

41. "Los Angeles City Annual Health Officer's Report, November 13, 1879," 3.

42. A similar process had already occurred in San Francisco. See Shah, *Contagious Divides;* Alexander Saxton, *The Indispensable Enemy: Labor and the Anti-Chinese Movement in California* (Berkeley: University of California Press, 1970).

43. The 1889 Los Angeles City Charter created the BHC, assigning responsibility for appointing the commissioners to the mayor. Burton L. Hunter, *The Evolution of Municipal Organization and Administrative Practice in the City of Los Angeles* (Los Angeles: Parker, Stone, and Baird, 1933).

44. Thus both the health officer and his department were under the supervision of the board. Burton Hunter, *Evolution of Municipal Organization.*

45. The commissioners discussed the appointment of additional sanitary inspectors and related personnel, as well as positions they wished to create. They also decided to meet twice a month in the mayor's office. "City Briefs," *Los Angeles Times,* April 15, 1890, 8. The city health officer regularly attended the bimonthly meetings and reported on public health conditions, which the commissioners used as a springboard for discussion. "Board of Health: Flags for Infectious Diseases Explained," *Los Angeles Times,* July 19, 1889, 5.

46. BHC/M, December 29, 1897, 1:76–77.

47. Robert Lee, *Orientals: Asian Americans in Popular Culture* (Philadelphia: Temple University Press, 1999), 22. For an overview of Chinese in the United States, see Sucheng Chan, *Asian Americans: An Interpretive History* (Boston: Twayne, 1991); Roger Daniels, *Asian America: Chinese and Japanese in the United States since 1850* (Seattle: University of Washington Press, 1988).

48. Leonard Pitt and Dale Pitt, *Los Angeles A to Z: An Encyclopedia of the City and County* (Berkeley: University of California Press, 1997), 89.

49. In 1877, Calle de los Negros was renamed Los Angeles Street. Although Mexicans and a few African Americans also lived in this vicinity, ethnic and racial groups tended to live separately. For a brief description of the groups who lived in and around the Plaza, see William Spalding, *History and Reminiscences: Los Angeles City and County, California* (Los Angeles: J. R. Finnell and Sons, 1931), 1:138; Greenwood, *Down by the Station,* 2, 10. For descriptions of Chinese living outside Chinatown, see Ervin King, "Boys' Thrills in Los Angeles of the 70s and 80s," *Southern California Quarterly* 30 (1948): 303–16.

50. Almaguer, *Racial Fault Lines,* 6. For a detailed look at extralegal ways in which Chinese were circumscribed in California preceding the 1882 Exclusion Act, see Mildred Wellborn, "The Events Leading to the Chinese Exclusion Acts," *Southern California Quarterly* 9 (1912–13): 49–58.

51. The accounts do not mention the race of the participants. For accounts of the Chinese Massacre of 1871, see C. P. Dorland, "Chinese Massacre at Los Angeles in 1871," *Publications of the Historical Society of Southern California* 3 (1893): 22–26; William Spalding, *History and Reminiscences,* 1:179–82; Ivan Light, "From Vice District to Tourist Attraction: The Moral Career of American Chinatowns," *Pacific Historical Review,* 43, no. 8 (1974): 367–94; Locklear, "Celestials and the Angels," 244; Lucie Cheng and Suellen Cheng, *Linking Our Lives: Chinese Women of Los Angeles* (Los Angeles: Chinese Historical Society of Southern California, 1984), 6.

52. Robert Lee, *Orientals,* ch. 1, "The 'Heathen Chinee' on God's Free Soil," and ch. 2, "The Coolie and the Making of the White Working Class," 15–82. Alexander Saxton's examination of labor and city politics in nineteenth- and early-twentieth-century San Francisco traces how white workers established a racialized hierarchy of job categories. Certain jobs were considered available to whites only; other, lower-tiered jobs were reserved for Chinese. Saxton, *Indispensable Enemy.*

53. Robert Lee argues that debates over admitting California as a free state were also about making California racially pure, which necessitated the exclusion of Chinese. Robert Lee, *Orientals,* 9.

54. Saxton, *Indispensable Enemy,* 127–39; Locklear, "Celestials and the Angels," 248–49.

55. For historical stereotypes of Chinese as disease carriers, see Kraut, *Silent Travelers,* 80–83. Few Chinese were successful in entering the medical profession during this period. Margaret Chung represents a rare example of a Chinese woman becoming a doctor. Chung graduated from the University of Southern California's College of Physicians and Surgeons in 1916. In the early 1920s, she opened one the first Western medical clinics in San Francisco's Chinatown. See Judy Tzu-Chun Wu, "Mom Chung of the Fair-Haired Bastards: A Thematic Biography of Doctor Margaret Chung, 1889–1959" (PhD diss., Stanford University, 1998).

56. Robert Lee, *Orientals,* 9.

57. Mary Douglas explores the connections between dirt, disease, and disorder in *Purity and Danger: An Analysis of Concepts of Pollution and Taboo* (New York: Praeger, 1970).

58. In the early twentieth century, Mexicans were similarly stereotyped as "dirty." David Montejano shows how in the 1920s and 1930s the stereotype of "dirty Mexicans" came to encompass a range of meanings from notions of hygiene to race, class, and living conditions. In Texas, these notions justified racially segregating Mexicans from whites. David Montejano, *Anglos and Mexicans in the Making of Texas, 1836–1986* (Austin: University of Texas Press, 1987), 225–35.

59. "Los Angeles City Annual Health Officer's Report, November 13, 1879," 3. The original is handwritten with "our" written in letters larger than the rest of the text.

60. The act was to remain in force for ten years, but it also included a provision for renewal every ten years. It was renewed in 1892 and then in 1920 was renewed indefinitely. It was not repealed until 1943.

61. These included the Sidewalk Ordinance (1870), which prohibited residents from using the sidewalks when they were carrying loads on poles; the Queue Ordinance (1873), which mandated cutting the hair of all Chinese prisoners to a one-inch length; and the Laundry Ordinance (1873), which levied a quarterly tax of $1 on laundries that used horse-drawn vehicles and a $15 tax per quarter on laundries without vehicles. (The mayor eventually vetoed the queue and laundry ordinances.)

62. Nancy Tomes, "The Private Side of Public Health: Sanitary Science, Domestic Hygiene, and the Germ Theory, 1870–1900," *Bulletin of the History of Medicine* 64, no. 4 (1990): 522.

63. Shaffer notes that "the growing problem of sewer waste disposal became one of the major topics among the city's residents during the 1880s." In "Letters from the People," introduction to the "Sewers" section.

64. *Los Angeles Times*, October 13, 1882, 3, in Shaffer, "Letters from the People."

65. BHC/M, April 10, 1893, 1:160. On the embedded meanings of race in an urban landscape, see Kay J. Anderson, "The Idea of Chinatown: The Power of Place and Institutional Practice in the Making of a Racial Category," *Annals of the Association of American Geographers* 77, no. 4 (1987): 580–98. On the relationship between place and social relations, see Dolores Hayden, *The Power of Place: Urban Landscapes as Public History* (Cambridge, MA: MIT Press, 1995).

66. In a June 26, 1899, letter to the LACC (Health Officer File, LACA), Robert Day, acting health officer, lists Idelfonso Sepúlveda and Mr. Shaeffer (no first name) as the two major landowners in Chinatown. William Spalding, *History and Reminiscences*, also names Juan Apablasa as owning a large amount of land in Chinatown (1:138). A street in old Chinatown was named after Apablasa, though it appears that it was actually Apablasa's widow who owned the land (which included vineyards) by the time the Chinese leased it to live on and farm.

67. In 1906, city officials in Santa Ana, California, used public health concerns to justify burning down that city's Chinatown. Ostensibly, a case of leprosy had been reported, although that claim was never confirmed. City officials had considered Chinatown, which covered barely two blocks, a nuisance for years. See Lisbeth Haas, *Conquests and Historical Identities in California, 1769–1936* (Berkeley: University of California Press, 1995), 177–78.

68. Saxton, *Indispensable Enemy,* 243–244. Charles McClain, "Of Medicine, Race, and American Law: The Bubonic Plague Outbreak of 1900," *Law and Social Inquiry* 13, no. 3 (1988): 447–513.

69. BHC/M, February 17, 1903, 1:371.

70. "Guarding against Invasion of Plague," *Los Angeles Times*, January 28, 1903, A2. There were no reports of L.A. residents who died of the plague in 1903.

71. BHC/M, January 1, 1904, 1:402.

72. Chinatown would be known as a tourist center in the twentieth century, but in the late 1800s it was extralegal activities that drew outsiders to Chinatown. See Light, "From Vice District," 367–94.

73. Logan and Moltoch argue that poor people do not control the use value of their neighborhoods. John R. Logan and Harvey L. Moltoch, *Urban Fortunes: The Political Economy of Place* (Berkeley: University of California Press, 1987), 111–16.

74. Nayan Shah provides a clear example of how Chinese but not whites were marked by vice businesses. Shah argues that in relationships between Chinese female prostitutes and their white male clients the police portrayed Chinese women as seducing white men (referred to as "boys"). Shah, *Contagious Divides*, 85–88.

75. "Removing Chinatown," *Los Angeles Times*, October 8, 1887.

76. "City Briefs."

77. BHC/M, December 29, 1897, 1:76.

78. Shaffer, "Letters from the People," introduction to the "Anti-Chinese" section.

79. "Contra-Coolie: Large Mass Meeting in the Tabernacle Last Night," *Los Angeles Times*, February 28, 1886, 8.

80. Ibid.

81. See Shaffer's "Waning on the Chinese Issue" in his "Letters from the People."

82. *Los Angeles Times*, March 2, 1886, 2. This letter was signed "Jordan Cox." See Shaffer, "Letters from the People."

83. LACHD/City, *Annual Report of Department of Health of the City of Los Angeles, California, for the Year Ended June 30, 1913*, 72–77, SRLF; hereafter cited as *AHR, 1913*. My discussion of the Chinese fruit and vegetable vendors relies mainly on city health department reports for 1910–20. I found only five complaints recorded in the LACC/M that came before the city council regarding the marketplace during this time period, 1913–20. The BHC/M were not preserved for this time period.

84. Framing concerns over social boundaries and jobs as public health issues occurred in various cities in the early twentieth century. In hopes of eliminating their Chinese competitors from the marketplace, Anglo cigar makers in San Francisco depicted them as disease carriers whose products would bring illnesses into white homes. See Shah, *Contagious Divides*, 158–71. Similarly, in an effort to fortify racial boundaries in the Jim Crow South, whites in Atlanta in the early twentieth century portrayed African American female house servants as tuberculosis carriers who posed a public health threat to the white community. See Tera Hunter, *To 'Joy My Freedom*, 187–218.

85. The quote in the heading comes from "Chinese Must Clean Up," *Los Angeles Times*, April 15, 1914, II3. Municipal reform concerns chiefly involved public utilities and city planning. See Fogelson, *Fragmented Metropolis*, 229–72.

86. The two main public markets were the Los Angeles City Market, located at Sixth and Alameda Streets, and the City Market of Los Angeles, located at Ninth and San Pedro. The ethnicity of the vendors at the public markets is not discussed in any city reports. My assertion regarding the vendors' race and ethnicity is based on health department photographs of the marketplaces in which only "whites" appear.

87. LACHD/City, *AHR, 1913,* 73.

88. Ibid.

89. Since the Chinese were singled out for poor treatment in other forums, it seems unlikely that they would have been welcomed into either of the two city markets.

90. LACHD/City, *Annual Report of Department of Health of the City of Los Angeles, California, for the Year Ended June 30, 1912,* 60, SRLF; hereafter cited as *AHR, 1912.* Since Chinese had first begun to immigrate to the United States in the mid–nineteenth century, whites had been employing Chinese as house-boys, launderers, and cooks. Whites overlooked the constant prejudices against Chinese as heathens and disease carriers in favor of employing them at low wages. Similarly, Angelenos' apparent willingness to buy fresh produce from Chinese vendors, given both the stereotypes of Chinese as dirty and the specific warnings from the health department, seems to reflect a case of consumerism overcoming all.

91. "John Chinaman Called Menace," *Los Angeles Times,* April 14, 1914, II1.

92. LACHD/City, *AHR, 1912,* 60.

93. Raymond Lou, "Chinese American Vendors of Los Angeles: A Case of Resistance, Political Organization and Participation," *Integrated Education* 19, nos. 3–6 (1982): 88–91.

94. 1912 is the first year the LACHD/City included the fruit and vegetable inspector's report.

95. LACHD/City, *AHR, 1912,* 59.

96. LACHD/City, *AHR, 1913,* 73.

97. For a comparative example of public health and Mexicans in Los Ange-les, see Natalia Molina, "Illustrating Cultural Authority: Medicalized Repre-sentations of Mexican Communities in Early Twentieth Century Los Angeles," *Aztlán: A Journal of Chicano Studies* 28 (Spring 2003).

98. LACHD/City, *AHR, 1912,* 74.

99. LACHD/City, *Annual Report of Department of Health of the City of Los Angeles, California, for the Year Ended June 30, 1915,* 58, SRLF; hereafter cited as *AHR, 1915.*

100. Initially, the city constructed three new market buildings on city prop-erty, with plans to build more. On ordinances relating to the marketplace, see L.A. City Ordinance (hereafter cited as Ord.) No. 27371, New Series (hereafter cited as N.S.); Ord. No. 26146, N.S.; and Ord. 28972, N.S. The first ordinance related to fruits and vegetables was No. 26146, which was then superseded by No. 27371 and then No. 28972. All ordinances can be found in LACA.

101. Burton Hunter, an employee of the city's Bureau of Budget and Effi-ciency, described the ordinance regulating prices as "an emergency measure, it being equipped for the immediate preservation of the public peace, health and safety." He provided no further elaboration. Hunter, *Evolution of Municipal Organization,* 151.

102. Ord. No. 27371, N.S. It is unclear how the public market vendors were able to reduce their prices so dramatically and still survive financially. It may be that the city lowered the stall rental rates.

103. LACHD/City, *AHR, 1913,* 73.

104. LACHD/City, *AHR, 1915,* 59.

105. "Chinese Must Clean Up"; "John Chinaman Called Menace."

106. LACHD/City, *AHR, 1915,* 59, 63.

107. Ord. No. 40783, N.S., September 3, 1920.

108. In his 1918 report, Frank Mefford makes no mention of Chinese but comments on the markup of strawberry prices by the Japanese Berry Growers Association. LACHD/City, *Annual Report of Department of Health of the City of Los Angeles, California, for the Year Ended June 30, 1918,* 82, SRLF.

109. Marc Weiss makes this point very clearly. He argues that in Los Angeles, "because the beauty of the surroundings and luxuriance of the lifestyle were such an important part of the sales pitch, which was carefully targeted to the middle and upper classes of the rural and urban American and middle west, public action to preserve physical image was a key element of the growth and sales strategy of the real estate sector." See Marc Weiss, *The Rise of the Community Builders: The American Real Estate Industry and Urban Land Planning* (New York: Columbia University Press, 1987), 81.

110. Ord. No. 17136, N.S., Section 12.

111. The history of zoning in Los Angeles usually begins with *Ex parte Hadacheck,* the case of J. C. Hadacheck, a brickyard owner who fought to keep his business in operation after the area was rezoned. See Weiss, *Rise of the Community Builders,* and Fogelson, *Fragmented Metropolis,* 254–62. For studies that address the racialization of space in Los Angeles, see Avila, *Popular Culture.*

112. "Chink Laundries Given More Time to Vacate Sites," *Labor Press,* 20 September 1912. In other respects, the paper was indisputably anti-Chinese. Anti-Asian immigration sentiment, for instance, is present in many articles that appeared during this same period.

113. Weiss, *Rise of the Community Builders,* 84.

114. Paul Ong describes how Chinese laundries emerged as an important business in the segmented labor market of late-nineteenth-century California. He argues that because of their location and dominance in the field Chinese laundries threatened white businessmen. Ong posits that Chinese laundries ceased to be a significant threat to the white community by the late 1800s, but my research shows that in Los Angeles Chinese laundries generated these kinds of conflicts again in the 1910s. Paul Ong, "An Ethnic Trade: The Chinese Laundries in Early California," *Journal of Ethnic Studies* 8, no. 4 (1981): 95–113.

115. Ord. No. 19563, N.S. All appeals to the city council I have been able to locate were initiated by Chinese launderers, with one exception. In 1915, the neighbors of a Japanese laundry petitioned the city council to close the laundry because it violated the residential district ordinance. The petitioners claimed that the Japanese laundry lowered their property values. CP 1424 (1915), LACA.

116. 118 U.S. 356, 374, 6 S. Ct. 1064. The court ruled unconstitutional local legislation that existed only because of "hostility to the race and nationality to which the [Chinese launderers] belonged."

117. David Bernstein, "Lochner, Parity, and the Chinese Laundry Cases," *William and Mary Law Review* 41, no. 1 (1999): 211–94.

118. *Ex parte Quong Wo*, California Supreme Court, October 19, 1911, 220–34.

119. *In the Matter of the Petition of San Chung, for Writ of Habeus Corpus*, California Appellate Court, vol. 11, October 1909, 511–23. I thank Ian Fusselman for bringing this case to my attention and for sharing his legal expertise with me.

120. CP 150 (1912), LACA.

121. CP 154 (1912), LACA.

122. LACC/M, January 30, 1912.

123. The council meeting minutes do not provide a citation for this case, and I have been unable to locate it.

124. CP 886, (1912), LACA.

125. CP 2446 (1912), LACA.

126. Lee describes aliens as "outsiders who are inside, [who] disrupt the internal structure of cultural formation as it defines itself vis-à-vis the Other; their presence constitutes a boundary crisis. Aliens are always a source of pollution." Robert Lee, *Orientals*, 3. Lee builds on the work of Douglas, *Purity and Danger*.

127. According to the ordinance, the city council should have referred the petition to the fire commissioner, not the health commissioner. Dr. Powers acknowledged this misdirection only *after* he had given his approval of the French laundry. CP 2446 (1912), LACA.

128. Mrs. Snodgrass claimed that the signatures represented 60 percent of her neighbors. The council file does not contain a copy of this petition, although Snodgrass's formal request for an exemption refers to it.

129. CP 416 (1912), LACA.

130. CP 807 (1912), LACA.

131. The Chinese Consolidated Benevolent Association, or Chinese Six Companies, its mainstream name, was founded in 1882, the same year as the Chinese Exclusion Act. The organization was an alliance of six companies functioning as a benevolent association. The Chinese Six Companies worked with the Chinese consul in the United States to achieve its goals. Its leadership was composed of diplomats and scholars from China, as well as merchants and businessmen. Sheong Chen, *Being Chinese, Becoming Chinese American* (Urbana: University of Illinois Press, 2002), 12–13.

132. Chinese Six Companies secretary Wong Ngi Tong to Mayor George Alexander, May 1, 1912, filed with CP 809 (1912), LACA.

133. CP 809 (1912), LACA.

134. Ibid.

135. CP 808 (1912).

136. LACC/M, September 10, 1912.

137. The records of the city health department for this period do not mention Native Americans. Since my focus is on the role of public health in shaping racial categories, I limit the discussion here to Mexicans and Chinese.

138. For more on Manifest Destiny, see Horsman, *Race and Manifest Destiny*.

139. Quoted in Robert F. Heizer and Alan M. Almquist, *The Other Californians: Prejudice and Discrimination under Spain, Mexico, and the United States*

to 1920 (Berkeley: University of California Press, 1971), 140. First quoted in Horsman, *Race and Manifest Destiny*, 210.

140. William S. Bennett and William Paul Dillingham, *Abstracts of Reports of the Immigration Commission*, vol. 1 of the Dillingham Commission Reports to the U.S. Senate (Washington, DC: Government Printing Office, 1911), 256.

141. Richard Griswold del Castillo, *La Familia: Chicano Families in the Urban Southwest, 1848 to the Present* (Notre Dame, IN: University of Notre Dame Press, 1984), 93, 96–97, 102.

142. Albert Camarillo, *Chicanos in a Changing Society: From Mexican Pueblos to American Barrios in Santa Barbara and Southern California, 1848–1930* (Cambridge, MA: Harvard University Press, 1979), 105, 109, 113, 118–20. Raquel Casas places women at the center of her analysis of the transition that took place after the U.S. annexation of California. She argues that Mexican women who married white men were often able to retain their culture and raise their children in bicultural and bilingual households. See Maria Raquel Casas, " 'In Consideration of His Being Married to a Daughter of the Land': Interethnic Marriages in Alta California, 1825–1875" (PhD diss., Yale University, 1998).

143. Records for the period immediately before the turn of the century contain only one complaint involving Mexicans, which was lodged against a Mexican tamale vendor. LACC/M, 1890–1900.

144. The records of the BHC were not preserved from 1911 to 1935.

145. Unlike most other city departments and agencies, the Los Angeles City Housing Commission did note the presence of Mexicans. The commission discusses Mexicans beginning with its first annual report, in 1907. See Housing Commission Reports, LACA.

2. CAUGHT BETWEEN DISCOURSES OF DISEASE, HEALTH, AND NATION

1. LACHD/County, untitled two-page addendum (cover page reads, "I beg to transmit herewith report of our department for inclusion in the annual report") to "First Annual Report of the Health Officer of Los Angeles County, California, for the Year Ending June 30, 1917" (handwritten version), DHS, hereafter cited as "AHR, 1917 (handwritten)" (addendum hereafter cited as "addendum to AHR, 1917").

2. For other studies that link nationalism and racism, see Mark Reisler, *By the Sweat of Their Brow: Mexican Immigrant Labor in the United States, 1900–1940* (Westport, CT: Greenwood Press, 1976); Ghassan Hage, *White Nation: Fantasies of White Supremacy in a Multicultural Society* (Annandale, NSW: Pluto Press, 1998).

3. In discussing the fortification of the U.S.-Mexican border in the 1920s, George Sánchez points out the irony of a process that turned Mexicans into outsiders in the Southwest, an area that had once belonged to Mexico. George Sánchez, *Becoming Mexican American*, ch. 4.

4. The different interests and agendas represented in the search for order during the early twentieth century are analyzed in Wiebe, *Search for Order;*

Rodgers, "In Search of Progressivism"; Hofstadter, *Age of Reform;* William Deverell and Tom Sitton, *California Progressivism Revisited* (Berkeley: University of California Press, 1994).

5. The sources shaping public opinion were varied: "[N]ewspaper editorials, magazine articles, and books alerted readers to the perceived dangers of this influx. Anti-immigrant hyperbole, including Massachusetts Republican Senator Henry Cabot Lodge's 'Efforts to Restrict Undesirable Immigration,' sociologist Guy Halifax's 'The Immigrant Scourge,' and Immigration Restriction League spokesman Prescott Hall's 'Selection of Immigration,' captivated nativists' imagination by emphasizing the undesirability of southern and eastern Europeans. Their arguments fueled the fear inherent in the demand for greater restriction and persuaded many to put aside the ideal of America as an asylum for the oppressed." See John Lund, "Boundaries of Restriction: The Dillingham Commission," *History Review* 6 (December 1994): 40–57.

6. "The provision providing for the commission stipulated that it consist of nine members; three Senators, three Congressmen, and three individuals to be appointed by the President. The bi-partisan commission formed in the following weeks. . . . [President Theodore] Roosevelt appointed Charles P. Neill from the Department of Labor, California Commissioner of Immigration William R. Wheeler, and political economy professor Jeremiah Jenks of Cornell University." Ibid.

7. William S. Bennet and William Paul Dillingham, *Abstracts of Reports of the Immigration Commission,* vols. 1–2 of the Dillingham Commission Reports to the U.S. Senate (Washington, DC: Government Printing Office, 1911).

8. Ibid.

9. The quote in the heading is drawn from Francis A. Walker, "Restriction of Immigration," *Atlantic Monthly* 77 (June 1896): 828.

10. For perspectives on Social Darwinism, see Robert C. Bannister, *Social Darwinism: Science and Myth in Anglo-American Thought* (Philadelphia: Temple University Press, 1979), and Mike Hawkins, *Social Darwinism in European and American Thought, 1860–1945* (Cambridge: Cambridge University Press, 1997).

11. Walker, "Restriction of Immigration," 828. Walker was director of the 1870 and 1880 U.S. censuses, commissioner of Indian Affairs, an educator, and president of MIT from 1881 to 1897.

12. By 1917, the U.S. Public Health Service had formalized these procedures and published examination guidelines. See U.S. Public Health Service, *Regulations Governing the Medical Inspection of Aliens* (Washington, DC: Government Printing Office, 1917).

13. Bennet and Dillingham, *Abstracts,* 1:26–27.

14. Ibid., 1:34–35.

15. Those volumes focused primarily on the Japanese. As this chapter will show, despite the passage of the Gentlemen's Agreement in 1907–8, curtailing most future immigration from Japan, yellow peril fears persisted. Mexicans, on the other hand, were not perceived as especially threatening. Thus, even when the commission focused on the Southwest, relatively little attention was paid to Mexicans. They were dismissed as sojourners. William P. Dillingham, Harry A.

Millis, and U.S. Immigration Commission, *Immigrants in Industries: Pt. 25. Japanese and Other Immigrant Races in the Pacific Coast and Rocky Mountain States*, vols. 23–25 of the Dillingham Commission Reports to the U.S. Senate (Washington, DC: Government Printing Office, 1911); Bennet and Dillingham, *Abstracts.*

16. Despite the intense focus on Asians and Mexicans, at least one Los Angeles public health official raised concerns over the new breed of European immigrants. In 1914, Arthur Potts, chief sanitary inspector for the city health department, appealed to Los Angeles Health Commissioner Dr. L. M. Powers to fund three additional sanitary inspectors. Potts feared an influx of immigrants due to the opening of the Panama Canal. He singled out southern European immigrants as having "absolutely no idea of modern sanitation." No additional inspectors were appointed, however, and Potts's concern seems to have dissolved promptly. See LACHD/City, *Annual Report of Department of Health of the City of Los Angeles, California, for the Year Ended June 30, 1914,* SRLF.

17. See ch. 1 for a discussion of the Chinese Exclusion Act.

18. Almaguer, *Racial Fault Lines,* 181. See also Yuji Ichioka, *The Issei: The World of the First Generation Japanese Immigrants, 1885–1924* (New York: Free Press, 1988). On intergenerational differences in Japanese communities, see Lon Kurashige, *Japanese American Celebration and Conflict: A History of Ethnic Identity and Festival in Los Angeles, 1934–1990* (Berkeley: University of California Press, 2002); David Yoo, *Growing up Nisei: Race, Generation, and Culture among Japanese Americans of California, 1924–49* (Urbana: University of Illinois Press, 2000).

19. Weber, *Dark Sweat,* 48–53.

20. Ricardo Romo, *East Los Angeles: History of a Barrio* (Austin: University of Texas Press, 1983), 61. See ch. 1 for a discussion of the settlement patterns of Los Angeles's nonwhite populations. George Sánchez, *Becoming Mexican American,* 70–72.

21. Albert Camarillo refers to this movement to the East Side as the barrioization of the Mexican community. Camarillo, *Chicanos,* 53. For other histories of East Los Angeles, see Rodolfo Acuña, *A Community under Siege: A Chronicle of Chicanos East of the Los Angeles River, 1945–1975* (Los Angeles: Chicano Studies Research Center Publications, University of California, Los Angeles, 1984), *Occupied America: A History of Chicanos* (New York: Harper and Row, 1988), and *Anything but Mexican: Chicanos in Contemporary Los Angeles* (New York: Verso Press, 1996); Richard Griswold del Castillo, *The Los Angeles Barrio, 1850–1890: A Social History* (Berkeley: University of California Press, 1979); David Gutiérrez, *Walls and Mirrors: Mexican Americans, Mexican Immigrants, and the Politics of Identity* (Berkeley: University of California Press, 1995); George Sánchez, *Becoming Mexican American.* For a fictional account of life in East Los Angeles, see Helena Maria Viramontes, *The Moths and Other Stories* (Houston, TX: Arte Público Press, 1985).

22. Kim, *Bitter Fruit.*

23. A special county charter (adopted June 2, 1913) placed the LACHD/County under civil service regulations. Dr. Pomeroy was hired under these regulations. See LACHD/County, "History and Functions," pamphlet, July 1970, 6, DHS.

24. Dr. Pomeroy hired two full-time employees, a sanitary inspector, a stenographer, a deputy health officer, and a rural nurse. The advisory council was likely composed of members of agencies that worked with the LACHD/County, including the Red Cross, life insurance companies, and railroad companies. LACHD/County, "Progress Report, Health Officer, March 1 to June 30 1917," 2–4, 7, DHS; hereafter cited as Progress Report, 1915–17.

25. LACHD/County, "First Annual Report of the Health Officer of Los Angeles County, California, for the Year Ending June 30, 1917" (typed version), 2, B of S/R; hereafter cited as "AHR, 1917 (typed, B of S/R)."

26. Pomeroy was born in 1883 and grew up in Louisville, Kentucky.

27. Briggs was one of the main public health investigators in the case of Mary Malone, more popularly known as "Typhoid Mary." Judith Leavitt argues that a range of institutional actors, including public health officials, prosecutors, and journalists, singled out Mary Malone from among the thousands of typhoid carriers then present in New York because she was Irish. The Irish occupied a low position within the racial hierarchy that dominated the East Coast. In Dr. Pomeroy's public health work on the West Coast, however, he rarely mentioned the Irish. Other West Coast officials were similarly silent. The presence of Mexicans may have helped the Irish become white more quickly than in other regions of the country. See Judith Walzer Leavitt, *Typhoid Mary: Captive to the Public's Health* (Boston: Beacon Press, 1996).

28. "Dr. J. L. Pomeroy Dead from the Flu," *Los Angeles Herald Examiner,* March 25, 1941.

29. The county also included cities incorporated under the laws of the state of California but not incorporated into the city of Los Angeles. I use the terms *urban* and *rural* as general descriptors; the areas referenced do not necessarily correspond to the terms *incorporated* and *unincorporated*. Driving was such a routine part of health inspectors' jobs that Ventura Motor Oil used Jonathan Kirkpatrick, a Los Angeles County Health Department inspector, as their poster boy in an ad entitled "25,000 Miles without Motor Repair," *Los Angeles Times,* May 25, 1924, F14.

30. It is not clear how these cases came to the attention of the LACHD/County. Only the requests for payments to the physicians from the LACHD/County to the B of S remain, not the case files.

31. The services provided by the LACHD/County were intended as a form of preventative care. The Charities Department oversaw both the county hospital and relief services. For residents in outlying areas, lack of transportation could prove a formidable obstacle in seeking medical services at the county hospital.

32. Diphtheria is a bacterial disease that infects the body in the throat or under the skin. A vaccine was developed in the 1930s that virtually eradicated the disease.

33. LACHD/County, Progress Report, 1915–17, 1.

34. LACHD/County, addendum to AHR, 1917, 4.

35. Ibid., 3.

36. Ibid.

37. LACHD/County, "Annual Report (Incomplete) of the Los Angeles County Health Department for the Year Ending June 30, 1917" (typed), 16, DHS; hereafter cited as "AHR, 1917 (incomplete, typed, DHS)."

38. Ibid., 17.

39. Ibid.

40. Ibid.

41. LACHD/County, AHR, 1917 (typed, B of S/R), 15.

42. I do not have a precise count of the number of African Americans in Los Angeles County during this period. Birth and death rates give some indication of how small the population was, however. From June 1916 to July 1917, health officials recorded only 1 "Negro" birth out of 1,543 total births, and only 9 deaths out of 1,377 total deaths. Ibid. Secondary literature on African Americans in Los Angeles is sparse but seems to confirm that the population was not large. Faced with institutional racism, African Americans provided for their own communities through various institutions, including churches, settlement houses, and clubhouses. This practice of turning inward to their own communities partially explains the lack of institutional records regarding African Americans in the county. See Evelyn Brooks Higginbotham, *Righteous Discontent: The Women's Movement in the Black Baptist Church, 1880–1920* (Cambridge, MA: Harvard University Press, 1993). My research on African American women in Los Angeles concurs with the findings of these studies. Natalia Molina, " 'A Monument to the Race Women': The Sojourner Truth Industrial Home," unpublished paper.

43. I do not have figures for Chinese in Los Angeles County. Health officials note that they composed a small percentage in the county's population. Birth and death rates give an indication of the size of the Chinese population in the county. From June 1916 to July 1917, health officials recorded only 1 Chinese birth out of 1,543 total births. Out of 1,377 deaths during this same time period, health officials recorded 2 deaths. Ibid.

44. The agreement also allowed newly married women ("picture brides") whose marriages had been arranged from a distance to join their husbands in the United States. For an analysis of Japanese immigration policy, see Roger Daniels, *The Politics of Prejudice: The Anti-Japanese Movement in California and the Struggle for Japanese Exclusion* (Berkeley: University of California Press, 1977), 58–64.

45. Japanese were able to circumvent the laws by purchasing land in the name of their American-born children and then holding the land in the name of a corporation. Kevin Leonard, " 'Is That What We Fought For?' Japanese Americans and Racism in California: The Impact of World War II," *Western Historical Quarterly* 21, no. 4 (1990): 464.

46. John Modell, *The Economics and Politics of Racial Accommodation: The Japanese of Los Angeles, 1900–1942* (Urbana: University of Illinois Press, 1977), 99.

47. Ibid., 39. For a history of Japanese in Los Angeles, see Donald Teruo Hata and Nadine Ishitani Hata, "Asian-Pacific Angelenos: Model Minorities and Indispensable Scapegoats," in *20th Century Los Angeles: Power, Promotion, and Social Conflict*, ed. Norman M. Klein and Martin J. Schiesel (Claremont, CA: Regina, 1990); Brian Hayashi, *For the Sake of Our Japanese Brethren: Assimilation, Nationalism, and Protestantism among the Japanese of Los Angeles, 1895–1942* (Stanford, CA: Stanford University Press, 1995); Kurashige, *Japanese American Celebration;* Leonard, " 'Is That What We Fought For?' "

48. See the February 1920 issue of the *Grizzly Bear*. Pomeroy originally prepared this article as a talk, which he presented at the San Dimas Church (n.d.). San Dimas was known for its orange and lemon groves. The now famous "Sunkist" name originated in San Dimas, although it was first spelled "Sunkissed." See "A Brief History of San Dimas, CA," retrieved May 4, 2005, from www.wemweb.com/traveler/towns/27sandim/27histor/history.html.

49. Dr. John Pomeroy, "The Japanese Evil in California" (talk presented at the San Dimas Church, n.d.), DHS. It is unclear if Dr. Pomeroy meant "worked in groups" when he wrote "formed work cooperatives." In this case, they could have driven up wages by banding together. The definition of *cooperatives* meant that the Japanese had control over the entire process—from planting to harvesting to distributing to selling their crops. In this case, they might have driven up prices through competition, not wages. I cite both the unpublished version of this talk and the article because they are slightly different. Also, the unpublished talk has handwritten notes discussed in the following point.

50. Ibid., 2.

51. Pomeroy and others apparently saw no irony in their use of American gender ideology to judge a group they considered inassimilable. Ibid.; Ralph Fletcher Burnight, *The Japanese in Rural Los Angeles County*, Sociological Monograph 16 (Los Angeles: Southern California Sociological Society, University of Southern California, 1920).

52. John Pomeroy to B of S, May 16, 1918, OD 1333 H, B of S/R. There is no indication of whether the Children's Bureau came to the aid of the health department. For a history of the development of the Children's Bureau, see Robyn Muncy, *Creating a Female Dominion in American Reform, 1890–1935* (New York: Oxford University Press, 1991). See also the Children's Bureau Records, National Archives, College Park, MD.

53. For a fascinating analysis of France's population campaign, see Cheryl Koos, "Engendering Reaction: The Politics of Pronatalism and the Family in France, 1919–1944" (PhD diss., University of Southern California, 1996).

54. Theodore Roosevelt, "The Strenuous Life," in *The Strenuous Life: Essays and Addresses* (1901; reprint, St. Claire Shores, MI: Scholarly Press, 1970), quoted in Gail Bederman, *Manliness and Civilization: A Cultural History of Gender and Race in the United States, 1880–1917* (Chicago: University of Chicago Press, 1995), 94.

55. See, for example, "Phelan Ends So. Cal. Tour with Anti-Japanese Plea, Warns of Subtle Invasion and Predicts Victory of Land Bill," *Los Angeles Evening Herald*, October 25, 1920.

56. Burnight, *Japanese*.

57. Reisler, *By the Sweat*.

58. William Deverell, "Plague in Los Angeles, 1924: Ethnicity and Typicality," in *Over the Edge: Remapping the American West,* ed. Valerie Matsumoto and Blake Allmendinger (Berkeley: University of California Press, 1999), 172–74.

59. Pomeroy, in making this comment in a letter to the B of S, blithely linked all Japanese in the United States to those in Japan, regardless of generation, citizenship, or time spent in the United States. John Pomeroy to B of S, June 19, 1919, B of S/R.

60. Typhoid fever is caused by bacteria *(Salmonella typhi)* and typically is transmitted through contaminated water or food. Symptoms include a sudden sustained fever, severe headache, nausea, and prolonged loss of appetite. Untreated, typhoid cases can be fatal. In developed countries, vaccinations have reduced both the risk and the incidence of typhoid fever, but it remains a deadly problem in many parts of the developing world.

61. The unstated agenda underlying health officials' decision to regulate Japanese farmers because of the alleged unsanitary conditions of the farms was likely an effort to protect local white farmers from having to compete with the Japanese.

62. Ord. No. 26146, cited in John Pomeroy to B of S, June 19, 1919, B of S/R.

63. John Pomeroy to B of S, June 19, 1919, B of S/R.

64. John Pomeroy to B of S, August 4, 1922, B of S/R.

65. Reisler, *By the Sweat,* 25.

66. Sánchez, *Becoming Mexican American,* 55. See also Howard Markel and Alexandra Stern, "Which Face? Whose Nation? Immigration, Public Health, and the Construction of Disease at America's Ports and Borders, 1891–1928," *American Behavioral Scientist* 42, no. 9 (1999): 1314–31; Alexandra Stern, "Buildings, Boundaries."

67. Gutiérrez, *Walls and Mirrors,* 46–48; Camille Guerin-Gonzales, *Mexican Workers and American Dreams: Immigration, Repatriation, and California Farm Labor, 1900–1939* (New Brunswick, NJ: Rutgers University Press, 1994), 24. Neil Foley also sees Mexicans' positionality as more fluid in relation to whites and African Americans in central Texas. Foley argues that Mexicans were not white enough to claim equality with white Americans but were white enough to escape the worst features of Jim Crow South. Foley, *White Scourge.*

68. LACHD/County, AHR, 1917 (typed, B of S/R).

69. *CSBHMB,* October 1916, 202.

70. LACHD/County, addendum to AHR, 1917, 3.

71. The quote in the heading is drawn from *CSBHMB,* November 1916, 239. Typhus symptoms can include high fever, headaches, chills, and severe muscular pain, followed by the appearance of a rash. The disease is serious and can be fatal for the very young, the elderly, and those already in poor health. See Encyclopedia Britannica Online, "Typhus," retrieved June 18, 2005, from http://search.eb.com/eb/article?tocId=9074006&query=typhus=typhus.

72. Encyclopedia Britannica Online, "Typhus."

73. In addition to the twenty-two Mexican railroad workers, one person in the city of Los Angeles contracted typhus; two people in the county (but not from the railroad camps) were affected; and no details are available regarding the one remaining case. There were also outbreaks in areas outside the county, including seven cases in Banning (Riverside County); one in Livermore (Alameda County); one in Bakersfield (Kern County); and three in Tulare (Tulare County). *CSBHMB,* June through December 1916.

74. LACHD/County, "Memorandum for Article on the Los Angeles County Health Office in 1917 Anniversary Number *Los Angeles Tribune,*" DHS.

75. The emergency staff included quarantine guards, special nurses, physicians, health officers, and a bacteriologist. LACHD/County, Progress Report,

1915–17, 6. Also, in October 1916, Pomeroy appointed Dr. Charles Dirks health officer and placed him in charge of assessing the occurrence of communicable diseases in the county. Dirks's epidemiological mapping was based on surveys of county pharmacists and school districts. See LACHD/County, AHR, 1917 (typed, B of S/R), 7; and John Pomeroy, "Efficient Public Health Service for Rural Districts and Small Towns" (unpublished paper, n.d., c. 1920), 4, DHS.

76. LACHD/County, "Calender [sic] of Progress, County Health Office, Los Angeles," n.d. (but dates range from April 21, 1915, to June 30, 1917), DHS. Delousing procedures at this time typically involved routine baths, laundering clothes, and cleaning living quarters. Using cyanide gas was not common because of the effects chemical gases could have on the central nervous system. In Prussia, however, the military did use hydrocyanic acid (HCN) to fumigate gypsy dwellings and railway carriages. The key ingredient was sodium cyanide and also included sulfuric acid and water. See Paul Julian Weindling, *Epidemics and Genocide in Eastern Europe* (New York: Oxford University Press, 2000), especially ch. 4, "The First World War and Combating Lice."

77. LACHD/County, "Memorandum for Article." Dr. Pomeroy did not reference any other county studies or surveys that focused on these communities, nor do the B of S/R refer to any studies.

78. What may have appeared to health officials as random movements may in fact have been Mexican laborers resisting inferior working conditions by searching for better employment elsewhere. LACHD/County, AHR, 1917 (incomplete, typed, DHS), 15.

79. Dr. Howard D. King, "Some Sanitary Aspects of the Mexican Revolution," *Southern California Practitioner* 29, no. 3 (1914): 63.

80. Dr. King also wrote about the problems of miscegenation and how "negro" laundresses spread tuberculosis. See his "Frequency of Tuberculosis among Negro Laundresses," *Journal of Outdoor Life*, 11, no. 275 (1914), and "Miscegenation: An Old Social Problem," *New Orleans Medical and Surgical Journal* 66, no. 534 (1914).

81. The health reports do not specify if there were any connections between the neighborhoods they investigated and the workers in the camps. It was not uncommon for men who worked in the railway yards to return home to a neighboring barrio at night. Jeff Garcilazo argues that railway employees preferred work in the railroad yards because it allowed them to work for the railroad company but keep a separate residence outside the company housing. These jobs often went to married men with families. Jeffrey Marcos Garcilazo, "Traqueros: Mexican Railroad Workers in the United States, 1870 to 1930" (PhD diss., University of California, Santa Barbara, 1995), 150–51.

82. LACHD/County, "Quarterly Report for the Period Ending December 31, 1916," 2, B of S/R; hereafter cited as QHR, December 1916.

83. *CSBHMB*, November 1916.

84. In Los Angeles, the house court form of housing was generally associated with Mexicans. In a report that equated West Coast house courts with East Coast tenement houses, one housing inspector noted, "The Mexican [is] condemned to a one room shack." Los Angeles City Housing Commission, Second Annual Report, June 1909, 12, Housing Commission Reports, LACA.

85. H. F. Senftner, MD, Assistant Epidemiologist, Bureau of Communicable Disease, Special Report to James G. Cumming, MD, Director, Bureau of Communicable Disease of California State Board of Health, "A Report on the Investigations and Regulation of the Incident of Typhus Fever in Mexican Labor Camps in the Santa Fe System in California from October 5th to 18th, 1916, inclusive," by November 1, 1916, 2, DIHR. The first outbreak of typhus was at a Southern Pacific Railroad camp. There are no preserved records as to why Santa Fe camps were selected for this survey.

86. The floating camps were so named because they could be easily moved along the railroad lines to spots where the track needed replacement or repair.

87. Senftner, Special Report, 4.

88. Ibid.

89. "Regulations of the State Board of Health, to be adopted by the Railroads for the Control and Prevention of Typhus Fever," October 4, 1916, DIHR.

90. Like the Residence District Ordinance that disproportionately affected Chinese living in the city of Los Angeles, this regulation was racialized upon enforcement. See ch. 1 for a discussion of Los Angeles's nineteenth-century residential zoning laws.

91. Less than 10 percent of the camps had "any bathing facilities whatsoever." See Senftner, Special Report, 6.

92. County health officials reported "compelling" railroad laborers to take weekly baths in coal oil and hot water, implying, erroneously, that Mexicans had facilities for bathing but used them only when forced to do so. LACHD/County, QHR, December 1916, 2.

93. LACHD/County, "Memorandum for Article."

94. *CSBHMB*, December 1916, 337.

95. The quote in the heading is drawn from a letter from Mexican railroad laborers (Felipe Vaiz et al.) to the Mexican consul of Los Angeles, October 17, 1916, Foreign Consulate Records for Los Angeles, SRE/A. Senftner notes the delousing procedures as his sole contact with Mexicans.

96. Senftner, Special Report, 2.

97. *CSBHMB*, November 1916, 255.

98. Felipe Vaiz et al. to Mexican consul, October 17, 1916, SRE/A, translation mine.

99. Ibid.

100. Ibid.

101. LACHD/County, AHR, 1917 (incomplete, typed, DHS).

102. LACHD/County, Progress Report, 1915–17, 5.

103. Paul Taylor, *Mexican Labor in the United States Imperial Valley* (Berkeley: University of California Press, 1930), 56–58.

104. Jeff Garcilazo argues that the Santa Fe and other railroad companies encouraged Mexican men to bring their families to live in company housing rent free in order to increase efficiency and loyalty from their workers. Garcilazo, "Traqueros," 85–86.

105. *CSBHMB*, October 1916, cover.

106. Vicente Rafael, "White Love: Surveillance and National Resistance in the U.S. Colonization of the Philippines," in *Cultures of United States Imperialism,* ed. Amy Kaplan and Donald Pease (Durham, NC: Duke University Press, 1993), 185–218. Rafael argues that these types of photographs flatten out identity, causing individuals to be seen merely as racial types.

107. *CSBHMB,* November 1916, 239.

108. "Precautionary Measures Taken by Board of Health in Mexico City to Prevent Spread of Typhus," *New York Times,* November 7, 1915; "Typhus in Mexico," *New York Times,* December 27, 1915.

109. LACHD/County, AHR, 1917 (typed, B of S/R), 12.

110. The BHC routinely blamed the origins of diseases on specific countries. The commissioners explained that the origins of Asiatic cholera were always in India. While this was accurate, the health commissioners seemed more concerned with accessing blame than preventing the disease as they made this assertion before explaining prevention, warning signs, or cures. BHC/M, March 1, 1893, 1:353. On the origins of cholera, see Rosenberg, *Cholera Years;* LACHD/County, untitled report that opens with "I hereby submit my report of work done for quarter ending September 30, 1916," 4, DHS; hereafter cited as QHR, September 1916.

111. *CSBHMB,* November 1916, 278.

112. Ibid.

113. LACHD/County, QHR, September 1916, 5.

114. Markel and Stern, "Which Face?"; McKiernan-Gonzalez, "Fevered Measures"; Stern, *Eugenic Nation.*

115. LACHD/County, AHR, 1917 (typed, B of S/R), 17.

116. The year of the typhus outbreak, county health workers also discovered that wells in the San Gabriel Valley contained contaminated water that caused dysentery. The report notes only that the department "discovered and corrected" the source of the water's pollution. LACHD/County, "Calender [sic] of Progress," 6.

117. LACHD/County, QHR, September 1916.

118. LACHD/County, AHR, 1917 (typed, B of S/R), 16–17.

119. LACHD/County, "Calender [sic] of Progress."

120. Health officials espoused hygiene as the first step in physical and social improvement. Whorton, *Crusaders for Fitness.*

121. LACHD/County, AHR, 1917 (typed, B of S/R), 16–17.

122. LACHD/County, "Quarterly Report for the Period Ending March 31, 1917," 4, B of S/R.

123. George Sánchez, *Becoming Mexican American,* 94.

124. California State Immigration and Housing Commission officials considered Mexicans to be an "indispensable" part of the workforce. They hoped to improve housing conditions for Mexicans. See "Talk delivered by L. T. Mott, Chief Housing Inspector, Fifth Conference of the 'Friends of the Mexicans,' Pomona College, December 5–6, 1925," folder 13, carton 46, DIHR.

125. LACHD/County, AHR, 1917 (typed, B of S/R), 16.

126. LACHD/County, AHR, 1917 (incomplete, typed, DHS), 14.

127. Romo, *History of a Barrio,* 61. See ch. 1 for a discussion of the settlement patterns of L.A.'s nonwhite populations.

128. LACHD/County, AHR, 1917 (typed, B of S/R), 16–17.

129. Ibid., 16.

130. Taylor, *Mexican Labor,* 40–41.

131. M. Ganiey, "Characteristics of the Mexican," *Railway Age Gazette,* November 20, 1912, 529.

3. INSTITUTIONALIZING PUBLIC HEALTH IN ETHNIC LOS ANGELES

1. "Mexican Situation Is Considered Here," *Riverside Enterprise,* June 17, 1924.

2. Cited in Reisler, *By the Sweat,* 185 n. 21.

3. For a discussion of the growth of industry in Los Angeles after 1920, see Bernard Marchand, *The Emergence of Los Angeles: Population and Housing in the City of Dreams, 1940–1970* (London: Pion, 1986), 65–67. Mark Reisler describes the movement of Mexicans into industrial jobs and the hostile reaction by organized labor to Mexicans' entrance into the industrial workforce. Reisler, *By the Sweat,* 96–117, 67–68.

4. "Mexican Situation."

5. LACHD/County, "First Annual Report of the Health Officer of Los Angeles County, California, for the Year Ending June 30, 1917" (typed version), 16–17, B of S/R; hereafter cited as "AHR, 1917 (typed, B of S/R)." See ch. 2 for details about interactions between health officials and Mexicans prior to 1920.

6. "Mexicans in Los Angeles," *Survey* 44 (1920): 715–16.

7. "Better Babies Their Slogan," *Los Angeles Times,* September 23, 1917.

8. Kenneth Neubeck and Noel Cavenaze provide a helpful discussion of gendered racism within the context of welfare. Kenneth Neubeck and Noel Cazenave, *Welfare Racism: Playing the Race Card against America's Poor* (New York: Routledge, 2001), 29–35.

9. "Better Babies Their Slogan."

10. "Filth, Disease, and Poverty Rampant at Old San Gabriel," *Los Angeles Times,* January 21, 1917.

11. See ch. 2 for details.

12. "Housing in Belvedere and Maravilla," *Monthly Labor Review* 16 (1925): 161.

13. Guerin-Gonzales, *Mexican Workers,* 45.

14. Quoted in Luis Leobardo Arroyo, "Power and Place: Re-Shaping Mexican Identities in Los Angeles, 1900–1930" (Working Paper 25, Julian Samora Research Institute, Michigan State University, East Lansing, 1996), 3.

15. Vicki Ruiz demonstrates that although Japanese farmers may have sometimes employed Mexicans, both still occupied a lower position in the racial hierarchy. In 1930s El Monte, for example, both groups attended segregated schools and were not allowed to sit next to whites in the town's movie theater. Nonetheless, during the 1933 El Monte Berry Strike, similarly aggrieved Japanese employers and Mexican laborers fought against one another rather than work together against common oppression. Ruiz, *Cannery Women,* 75–77.

16. LACHD/County, untitled report that begins with "I beg to transmit herewith report of the County Health Department for the Calendar Year ending January 1, 1921," 20, DHS, hereafter cited as AHR, 1920.

17. John Pomeroy to B of S, April 1, 1924, B of S/R. A ditch in Belvedere, for example, became a prime site for dumping waste, to the chagrin of nearby residents.

18. LACHD/County, AHR, 1920, 17.

19. John Pomeroy to B of S regarding request for establishment of local offices of supply stations at Sherman and Belvedere, April 16, 1919, B of S/R.

20. LACHD/County, "Calender [sic] of Progress, County Health Office, Los Angeles," n.d. (but dates range from April 21, 1915, to June 30, 1917), 2, DHS.

21. Romo, East Los Angeles, 81.

22. The historian Ricardo Romo describes this area as becoming predominantly Mexican in the early 1920s. Romo, East Los Angeles. Real estate and manufacturing developers had tried to gain municipality status for Belvedere in 1927. Such a move would have resulted in increased costs in the form of taxes and would have likely made it more difficult for working-class Mexicans to afford the area. George Sánchez, Becoming Mexican American, 3.

23. Robert McLean, That Mexican as He Really Is, North and South of the Rio Grande (New York: Fleming H. Revell, 1928), 147.

24. Los Angeles City School System Research Department, "Ethnological Study of the Mexicans," unpublished paper, quoted in Mexican Fact-Finding Committee, Mexicans in California: Report of Governor C. C. Young's Mexican Fact Finding Committee (Sacramento: California State Printing Office, 1930), 176.

25. In 1920, the county estimated total population (including the city) at 936,455; in 1927, the total was 2,206,694. See Ira V. Hiscock, A Survey of Public Health Activities in Los Angeles County, California (Los Angeles: Los Angeles County Bureau of Efficiency, 1928), 11–12. This was the first analytical survey of the activities of the LACHD/County. The Los Angeles Board of Efficiency commissioned Hiscock (who was a professor in the Department of Public Health at Yale University and the author of evaluations of numerous health departments throughout the country) to do the study.

26. LACHD/County, "Annual Report of County Health Office to Board of Supervisors for Calendar Year 1923," 34, DHS, hereafter cited as AHR, 1923.

27. LACHD/County, untitled report that begins with "I beg to submit herewith, annual report of the Health Department, Los Angeles County, for the year ending December 31, 1921," 8, DHS; hereafter cited as AHR, 1921.

28. Ibid.

29. See ch. 2 for a discussion of this epidemic.

30. Memo, John Pomeroy to B of S regarding "cleanup" work in the Belvedere and Laguna districts, August 12, 1916, B of S/R.

31. "Development of East Side Shows Phenomenal Gain in Eight Years," Health News (California Department of Public Health), April 1929, 3.

32. Hiscock, Survey of Public Health, 13.

33. House Committee on Immigration and Naturalization, Hearings before the Committee on Immigration and Naturalization, House of Representatives, 70th Cong., 1st sess., 1928, 52.

34. Bubonic plague attacks the lymph nodes. Typically, the plague bacterium is spread through flea bites. Fleas feed on the blood of rats and squirrels that carry the *Yersinia pestis* bacteria and then pass the bacteria on to humans. In addition to enlarged lymph glands, bubonic plague symptoms include high fever, shivering, vomiting, and headaches. Pneumonic plague, which attacks the lungs, is also caused by *Yersinia pestis*, but it is not commonly spread through flea bites. Instead, it develops when plague bacilli introduced into the air as spray droplets (emitted when an infected individual coughs) lodge in people's respiratory tracts. Even today, pneumonic plague is deadly. If left untreated, it claims the lives of nearly 100 percent of its victims (for untreated bubonic plague, the fatality figure is 50 percent).

35. "Disease Spread Checked," *Los Angeles Times,* November 6, 1924, A1–A2.

36. Guadalupe Samarano, Luciana's husband, died on October 25. A neighbor who had attended Luciana's funeral also died on October 25. Five days later, two more members of the Samarano family died. The next day, four more friends and family members of the Samaranos died. They all lived at one of four residences in the Clara Street neighborhood. "Governor Gratified at End of Plague Menace," *Los Angeles Times,* November 16, 1924, A1–A2. For an insightful analysis of the plague, see Deverell, *Whitewashed Adobe,* ch. 5, "Ethnic Quarantine." Deverell argues that city leaders promoted two dichotomous images of Los Angeles—the salubrious, sunny city advertised across the country and the shack-filled, disease-ridden areas inhabited by Mexicans. According to this line of reasoning, the plague came to be seen as "typical" as the inferior housing that had come to be so closely linked to this community.

37. "Pneumonic Plague Quarantine," *Monthly Bulletin of the Los Angeles Health Department,* November 1924, 3–5. The quarantined area was bordered by the Los Angeles River and by Alameda, Macy, and Alhambra Streets. "Quarantine for Plague Area Lifted," *Los Angeles Times,* November 14, 1924, A1–A2.

38. Ibid.

39. Memo, John Pomeroy to B of S, December 10, 1923, B of S/R.

40. John Pomeroy to B of S, December 24, 1924, B of S/R.

41. "Pneumonic Plague Quarantine," *Monthly Bulletin of the Los Angeles Health Department,* November 1924, 4.

42. Ibid., 3–5.

43. Both victims had attended the Samarano funeral. John Pomeroy, "Report on the Expenditures of Plague Prevention," submitted to B of S, December 15, 1924, B of S/R.

44. "Pneumonic Plague Quarantine." The article describes how the nurses "set aside about six square blocks as a quarantined area." A memo to the B of S from Dr. Pomeroy states that a three-block quarantine of this area had already been initiated on November 1, 1924. Memo, John Pomeroy to B of S, December 10, 1924, B of S/R.

45. Memo, John Pomeroy to B of S, December 10, 1923, B of S/R.

46. "Pneumonic Plague Quarantine." The newspaper articles focused mainly on the area of the original quarantine. An article entitled "No Spread of Disease" in the *Los Angeles Times* (November 7, 1924), for instance, referred to the Belvedere restricted area, almost in passing, as "a few city blocks also under

quarantine." It is unclear why the media focused less on Belvedere. The area may have seemed less noteworthy at the time, given the low number of plague victims and the near certainty that these represented "contact cases" rather than new outbreaks. Or perhaps it was Belvedere's outlying position, distant from the city center, that lessened health officials' concern.

47. "Three Plague Deaths and Four New Cases in Los Angeles as Epidemic Revives Again," *New York Times*, November 7, 1924.

48. For an analysis of the rumors that circulated among Chinese during the 1900 bubonic plague epidemic in San Francisco, see Shah, *Contagious Divides*, 133, 35–36.

49. "Pneumonic Plague Takes Seven More Victims," *New York Times*, November 3, 1924, 14.

50. "Rat Clean-up in City Urged," *Los Angeles Times*, November 19, 1924, A3.

51. "No Spread of Disease," A1–2, 2.

52. "Disease Spread Checked," A2.

53. "No New Pneumonic Cases," *Los Angeles Times*, November 8, 1924, 2.

54. During San Francisco's 1900 bubonic plague epidemic, Chinese residents were suspected of spreading the disease. Chinatown was quarantined (in Los Angeles, the Chinatown area was not closed off in 1900, but health officials did conduct an investigation). In *Contagious Divides*, the historian Nayan Shah makes a compelling argument that in the early twentieth century medical racial profiling put all Asian immigrants under suspicion, which in turn made them subject to heightened medical and public health screenings. For example, Chinese immigrants on Angel Island (the West Coast's foremost immigration station for Asian immigrants) underwent prolonged bacteriological testing. Newly arrived immigrants could be detained for weeks. Shah also forcefully demonstrates how health officials quarantined Chinatown not just because the first plague victim resided there but also because they suspected Chinese bodies and homes to be more likely to harbor disease. Many of the same health officials who had been involved in the 1900 episode in San Francisco played prominent roles during the 1924 outbreak in Los Angeles. Wilfred Kellogg, for example, was the San Francisco City Health Department's bacteriologist and the first person to suspect that Wing Chung Ging, a Chinese laborer who lived in Chinatown, was the bubonic plague's first victim. In 1924, Kellogg was the director of the California State Department of Health's hygiene laboratory. U.S. Public Health Service employee Dr. N. E. Wayson, who had served as chief medical officer on Angel Island earlier in the century, was directly involved in plague containment efforts in 1924. See Shah, *Contagious Divides*, 179–203, 120.

55. "Disease Spread Checked," A2.

56. "Los Angeles Plague of 1924–25," in *Encyclopedia of Plague and Pestilence*, ed. George C. Kohn (New York: Facts on File, 1995), 206.

57. "Pneumonic Plague Takes More Victims," *New York Times*, November 3, 1924, 14.

58. "Disease Spread Checked," A1.

59. John Pomeroy to B of S regarding "Report of Special Programs on Sanitary Work in relation [*sic*] to Plague Prevention," February 9, 1925, B of S/R.

60. "Harbor Health Survey," January 29, 1925, *Los Angeles Times*, A2.

61. John Pomeroy, "Efficient Public Health Service for Rural Districts and Small Towns" (unpublished paper, n.d., c. 1920, DHS), 6.

62. John Pomeroy, "The Public Health Center," *California and Western Medicine* 35, no. 3 (September 1931): 4. From their inception, the health centers created conflict between public health officials and private physicians. Physicians labeled the health centers a socialist experiment because they provided free medical care to those in need. Many private physicians feared that the centers would take away paying clients. The county health department's responsibilities were limited to the unincorporated communities in the county. When incorporated cities began contracting the department's services, tensions between private physicians and county health officials increased further and threatened to culminate in the loss of key public services (see ch. 4 for details).

63. LACHD/County, AHR, 1920, 30.

64. Ibid., 20.

65. Ibid., 21.

66. John L. Pomeroy, "The Principles of the Health Center Movement and Their Application in Los Angeles County" (paper presented at a meeting of the League of California, Health Officers' Section, September 20, 1927).

67. Interestingly, the superintendent of charities, who oversaw the county hospital, blamed the increase in patients not on Mexicans, as other reports had, but on the successful effects of Los Angeles boosters in enticing Easterners to move to Los Angeles. Superintendent of Charities to B of S, regarding the Over-Crowded Conditions at the County Hospital and Farm, October 27, 1921, B of S/R.

68. Health centers were prepared to provide only preventative care, so the county hospital should not have directed any individuals already in need of medical attention to the health centers. Ira Hiscock, *Survey of Public Health,* 13.

69. A 1925 county health department memo describes Simons Brick Yard as adjacent to Belvedere, with "a population of 1,052 persons, living in 235 buildings, making 4.4 persons per building." Memo, E. J. Bumiller, Sanitary Officer, to John Pomeroy, regarding "Plague Campaign Survey for the month of June, ending June 30, 1925," August 26, 1925, B of S/R. Simons Brick Company was considered one of the six largest company employers of Mexicans. "L.A. Tenements and the Bubonic-Pneumonic Plagues," *Municipal League of Los Angeles Bulletin* 2, no. 7 (1925): 3. William Deverell provides an insightful analysis of Simons Brick Yard in Deverell, *Whitewashed Adobe,* ch. 4, "The Color of Brickwork Is Brown." For a fictional account of Simons Brick Yard, see Alejandro Morales, *The Brick People* (Houston, TX: Arte Público Press, 1992).

70. LACC/M, April 15, 1920.

71. John Pomeroy to B of S, April 25, 1921, B of S/R. Population demographics were not included in the letter; thus it is hard to say how many Mexicans and African Americans lived in Duarte. Overall, African Americans did not exceed 1 percent of the population in the county.

72. John Pomeroy to B of S, October 14, 1923, B of S/R.

73. LACHD/County, "Annual Report 1925 Los Angeles County Health Department," 39, 40, DHS; hereafter cited as AHR, 1925.

74. LACHD/County, AHR, 1923, 40.

75. John Pomeroy to B of S, October 14, 1923, B of S/R.

76. Ibid.

77. LACHD/County, "History and Functions," pamphlet, July 1970, 7.

78. John Pomeroy to B of S, March 12, 1923, and June 6, 1923, B of S/R. Dr. Pomeroy made his request to lease land in Maravilla to the B of S twice.

79. John Pomeroy to B of S, October 14, 1923, B of S/R.

80. "Welfare Center Will Be Opened with Ceremony," April 13, 1929, *Los Angeles Times,* 3.

81. Notable officials included Dr. W. M. Dickie, Director of the State Department of Public Health, Surgeon S. B. Grunn of the U.S. Public Health Service, council members and mayors of area cities, and heads of medical organizations. See "Health Center Opened: Ceremony Conducted at New East Unit with Many Public Welfare Workers Attending," *Los Angeles Times,* April 17, 1929, A3.

82. LACHD/County, AHR, 1921, 11.

83. Richard Meckel, *Save the Babies: American Public Health Reform and the Prevention of Infant Mortality* (Baltimore: Johns Hopkins University Press, 1990), 26–32.

84. Pomeroy's part-time predecessor had not collected any data. The year 1915 marks the beginning of health-related data collection for the county.

85. LACHD/County, "Annual Report (Incomplete) of the Los Angeles County Health Department for the Year Ending June 30, 1917" (typed), 9, DHS; hereafter cited as "AHR, 1917 (incomplete, typed, DHS)."

86. I use 1927 as a cutoff date here because the LACHD/County AHRs for the years 1929–30 and 1930–31 (the reports run from July 1 to June 30) do not include a birth chart in their vital statistics reports, which are on pp. 81–82 and 26–27, respectively.

The figures for African Americans appear to be a statistical artifact of the very small size of the black population. There is no discussion of African American IMRs, and very little regarding African Americans in general, in the LACHD/County AHRs for this period.

87. At one point, the combined problem of gastrointestinal and communicable diseases accounted for about half the IMR cases in the Los Angeles area. "Analysis of Vital Statistics Showing the Most Economical and Efficient Method to Reduce Infant Mortality," September 27, 1918, 7, B of S/R; Hiscock, *A Survey of Public Health,* 44.

88. Health officials attributed the 1920 rise in IMRs among Mexicans to this epidemic. LACHD/County, AHR, 1920, 35.

89. LACHD/County, AHR, 1925, 80.

90. LACHD/County, AHR, 1917 (incomplete, typed, DHS), 9.

91. Japanese IMRs were only slightly higher than whites'. Health officials rarely did more than mention this fact in passing.

92. LACHD/County, "Annual Report of County Health Officer to Board of Supervisors, for Calender [sic] Year 1919," 15, DHS; hereafter cited as AHR, 1919.

93. In 1936, the city registrar and city health officer of El Paso attempted to reclassify Mexicans' racial status from "white" to "colored" in birth and death records. While they claimed they were trying to keep in accordance with U.S.

Census guidelines, members from the Mexican American community protested on grounds that such a reclassification would further marginalize them. See Mario T. García, "Mexican Americans and the Politics of Citizenship: The Case of El Paso, 1936," *New Mexico Historical Review* 59, no. 2 (1984): 187–204; Neil Foley, "Partly Colored or Other White: Mexican Americans and Their Problem with the Color Line," in *Beyond Black and White: Race, Ethnicity, and Gender in the U.S. South and Southwest* (College Station: Texas A&M University Press, 2004), 130.

94. For instance, in 1920 health providers concluded that both of these factors contributed to that year's epidemic of infantile diarrhea. LACHD/County, AHR, 1920, 35.

95. Ibid., 17.

96. Ibid., 35.

97. LACHD/County, untitled report that begins with "I herewith submit my report of work done for quarter ending September 30, 1916," 4, DHS.

98. Mexican Fact-Finding Committee, *Mexicans in California*, 184.

99. LACHD/County, AHR, 1920, 20.

100. LACHD/County, AHR, 1923.

101. LACHD/County, AHR, 1920, 20.

102. Foley, *White Scourge;* Montejano, *Anglos and Mexicans*, 223–25.

103. Such strategies were very much in keeping with the attitudes of the time. Pearl Ellis, who worked in the Americanization Department of the Covina City School District (in Los Angeles County), wrote a book based on her experiences working with Mexicans that advocated the same sorts of policies the LACHD/County did. She advocated training Mexican girls in the areas of sewing, food preparation, home nursing, and parenting skills. According to Ellis, such training would be a "safeguard to the community." See Pearl Ellis, *Americanization through Homemaking* (Los Angeles: Wetzel, 1929).

104. Linda K. Kerber, *Women of the Republic: Intellect and Ideology in Revolutionary America* (Chapel Hill: University of North Carolina Press, 1980).

105. Gayle Gullett examines the various strategies used by women's groups to gain the vote in California, including drawing on their moral authority. Gullett, *Becoming Citizens*.

106. Paula Baker, "The Domestication of Politics: Women and American Political Society, 1780–1920," *American Historical Review* 89, no. 3 (1984): 620–47.

107. The quote in the heading is drawn from "Analysis of Vital Statistics," 8. The quote from Pomeroy appears in LACHD/County, AHR, 1917 (incomplete, typed, DHS), 9–10.

108. Most of the WBCs and childbirth programs that the county developed were for Mexicans, again highlighting the lower status of the Japanese in the regional racial hierarchy.

109. Pure-milk stations offered pasteurized milk, which was not otherwise readily available. The program developed when physicians began stressing the need for doctors to become more involved in directing mothers in the area of proper feeding of their babies in the late 1800s (a position sure to bolster their profession). As such, they began to advocate that nursing mothers both breast-feed and bottle-feed their babies. Because cow's milk was not pasteurized at this

time, municipal reformers, including doctors, established milk stations to distribute pasteurized milk. See Rima D. Apple, *Mothers and Medicine: A Social History of Infant Feeding, 1890–1950* (Madison: University of Wisconsin Press, 1987), 56–60.

110. Meckel, *Save the Babies,* 94–96.

111. LACHD/County, AHR, 1920, 43.

112. LACHD/County, "Memorandum for Article on the Los Angeles County Health Office in 1917 Anniversary Number *Los Angeles Tribune,*" DHS.

113. For example, the Pacific Electric Company, which had participated in the Belvedere cleanup (see ch. 2), joined forces with the health department to teach hygienic standards to their employees in accordance with WBC tenets. LACHD/County health officials also established WBCs in agricultural work camps. See "Analysis of Vital Statistics," 2–3.

114. LACHD/County, AHR, 1920, 20.

115. LACHD/County, AHR, 1917 (incomplete, typed, DHS), 11.

116. John Pomeroy to B of S, February 17, 1916, 1, B of S/R.

117. Settlement workers at the Rose Gregory Houchen Settlement, a Methodist community center in El Paso, did learn to speak Spanish to communicate with their Mexican clientele and offered a bilingual kindergarten program. Ruiz, *From out of the Shadows.* Historian Eve Carr also argues that "[a]lthough Houchen's programs were ultimately driven by goals of Americanization and religious conversion, the missionaries appear to have remained aware of the community's Mexican identity" and "worked to find a point of connection." Eve Carr, "Missionaries and Motherhood: Sixty-Six Years of Public Health Work in South El Paso" (PhD diss., Arizona State University, 2003), 134–35.

118. By contrast, workers at the Houchen settlement embraced a "melting pot" ideology. One missionary explained, "We assimilate the best of their culture, their art, their ideals, and they in turn gladly accept the best America has to offer." Quoted in Ruiz, *From out of the Shadows,* 37.

119. John Pomeroy to B of S, February 17, 1916, 1, B of S/R. In this letter, Pomeroy identified *both* Japanese and Mexican residents as threats. In practice, however, the county directed very few services toward the Japanese (the department's approach to the county's Japanese communities is discussed later in this chapter). Pomeroy also asserted that his estimation of the health threat posed by Mexicans was backed up by the independent assessments of staff from the California State Housing Commission, the Los Angeles County Department of Charities, and various local schoolteachers.

120. Mary Coman to B of S, July 20, 1916, B of S/R.

121. John Pomeroy to B of S, February 17, 1916, 2, B of S/R. In 1946, Latina/o parents sued four school districts in Orange County for segregating Mexican children. One of the school superintendents cited Mexicans' purported inferior hygienic standards as justification for segregation. Vicki Ruiz, " 'We Always Tell Our Children They Are American': Méndez v. Westminster and the California Road to Brown," *College Board Review,* no. 200 (Fall 2003): 26.

122. A similar charge of deliberate subterfuge was leveled against Chinese communities in San Francisco during the 1900 bubonic plague epidemic. See Shah, *Contagious Divides,* 133.

123. Mary Coman to B of S, July 20, 1916, B of S/R.

124. During the early twentieth century, infant welfare work was under-funded and had to rely heavily on volunteers. The increase of the number of WBCs in Los Angeles was made possible in part by the volunteer efforts of a phalanx of female reformers and middle- and upper-middle-class clubwomen who tackled an array of issues in their quest for social change. In the Midwest and on the East Coast, clubwomen and settlement house workers first began working with southern and eastern European immigrants in the 1890s. Meckel, *Save the Babies,* 124. The settlement house movement, and the involvement of white middle-class female reformers with immigrant women, has been thoroughly examined. The public health aspects of these reformers' work is less studied. Robyn Muncy, however, has traced the ways in which Hull House reformers were able to institutionalize their local reform efforts at the national level through the Children's Bureau, in part by "providing the Bureau with a scientific foundation for its authority." Muncy, *Creating a Female Dominion,* 86. For an examination of social reformers' many agendas, see Gwendolyn Mink, "The Lady and the Tramp: Gender, Race and the Origins of the American Welfare State," in *Women, the State, and Welfare,* ed. Linda Gordon (Madison: University of Wisconsin Press, 1990); Baker, "Domestication of Politics"; and Theda Skocpol, *Protecting Soldiers and Mothers: The Political Origins of Social Policy in the United States* (Cambridge, MA: Harvard University Press, 1992).

125. For more on Americanization programs geared toward women, see Sarah Deutsch, *No Separate Refuge: Culture, Class, and Gender on an Anglo-Hispanic Frontier in the American Southwest, 1880–1940* (New York: Oxford University Press, 1987); George Sánchez, " 'Go after the Women' "; Linda Gordon, *The Great Arizona Orphan Abduction* (Cambridge, MA: Harvard University Press, 1999); Ellis, *Americanization through Homemaking.*

126. Mary Bryant Dale, "Annals of the Maternal and Child Hygiene Bureau of the Los Angeles County Health Department: A Historical Survey, 1915–1944" (PhD diss., Yale University, 1945), 37.

127. In Los Angeles, where the regional racial lexicon defined Mexicans as the racial "others," clubwomen tended to focus their attentions on Mexican women rather than southern and eastern European immigrants. Members of the Montebello Women's Club, for example, volunteered at the Simons Brick Yard clinic. The Parent-Teachers' Association assisted with the predominantly Mexican users of the Duarte clinic. The El Monte clinic received the support of the vice consul of Mexico, the Cruz Azul (Blue Cross), and the Woman's Club of El Monte. The Cruz Azul was the Mexican equivalent of the Red Cross. Mexican women organized and operated chapters located throughout Mexican communities in California and Texas. In my research in the Foreign Consulate Records for Los Angeles, SRE/A, and the *El Heraldo de México* newspaper, the Cruz Azul did not become very involved in Los Angeles until the Depression. See also Francisco E. Balderrama and Raymond Rodríguez, *Decade of Betrayal: Mexican Repatriation in the 1930s* (Albuquerque: University of New Mexico Press, 1995), 37–39, 46–49; Gilbert G. González, *Mexican Consuls and Labor Organizing: Imperial Politics in the American Southwest* (Austin: University of Texas Press, 1999).

128. Alejandro Portes and Rubén G. Rumbaut, *Immigrant America: A Portrait* (Berkeley: University of California Press, 1990); Gary Gerstle and John Mollenkopf, eds., *E Pluribus Unum? Contemporary and Historical Perspectives on Immigrant Political Incorporation* (New York: Russell Sage Foundation, 2001).

129. Hiscock, *Survey of Public Health*, 42.

130. Ibid., 5. The Medical College of Evangelists, later renamed White Memorial Hospital, did not archive the records of the home delivery program. This Seventh Day Adventist College was founded in 1905–6 and was renamed Loma Linda University in 1961. Metropolitan Life Insurance also sponsored a home visiting nurse program for its Los Angeles area policyholders. The company began its visiting nurse program in East Coast cities in 1909. Meckel, *Save the Babies*, 129–30; Hoy, *Chasing Dirt*, 110–13.

131. LACHD/County, AHR, 1925, 60. The report does not give any indication of who paid and who did not. Patients made their own arrangements regarding confinement. Hiscock, *Survey of Public Health*, 41. An advertisement in *The Belvedere Citizen* in January 25, 1935, listed the cost of home delivery service by a doctor and trained nurse at $30 and compared that price to the hospital rate, which ranged from $35 to $65.

132. See "A History of Caring: The Early Years, 1913–1939," retrieved May 7, 2005, from the White Memorial Hospital Web site: www.whitememorial.com/content/about/history/early_years.asp.

133. I have been unable to locate specific information on the Orange Packers Association. The California Fruit Growers Exchange, incorporated in 1905, was the region's most well-known cooperative for marketing citrus. In 1952, the organization changed its name to Sunkist Growers, Inc. Each grower-member in the cooperative organization also belonged to a local association or district exchange. The Orange Packers may have been one of these local units. See Pitt and Pitt, *Los Angeles A to Z*.

134. LACHD/County, AHR, 1920, 40.

135. Charles J. Lang, *Who's Who in Los Angeles County, 1928–1929* (Los Angeles: Charles J. Lang, 1929).

136. LACHD/County, AHR, 1920, 40.

137. The original county hospital operated on a $4,000 budget with six staff members. The hospital contained one hundred beds and forty-seven patients. In 1930 the cornerstone for the current hospital building was laid, and construction was completed three years later. In 1968, to reflect the affiliation to the USC School of Medicine, the name was changed to Los Angeles County Hospital + USC Medical Center. I will refer to the facility as county hospital, as it was referred to during this period. See "Los Angeles County-USC Medical Center," retrieved May 7, 2005, from the Los Angeles Almanac Web site: www.losangelesalmanac.com/topics/Health/heo1.htm.

138. The birth registers were not preserved chronologically. The county hospital does not have an official archive. Administrators allowed me access to the records for research purposes. I did not have an entire set of registers to research, but this sample gives some indication of Mexicans' experiences with the hospital.

139. Although these were institutional reports, they circulated in the general public and contributed to an anti-Mexican sentiment. One letter to the *Los Angeles Times* reflects these attitudes. Under the headline "Expensive Neighbors," the writer, known only as "Much Discouraged," rhetorically asks why Mexicans do not naturalize at higher rates. He answers by asserting, "Our General Hospital, free clinics and half our schools are for our Mexican brother." *Los Angeles Times*, June 13, 1930, A4.

140. Emory S. Bogardus, "The Mexican Immigrant," *Journal of Applied Sociology* 11 (May–June 1927): 470–88.

141. I examined individual birth records and birth registers at Los Angeles County Hospital for 1920–25. I chose these years to assess the validity of the 1925 report.

142. Los Angeles County Hospital birth records for a six-month period between October 1921 and March 1922, Los Angeles County Hospital.

143. On the history of midwifery, see Frances Korbin, "The American Midwife Controversy: A Crisis of Professionalization," in Leavitt and Numbers, *Sickness and Health*, 217–25; Judith Walzer Leavitt, *Brought to Bed: Childbearing in America, 1750–1950* (New York: Oxford University Press, 1986); Judy Barrett Litoff, *American Midwives, 1860 to the Present* (Westport, CT: Greenwood Press, 1978); Joyce Antler and Daniel Fox, "Movement toward a Safer Maternity: Doctor Accountability in New York City, 1915–1940," *Bulletin of the History of Medicine* 50 (Winter 1976): 569–95; Natalia Molina, "Birthing with Their Hands: Mamás, Parteras, y Comadres—y Doctors, Tambien," unpublished paper, 1996.

144. One notable exception is Charlotte Borst's work, which examines European immigrant midwives in Milwaukee. Charlotte Borst, *Catching Babies: The Professionalization of Childbirth, 1870–1920* (Cambridge, MA: Harvard University Press, 1995). Another important reason for researchers' failure to evaluate the role of women of color in history is the bias that characterized the field of women's studies as it first emerged in the United States and lingers today. Women's history tended to focus mainly on middle-class white women from the East Coast. Antonia Castañeda addresses the fact that women of color have not been dealt with on their own terms. Gender is often taken as a monolith in women's history and in regionally specific Western history. Castañeda urges scholars to begin to correct these biases by crossing disciplinary boundaries and turning to postcolonial studies, critical theory, and third world feminist theory. See Antonia Castañeda, "Women of Color and the Rewriting of Western History: The Discourse, Politics, and Decolonization of History," *Pacific Historical Review* 61, no. 4 (November 1992): 501–34.

145. The two best-known studies examine African American midwives in the South and *Hispana* midwives in New Mexico. See Onie Lee Logan as told to Katherine Clark, *Motherwit: An Alabama Midwife's Story* (New York: E. P. Dutton, 1989) and Fran Leeper Buss, *La Partera: Story of a Midwife* (Ann Arbor: University of Michigan Press, 1980). The crucial role *parteras* play in contemporary immigrant communities in the United States has also begun to receive attention. Aída Hurtado, "A View from Within: Midwife Practices in South Texas," *International Quarterly of Community Health Education* 8, no. 4 (1987–88): 317–39.

146. See Sánchez, *Becoming Mexican American,* and Balderrama and Rodríguez, *Decade of Betrayal.*

147. Dr. Blanche Harris, director of the LACHD/County's Division of Maternity and Infant Hygiene, argued that decisions regarding midwifery should take into account local needs. Harris to Harold Fuller, Office of the Assistant to the Chancellor, New York University, April 28, 1930, National Archives, Washington, DC, RG 102, Entry #3 4-1-1-6, Central File 1929-32, box 373. For example, in 1920, Massachusetts revised its laws regarding notification of births to omit the mention of midwives. This revision made midwifery a nonlegal issue as long as midwives practiced only among "foreign born populations." Anna Rude, MD, "The Midwife Problem in the United States," *Journal of the American Medical Association* 81 (September 1923): 998.

148. Dr. H. N. Barnett, Director of Bureau of Child Hygiene, Texas, to Miss Ora Marshino, Division of Maternity and Infant Hygiene, Children's Bureau, July 10, 1930. National Archives, Washington, DC: RG 102, stack 530, row 46, cmpt. 2, shelf 2, box 413, entry, central file, 1929-32, box 367.

149. Anna Rude, MD, "The Midwife Problem in the United States" (paper presented at the annual meeting of the American Medical Association, San Francisco, June 1923), 1.

150. In Chicago, for example, midwives, and particularly immigrant midwives, had been at the center of controversies since the Progressive Era, when they were labeled as abortionists. See Leslie Reagan, "Linking Midwives and Abortion in the Progressive Era," *Bulletin of the History of Medicine* 69 (1995): 569-98.

151. From 1919 to 1920, the subject of midwifery came before the LACC only with regard to the amendment of the midwifery law, which was denied. CP 2902 (1919), LACA.

152. The minutes of the B of S make no mention of midwives during the years 1920-30. The indexes do not list midwives for these years, and I examined the minute books for 1920-23.

153. The BHC approved midwifery licenses until it was dismantled in 1911, after which point the city council approved midwifery licenses. In 1917, the California Medical Practice Act established midwifery law for the entire state. The act outlined the qualifications needed to obtain a midwife license. Educational requirements included four years of high school education and a year of instruction at a board-approved hospital, or an equivalent education. Applicants also needed to pass an exam and follow specified professional training and medical practice restrictions. All of the requirements privileged midwives who spoke English and had received their training in the United States. Unless a midwife already possessed these credentials before migrating to Los Angeles, formal training would have been difficult to obtain, as Los Angeles had no midwifery schools.

154. For the period 1900 to 1938, I located only one application denied by the city council, which was submitted by Mrs. George Wagner. The city council stated that while "[Mrs. Wagner] may have received a license to practice in Missouri and graduated at the School of midwifery in St. Louis, [this did] not necessarily qualify her for practicing midwifery in Los Angeles." Nonetheless, the

city council's position was irrelevant, since only one month earlier, the state legislature had passed a bill requiring all midwives to secure a state license from the state board of medical examiners. CP 2046 (1917), LACA.

155. LACHD/County, AHR, 1925, 71–72.

156. LACHD/County, untitled report that begins with "Subject: Annual Report for year 1924. I beg to transmit herewith, statistical report of the County Health Department," 42, DHS; hereafter cited as AHR, 1924.

157. California State Board of Health, *Twenty-eighth Biennial Report of the State Board of Health of California for the Fiscal Years from July 1, 1922, to June 30, 1924* (Sacramento: California State Printing Office, 1925), 108.

158. By contrast, the health workers at the clinic housed in the Houchen settlement actively discouraged the use of midwives. By 1930 the settlement house had opened up a six-bed maternity ward. Ruiz, *From out of the Shadows*, 38.

159. LACHD/County, AHR, 1925, 72.

160. LACHD/County, AHR, 1924, 35.

161. Rude, "Midwife Problem" [*JAMA* version], 987–92.

162. Ibid., 989.

163. The quote in the heading is drawn from *Boston Herald,* June 16, 1907. See ch. 2 for a discussion of Japanese settlements in the 1910s.

164. Pitt and Pitt, *Los Angeles A to Z.*

165. From 1910 to 1920, 25,592 Japanese immigrants settled in California. "The Jap Menace in California," *Los Angeles Times,* July 25, 1920, II1.

166. Ibid.

167. U.S. Bureau of the Census, *Sixteenth Census of the United States, 1940: Population, Characteristics of the Population,* vol. 2 (Washington, DC: Government Printing Office, 1943), 252.

168. LACHD/County, AHR, 1920, 35.

169. Ellis, *Americanization through Homemaking.* The article does not mention if Dr. Pomeroy also fired Dr. Hara. Because Dr. Pomeroy found out about the marriage months later, it is likely that Dr. Hara had finished the investigation and was no longer working for the county. The details surrounding the case speak to both the legal and informal rules surrounding race relations in the region. The couple first married at sea in hopes of having their interracial marriage recognized. When questions arose as to the legality of their marriage, they traveled to New Mexico to marry, since New Mexico had no statutes related to marriage between an "Oriental" and an American citizen. This highlights the different ideologies that informed other regional racial lexicons.

170. An average of 443 Japanese children were born each year from 1915 to 1920. On the basis of a typical birth rate of 64 per 1,000, there were 6,924 Japanese in the county. Pomeroy rounded up and down by a thousand to come up with the estimate of six thousand to eight thousand. LACHD/County, AHR, 1920, 31–32.

171. Ibid., 31.

172. "Analysis of Vital Statistics," 2.

173. LACHD/County, AHR, 1919.

174. Ibid.

175. Ibid.

176. The LACHD/County held sixteen WBCs, which they labeled "special conferences," for Japanese residents in the summer of 1918. Since they were designated as Japanese conferences, the clinics were most likely segregated. See "Conferences held from June 9th to October 1918," front matter in "Analysis of Vital Statistics."

177. Clinic staff examined 103 children and spoke to 68 mothers. LACHD/County, AHR, 1923, 27. The AHR does not state if this was a private school used by a public agency or a segregated public school.

178. LACHD/County, AHR, 1923, 31.

179. The county's Japanese residents tended to live in the rural areas, not the incorporated cities. So this approach only increased the illusion of a large Japanese presence in the county.

180. LACHD/County, "Memorandum for Article." The department was contradicting itself, however: the birth chart in LACHD/County, AHR, 1917 (typed, B of S/R), 28, shows that Japanese births constituted one-third of the births in the county, not the one-fourth noted in this memo.

181. LACHD/County, AHR, 1919, 9.

182. LACHD/County, AHR, 1920, 31.

183. The text for this talk (presented at a church in San Dimas, about thirty miles east of downtown Los Angeles) on the Japanese threat became the basis for a journal article Pomeroy published in 1920. See ch. 2 for further details.

184. The quote in the heading is drawn from "Jap Births Alarm Phelan," *Los Angeles Times,* July 6, 1919, IV11.

185. While President Roosevelt considered it the duty of middle- and upper-class white women to procreate, he also believed in sterilization for those who threatened the nation's "racial stock," including immigrants and the disabled. Daniel Kelves, *In the Name of Eugenics: Genetics and the Uses of Human Heredity* (Cambridge, MA: Harvard University Press, 1995), 73–74, 85–88, 93–94; Bederman, *Manliness and Civilization.*

186. Quoted in Allison Berg, *Mothering the Race: Women's Narratives of Reproduction, 1890–1930* (Urbana: University of Illinois Press, 2002), 1.

187. Wendy Kline, *Building a Better Race: Gender, Sexuality, and Eugenics from the Turn of the Century to the Baby Boom* (Berkeley: University of California Press, 2001); Stern, *Eugenic Nation.* For other important works on eugenics, see Martin Pernick, *The Black Stork: Eugenics and the Death of "Defective" Babies in American Medicine and Motion Pictures since 1915* (New York: Oxford University Press, 1996); Nancy Stepan, *The Hour of Eugenics: Race, Gender, and Nation in Latin America* (Ithaca, NY: Cornell University Press, 1991); Kelves, *In the Name.*

188. The precedent-setting case for forced sterilization involved a poor white seventeen-year-old woman named Carrie Buck. The Supreme Court upheld Virginia's decision to forcibly sterilize Buck because she was considered feeble-minded. See *Buck v. Bell* (1927).

189. Martin Pernick, "Eugenics and Public Health in American History," *American Journal of Public Health* 87, no. 11 (1997): 1767–72.

190. "Analysis of Vital Statistics," 2.

191. Ibid.

192. LACHD/County, "Quarterly Report for the Period Ending March 31, 1917," 4, B of S/R.

193. Modell, *Economics and Politics*. Lon Kurashige argues that some Japanese in Los Angeles engaged in processes of racial rearticulation in which they attempted to diffuse negative images of their communities. See Kurashige, *Japanese American Celebration*.

194. I am grateful for discussions with Charles Briggs, John McKiernan-Gonzalez, and David Sloane, which helped me tease out the possible motives involved in the Japanese Association's decisions.

195. "Babies Are Safe in Los Angeles," *Los Angeles Times,* October 28, 1934.

196. Ibid. Although it was written in 1934, I use this article to discuss the WBCs in the 1920s because it includes information regarding the opening of the WBCs.

197. LACHD/County, AHR, 1925, 71.

198. LACHD/County, AHR, 1920, 40.

199. Ibid., 42.

200. Ruiz, *From out of the Shadows,* 38; George Sánchez, " 'Go after the Women.' " Richard Meckel describes how health officials directed programs at mothers because health officials considered mothers the "natural caretakers of children." Meckel, *Save the Babies,* 119–23.

201. Ruiz, *From out of the Shadows.*

202. "Babies Are Safe."

203. Emory S. Bogardus, *The Mexican in the United States* (Los Angeles: University of Southern California, School of Research Studies, 1934).

204. Rude, "Midwife Problem" (paper version).

205. "Babies Are Safe."

206. Ibid.

207. LACHD/County, AHR, 1920, 42, emphasis in the original.

208. Ruiz, *From out of the Shadows.*

209. LACHD/County, AHR, 1924, 43.

210. Hiscock, *Survey of Public Health,* 42. LACHD/County, AHR, 1925, 62.

211. Interview with Wenceslao Orozco in Manuel Gamio, *The Mexican Immigrant, His Life Story* (Chicago: University of Chicago Press, 1931), 168. These issues continue to be salient today. In the late 1970s, ten working-class Chicanas sued Los Angeles County Hospital, claiming they had undergone forced sterilization. When the case went to court, the judge ruled on behalf of the hospital, citing language barriers and the breakdown of communication in his ruling. Carlos Vélez-Ibáñez, " 'Se Me Acabó la Canción': An Ethnography of Non-Consenting Sterilizations among Mexican Women in Los Angeles," in *Mexican Women in the United States: Struggles Past and Present,* ed. Magdalena Mora and Adelaida Del Castillo, 71–91 (Los Angeles: Chicano Studies Research Center, University of California, Los Angeles, 1980); Elaine Tyler May, *Barren in the Promised Land: Childless Couples and the Pursuit of Happiness* (New York: Basic Books, 1995), 123.

4. "WE CAN NO LONGER IGNORE THE PROBLEM OF THE MEXICAN"

1. The quote in the chapter title is drawn from BHC [LACHD/City], untitled annual report of the Board of Health Commissioners for the year ending June 30, 1937, 11, SRLF; hereafter cited as *AHR, 1937*. In an unusual departure from ordinary procedure, the board submitted a report on behalf of the city health department, apparently because the health department could not, due to the Depression.

2. MAM, 1930.

3. Tuberculosis is caused by slow-growing bacteria that thrive in the presence of abundant oxygen and blood. Thus the infection often targets the lungs. Pulmonary TB is the most common form of TB in the United States. A TB infection can be either latent or active. See "Tuberculosis," retrieved May 7, 2005, from the WebMD Web site: http://mywebmd.com/content.

4. The mayor's message stated that Mexicans' TB rates were high in comparison to rates among other groups, but the text provided neither a source for that assertion nor the raw data that would have allowed readers to make rate comparisons. MAM, 1930, 23.

5. Ibid.

6. Ruiz, *From out of the Shadows*.

7. The 1921 Immigration Act had initiated a quota system that became known as the national origins principle. Immigration from eastern and southern Europe was limited to 3 percent of the population of each designated European country's citizens in the United States at the time of the 1890 census. That amount was reduced to 2 percent under the 1924 Immigration Act.

8. The Box bill, HR 6741, proposed extending the quota restrictions to countries in the Western Hemisphere. Reisler, *By the Sweat*, 19 n. 19.

9. Later in this chapter, I discuss how both my research and the work of others do not support Box's statements. U.S. Congress, House Committee on Immigration and Naturalization, *Seasonal Agricultural Laborers from Mexico. Hearings January 28 and 29, February 2, 9, 11, and 23, 1926 on H.R. 6741, H.R. 7559, H.R. 9036*, 69th Cong., 2nd sess., 1926, 14, 15.

10. Similarly, Lisa Lowe examines how Asian Americans have been excluded from full social membership in the United States. Their exclusion began when they were allowed to immigrate to the United States during specific historical time periods as low-wage workers but were barred from citizenship, but it has continued long after immigration restrictions ceased. Nonetheless, the United States maintains the fiction of cultural and racial homogeneity for political and ideological reasons. Lisa Lowe, *Immigrant Acts: On Asian American Cultural Politics* (Durham, NC: Duke University Press, 1996).

11. Reisler, *By the Sweat*, 202–4.

12. Ibid., 207.

13. U.S. Congress, House Committee on Immigration and Naturalization, *Hearings before the Committee*, 60.

14. Reisler, *By the Sweat*, 210–11.

15. See ch. 2 for more on the *Grizzly Bear.*

16. Clarence Hunt's parents were from Virginia and Arkansas, but Hunt was a native Californian. Hunt was a thirty-second-degree Scottish Rite Mason. He was also on the board of directors of the Los Angeles County Anti-Asiatic Society beginning in 1919. Modell, *Economics and Politics,* 53 n. 73; Rockwell Dennis Hunt, *California and Californians* (Chicago: Lewis Publishing, 1926), 4:479.

17. *Grizzly Bear,* December 1927, 3.

18. Of course, race relations overall worsened within the context of the Depression. But we must be careful not to assume that the quality of race relations rises and falls with the state of the economy. Omi and Winant argue that "efforts to explain racial inequality as a purely social structure phenomenon are unable to account for the origins, patterning, and transformation of racial difference." See Omi and Winant, *Racial Formation,* 56. We must also be wary of arguments that privilege class as a driving force in history but classify race as ideological and epiphenomenal. See Barbara Fields, "Ideology and Race in American History," in *Region, Race, and Reconstruction: Essays in Honor of C. Vann Woodward,* ed. J. Morgan Kousser and James McPherson (New York: Oxford University Press, 1982), 143–77.

19. By contrast, Stephen Jay Gould carefully details the history of craniometry and IQ testing and how they were used to argue for the racial inferiority of certain groups. See Stephen Jay Gould, *The Mismeasure of Man* (New York: Norton, 1981).

20. Public health as a race-making institution did not function in isolation. The fortification of the border and the development of the Border Patrol were amongst the most significant racializing processes and institutions that developed at this same time. See Kathleen Anne Lytle Hernández, "Entangling Bodies and Borders: Racial Profiling and the U.S. Border Patrol, 1924–1955" (PhD diss., University of California, Los Angeles, 2002); Mae M. Ngai, "The Strange Career of the Illegal Alien: Immigration Restriction and Deportation Policy in the United States, 1921–1965," *Law and History Review* 21, no. 1 (2003): 69–108; Mae M. Ngai, *Impossible Subjects: Illegal Aliens and the Making of Modern America* (Princeton, NJ: Princeton University Press, 2004).

21. Edythe Tate-Thompson, *A Statistical Study of Sickness among the Mexicans in the Los Angeles County Hospital, from July 1, 1922 to June 30, 1924* (Sacramento: California State Board of Health, 1925).

22. The first LACHD/County AHR to mention Mexicans with TB was in 1920; see LACHD/County, untitled report that begins with "I beg to transmit herewith report of the County Health Department for the Calendar Year ending January 1, 1921," 19, 44, DHS; hereafter cited as AHR, 1920. The reports were usually brief and mainly qualitative.

23. "Mexicans in Los Angeles."

24. Frances Reeves, "Housing Problems of the Tuberculosis Clients in the Los Angeles County Central Welfare District" (master's thesis, University of Southern California, 1936); James Kincaid, "A Survey of 180 Unattached Tuberculosis Male Indigents in Los Angeles with the Emphasis on the Public Health Problem" (master's thesis, University of Southern California, 1939); Marian Oshrenko, "The Social Implications of Delay in Sanatorium Placement for Tuberculosis; A Study of Cases in Los Angeles County" (master's thesis, University of Southern California, 1941).

25. LACHD/County, "First Annual Report of the Health Officer of Los Angeles County, California, for the Year Ending June 30, 1917" (typed version), B of S/R.

26. U.S. Congress, Senate Committee on Public Health and National Quarantine, *Standardization of Treatment of Tuberculosis: Hearings before the United States Senate Committee on Public Health and National Quarantine,* 64th Cong., 1st sess., January 17, 1916.

27. Edythe Tate-Thompson to B of S, April 24, 1929, B of S/R. She also stated that she was concerned that migrants were coming to Los Angeles to seek free medical care at the facility, even though they had not resided in California for very long and thus had not yet paid taxes to the state. Among the patients Tate-Thompson used as an example of this reprehensible behavior were migrants from Iowa and Kansas.

28. Supervisor W. H. Holland of Olive View, Holland, to B of S, February 4, 1927, B of S/R.

29. Tate-Thompson, *Statistical Study of Sickness.*

30. See ch. 2.

31. Increasing standards of public health to fortify the border was not entirely new. Health officials in El Paso, which served as the major point of entry from Mexico to the United States, made similar pleas in 1917 during a typhus epidemic. Stern, "Buildings, Boundaries."

32. Edythe Tate-Thompson, "Migration of Indigent Tuberculosis Is Serious Problem," *Weekly Bulletin of the California State Department of Public Health* 8, no. 19 (June 15, 1929): 73–74.

33. California State Department of Public Health, *Thirty-First Biennial Report for the Fiscal Years July 1, 1928, to June 30, 1930* (Sacramento: California State Printing Office, 1931).

34. Ibid.

35. *Grizzly Bear,* December 1927, 3.

36. U.S. Congress, *Hearings before the Committee on Immigration and Naturalization, House of Representatives,* 70th Cong., 1st sess.

37. "For Control of Mexicans' Health," *Weekly Bulletin of the California State Department of Public Health* 7, no. 1 (1928): 2–3.

38. For a history of immigration to these ports of entry, see Markel and Stern, "'Which Face?'"; Kraut, *Silent Travelers;* Shah, *Contagious Divides;* Amy Fairchild, *Science at the Borders: Immigrant Medical Inspection and the Shaping of the Modern Industrial Labor Force* (Baltimore: Johns Hopkins University Press, 2003).

39. Douglas Baynton, "Disability and the Justification of Inequality in American History," in *The New Disability History: American Perspectives,* ed. Paul Longmore and Lauri Umansky (New York: New York University Press, 2001), 33–57.

40. Remsen Crawford, "The Menace of Mexican Immigration," *Current History* 31 (1930): 907.

41. Madison Grant, "Editorial: Immigration," *Eugenics: A Journal of Race Betterment* 3 (1930): 74.

42. Kenneth Roberts, "Wet and Other Mexicans," *Saturday Evening Post,* February 4, 1928, 10–11, 137–38, 41–42, 46; Kenneth Roberts, "The Docile Mexican," *Saturday Evening Post,* March 10, 1928, 40–41, 165–66; Kenneth

Roberts, "Mexicans or Ruin," *Saturday Evening Post,* February 18, 1928, 14–5, 142, 45–46, 49–50, 54.

43. Samuel J. Holmes, "Perils of the Mexican Invasion," *North American Review* 227 (May 1929): 615–23. There are no reports by the LACHD/County on how many Mexicans may have had tuberculosis *before* they entered the United States.

44. Crawford, "Menace of Mexican Immigration," 904.

45. By 1920, the sex ratio between Mexican-born men and women living in the United States was becoming more even, with the two groups numbering 276,526 and 209,892, respectively, according to the U.S. Census. Cited in Reisler, *By the Sweat,* 185 n. 20.

46. C. M. Goethe, "Other Aspects of the Problem," *Current History* 28 (August 1928): 767.

47. Samuel J. Holmes, "Peon Immigrants," *Eugenics: A Journal of Race Betterment* 1 (November 1928): 36.

48. Holmes, "Perils."

49. Goethe, "Other Aspects," 767–68.

50. Ibid., 768. Goethe does not cite where he obtained this information.

51. Crawford, "Menace of Mexican Immigration," 905.

52. Clark Davis argues that the Depression hit Los Angeles harder than any other city in the West. Clark Davis, *Company Men: White-Collar Life and Corporate Cultures in Los Angeles, 1892–1941* (Baltimore: Johns Hopkins University Press, 2000), 198.

53. Fogelson, *Fragmented Metropolis,* 79, 143.

54. Edward J. Escobar, *Race, Police, and the Making of a Political Identity: Mexican Americans and the Los Angeles Police Department, 1900–1945* (Berkeley: University of California Press, 1999), 79.

55. Lee Shippey, "Lee Side O' L.A.," *Los Angeles Times,* June 18, 1931.

56. Quoted in Balderrama and Rodríguez, *Decade of Betrayal,* 75.

57. CP 10789 (1931), LACA.

58. Mexican immigrants did not exceed 1 percent of the total immigrant population in the United States until 1910. In 1910 there were 221,915 Mexican immigrants (1.6 percent of the immigrant population); in 1920, 486,418 (3.5 percent); and in 1930, 641,462 (4.5 percent). In 1930, 38 percent (541,197) were second generation and almost 19 percent were third generation or more. Homer L. Hitt and Wilson T. Longmore, "A Demographic Analysis of First and Second Generation Mexican Population," *Southwestern Social Science Quarterly* 24 (1943): 138–49.

59. "State against Mexican Bars," February 24, 1921, 5.

60. Balderrama and Rodríguez, *Decade of Betrayal,* 45.

61. LACHD/County, "Health Department of Los Angeles County Annual Report Year Ended June 30, 1931," 1, DHS; hereafter cited as AHR, 1931.

62. Ibid.

63. Zdenka Buben, "Medical Social Work in a Public Health Department" (paper presented at the Conference of Social Work, 1930), DHS.

64. Discussing communicable diseases for all the preceding years was itself a significant departure from established reporting protocol. Dr. John Pomeroy,

"Remarkably Healthy Conditions Revealed by Vital Statistics Report—1931," 3, DHS.

65. LACHD/County, AHR, 1931 contained reports on "communicable diseases and race" and only referenced Mexicans. In LACHD/County, "Health Department of Los Angeles County Annual Report Year Ended June 30, 1937," DHS, hereafter cited as AHR, 1937, the Medical Social Service, Tuberculosis, Sanitation, and Vital Statistics Divisions all included special reports on Mexicans but no other racialized group.

66. Office of the Chief Administrative Officer, Department of Charities, January 26, 1939, box 64, B 111 c bb aaa (6), JAF.

67. LACHD/County, AHR, 1931, 76.

68. Buben, "Medical Social Work."

69. Interestingly, the report goes on to say, "On the other hand, the incidence of contagious diseases among Japanese is relatively low." Pomeroy, "Remarkably Healthy Conditions," 3.

70. This number was very large compared to 201 and 1,623 in 1923 and 1925, respectively. LACHD/City, *Annual Report of Department of Health of the City of Los Angeles, California, for the Year Ended June 30, 1924*, 12, SRLF; LACHD/City, *Annual Report of Department of Health of the City of Los Angeles, California, for the Year Ended June 30, 1923*, 10, SRLF; LACHD/City, *Annual Report of Department of Health of the City of Los Angeles, California, for the Year Ended June 30, 1925*, 18, SRLF.

71. The LACHD/City went before the LACC on February 26, 1926, and April 8, 1926, to ask for $15,000 each time to help fight the smallpox epidemic. LACC/M, February 23, 1926, and April 8, 1926.

72. El Paso had special significance, as the city was the major port of entry for Mexicans coming to the United States in the early twentieth century. George Sánchez, *Becoming Mexican American.*

73. LACC/M, January 2, 1934.

74. As noted in the introduction, county cities located outside Los Angeles city limits were unincorporated with respect to that city; they were, however, incorporated under the laws of the state of California. The county's unincorporated cities had to pay to contract public health services. Private physicians groups alleged that the county's public health centers took away their paying clientele. John L. Pomeroy, "Huntington Park Public Health Problem," in *Administration of Public Health: Viewpoints of Public Health Experts and Los Angeles County Medical Society*, ed. John L. Pomeroy (Los Angeles: Los Angeles County Health Department, 1934), 57–62.

75. Pomeroy, "Huntington Park."

76. CP 349 (1938), LACA. It is interesting that Mrs. Duncan used a derogatory term historically ascribed to African Americans. This suggests that her racial ideology was framed by a black and white paradigm, so perhaps she was not herself a native Angeleno.

77. The Mother's Bureau was a special all-female division of the police department; the officers used social work methods in their police work. Janis Appier, *Policing Women: The Sexual Politics of Law Enforcement and the LAPD* (Philadelphia: Temple University Press, 1998), 78–85.

78. CP 349 (1938), LACA.

79. Ruiz, " 'We Always Tell Our Children.' " Racialized communities fought for desegregation. Just a few years before Mrs. Duncan issued her complaint to the health department, a group of Mexican parents in Lemon Grove (in San Diego) refused to send their children to school when the school board proposed separate facilities—in a barn—for their children. The parents sued and won their case. See the documentary *The Lemon Grove Incident* (1985), dir. Frank Christopher, prod. Paul Espinosa, available from Espinosa Productions, espinosa@electriciti.com. Also see "School Segregation: The Social Reproduction of Inequality, 1870–1934," ch. 3, in Martha Menchaca, *The Mexican Outsiders: A Community History of Marginalization and Discrimination in California* (Austin: University of Texas Press, 1995).

80. BHC/M, April 27, 1938, 40.

81. Mary Odem's work challenges the notion of a monolithic "state" by showing the ways in which courts and parole officers enforced laws differently than lawmakers intended. Mary Odem, *Delinquent Daughters: Protecting and Policing Adolescent Female Sexuality in the United States, 1885–1920* (Chapel Hill: University of North Carolina Press, 1995).

82. The quote in the heading is drawn from Benjamin Goldberg, "Tuberculosis in Racial Types with Special Reference to Mexicans," *American Journal of Public Health* 19, no. 3 (1929): 274–84.

83. California Department of Public Health, *Thirty-Second Biennial Report for the Fiscal Years from July 1, 1930, to June 30, 1932* (Sacramento: California State Printing Office, 1933), 24.

84. The report's failure to note the total number of cases and the rates of other racial groups over the same time period exemplifies the uneven treatment accorded to Mexicans. Pomeroy, "Remarkably Healthy Conditions," 3.

85. California Department of Public Health, *Thirty-First Biennial Report*.

86. Baur, *Health Seekers*.

87. California Department of Public Health, *Thirty-Fourth Biennial Report for the Fiscal Years from July 1, 1934, to June 30, 1936* (Sacramento: California State Printing Office, 1937), 127.

88. California Department of Public Health, *Thirty-First Biennial Report*, 277.

89. Tate-Thompson, "Migration of Indigent Tuberculosis," 73.

90. LACHD/County, AHR, 1931, 18.

91. Aaron Zitner, "Davis' Apology Sheds No Light on Sterilizations in California," *Los Angeles Times*, March 16, 2003, A26.

92. Goldberg, "Tuberculosis," 275, 76.

93. These arguments are reminiscent of the paternalistic reasoning used during Reconstruction. Both scientists and everyday citizens contended that African Americans were incapable of taking care of themselves outside slavery. See Tera Hunter, *To 'Joy My Freedom*, 188–89. David McBride uses the term *sociomedical racialism* to describe the process by which people attributed high rates of tuberculosis and syphilis in African Americans in the early twentieth century to racial traits. David McBride, *From TB to AIDS: Epidemics among Urban Blacks since 1900* (Albany: State University of New York Press, 1991). James Jones

examines the Tuskegee study, from 1932 to 1972, in which a group of physicians claimed to be treating a group of black men with syphilis but were actually just studying the advanced effects of the disease. James H. Jones, *Bad Blood: The Tuskegee Syphilis Experiment* (New York: Free Press, 1981). For more on how the black body has been linked with specific epidemiological patterns, see Keith Wailoo, *Drawing Blood: Technology and Disease Identity in Twentieth-Century America* (Baltimore: Johns Hopkins University Press, 1999), and *Dying in the City*.

94. Emil Bogen, "Racial Susceptibility to Tuberculosis," *American Review of Tuberculosis* 24, no. 5 (1931): 522–31.

95. Report of the Los Angeles County Department of Charities, February 1938, box 64, B III 14 c bb aaa 6, p. 4, JAF. The report mentioned no other vector for infection, nor did it identify the methods used in conducting the investigation, thus leaving the scientific validity of the findings open to considerable question.

96. Report of the Bureau of Indigent Relief, September 1937, box 64, B III 14 c bb aaa (5), 5, JAF. The Mexican consul received a letter around this same time from a Mexican national who was a patient in the county hospital complaining of neglect in the hospital. Mexican consul to C. José Noriega, July 14, 1932, SRE/A.

97. Report of the Bureau of Indigent Relief, September 1937, box 64, B III 14 c bb aaa (5), 5, JAF.

98. Report to B of S from the Superintendent of Charities, August 7, 1933, p. 4, box 64, 14 a, bb, aaa (1), JAF. The county Charities Department did not track medical and charity cases separately.

99. After the passage of the Tydings-McDuffie Act in 1934, Filipinas/os in the United States were vulnerable to deportation campaigns since they were no longer considered nationals. See Dorothy Fujita-Rony, *American Workers, Colonial Power: Philippine Seattle and the Transpacific West, 1919–1941* (Berkeley: University of California Press, 2003). Health issues, such as tuberculosis, were one reason U.S. officials used as rationale to deport Filipinas/os. Emily Abel, " 'Only the Best Class of Immigration': Public Health Policy toward Mexicans and Filipinos in Los Angeles, 1910–1940," *American Journal of Public Health* 94, no. 6 (2004): 932–39.

100. At the time, the Bureau of Immigration was part of the Labor Department. Doak ordered the bureau to rid the country of illegal aliens who were using up taxpayers' dollars. Guerin-Gonzales, *Mexican Workers*, 79.

101. Abraham Hoffman, *Unwanted Mexican Americans in the Great Depression: Repatriation Pressures, 1929–1939* (Tucson: University of Arizona Press, 1974), 42.

102. George Sánchez, *Becoming Mexican American*, 215.

103. González argues that the Mexican consul took an active role in the repatriation of Mexicans by establishing the *Beneficencia Mexicana* to assist those Mexicans who wanted to repatriate. The consul did so to ensure that Mexicans would not join any Communist Party organizations, which were acting to protect the rights of Mexicans by protesting the Mexican government's denouncement of leftist unions, Mexicans' unemployment rates, and U.S. repatriation

programs. Gilbert G. González, *Mexican Consuls,* 78–81. On the role of the Mexican consulate in Los Angeles, also see Francisco Balderrama, *In Defense of La Raza: The Los Angeles Mexican Consulate and the Mexican Community, 1929–1936* (Tucson: University of Arizona Press, 1982).

104. Gardner Jackson, "Doak the Deportation Chief," *Nation,* March 18, 1931, 295–96, quoted in Guerin-Gonzales, *Mexican Workers,* 79. L.A. officials deliberately created an atmosphere of fear in hope that Mexicans would then voluntarily return to Mexico. For example, Director Visel strategically advertised an impending deportation roundup. Guerin-Gonzales, *Mexican Workers,* 80–81; Hoffman, *Unwanted Mexican Americans,* 44.

105. Hoffman, *Unwanted Mexican Americans,* 100–104, 26.

106. See Guerin-Gonzales, *Mexican Workers;* Hoffman, *Unwanted Mexican Americans;* Balderrama, *In Defense of La Raza;* Balderrama and Rodríguez, *Decade of Betrayal.* George Sánchez and David Gutiérrez's discussions of the Depression and repatriation provide insight into how these events helped shape ethnic identity, which I address in ch. 5. See George Sánchez, *Becoming Mexican American;* Gutiérrez, *Walls and Mirrors.*

107. Ngai, "Strange Career," 69. In 1930, six years after its formation, the Border Patrol came under scrutiny because of its uncontested practice of patrolling up to two hundred miles into the interior. While the House Immigration Committee viewed this practice as overstepping their power, the Transportation Section performed similar duties without any discussion outside of their department. In comparison, the county Department of Charities was allowed to function as an independent immigration bureau without any apparent check and balance system.

108. County Department of Charities to B of S, February 10, 1938, B of S/R.

109. County Department of Charities to B of S, October 18, 1938, B of S/R.

110. County Department of Charities to B of S, August 9, 1938, B of S/R.

111. Guerin-Gonzales, *Mexican Workers,* 90. For more on Mexicans' resettlement experience in Mexico, see 97–109. See also Balderrama and Rodríguez, *Decade of Betrayal.*

112. County Department of Charities to B of S, May 16, 1938, August 9, 1938, B of S/R.

113. During this same time period, the Mexican consul contacted the U.S. Immigration Service in Los Angeles to inform them that the Vice-Consul Ricardo Hill was having difficulty interviewing Mexican prisoners before they were deported and they wanted the problem rectified. Mexican consul to U.S. Immigration Service in Los Angeles, July 25, 1932, IV-329–1, SRE/A.

114. Harry E. Hull to J. C. Brodie, March 23, 1933, Immigration Bureau File, 55739/674, RG 85, NA, quoted in Reisler, *By the Sweat,* 231. The year 1882 marked the first federal Immigration Act. The act denied entry to any "lunatic, idiot, or any person unable to take care of himself or herself without becoming a public charge." In 1891, the federal government changed the wording from *unable* to *"unlikely* to take care of himself or herself without becoming a public charge." A 1907 law denied entry to anyone judged "mentally or physically defective." Changes to the act in 1917 added that immigrants with

certain abnormalities, including asthma, bunions, poor eyesight, and varicose veins, could be denied entry into the United States. See Baynton, "Disability." These laws were very important to a country that looked at incoming immigrants as a potential workforce. See Fairchild, *Science at the Borders.*

115. County Department of Charities to B of S, February 10, 1939, B of S/R.

116. Alfonso Pesquería to U.S. Immigration Service in Los Angeles, January 20, 1930, file 241.215.4, SRE/A.

117. County Department of Charities to B of S, February 10, 1938, B of S/R.

118. In 1923, Mexican Consul Lupián made a report to the SRE in Mexico regarding Mexican laborers who used hospital services in Chicago. He argued that although there were no formal studies regarding hospitalized Mexicans in the United States, the majority of these patients had suffered work-related accidents. Various letters throughout the 1920s from Mexican laborers across the Southwest to the consulate regarding their stays in hospitals because of work-related accidents support his statement. Mexicans who had been in the United States for at least one year were admitted into public hospitals without any problems. In the ideal scenario, their employers paid the hospital bills and then docked the injured employees half their pay until the hospital bills were paid off. But the various letters to the consulate from Mexican laborers who went to the hospital for work-related injuries and were later fired and then saddled with their medical bills prove otherwise. The consulate often served as an intermediary, contacting the employer on behalf of the laborer. Consul Lupián to the SRE, August 5, 1923, 27-4-59, 27-4-58, SRE/A.

119. County Department of Charities to B of S, August 9, 1938, B of S/R.

120. County Department of Charities to B of S, August 9, 1938, May 16, 1938, B of S/R.

121. County Department of Charities to B of S, February 10, 1939, B of S/R.

122. Report of the Bureau of Indigent Relief, September 1937, box 64, 5, JAF.

123. Ibid.

124. Ibid.

125. Hoffman argues that the intense drives for deportation ended in March 1931. He maintains that by 1935 Mexicans chose to remain in the United States rather than repatriate. Hoffman, *Unwanted Mexican Americans,* 64, 112. Sánchez argues that by 1935 the Mexican community in Los Angeles had been substantially transformed by deportations and repatriation. George Sánchez, *Becoming Mexican American,* 224–25. Guerin-Gonzales sees repatriations as slowing after 1932. Guerin-Gonzales, *Mexican Workers,* 94.

126. Guerin-Gonzales, *Mexican Workers,* 113–15.

127. For an insightful analysis of the Bracero Program, see Kitty Calavita, *Inside the State: The Bracero Program, Immigration, and the I.N.S, After the Law* (New York: Routledge, 1992).

128. LACHD/County, AHR, 1931, 26.

129. Pomeroy's cover letter for this report stated that the AHR for the year was not finished and they were therefore submitting this report. There is no pre-

served copy of the LACHD/County's AHR for 1927, and it is unclear if it was ever finished. LACHD/County, "Preliminary Report of the County Health Department for the Calendar Year 1927," May 17, 1928, B of S.

130. LACHD/County, untitled annual health report covering 1929–30, 82, DHS; hereafter cited as AHR, 1929–30, 82.

131. Ibid., 81.

132. LACHD/County, AHR, 1931, 77.

133. Ibid.

134. Shippey, "Lee Side O' L.A."

135. *Grizzly Bear,* April 1933, 4.

136. Submitted to the B of S by the Investigating Committee of the County Welfare Department, Report on the Expenditures of the County Welfare Department, box 63, JAF.

137. County Department of Charities, box 63, JAF.

138. Pomeroy, "Remarkably Healthy Conditions," 5.

139. Giles Porter, "Mexicans Gone, Disease and Birth Rates Down," *Weekly Bulletin of the California State Department of Public Health* 12, no. 49 (1934).

140. Zitner, "Davis' Apology," 15.

141. IMR = total infant deaths/total living births × 1,000.

142. Duffy, *The Sanitarians;* Alisa Klaus, *Every Child a Lion: The Origins of Maternal and Infant Health Policy in the United States* (Ithaca, NY: Cornell University Press, 1993).

143. "Parrish Heads Health Group," *Los Angeles Times,* February 15, 1930; "Health Centers to Be Copied, Says Pomeroy," *Los Angeles Times,* July 23, 1929.

144. LACHD/City, *Annual Report of Department of Health of the City of Los Angeles, California, for the Fiscal Year Ended June 30, 1936,* 18, SRLF.

145. Mary June Burton, "Babies Are Safe in Los Angeles," *Los Angeles Times,* October 18, 1934.

146. LACHD/City, *Annual Report of Department of Health of the City of Los Angeles, California, for the Year Ending June 30, 1930,* 11, SRLF.

147. "Tennesseean Takes Helm of Health Association," *Los Angeles Times,* September 6, 1934.

148. Some eugenicists even favored a high IMR among immigrant groups. Meckel, *Save the Babies;* Kelves, *In the Name of Eugenics.*

149. BHC [LACHD/City], *AHR, 1937,* 11.

150. *Nonresident* referred to women from anywhere outside of California.

151. BHC [LACHD/City], *AHR, 1937,* 28.

152. Roberts examines how the media have constructed black women's bodies to advance certain agendas. Dorothy Roberts, *Killing the Black Body: Race, Reproduction, and the Meaning of Liberty* (New York: Vintage, 1997). For more on these cultural constructions, see Laura Briggs, *Reproducing Empire;* Robin D. G. Kelley, *Yo' Mama's Disfunktional! Fighting the Culture Wars in Urban America* (Boston: Beacon Press, 1997); Lisa Sun-Hee Park, "Perpetuation of Poverty through Public Charge," *Denver University Law Review* 78 (2001): 1161–77; Laura E. Gomez, *Misconceiving Mothers: Legislators, Prosecutors, and the Politics of Prenatal Drug Exposure* (Philadelphia: Temple Uni-

versity Press, 1997); Rickie Solinger, *Beggars and Choosers: How the Politics of Choice Shapes Adoption, Abortion, and Welfare in the United States* (New York: Hill and Wang, 2001); Carmen Whalen, *From Puerto Rico to Philadelphia: Puerto Rican Workers and Postwar Economies* (Philadelphia: Temple University Press, 2001). We mainly think of the stereotype of the welfare queen emerging in the 1960s, but it is also important to trace these precursors to the stereotype as we know it today. For studies of the emergence of this pervasive stereotype, see Rickie Solinger, *Wake up Little Susie: Single Pregnancy and Race before Roe v. Wade* (New York: Routledge, 1992).

153. Proposition 187 proposed denying undocumented immigrants medical, educational and public services. While the proposition stated that this applied to all immigrants, in California, where it passed, it was widely conceived as directed at Mexicans. Pierrette Hondagneu-Sotelo goes further and argues that the law would have affected women and children disproportionately. See Pierrette Hondagneu-Sotelo, "Women and Children First: New Directions in Anti-Immigrant Politics," *Socialist Review* 25, no. 1 (1995): 169–90. The proposition passed in November 1994 but was immediately declared unconstitutional.

154. Stern, *Eugenic Nation.*

155. In 2003, Governor Gray Davis issued an apology for California's aggressive sterilization policy that had both sterilized women against their will and advocated sterilizations for those deemed unworthy to reproduce, such as poor women. Tony Platt, "Eugenics: Excavate the Past to Make Amends for an Old Sin," *Los Angeles Times,* July 6, 2003, M3; Zitner, "Davis' Apology."

156. Wendy Kline, in *Building a Better Race,* skillfully demonstrates how women who transgressed sexual boundaries could be labeled as immoral and thus be vulnerable to sterilizations procedures.

157. Paul Popenoe, "Eugenic Sterilization in California: The Insane," *Journal of Social Hygiene* 13, no. 6 (1927): 257–68. According to Popenoe, 3.72 percent of the men and 1.171 percent of the women were deported. The cases represented in his study do not include all the sterilizations performed at the two state hospitals. Only the cases that had complete records were used. The study contained 462 sterilization cases from Patton State Hospital and 723 from Stockton State Hospital. Popenoe writes that Ezra Gosney, another leading eugenicist of the time, undertook the study, although he is the single author of this article.

158. I did not find one letter pertaining to sterilization in the consulate's records prior to the Depression. Foreign Consulate Records for Los Angeles, 1909–30, SRE/A.

159. Tests done in the same time period at the Whittier School for Boys yielded test scores for Mexicans and African Americans that consistently defined them as feeble-minded while white boys' scores were regularly average or above average, thereby raising the specter of racial bias. Alexandra Stern, speech presented at the Center for Race and Ethnicity, University of California, San Diego, fall 2000.

160. Vice-Consul Bravo to Mr. Thomas H. Leonard, July 9, 1930, SRE/A.

161. Vice-Consul Joel Quiñones to Ho. F. A. Leonard, July 25, 1930, SRE/A. The documents do not state why he was sentenced. Youth could be sentenced to state homes, such as Pacific Colony, for a range of "delinquent"

behaviors, including stealing, assault, or what was deemed sexually inappropriate behavior. For a fascinating analysis of how women and girls, mainly white, who were labeled as mentally deficient or seen as transgressing proper gender roles became targeted for sterilizations or lifelong internment in state homes, see Kline, *Building a Better Race.*

162. Consul Rafael de la Colina to Mrs. W. J. Holland, Chief Probation Officer, December 8, 1930, SRE/A.

163. Escobar, *Race, Police.*

164. Consul Rafael de la Colina to the director of *El Heraldo de México,* November 29, 1930, IV-73–1, SRE/A.

165. Consul Rafael de la Colina to the SRE, February 11, 1931, SRE/A; Balderrama, *In Defense of La Raza,* 18.

166. See ch. 1 for details.

167. Greenwood, *Down by the Station,* 9.

168. Chinese moved to the areas below downtown for better entrepreneurial opportunities. Cheng and Cheng describe these areas as located around Ninth Street and South San Pedro and mention another area as bounded by Main Street to Central Avenue and Jefferson to Pico Boulevard. Cheng and Cheng, *Linking Our Lives,* 14–15.

169. Myra Paule, "Chinese Mission Thrives amid Squalor," *Los Angeles Times,* January 24, 1926, C20; Gordon L'Allemand, "Chinatown Passes," *Los Angeles Times,* March 19, 1933, I12.

170. See ch. 1 for a discussion of earlier efforts to cripple Chinese businesses in Los Angeles.

171. In the history of Chinese labor recruitment to the United States, there are repeated examples of white working-class laborers and small business owners accusing Chinese laborers of taking away their livelihoods, reflecting a free labor ideology. Saxton, *Indispensable Enemy.* Conflicts between whites and Chinese workers often arose as Chinese moved into urban areas in search of jobs. Richard White, *"It's Your Misfortune and None of My Own": A History of the American West* (Norman: University of Oklahoma Press, 1991), 340–42.

172. The commissioners were appointed by the mayor and confirmed by the city council. The commissioners, in turn, appointed the city health officer. It is unclear why the board proposed the amendments. Neither the LACHD/City nor the LACHD/County discussed Chinese launderers in their annual health reports during the 1930s.

173. BHC to LACC, in reference to Sanitary Ordinance 68,600, August 20, 1931; CP 5683 (1931), LACA.

174. Robert Lee, *Orientals.*

175. Section 311 of the Sanitary, Health and Food Code of the City of Los Angeles.

176. Sun Chong to LACC, forwarded by Sun Chong's landlord, July 1932, filed with CP 3605 (1932), LACA. See ch. 1 for a discussion on earlier legislation affecting Chinese launderers.

177. BHC to LACC, April 28, 1932, filed with CP 5683 (1931), LACA.

178. BHC to LACC, September 21, 1932, filed with CP 3877 (1932), LACA.

179. Chinese Consolidated Benevolent Association to LACC, August 12, 1932, filed with CP 3877 (1932), LACA.

180. See ch. 1 for more on the 1910s struggles of Chinese launderers and the CCBA.

181. Chen, *Being Chinese*, 83.

182. Chinese Consolidated Benevolent Association to LACC, August 12, 1932 (emphasis in the original), filed with CP 3877 (1932), LACA.

183. CP 1835 (1932), LACA.

184. Such was the case for one of the members of the East-Side Taxpayers' Protective League. Letter to LACC, April 18, 1932, filed with CP 1835 (1932), LACA.

185. Resolution to LACC, July 11, 1932, filed with CP 3448 (1932), LACA.

186. Chinese American Citizens Alliance to LACC, August 26, 1932, filed with CP 4068 (1932), LACA.

187. CP 5683 (1931), LACA.

188. Palmer Gillette of Gillette Holding Corporation to LACC, October 25, 1932, and David Granas, importer exporter, to LACC, October 26, 1932, both filed with CP 5683 (1932), LACA. One of Baker's supporters, the attorney Hiram McTavish, voiced his concern for washerwomen in the city who would also be affected by the ordinance and asked the city council if they realized that the ordinance also affected this group. Hiram McTavish to LACC, October 21, 1932, filed with CP 5683 (1931), LACA.

189. Steam laundries tended to be operated by whites, while the majority of hand laundries were operated by Chinese.

190. BHC to LACC, September 21, 1932, filed with CP 3877 (1932), LACA.

191. Ibid.

192. Ibid.

193. The 1924 Immigration Act prevented Chinese wives of American citizens from immigrating. With the decrease in immigration of Chinese wives, the population of Chinese women in the United States did not exceed 9 percent until after 1943, when the 1882 Chinese Exclusion Act was finally repealed. See Cheng and Cheng, *Linking Our Lives*, 9–10.

194. Chan, *Asian-Americans;* Ronald Takaki, *Strangers from a Different Shore: A History of Asian Americans* (Boston: Little Brown, 1991), 234–35.

195. BHC to LACC, September 21, 1932, filed with CP 3877 (1932), LACA.

196. Charles Decker to LACC, January 11, 1933 (emphasis added), filed with CP 4264–3877 (1932), LACA. Californian opponents of Asian immigration also began to be more concerned with Filipinas/os in California during the early 1930s. *Grizzly Bear,* January 1931, 10; August 1931, 3; and February 1934, 3.

197. Charles Decker to LACC, January 11, 1933, filed with CP 4264–3877 (1932), LACA.

198. *Grizzly Bear,* November 1932, 24.

199. Chinese American Citizens Alliance to LACC, August 26, 1932, filed with CP 4068 (1932), LACA.

200. BHC to LACC, September 21, 1932, 2, filed with CP 3877 (1932), LACA.

201. A letter from Erwin P. Werner, City Attorney, September 22, 1932, filed with CP 5683 (1931), LACA, addresses the city council's request to draft an ordinance.

202. A letter (May 10, 1937) from the Chinese Laundryowners' Association to the City Council cites these cases; filed with CP 1959 (1937), LACA. The records from the Los Angeles Municipal Court where the cases were tried have been destroyed.

203. Neither the LACC nor the BHC mentions the court ruling. Both bodies continued to discuss the ordinance until January 1933. Dr. Charles Decker to LACC, January 11, 1933, filed with CP 4264 (1932), LACA.

204. Jacobson, *Whiteness*, 3.

5. THE FIGHT FOR "HEALTH, MORALITY, AND DECENT LIVING STANDARDS"

1. The quote in the chapter title is drawn from CP 1070 (1939), LACA. In this chapter, I use the term *Mexican Americans* to signal the beginning of the demographic shift from first-generation to second-generation dominance.

2. George Sánchez discusses the increasing political mobilization of Mexican Americans in the late 1930s in "Forging a New Politics of Opposition," ch. 11 in George Sánchez, *Becoming Mexican American*.

3. Gutiérrez, *Walls and Mirrors*, 94–95. Mexican Americans' struggles over public housing have much in common with the struggles that African Americans faced over claiming public space. Robin D. G. Kelley, *Race Rebels: Culture, Politics, and the Black Working Class* (New York: Free Press, 1994).

4. George Sánchez, *Becoming Mexican American*, 224–25. "Mexicans, First Here, Leave Mark of Customs on City," *Los Angeles Times*, August 8, 1937, A2.

5. The Hoover administration initiated studies on various social issues. The first study began with the White House Conference on Child Health and Protection.

6. "Pupils Found to Be Starved," *Los Angeles Times*, May 4, 1933.

7. Pellagra is a vitamin-deficiency disease generally associated with poor diet. Cases had increased from seven to twenty-one; five ended in death. Pellagra cases occurred mainly in the county's Mexican population. LACHD/County, "Health Department of Los Angeles County Annual Report Year Ended June 30, 1936," 45, DHS; hereafter cited as AHR, 1936.

8. LACHD/County, AHR, 1936, 4. No thorough examination of the declining birth rate was conducted by the agency. I suggest that deportations sorely disrupted Mexican communities and that this in turn lowered the birth rate. By December 1933, deportations and repatriations had decreased the Mexican population in the county by nearly 29 percent, from 175,000 to 125,000. See "Why Has Los Angeles So Many on Relief," *Los Angeles Times*, December 1, 1933.

9. LACHD/County, AHR, 1936, 58. The LACHD/County AHR for 1937 discusses decreasing Mexican birth rates as well. LACHD/County, "Health Department of Los Angeles County Annual Report Year Ended June 30, 1937," 10, DHS; hereafter cited as AHR, 1937.

10. Tuberculosis ranked as the seventh leading cause of death in the nation and the fifth leading cause of death in Los Angeles. LACHD/County, AHR,

1937, 7. In addition, Dr. Pomeroy stated that there were more cases of tuberculosis in the county in 1936 than in 1920. Dr. Pomeroy cited the reallocation of taxes to relief efforts as hampering the funds allocated for public health. "Relief Impairs Health Work," *Herald Examiner,* January 16, 1933.

11. LACHD/County, AHR, 1937, 160.

12. Ibid., 7.

13. LACHD/County, "Los Angeles County Health Department Annual Report 1939[–]1940," 62, DHS.

14. LACHD/County, "Annual Report Los Angeles County Health Department 1938[–]1939," 26, DHS; hereafter cited as AHR, 1938–39.

15. LACHD/County, AHR, 1937, 9.

16. LACC/M, October 18, 1932.

17. LACHD/County, AHR, 1936, 52. While the Mexican and Asian communities were composed of both citizens and recent immigrants, the overwhelming majority of African Americans were U.S. citizens. Nonetheless, their position in the regional racial hierarchy effectively barred them from accessing much-needed public programs.

18. LACHD/County, AHR, 1936, 48.

19. Ibid., 2.

20. LACHD/County, AHR, 1936, 48–52. The study does not explain how the schools or the students attending them were selected.

21. Considering that certain public schools in Los Angeles were readily identified as "Mexican schools" because of their large Mexican population, finding Mexican children to test should not have been a problem.

22. The B of S ordered the chief county administrative officer, the superintendent of charities, and the General Hospital Advisory Committee to study the grand jury's criticisms of the hospital. "Digest of Official Acts," 1939, box 53, B III 12 d gg, JAF.

23. LACHD/County, AHR, 1937, 108–9.

24. In the early 1930s, health officials tended to trace Mexicans' high rates of TB to genetic inferiority. Studies in the latter half of the 1930s tended to cite Mexican culture, thereby still placing the blame squarely on Mexicans.

25. LACHD/County, AHR, 1937, 27.

26. Twenty-one percent of families were on work relief, and 49 percent of families were on direct relief. Ibid., 3. Readers might find useful some of the following information from "General Relief (GR) and LACEH&H Recommendations," retrieved May 7, 2005, from the Web site of the Los Angeles Coalition to End Hunger and Homelessness (www.lacehh.org/factsheetB-GR.htm): "Los Angeles County has administered public assistance programs for able-bodied adults since the passage of California's Indigent Act of 1901. In 1931, California passed the Welfare and Institutions Code that mandated that all counties in CA assist indigent adults. In 1938, the County's Bureau of Indigent Relief administered General Relief (GR) for 'employables' and 'unemployables' in LA County."

27. Pitt and Pitt, *Los Angeles A to Z,* 365.

28. John Pomeroy to B of S, April 10, 1935, p. 1, box 29, 5-f-1, JAF.

29. LACHD/County, AHR, 1937, 32.

30. President Roosevelt's New Deal was a domestic initiative that generally embraced the concept of a government-regulated economy and created many programs that affected the daily lives of millions of Americans. For example, the Works Progress Administration (WPA) created programs that employed approximately 8.5 million people over eight years.

31. Duffy, *The Sanitarians,* 258.

32. John Pomeroy to B of S, April 10, 1935, p. 2, box 29, 5-f-1, JAF.

33. Tate-Thompson's title had changed from director to chief by 1941.

34. Edythe Tate-Thompson to B of S, March 13, 1941, box 29, 5-f-1, JAF. In 1929, in a letter to the B of S, Tate-Thompson stated that she was concerned that migrants were coming to Los Angeles to seek free medical care, even though they had not resided in California for very long and thus had not yet paid taxes to the state. Among the patients Tate-Thompson used as an example of this reprehensible behavior were migrants from Iowa and Kansas. Yet twelve years later Tate-Thompson argued the opposite.

35. LACHD/County, AHR, 1937, 28.

36. "Stay Away from California: Warning to Transient Hordes," *Los Angeles Herald,* August 24, 1935.

37. "Indigents Barred at Arizona Line," *Los Angeles Herald,* February 4, 1936.

38. "Rule Guard at Border Legal," *Los Angeles Herald,* February 6, 1936.

39. LACHD/County, AHR, 1937, 32.

40. The quote in the heading is drawn from LACHD/City, *Annual Report of Department of Health of the City of Los Angeles, California, for the Year Ended June 30, 1925,* 61, SRLF; hereafter cited as *AHR, 1925.*

41. For an excellent example of how homes could signal social membership for disenfranchised groups, see Sugrue, *Origins.*

42. According to the historian George Sánchez, ownership was more likely for Mexican Americans than for Mexicans. Also, Mexicans tended to own homes in the county where property was more affordable. George Sánchez, *Becoming Mexican American,* 198.

43. Camarillo, *Chicanos,* 202.

44. President's Conference on Home Building and Home Ownership, *Housing of the Community—Home Repair and Remodeling* (Washington, DC: National Capital Press, 1932), 6, cited in Reeves, "Housing Problems," 2. See also *Slums and Blighted Areas in the United States,* Housing Division Bulletin no. 1, Federal Emergency Administration of Public Works (Washington, DC: Government Printing Office, 1935).

45. The Housing Commission existed within the city health department. Its members were appointed by the health commissioner and received no salary. Burton L. Hunter, *Evolution of Municipal Organization,* 147.

46. Report of the Housing Commission, 1910–13, Housing Commission Reports, LACA.

47. Elizabeth Fuller, *The Mexican Housing Problem in Los Angeles,* Studies in Sociology 5, no. 1 (Los Angeles: Southern California Sociological Society, University of Southern California, 1920), 7.

48. Ibid., 2.

49. California Commission of Immigration and Housing, *A Community Survey Made in Los Angeles City* (San Francisco, 1919), 14.

50. The Federal Housing Administration, established three years earlier, provided loans to institutions that would in turn build low-rent housing.

51. U.S. Housing Authority to LACC, September 14, 1938, filed with CP 3900 (1938), LACA.

52. The county already had a housing authority, but the city wanted to operate independently from the county on this as on most other matters. See "City Housing Action Urged," *Los Angeles Times*, May 25, 1938, A1, and "Delay on Slum Projects Brings Criticism of City," *Los Angeles Times*, June 13, 1939, 18; Mayor Frank Shaw to LACC, May 15, 1938, filed with CP 1241 (1938), LACA. The 1925 City Charter had established a Municipal Housing Commission that had the power to negotiate bonds for the city and acquire and oversee its properties. Negotiating federal monies for public housing, however, was outside the scope of its duties. Fred Crawford, *Organizational and Administrative Development of the Government of the City of Los Angeles: During the Thirty-Year Period July 1, 1925 to September 30, 1955* (Los Angeles: School of Public Administration, University of Southern California, 1955), 107–8.

53. The ways in which slum clearance projects act to divide and destroy social (as opposed to physical) communities raise important questions. Poor communities often faced very difficult choices when their neighborhoods were targeted for municipal "cleanup." Better, cleaner, safer homes typically meant the razing of their neighborhoods. These issues came to light often during slum clearance and urban renewal programs and continue into the twenty-first century. See Avila, *Popular Culture;* Dana Cuff, *The Provisional City: Los Angeles Stories of Architecture and Urbanism* (Cambridge, MA: MIT Press, 2000).

54. Timothy McDonnell, *The Wagner Housing Act* (Chicago: Loyola University Press, 1957), 17, quoted in Don Parson, "Los Angeles' 'Headline-Happy Public Housing War,' " *Southern California Quarterly* 65 (1983): 251–85.

55. "Proposed Resolution of the Special Slum Clearance Committee of the California Real Estate Association," March 24, 1939, filed with CP 3900 (1938), LACA.

56. Don Parson, "Making a Better World: Public Housing and the Direction of Modern Los Angeles," unpublished manuscript, 95–97. For much of Shaw's administration, allegations of corruption were leveled at city hall. In 1938, after the mayor was implicated in bombing a car owned by a private investigator who was looking into these charges, Los Angeles held a recall election and voted Shaw out. Shaw was the first U.S. mayor to be removed from office by recall. See "Frank Shaw—First U.S. Mayor Successfully Recalled From Office," retrieved May 7, 2005, from the Los Angeles Almanac Web site: www.losangelesalmanac.com/topics/History/hi06f.htm.

57. "Slum Drive Hits Obstacle," *Los Angeles Times*, May 4, 1938, A3.

58. The city council needed to appropriate funds for slum clearance surveys before the mayor could act. CP 4879 (1938), LACA.

59. Willetta H. Wolf to LACC, filed with CP 4346 (1938), LACA.

60. "Scotching the 'Slum' Story," *Los Angeles Times*, April 18, 1938, A4.

61. "City Housing Urged," *Los Angeles Times*, May 25, 1938, A1.

62. "Delay on Slum Projects Brings Criticism of City," *Los Angeles Times,* June 13, 1939, 18.

63. Years later, the LACHD/City recalled Jacob's scathing assessment as they attempted to deal with the "stain of the slum." LACHD/City, *AHR, 1925,* 6. Los Angeles Municipal Housing Commission Annual Report, 1910, 8, quoted in Sophie Spalding, "The Myth of the Classic Slum: Contradictory Perceptions of Boyle Heights Flats, 1900–1991," *Journal of Architectural Education* 45, no. 2 (February 1992): 108. Jacob A. Riis exposed L.A.'s slum tenement housing conditions in his book *How the Other Half Lives: Studies among the Tenements of New York* (New York: C. Scribner's Sons, 1890).

64. Sophie Spalding, "Myth of the Classic Slum," 107–8.

65. "Scotching the 'Slum' Story."

66. Ibid.

67. LACHD/City, *Annual Report of Department of Health of the City of Los Angeles, California, for the Fiscal Year 1938–1939,* 32, SRLF. The health department's report to the LACC is not included in the AHR. The BHC/M describe the report as "lengthy." The report contained seventy-five photographs of the surveyed areas. BHC/M, January 5, 1938, 1.

68. CP 3900 (1938), LACA.

69. "Health Department Begins Pneumonia-Typing Service," *Los Angeles Times,* December 31, 1937, A2.

70. "Tenements' End Sought," *Los Angeles Times,* March 12, 1936, A10.

71. LACHD/County, AHR, 1937, 3.

72. The report was by the Bureau of Housing and Sanitation, an agency that sometimes worked in conjunction with the LACHD/County to examine the relationship between poor housing and high rates of disease in the county. The bureau enforced ordinances involving housing, food establishments, industrial establishments, and community sanitation; it enforced regulations regarding smoke and soot, swimming pools, water supply, and beverages; and it investigated food-poisoning cases. LACHD/City, *Annual Report of Department of Health of the City of Los Angeles, California, for the Year Ended June 30, 1936,* 31, SRLF.

73. C. G. Kahlert, "Housing Survey," Los Angeles County, Division of Sanitation Report, Housing and Institutions, September 1, 1937, Addendum 2, JAF.

74. LACHD/County, AHR, 1937, 3.

75. "Disease Laid to Poor Housing," *Los Angeles Times,* November 27, 1938, 16.

76. LACHD/County, AHR, 1938–39, 14. By shifting the source of high tuberculosis rates from Mexicans' genetic inferiority to poor housing conditions, Pomeroy bolstered the need for federal funds to be invested in the county.

77. "Council Votes Slum Projects," *Los Angeles Times,* November 9, 1940, A1.

78. Panel Discussion on Public Housing in Los Angeles (Los Angeles County), April 3, 1939, box 65, folder d aaa (3), JAF.

79. Those who live in public housing today are often stigmatized as a delinquent population. Arnold R. Hirsch, *Making the Second Ghetto: Race and*

Housing in Chicago, 1940–1960 (Chicago: University of Chicago Press, 1998); Douglas Massey and Nancy Denton, *American Apartheid: Segregation and the Making of the Underclass* (Cambridge, MA: Harvard University Press, 1993); Sugrue, *Origins*.

80. CP 1241 (1938), LACA.

81. "Belvedere Residents Fight Maravilla Park Slum Project," *Los Angeles Times*, March 7, 1940, 9.

82. Petition dated April 16, 1938, filed with CP 1231 (1938), LACA.

83. Bureau of Housing and Sanitation Report, filed with CP 1231 (1938), LACA.

84. The IWO provided members with both sickness insurance and tuberculosis insurance. Roger Keeran describes the IWO as being formed in 1930 by left-wing and communist members of another fraternal organization, the Workmen's Circle. "International Workers Order," in *Encyclopedia of the American Left*, ed. Mari Jo Buhle, Paul Buhle, and Dan Georgakas (New York: Garland Publishing, 1990), 379.

85. CP 1070 (1939), LACA.

86. Ibid.

87. Mario T. García, *Memories of Chicano History: The Life and Narrative of Bert Corona* (Berkeley: University of California Press, 1994), 75–76.

88. Ibid., 88–89.

89. George Sánchez, *Becoming Mexican American*; Ruiz, *Cannery Women*; Gutiérrez, *Walls and Mirrors*.

90. For histories of El Congreso during the Depression, see Escobar, *Race, Police*, 150–54, Gutiérrez, *Walls and Mirrors*, 110–16, Ruiz, *From out of the Shadows*, 95–97; George Sánchez, *Becoming Mexican American*, 245–49.

91. CP 444 (1939), LACA.

92. David Gutiérrez describes the start-up of El Congreso. See Gutiérrez, *Walls and Mirrors*, 110–11. The organization's first national meeting did not occur until April 28–30, 1939; the petition was submitted to the city council in February 1939. The only member's name mentioned in the petition is Ramón Welch, the provisional general secretary, who signed the petition. CP 1070 (1939), LACA.

93. The claim that El Congreso had fifty thousand members may have been based on looking ahead to the national convention. The delegates at the convention represented 136 union locals and Latino groups. George Sánchez, *Becoming Mexican American*, 245. See also "Spanish Assembly Will Open Today," *Los Angeles Times*, April 29, 1939, A1.

94. First National Congress of Spanish Speaking Peoples of the United States, "Digest of Proceedings," April 28–30, 1939, p. 5, MSS0224, box 13, folder 9, Ernesto Galarza Papers, Stanford University.

95. C.P. 1070 (1939), LACA.

96. During this same time period, Chinese in San Francisco also appropriated public health discourse in their demands for better housing. See Shah, *Contagious Divides*, 225–50.

97. CP 1070 (1939), LACA.

98. Ibid.

99. Ibid.

100. The president of the National Organization Committee, Eduardo Quevedo, presided over the subsession on health and housing. "Digest of Proceedings," 2.

101. For more on these important figures, see Acuña, *Occupied America;* Ruiz, *Cannery Women;* Camarillo, *Chicanos.*

102. "Digest of Proceedings," 14.

103. Ibid., 7.

104. Ibid.

105. Sarah Deutsch, George Sánchez, and Gary Y. Okihiro, "Contemporary Peoples/Contested Places," in *The Oxford History of the American West,* ed. Clyde A. Milner II, Carol A. O'Connor, and Martha A. Sandweiss (New York: Oxford University Press, 1994), 641.

106. "Resolutions Adopted by the Second Convention of the Spanish Speaking People's Congress of California," December 9–10, 1939, p. 5, MSS0224, box 13, folder 9, Ernesto Galarza Papers, Stanford University.

107. CP 444 (1939), LACA.

108. Some agricultural growers also used threats of deportation against their Mexican workers to prevent them from organizing through unions, as with the members of the Cannery and Agricultural Workers' Industrial Union (C & AWUI) in the San Joaquin Valley. In one circular, growers appropriated public health discourse, shaping it into a threat. Mexicans who did not return to work, the flyer warned, would be "deloused, defilthed, and if that [was not] enough, deported." See Carey McWilliams and Herbert Klein, "Cold Terror in California," *Nation,* July 15, 1934. For more on the C & AWUI, see Ruiz, *Cannery Women,* 49–51, 74.

109. CP 444 (1939), LACA.

110. Goetze had been involved in civic affairs regarding Mexican housing before. In 1925, he served on the Housing Subcommittee for the Municipal League (the league reported on conditions related to the 1924 plague). See "L.A. Tenements," 2.

Goetze designed the California bungalow belonging to actor Theodore Roberts. (Roberts was famous for his role as Simon Legree in a 1910 film version of *Uncle Tom's Cabin.*)

111. B of S, Minutes, August 8, 1938, Letter of introduction for Goetze, August 8, 1938, B of S/R.

112. Sigfried Goetze to B of S, October 24, 1938, Minutes, vol. 245, p. 275, B of S/R.

113. Rex Thompson to B of S, November 1, 1938, Minutes, vol. 245, p. 415, B of S/R.

114. CP 445 (1939), LACA, emphasis mine.

115. Ibid.

116. CP 3644 (1938), LACA. Club members may have been concerned with union backlashes that would have affected the waterfronts in San Diego, San Pedro, and San Francisco. See McWilliams and Klein, "Cold Terror."

117. Constructing Mexicans and American citizens of Mexican descent as threatening, even subversive, was not unprecedented. One of the most famous

examples occurred during the Mexican Revolution when Mexican nationals residing in the United States were suspected of plotting to overthrow the U.S. government in the Plan de San Diego. William M. Hager, "The Plan of San Diego: Unrest on the Texas Border in 1915," *Arizona and the West* 5 (1963): 327–36.

118. George Sánchez, *Becoming Mexican American;* Gutiérrez, *Walls and Mirrors;* Escobar, *Race, Police.*

119. Juan Gómez-Quiñones, *Roots of Chicano Politics, 1600–1940* (Albuquerque: University of New Mexico Press, 1994), 383–87; Gutiérrez, *Walls and Mirrors,* 105; Camarillo, *Chicanos,* 63–64; Mario T. García, *Mexican Americans: Leadership, Ideology and Identity, 1930–1960* (New Haven, CT: Yale University Press, 1989), 154–57; Ruiz, *Cannery Women,* 111–17.

120. Gutiérrez, *Walls and Mirrors.*

121. George Sánchez argues that Mexican American leaders in the late 1930s were from a working-class background, if not working class themselves, giving rise to their concerns about housing issues. See George Sánchez, *Becoming Mexican American,* 229.

122. CP 1070 (1939), LACA.

123. "Policy of Projects Changed Over from Slum Clearance to One of War Housing," *Los Angeles Times,* October 23, 1942.

124. For more on Chávez Ravine (where Dodger Stadium now stands) and the construction of the East Los Angeles Freeway, see Natalia Molina, "The Construction of the East Los Angeles Freeway" (undergraduate thesis, University of California, Los Angeles, 1993); Avila, *Popular Culture.*

EPILOGUE

1. Cuff, *Provisional City;* Kenneth T. Jackson, *Crabgrass Frontier: The Suburbanization of the United States* (New York: Oxford University Press, 1987); Avila, *Popular Culture;* Nicolaides, *My Blue Heaven;* Sugrue, *Origins;* Sides, *L.A. City Limits.*

2. All quotes from the City Surveys are taken from City Survey Files: Los Angeles, California, Fourth Grade/Red/ "D" Areas, 1939, U.S. Home Owners Loan Corporation, Record Group 195, National Archives, Washington, DC. I thank Becky Nicolaides for generously sharing her primary research in this area with me.

3. LACHD/County, untitled two-page addendum (cover page reads, "I beg to transmit herewith report of our department for inclusion in the annual report") to "First Annual Report of the Health Officer of Los Angeles County, California, for the Year Ending June 30, 1917" (handwritten version), 4, DHS; and Pomeroy, "Efficient Public Health Service for Rural Districts and Small Towns" (paper prepared for an unidentified society, n.d., circa 1920, DHS.

4. City Survey Files.

5. George Lipsitz, *Possessive Investment in Whiteness,* 5.

6. Kelley, *Yo' Mama's Disfunktional!* 9.

7. Cited in Mary S. Pardo, *Mexican American Women Activists: Identity and Resistance in Two Los Angeles Communities* (Philadelphia: Temple University Press, 1998), 265.

8. Avila, *Popular Culture*, 206–7.

9. U.S. Commission on Wartime Relocation and Internment of Civilians, *Personal Justice Denied: Report of the Commission on Wartime Relocation and Internment of Civilians* (Seattle: University of Washington Press, 1997).

10. Deutsch, Sánchez, and Okihiro, "Contemporary Peoples," 641.

11. Similarly, Lisa Sun-Hee Park examines how the use of the term *public charge* became racialized upon enforcement as seen in national policies such as the 1996 Welfare Reform Act and the 1996 Immigration Act and, in essence, criminalized low-income immigrant mothers. Park, "Perpetuation of Poverty."

12. Many saw the threat of withholding a public school education to children as paralleling earlier civil rights struggles. *Los Angeles Times* editor Frank del Olmo called then California Governor Pete Wilson a "[Orval] Faubus for the '90s," referring to Governor Orval Faubus of Arkansas who refused to desegregate schools after the *Brown v. Board of Education* court ruling in 1954. "A Cautionary Lesson for Our Governor: Prop. 187," *Los Angeles Times*, December 21, 1994. Although Proposition 187 was held up in the courts, it created a climate of fear and caused some children to stop attending school. See the documentary *Fear and Learning at Hoover Elementary* (1997), dir. Laura Angelica Simón, prod. Tracey Trench, POV Series, PBS.

13. See also Hondagneu-Sotelo, "Women and Children First."

14. "U.S. Seeks to Spur Use of Aid by Immigrants," *Los Angeles Times*, May 25, 1999.

15. "East Los Angeles Rally Staged Lauding Clinic's 187 Position," *Los Angeles Times*, December 18, 1994, 10.

16. Arthur Schlesinger Jr. argues that multiculturalism (which includes bilingual education programs) threatens a homogenous America. Arthur Schlesinger Jr., *The Disuniting of America: Reflections on a Multicultural Society* (New York: Norton, 1998).

17. Dorothy Roberts, *Shattered Bonds: The Color of Child Welfare* (New York: Basic Books, 2002), 59–67.

18. Deborah Gray White, *Ar'n't I A Woman? Female Slaves in the Plantation South* (New York: Norton, 1985).

19. The movie featured Jessica Lange as a white social worker who adopts a black baby abandoned by his crack-addict mother, played by Halle Berry. Berry's character spends most of her time in a drug-sustained haze.

20. Robin Kelley examines the origins of these stereotypes and their longevity and provides an insightful critique. Kelley, *Yo' Mama's Disfunktional!*

21. Dorothy Roberts, *Shattered Bonds*, 60.

22. Natalia Molina and Anne-Emanuelle Birn, "In the Name of Public Health," *American Journal of Public Health* 95 (July 2005): 1–3; Vélez-Ibáñez, " 'Se Me Acabó La Canción' "; Alexandra Stern, "Sterilized in the Name of Public Health and Population Policy: Race, Immigration, and Reproductive Control in Modern California," *American Journal of Public Health* (forthcoming). On the politics of sterilization in Puerto Rico, see Laura Briggs, *Reproducing Empire*.

23. *Fortnight Magazine*, August 18, 1954, 9, cited in Katherine Underwood, "Process and Politics: Multiracial Electoral Coalition Building and Representa-

tion in Los Angeles' Ninth District, 1949–1962" (PhD diss., University of California, San Diego, 1992), 96.

24. Pardo, *Mexican American Women Activists*.

25. Miguel Melendez, *We Took the Streets: Fighting for Latino Rights with the Young Lords* (New York: St. Martin's Press, 2003); Winona LaDuke, *All Our Relations: Native Struggles for Land and Life* (Cambridge, MA: South End Press, 1999); Laura Pulido, *Environmentalism and Economic Justice: Two Chicano Struggles in the Southwest* (Tucson: University of Arizona Press, 1996); Alondra Nelson, "Black Power, Biomedicine, and the Politics of Knowledge" (PhD diss., New York University, 2003).

Bibliography

ARCHIVAL AND MANUSCRIPT COLLECTIONS

California Department of Industrial Relations, Division of Immigration and Housing Records. Bancroft Library, University of California, Berkeley.

Center for Oral and Public History. Oral History Program, Mexican American Project, California State University, Fullerton.

Chamber of Commerce Collection. Regional History Center, University of Southern California.

Children's Bureau Records. National Archives, College Park, MD.

Fletcher Bowron Collection. Henry E. Huntington Library, San Marino, CA.

Foltz Collection. Henry E. Huntington Library, San Marino, CA.

Foreign Consulate Records for Los Angeles. Archives, Secretaría de Relaciones Exteriores, Mexico City, D.F., Mexico.

Galarza, Ernesto. Papers. Special Collections, Stanford University.

Herald Examiner Newspaper Clippings. Regional History Center, University of Southern California.

Immigration and Naturalization Records. National Archives, Laguna Niguel, CA.

John Anson Ford Collection. Henry E. Huntington Library, San Marino, CA.

Leslie T. Webster Collection. Rockefeller University Archives.

Lindley, Dr. Walter. Papers. Claremont College, Special Collections.

Los Angeles City Archives.

Los Angeles City Health Department Collection. Urban Archives, California State University, Northridge.

Los Angeles County Board of Supervisors, Records. Office of the Los Angeles County Board of Supervisors, Los Angeles.

Los Angeles County Health Department, Records. Los Angeles County Department of Health Services Library, Main Office, Los Angeles.

Los Angeles County Hospital, Birth Records.

McWilliams, Carey. Papers. Special Collections, University of California, Los Angeles.

Medical Journal Collection. Bio-Medical Special Collections, University of California, Los Angeles.

Nicholson Collection. Henry E. Huntington Library, San Marino, CA.

Park Collection. Henry E. Huntington Library, San Marino, CA.

Roybal, Edward. Papers. Special Collections, University of California, Los Angeles.

Severance Collection. Henry E. Huntington Library, San Marino, CA.

Shades of LA Collection. Los Angeles Public Library.

U.S. Public Health Service Records. National Archives, College Park, MD.

U.S. Senate and House Records. Washington, DC.

United Way Collection. Urban Archives, California State University, Northridge.

Visiting Nursing Program Archives. St. Vincent's Hospital, Los Angeles.

Watkins Collection. Henry E. Huntington Library, San Marino, CA.

YWCA Collection. Urban Archives, California State University, Northridge.

PUBLISHED PRIMARY SOURCES

Bennet, William S., and William Paul Dillingham. *Abstracts of Reports of the Immigration Commission, Reports of the Immigration Commission.* Vols. 1–2 of the Dillingham Commission Reports to the U.S. Senate. Washington, DC: Government Printing Office, 1911.

Bogardus, Emory S. "The Mexican Immigrant." *Journal of Applied Sociology* 11 (May–June 1927): 470–88.

———. *The Mexican in the United States.* Los Angeles: University of Southern California, 1934.

Bogen, Emil. "Racial Susceptibility to Tuberculosis." *American Review of Tuberculosis* 24, no. 5 (1931): 522–31.

Burnight, Ralph Fletcher. *The Japanese in Rural Los Angeles County.* Sociological Monograph 16. Los Angeles: Southern California Sociological Society, University of Southern California, 1920.

California Commission of Immigration and Housing. *A Community Survey Made in Los Angeles City.* San Francisco, 1919.

California Department of Public Health. *Thirty-First Biennial Report for the Fiscal Years July 1, 1928, to June 30, 1930.* Sacramento: California State Printing Office, 1931.

———. *Thirty-Fourth Biennial Report for the Fiscal Years from July 1, 1934, to June 30, 1936.* Sacramento: California State Printing Office, 1937.

———. *Thirty-Second Biennial Report for the Fiscal Years from July 1, 1930, to June 30, 1932.* Sacramento: California State Printing Office, 1933.

Crawford, Fred. *Organizational and Administrative Development of the Government of the City of Los Angeles: During the Thirty-Year Period July 1,*

1925 to September 30, 1955. Los Angeles: School of Public Administration, University of Southern California, 1955.

Crawford, Remsen. "The Menace of Mexican Immigration." *Current History* 31 (1930): 902–07.

Dillingham, William P., Harry A. Millis, and U.S. Immigration Commission. *Immigrants in Industries: Pt. 25. Japanese and Other Immigrant Races in the Pacific Coast and Rocky Mountain States.* Vols. 23–25 of the Dillingham Commission Reports to the U.S. Senate, Washington, DC: Government Printing Office, 1911.

Ellis, Pearl. *Americanization through Homemaking.* Los Angeles: Wetzel, 1929.

Fuller, Elizabeth. *The Mexican Housing Problem in Los Angeles.* Studies in Sociology 5, no. 1. Los Angeles: Southern California Sociological Society, University of Southern California, 1920.

Gamio, Manuel. *The Mexican Immigrant, His Life Story.* Chicago: University of Chicago Press, 1931.

Gates, W. Almont. *Oriental Immigration on the Pacific Coast.* San Francisco, 1909.

Goethe, C. M. "Other Aspects of the Problem." *Current History* 28 (August 1928): 767.

Goldberg, Benjamin. "Tuberculosis in Racial Types with Special Reference to Mexicans." *American Journal of Public Health* 19, no. 3 (1929): 274–84.

Grant, Madison. "Editorial: Immigration." *Eugenics: A Journal of Race Betterment* 3 (1930): 74.

Hiscock, Ira V. *A Survey of Public Health Activities in Los Angeles County, California.* Los Angeles: Los Angeles County Bureau of Efficiency, 1928.

Hitt, Homer L., and Wilson T. Longmore. "A Demographic Analysis of First and Second Generation Mexican Population." *Southwestern Social Science Quarterly* 24 (1943): 138–49.

Holmes, Samuel J. "Peon Immigrants." *Eugenics: A Journal of Race Betterment* 1 (November 1928): 36.

————. "Perils of the Mexican Invasion." *North American Review* 227 (May 1929): 615–23.

"Housing in Belvedere and Maravilla." *Monthly Labor Review* 16 (1925): 160–61.

Hunt, Rockwell Dennis. *California and Californians.* Vol. 4. Chicago: Lewis Publishing, 1926.

Hunter, Burton L. *The Evolution of Municipal Organization and Administrative Practice in the City of Los Angeles.* Los Angeles: Parker, Stone, and Baird, 1933.

King, Howard D. "Frequency of Tuberculosis among Negro Laundresses." *Journal of Outdoor Life,* 11, no. 275 (1914).

————. "Miscegenation: An Old Social Problem." *New Orleans Medical and Surgical Journal* 66, no. 534 (1914).

————. "Some Sanitary Aspects of the Mexican Revolution." *Southern California Practitioner* 29, no. 3 (1914): 63.

"L.A. Tenements and the Bubonic-Pneumonic Plagues." *Municipal League of Los Angeles Bulletin* 2, no. 7 (1925): 2–5.

Lang, Charles J. *Who's Who in Los Angeles County, 1928–1929.* Los Angeles: Charles J. Lang, 1929.

Lindley, Walter, and Joseph Pomeroy Widney. *California of the South.* New York: D. Appleton, 1896.

McLean, Robert. *That Mexican as He Really Is, North and South of the Rio Grande.* New York: Fleming H. Revell, 1928.

Mexican Fact-Finding Committee. *Mexicans in California: Report of Governor C. C. Young's Mexican Fact Finding Committee.* Sacramento: California State Printing Office, 1930.

"Mexicans in Los Angeles." *Survey* 44 (1920): 715–16.

Pomeroy, John. "Efficient Public Health Service for Rural Districts and Small Towns." Paper prepared for an unidentified society, n.d., circa 1920, DHSL.

———. "Huntington Park Public Health Problem." In *Administration of Public Health: Viewpoints of Public Health Experts and Los Angeles County Medical Society,* edited by John L. Pomeroy, 57–62. Los Angeles: Los Angeles County Health Department, 1934.

———. "The Principles of the Health Center Movement and Their Application in Los Angeles County." Paper presented at the League of California, Health Officers' Section, September 20, 1927.

———. "The Public Health Center." *California and Western Medicine* 35, no. 3 (September 1931): 4.

Popenoe, Paul. "Eugenic Sterilization in California: The Insane." *Journal of Social Hygiene* 13, no. 6 (1927): 257–68.

Porter, Giles. "Mexicans Gone, Disease and Birth Rates Down." *Weekly Bulletin of the California State Department of Public Health* 12, no. 49 (1934).

Riis, Jacob A. *How the Other Half Lives: Studies among the Tenements of New York.* New York: C. Scribner's Sons, 1890.

Roberts, Kenneth. "The Docile Mexican." *Saturday Evening Post,* March 10, 1928, 40–41, 165–66.

———. "Mexicans or Ruin." *Saturday Evening Post,* February 18, 1928, 14–15, 142, 45–46, 49–50, 54.

———. "Wet and Other Mexicans." *Saturday Evening Post,* February 4, 1928, 10–11, 137–38, 41–42, 46.

Rude, Anna, MD. "The Midwife Problem in the United States." Paper presented at the annual meeting of the American Medical Association, San Francisco, June 1923.

———. "The Midwife Problem in the United States." *Journal of American Medical Association* 81 (September 1923): 998.

Spalding, William. *History and Reminiscences: Los Angeles City and County, California.* Vol. 1. Los Angeles: J. R. Finnell and Sons, 1931.

Tate-Thompson, Edythe. "Migration of Indigent Tuberculosis Is Serious Problem." *Weekly Bulletin of the California State Department of Public Health* 8, no. 19 (June 15, 1929): 73–74.

———. *A Statistical Study of Sickness among the Mexicans in the Los Angeles County Hospital, from July 1, 1922 to June 30, 1924.* Sacramento: California State Board of Health, 1925.

Taylor, Paul. *Mexican Labor in the United States Imperial Valley.* Berkeley: University of California Press, 1930.

Truman, Benjamin Cummings. *Semi-Tropical California: Its Climate, Healthfulness, Productiveness, and Scenery.* San Francisco: A. L. Bancroft, 1874.

U.S. Congress, House Committee on Immigration and Naturalization. *Hearings before the Committee on Immigration and Naturalization, House of Representatives,* 70th Cong., 1st sess., 1928.

——— . *Seasonal Agricultural Laborers from Mexico. Hearings January 28 and 29, February 2, 9, 11, and 23, 1926 on H.R. 6741, H.R. 7559, H.R. 9036,* 69th Cong., 2nd sess., 1926.

U.S. Congress, Senate Committee on Public Health and National Quarantine. *Standardization of Treatment of Tuberculosis: Hearings before the United States Senate Committee on Public Health and National Quarantine,* 64th Cong., 1st sess., January 17, 1916.

U.S. Public Health Service. *Regulations Governing the Medical Inspection of Aliens.* Washington, DC: Government Printing Office, 1917.

Walker, Francis A. "Restriction of Immigration," *Atlantic Monthly* 77 (June 1896), 828.

Widney, Joseph. *Race Life of the Aryan Peoples.* 2 vols. New York: Funk and Wagnalls, 1907.

——— . *The Three Americas: Their Racial Past and the Dominant Racial Factors of Their Future.* Los Angeles: Pacific Publishing, 1935.

SECONDARY SOURCES

Abel, Emily. " 'Only the Best Class of Immigration': Public Health Policy toward Mexicans and Filipinos in Los Angeles, 1910–1940." *American Journal of Public Health* 94, no. 6 (2004): 932–39.

Abu-Lughod, Janet. *New York, Chicago, Los Angeles: America's Global Cities.* Minneapolis: University of Minnesota Press, 1999.

Acuña, Rodolfo. *Anything but Mexican: Chicanos in Contemporary Los Angeles.* New York: Verso Press, 1996.

——— . *A Community under Siege: A Chronicle of Chicanos East of the Los Angeles River, 1945–1975.* Los Angeles: Chicano Studies Research Center Publications, University of California, Los Angeles, 1984.

——— . *Occupied America: A History of Chicanos.* New York: Harper and Row, 1988.

Almaguer, Tomás. *Racial Fault Lines: The Historical Origins of White Supremacy.* Berkeley: University of California Press, 1994.

Anderson, Kay J. "The Idea of Chinatown: The Power of Place and Institutional Practice in the Making of a Racial Category." *Annals of the Association of American Geographers* 77, no. 4 (1987): 580–98.

Antler, Joyce, and Daniel Fox. "Movement toward a Safer Maternity: Doctor Accountability in New York City, 1915–1940." *Bulletin of the History of Medicine* 50 (Winter 1976): 569–95.

Appier, Janis. *Policing Women: The Sexual Politics of Law Enforcement and the LAPD.* Philadelphia: Temple University Press, 1998.

Apple, Rima D. *Mothers and Medicine: A Social History of Infant Feeding, 1890–1950.* Madison: University of Wisconsin Press, 1987.

Arnold, David. *Colonizing the Body: State Medicine and Epidemic Disease in Nineteenth-Century India.* Berkeley: University of California Press, 1993.

Arroyo, Luis Leobardo. "Power and Place: Re-Shaping Mexican Identities in Los Angeles, 1900–1930." Working Paper No. 24, Julian Samora Research Institute, 1996.

Austin, Joe, and Michael Willard. *Generations of Youth: Youth Cultures and History in Twentieth-Century America.* New York: New York University Press, 1998.

Avila, Eric. *Popular Culture in the Age of White Flight: Fear and Fantasy in Suburban Los Angeles.* Berkeley: University of California Press, 2004.

Baker, Paula. "The Domestication of Politics: Women and American Political Society, 1780–1920." *American Historical Review* 89, no. 3 (1984): 620–47.

Balderrama, Francisco. *In Defense of La Raza: The Los Angeles Mexican Consulate and the Mexican Community, 1929–1936.* Tucson: University of Arizona Press, 1982.

Balderrama, Francisco E., and Raymond Rodríguez. *Decade of Betrayal: Mexican Repatriation in the 1930s.* Albuquerque: University of New Mexico Press, 1995.

Bannister, Robert C. *Social Darwinism: Science and Myth in Anglo-American Thought.* Philadelphia: Temple University Press, 1979.

Baur, John. *The Health Seekers of Southern California, 1870–1900.* San Marino, CA: Huntington Library, 1959.

Baynton, Douglas. "Disability and the Justification of Inequality in American History." In *The New Disability History: American Perspectives,* edited by Paul Longmore and Lauri Umansky, 33–57. New York: New York University Press, 2001.

Bederman, Gail. *Manliness and Civilization: A Cultural History of Gender and Race in the United States, 1880–1917.* Chicago: University of Chicago Press, 1995.

Berg, Allison. *Mothering the Race: Women's Narratives of Reproduction, 1890–1930.* Urbana: University of Illinois Press, 2002.

Bernstein, David. "Lochner, Parity, and the Chinese Laundry Cases." *William and Mary Law Review* 41, no. 1 (1999): 211–94.

Borst, Charlotte. *Catching Babies: The Professionalization of Childbirth, 1870–1920.* Cambridge, MA: Harvard University Press, 1995.

Briggs, Charles L., and Clara Mantini-Briggs. *Stories in the Time of Cholera: Racial Profiling during a Medical Nightmare.* Berkeley: University of California Press, 2003.

Briggs, Laura. *Reproducing Empire: Race, Sex, Science, and U.S. Imperialism in Puerto Rico.* Berkeley: University of California Press, 2002.

Buhle, Mari Jo, Paul Buhle, and Dan Georgakas, eds. *Encyclopedia of the American Left.* New York: Garland Publishing, 1990.

Buss, Fran Leeper. *La Partera: Story of a Midwife.* Ann Arbor: University of Michigan Press, 1980.

Calavita, Kitty. *Inside the State: The Bracero Program, Immigration, and the I.N.S.* New York: Routledge, 1992.

Camarillo, Albert. *Chicanos in a Changing Society: From Mexican Pueblos to American Barrios in Santa Barbara and Southern California, 1848–1930.* Cambridge, MA: Harvard University Press, 1979.

Carr, Eve. "Missionaries and Motherhood: Sixty-Six Years of Public Health Work in South El Paso." PhD diss., Arizona State University, 2003.

Casas, Maria Raquel. " 'In Consideration of His Being Married to a Daughter of the Land': Interethnic Marriages in Alta California, 1825–1875." PhD diss., Yale University, 1998.

Castañeda, Antonia. "Engendering the History of Alta California, 1769–1848: Gender, Sexuality, and the Family." In *Contested Eden: California before the Gold Rush,* edited by Ramón Gutiérrez and Roberto Orsi, 230–59. Berkeley: University of California Press, 1998.

———. "Women of Color and the Rewriting of Western History: The Discourse, Politics, and Decolonization of History." *Pacific Historical Review* 61, no. 4 (November 1992): 501–34.

Chan, Sucheng. *Asian Americans: An Interpretive History.* Boston: Twayne, 1991.

Chávez-García, Miroslava. *Negotiating Conquest: Gender and Power in California, 1770s to 1880s.* Tucson: University of Arizona Press, 2004.

Chen, Sheong. *Being Chinese, Becoming Chinese American.* Urbana: University of Illinois Press, 2002.

Cheng, Lucie, and Suellen Cheng. *Linking Our Lives: Chinese Women of Los Angeles.* Los Angeles: Chinese Historical Society of Southern California, 1984.

Cuff, Dana. *The Provisional City: Los Angeles Stories of Architecture and Urbanism.* Cambridge, MA: MIT Press, 2000.

Daniels, Roger. *Asian America: Chinese and Japanese in the United States since 1850.* Seattle: University of Washington Press, 1988.

———. *The Politics of Prejudice: The Anti-Japanese Movement in California and the Struggle for Japanese Exclusion.* Berkeley: University of California Press, 1977.

Davis, Clark. *Company Men: White-Collar Life and Corporate Cultures in Los Angeles, 1892–1941.* Baltimore: Johns Hopkins University Press, 2000.

———. "From Oasis to Metropolis: Southern California and the Changing Context of American Leisure." *Pacific Historical Review* 61, no. 3 (1992): 357–86.

Davis, Mike. *City of Quartz: Excavating the Future in Los Angeles.* London: Verso Press, 1990.

de Graaf, Lawrence B. "Recognition, Racism, and Reflections on the Writing of Western Black History." *Pacific Historical Review* 44 (1975): 22–47.

Deutsch, Sarah. *No Separate Refuge: Culture, Class, and Gender on an Anglo-Hispanic Frontier in the American Southwest, 1880–1940.* New York: Oxford University Press, 1987.

Deutsch, Sarah, George Sánchez, and Gary Y. Okihiro. "Contemporary Peoples/ Contested Places." In *The Oxford History of the American West,* edited by

Clyde A. Milner II, Carol A. O'Connor, and Martha A. Sandweiss, 639–69. New York: Oxford University Press, 1994.

Deverell, William. "Plague in Los Angeles, 1924: Ethnicity and Typicality." In *Over the Edge: Remapping the American West,* edited by Valerie Matsumoto and Blake Allmendinger, 172–200. Berkeley: University of California Press, 1999.

――――. "Privileging the Mission over the Mexican." In *Many Wests: Place, Culture, and Regional Identity,* edited by David Wrobel and Michael Steiner, 235–58. Lawrence: University Press of Kansas, 1997.

――――. *Whitewashed Adobe: The Rise of Los Angeles and the Remaking of Its Mexican Past.* Berkeley: University of California Press, 2004.

Deverell, William, and Tom Sitton. *California Progressivism Revisited.* Berkeley: University of California Press, 1994.

Douglas, Mary. *Purity and Danger: An Analysis of Concepts of Pollution and Taboo.* New York: Praeger, 1970.

Duffy, John. *The Sanitarians: A History of American Public Health.* Urbana: University of Illinois Press, 1990.

Epstein, Steven. *Impure Science: AIDS, Activism, and the Politics of Knowledge.* Berkeley: University of California Press, 1996.

Escobar, Edward J. *Race, Police, and the Making of a Political Identity: Mexican Americans and the Los Angeles Police Department, 1900–1945.* Berkeley: University of California Press, 1999.

Fairchild, Amy. *Science at the Borders: Immigrant Medical Inspection and the Shaping of the Modern Industrial Labor Force.* Baltimore: Johns Hopkins University Press, 2003.

Farmer, Paul. *AIDS and Accusation: Haiti and the Geography of Blame.* Berkeley: University of California Press, 1992.

Ferguson, Roderick. *Aberrations in Black: Toward a Queer of Color Critique.* Minneapolis: University of Minnesota Press, 2004.

Fields, Barbara. "Ideology and Race in American History." In *Region, Race, and Reconstruction: Essays in Honor of C. Vann Woodward,* edited by J. Morgan Kousser and James McPherson, 143–77. New York: Oxford University Press, 1982.

Fogelson, Robert M. *The Fragmented Metropolis: Los Angeles, 1850–1930.* Berkeley: University of California Press, 1967.

Foley, Neil. "Partly Colored or Other White: Mexican Americans and Their Problem with the Color Line." In *Beyond Black and White: Race, Ethnicity, and Gender in the U.S. South and Southwest.* College Station: Texas A&M University Press, 2004.

――――. *The White Scourge: Mexicans, Blacks and Poor Whites in Texas Cotton Culture.* Berkeley: University of California Press, 1997.

Foucault, Michel. *The History of Sexuality.* Vol. 1. *An Introduction.* Translated by Robert Hurley. New York: Random House, 1976.

Fujita-Rony, Dorothy. *American Workers, Colonial Power: Philippine Seattle and the Transpacific West, 1919–1941.* Berkeley: University of California Press, 2003.

Gaines, Kevin Kelly. *Uplifting the Race: Black Leadership, Politics, and Culture in the Twentieth Century.* Chapel Hill: University of North Carolina Press, 1996.

García, Mario T. *Memories of Chicano History: The Life and Narrative of Bert Corona.* Berkeley: University of California Press, 1994.

———. "Mexican Americans and the Politics of Citizenship: The Case of El Paso, 1936." *New Mexico Historical Review* 59, no. 2 (1984): 187–204.

———. *Mexican Americans: Leadership, Ideology and Identity, 1930–1960.* New Haven, CT: Yale University Press, 1989.

García, Matt. *A World of Its Own: Race, Labor, and Citrus in the Making of Greater Los Angeles, 1900–1970.* Chapel Hill: University of North Carolina Press, 2001.

Garcilazo, Jeffrey Marcos. "Traqueros: Mexican Railroad Workers in the United States, 1870 to 1930." PhD diss., University of California, Santa Barbara, 1995.

George, Lynell. *No Crystal Stair: African-Americans in the City of Angels.* London: Verso, 1992.

Gerstle, Gary, and John Mollenkopf, eds. *E Pluribus Unum? Contemporary and Historical Perspectives on Immigrant Political Incorporation.* New York: Russell Sage Foundation, 2001.

Glenn, Evelyn Nakano. *Unequal Freedom: How Race and Gender Shaped American Citizenship and Labor.* Cambridge, MA: Harvard University Press, 2002.

Gomez, Laura E. *Misconceiving Mothers: Legislators, Prosecutors, and the Politics of Prenatal Drug Exposure.* Philadelphia: Temple University Press, 1997.

Gómez-Quiñones, Juan. *Roots of Chicano Politics, 1600–1940.* Albuquerque: University of New Mexico Press, 1994.

González, Deena J. *Refusing the Favor: The Spanish-Mexican Women of Santa Fe, 1820–1880.* New York: Oxford University Press, 1999.

González, Gilbert G. *Labor and Community: Mexican Citrus Worker Villages in a Southern California County, 1900–1950.* Urbana: University of Illinois Press, 1994.

———. *Mexican Consuls and Labor Organizing: Imperial Politics in the American Southwest.* Austin: University of Texas Press, 1999.

Gordon, Dudley. "Charles F. Lummis and Jack London: An Evaluation." *Southern California Quarterly* 46 (March 1964): 83–88.

Gordon, Linda. *The Great Arizona Orphan Abduction.* Cambridge, MA: Harvard University Press, 1999.

Gould, Stephen Jay. *The Mismeasure of Man.* New York: Norton, 1981.

Greenwood, Roberta S. *Down by the Station: Los Angeles Chinatown, 1880–1933.* Los Angeles: Institute of Archaeology, University of California, Los Angeles, 1996.

Griswold del Castillo, Richard. *La Familia: Chicano Families in the Urban Southwest, 1848 to the Present.* Notre Dame, IN: University of Notre Dame Press, 1984.

——— . *The Los Angeles Barrio, 1850–1890: A Social History.* Berkeley: University of California Press, 1979.

Guerin-Gonzales, Camille. *Mexican Workers and American Dreams: Immigration, Repatriation, and California Farm Labor, 1900–1939.* New Brunswick, NJ: Rutgers University Press, 1994.

Guglielmo, Thomas A. *White on Arrival: Italians, Race, Color, and Power in Chicago, 1890–1945.* New York: Oxford University Press, 2003.

Gullett, Gayle. *Becoming Citizens: The Emergence and Development of the California Women's Movement, 1880–1911.* Urbana: University of Illinois Press, 2000.

Gutiérrez, David. *Walls and Mirrors: Mexican Americans, Mexican Immigrants, and the Politics of Identity.* Berkeley: University of California Press, 1995.

Gutiérrez-Jones, Carl. *Rethinking the Borderlands: Between Chicano Culture and Legal Discourse.* Berkeley: University of California Press, 1995.

Haas, Lisbeth. *Conquests and Historical Identities in California, 1769–1936.* Berkeley: University of California Press, 1995.

Hage, Ghassan. *White Nation: Fantasies of White Supremacy in a Multicultural Society.* Annandale, NSW: Pluto Press, 1998.

Hager, William M. "The Plan of San Diego: Unrest on the Texas Border in 1915." *Arizona and the West* 5 (1963): 327–36.

Handlin, Oscar. *The Uprooted: The Epic Story of the Great Migrations That Made the American People.* Boston: Little, Brown, 1973.

Haney-Lopez, Ian. *White by Law: The Legal Construction of Race.* New York: New York University Press, 1996.

Harnagel, Edward E. "The Life and Times of Walter Lindley, M.D., 1852–1922, and the Founding of the California Hospital." *Southern California Quarterly* 53, no. 4 (1971): 303–15.

Hata, Donald Teruo, and Nadine Ishitani Hata. "Asian-Pacific Angelenos: Model Minorities and Indispensable Scapegoats." In *20th Century Los Angeles: Power, Promotion, and Social Conflict,* edited by Norman M. Klein and Martin J. Schiesel. Claremont, CA: Regina, 1990.

Hawkins, Mike. *Social Darwinism in European and American Thought, 1860–1945.* Cambridge: Cambridge University Press, 1997.

Hayashi, Brian. *For the Sake of Our Japanese Brethren: Assimilation, Nationalism, and Protestantism among the Japanese of Los Angeles, 1895–1942.* Stanford, CA: Stanford University Press, 1995.

Hayden, Dolores. *The Power of Place: Urban Landscapes as Public History.* Cambridge, MA: MIT Press, 1995.

Hays, Samuel P. *The Response to Industrialism, 1885–1914.* Chicago: University of Chicago Press, 1995.

Heizer, Robert F., and Alan M. Almquist. *The Other Californians: Prejudice and Discrimination under Spain, Mexico, and the United States to 1920.* Berkeley: University of California Press, 1971.

Higginbotham, Evelyn Brooks. *Righteous Discontent: The Women's Movement in the Black Baptist Church, 1880–1920.* Cambridge, MA: Harvard University Press, 1993.

Higham, John. *Strangers in the Land: Patterns of American Nativism, 1860–1925*. New Brunswick, NJ: Rutgers University Press, 1955.

Hirsch, Arnold R. *Making the Second Ghetto: Race and Housing in Chicago, 1940–1960*. Chicago: University of Chicago Press, 1998.

Hoffman, Abraham. *Unwanted Mexican Americans in the Great Depression: Repatriation Pressures, 1929–1939*. Tucson: University of Arizona Press, 1974.

Hofstadter, Richard. *The Age of Reform: From Bryan to F.D.R.* New York: Knopf, 1955.

Holston, James, ed. *Cities and Citizenship*. Durham, NC: Duke University Press, 1999.

Hondagneu-Sotelo, Pierrette. "Women and Children First: New Directions in Anti-Immigrant Politics." *Socialist Review* 25, no. 1 (1995): 169–90.

hooks, bell. *Talking Back: Thinking Feminist, Thinking Black*. Boston: South End Press, 1989.

Horsman, Reginald. *Race and Manifest Destiny: The Origins of American Racial Anglo-Saxonism*. Cambridge, MA: Harvard University Press, 1981.

Hoy, Suellen. *Chasing Dirt: The American Pursuit of Cleanliness*. New York: Oxford University Press, 1995.

Hunter, Tera. *To 'Joy My Freedom: Southern Black Women's Lives and Labors after the Civil War*. Cambridge, MA: Harvard University Press, 1997.

Hurtado, Aída. "A View from Within: Midwife Practices in South Texas." *International Quarterly of Community Health Education* 8, no. 4 (1987–88): 317–39.

Ichioka, Yuji. *The Issei: The World of the First Generation Japanese Immigrants, 1885–1924*. New York: Free Press, 1988.

Jackson, Kenneth T. *Crabgrass Frontier: The Suburbanization of the United States*. New York: Oxford University Press, 1987.

Jacobson, Matthew Frye. *Barbarian Virtues: The United States Encounters Foreign Peoples at Home and Abroad, 1876–1917*. New York: Hill and Wang, 2000.

————. *Whiteness of a Different Color: European Immigrants and the Alchemy of Race*. Cambridge, MA: Harvard University Press, 1998.

Jones, James H. *Bad Blood: The Tuskegee Syphilis Experiment*. New York: Free Press, 1981.

Kelley, Robin D. G. *Race Rebels: Culture, Politics, and the Black Working Class*. New York: Free Press, 1994.

————. *Yo' Mama's Disfunktional! Fighting the Culture Wars in Urban America*. Boston: Beacon Press, 1997.

Kelves, Daniel. *In the Name of Eugenics: Genetics and the Uses of Human Heredity*. Cambridge, MA: Harvard University Press, 1985.

Kerber, Linda K. *Women of the Republic: Intellect and Ideology in Revolutionary America*. Chapel Hill: University of North Carolina Press, 1980.

Kim, Claire Jean. *Bitter Fruit: The Politics of Black-Korean Conflict in New York City*. New Haven, CT: Yale University Press, 2000.

Kincaid, James. "A Survey of 180 Unattached Tuberculosis Male Indigents in Los Angeles with the Emphasis on the Public Health Problem." Master's thesis, University of Southern California, 1939.

King, Ervin. "Boys' Thrills in Los Angeles of the 70s and 80s." *Southern California Quarterly* 30 (1948): 303–16.

Kingsbury Jacobs, Josephine. "Sunkist Advertising: The Iowa Campaign." In *Los Angeles: Biography of a City,* edited by John Caughey and LaRee Caughey. Berkeley: University of California Press, 1977.

Klaus, Alisa. *Every Child a Lion: The Origins of Maternal and Infant Health Policy in the United States.* Ithaca, NY: Cornell University Press, 1993.

Kline, Wendy. *Building a Better Race: Gender, Sexuality, and Eugenics from the Turn of the Century to the Baby Boom.* Berkeley: University of California Press, 2001.

Kolko, Gabriel. *The Triumph of Conservatism: A Re-Interpretation of American History, 1900–1916.* New York: Free Press of Glencoe, 1963.

Koos, Cheryl. "Engendering Reaction: The Politics of Pronatalism and the Family in France, 1919–1944." PhD diss., University of Southern California, 1996.

Korbin, Frances. "The American Midwife Controversy: A Crisis of Professionalization." In *Sickness and Health in America: Readings in the History of Medicine and Public Health,* edited by Judith Walzer Leavitt and Ronald L. Numbers, 217–25. Madison: University of Wisconsin Press, 1978.

Kraut, Alan. *Silent Travelers: Germs, Genes, and the "Immigrant Menace."* New York: Basic Books, 1994.

Kropp, Phoebe. " 'All Our Yesterdays': The Spanish Fantasy Past and the Politics of Public Memory in Southern California, 1884–1939." PhD diss., University of California, San Diego, 1999.

Kurashige, Lon. *Japanese American Celebration and Conflict: A History of Ethnic Identity and Festival in Los Angeles, 1934–1990.* Berkeley: University of California Press, 2002.

LaDuke, Winona. *All Our Relations: Native Struggles for Land and Life.* Cambridge, MA: South End Press, 1999.

Leavitt, Judith Walzer. *Brought to Bed: Childbearing in America, 1750–1950.* New York: Oxford University Press, 1986.

———. *The Healthiest City: Milwaukee and the Politics of Health Reform.* Princeton, NJ: Princeton University Press, 1982.

———. *Typhoid Mary: Captive to the Public's Health.* Boston: Beacon Press, 1996.

Leavitt, Judith Walzer, and Ronald L. Numbers. *Sickness and Health in America: Readings in the History of Medicine and Public Health.* Madison: University of Wisconsin Press, 1978.

Lee, Erika. *At America's Gates: Chinese Immigration during the Exclusion Era, 1882–1943.* Chapel Hill: University of North Carolina Press, 2003.

Lee, Robert. *Orientals: Asian Americans in Popular Culture.* Philadelphia: Temple University Press, 1999.

Leonard, Kevin. " 'Is That What We Fought For?' Japanese Americans and Racism in California: The Impact of World War II." *Western Historical Quarterly* 21, no. 4 (1990): 463–82.

Light, Ivan. "From Vice District to Tourist Attraction: The Moral Career of American Chinatowns." *Pacific Historical Review,* 43, no. 8 (1974): 367–94.

Lipsitz, George. *The Possessive Investment in Whiteness: How White People Profit from Identity Politics*. Philadelphia: Temple University Press, 1998.

Litoff, Judy Barrett. *American Midwives, 1860 to the Present*. Westport, CT: Greenwood Press, 1978.

Locklear, William. "The Celestials and the Angels: A Study of the Anti-Chinese Movement in Los Angeles to 1882." *Southern California Quarterly* 42, no. 3 (1960): 113–31.

Logan, John R., and Harvey L. Moltoch. *Urban Fortunes: The Political Economy of Place*. Berkeley: University of California Press, 1987.

Logan, Onie Lee, as told to Katherine Clark. *Motherwit: An Alabama Midwife's Story*. New York: E. P. Dutton, 1989.

Lou, Raymond. "Chinese American Vendors of Los Angeles: A Case of Resistance, Political Organization and Participation." *Integrated Education* 19, nos. 3–6 (1982): 88–91.

Lowe, Lisa. *Immigrant Acts: On Asian American Cultural Politics*. Durham, NC: Duke University Press, 1996.

Lund, John. "Boundaries of Restriction: The Dillingham Commission." *History Review* 6 (December 1994): 40–57.

Lytle Hernández, Kathleen Anne. "Entangling Bodies and Borders: Racial Profiling and the U.S. Border Patrol, 1924–1955." PhD diss., University of California, Los Angeles, 2002.

Marchand, Bernard. *The Emergence of Los Angeles: Population and Housing in the City of Dreams, 1940–1970*. London: Pion, 1986.

Markel, Howard, and Alexandra Stern. "Which Face? Whose Nation? Immigration, Public Health, and the Construction of Disease at America's Ports and Borders, 1891–1928." *American Behavioral Scientist* 42, no. 9 (1999): 1314–31.

Massey, Douglas, and Nancy Denton. *American Apartheid: Segregation and the Making of the Underclass*. Cambridge, MA: Harvard University Press, 1993.

Matsumoto, Valerie. *Farming the Home Place: A Japanese American Community in California*. Ithaca, NY: Cornell University Press, 1993.

May, Elaine Tyler. *Barren in the Promised Land: Childless Couples and the Pursuit of Happiness*. New York: Basic Books, 1995.

McBride, David. *From TB to AIDS: Epidemics among Urban Blacks since 1900*. Albany: State University of New York Press, 1991.

McClain, Charles. "Of Medicine, Race, and American Law: The Bubonic Plague Outbreak of 1900." *Law and Social Inquiry* 13, no. 3 (1988): 447–513.

McKiernan-Gonzalez, John. "Fevered Measures: Race, Contagious Disease and Community Formation on the Texas-Mexico Border, 1880–1923." PhD diss., University of Michigan, 2002.

McWilliams, Carey. *Southern California: An Island on the Land*. Salt Lake City, UT: Gibbs Smith, 1946.

Meckel, Richard. *Save the Babies: American Public Health Reform and the Prevention of Infant Mortality*. Baltimore: Johns Hopkins University Press, 1990.

Meléndez, Miguel. *We Took the Streets: Fighting for Latino Rights with the Young Lords*. New York: St. Martin's Press, 2003.

Menchaca, Martha. "Chicano Indianism: A Historical Account of Racial Repression in the United States." *American Ethnologist* 20, no. 3 (1993): 583–603.

———. *The Mexican Outsiders: A Community History of Marginalization and Discrimination in California.* Austin: University of Texas Press, 1995.

Mink, Gwendolyn. "The Lady and the Tramp: Gender, Race and the Origins of the American Welfare State." In *Women, the State, and Welfare,* edited by Linda Gordon. Madison: University of Wisconsin Press, 1990.

Modell, John. *The Economics and Politics of Racial Accommodation: The Japanese of Los Angeles, 1900–1942.* Urbana: University of Illinois Press, 1977.

Molina, Natalia. "Birthing with Their Hands: Mamás, Parteras, y Comadres—y Doctors, Tambien." Unpublished manuscript, 1996.

———. "The Construction of the East Los Angeles Freeway." Undergraduate thesis, University of California, Los Angeles, 1993.

———. "Illustrating Cultural Authority: Medicalized Representations of Mexican Communities in Early Twentieth Century Los Angeles." *Aztlán: A Journal of Chicano Studies* 28 (Spring 2003): 129–43.

Molina, Natalia, and Anne-Emanuelle Birn. "In the Name of Public Health." *American Journal of Public Health* 95 (July 2005): 1–3.

Monroy, Douglas. *Rebirth: Mexican Los Angeles from the Great Migration to the Great Depression.* Berkeley: University of California Press, 1999.

Montejano, David. *Anglos and Mexicans in the Making of Texas, 1836–1986.* Austin: University of Texas Press, 1987.

Morales, Alejandro. *The Brick People.* Houston, TX: Arte Público Press, 1992.

Muncy, Robyn. *Creating a Female Dominion in American Reform, 1890–1935.* New York: Oxford University Press, 1991.

Nelson, Alondra. "Black Power, Biomedicine, and the Politics of Knowledge." PhD diss., New York University, 2003.

Neubeck, Kenneth, and Noel Cazenave. *Welfare Racism: Playing the Race Card against America's Poor.* New York: Routledge, 2001.

Ngai, Mae M. *Impossible Subjects: Illegal Aliens and the Making of Modern America.* Princeton, NJ: Princeton University Press, 2004.

———. "The Strange Career of the Illegal Alien: Immigration Restriction and Deportation Policy in the United States, 1921–1965." *Law and History Review* 21, no. 1 (2003): 69–108.

Nicolaides, Becky M. *My Blue Heaven: Life and Politics in the Working-Class Suburbs of Los Angeles, 1920–1965.* Chicago: University of Chicago Press, 2002.

Odem, Mary. *Delinquent Daughters: Protecting and Policing Adolescent Female Sexuality in the United States, 1885–1920.* Chapel Hill: University of North Carolina Press, 1995.

Omi, Michael, and Howard Winant. *Racial Formation in the United States from the 1960s to the 1980s.* New York: Routledge, 1986.

Ong, Aihwa. "Cultural Citizenship as Subject-Making: Immigrants Negotiate Racial and Cultural Boundaries in the United States." *Current Anthropology* 37, no. 5 (1996): 737–63.

———. *Flexible Citizenship: The Cultural Logics of Transnationality.* Durham, NC: Duke University Press, 1999.

Ong, Paul. "An Ethnic Trade: The Chinese Laundries in Early California." *Journal of Ethnic Studies* 8, no. 4 (1981): 95–113.

Oshrenko, Marian. "The Social Implications of Delay in Sanatorium Placement for Tuberculosis: A Study of Cases in Los Angeles County." Master's thesis, University of Southern California, 1941.

Pardo, Mary S. *Mexican American Women Activists: Identity and Resistance in Two Los Angeles Communities.* Philadelphia: Temple University Press, 1998.

Park, Lisa Sun-Hee. "Perpetuation of Poverty through Public Charge." *Denver University Law Review* 78 (2001): 1161–77.

Parson, Don. "Los Angeles' 'Headline-Happy Public Housing War.' " *Southern California Quarterly* 65 (1983): 251–85.

Perea, Juan F. *Immigrants Out: The New Nativism and the Anti-Immigrant Impulse in the United States.* New York: New York University Press, 1997.

Pernick, Martin. *The Black Stork: Eugenics and the Death of "Defective" Babies in American Medicine and Motion Pictures since 1915.* New York: Oxford University Press, 1996.

———. "Eugenics and Public Health in American History." *American Journal of Public Health* 87, no. 11 (1997): 1767–72.

Pitt, Leonard, and Dale Pitt. *Los Angeles A to Z: An Encyclopedia of the City and County.* Berkeley: University of California Press, 1997.

Portes, Alejandro, and Rubén G. Rumbaut. *Immigrant America: A Portrait.* Berkeley: University of California Press, 1990.

Pulido, Laura. *Environmentalism and Economic Justice: Two Chicano Struggles in the Southwest.* Tucson: University of Arizona Press, 1996.

Quadagno, Jill. *The Color of Welfare: How Racism Undermined the War on Poverty.* New York: Oxford University Press, 1994.

Rafael, Vicente. "White Love: Surveillance and National Resistance in the U.S. Colonization of the Philippines." In *Cultures of United States Imperialism,* edited by Amy Kaplan and Donald Pease, 185–218. Durham, NC: Duke University Press, 1993.

Reagan, Leslie. "Linking Midwives and Abortion in the Progressive Era." *Bulletin of the History of Medicine* 69 (1995): 569–98.

Reeves, Frances. "Housing Problems of the Tuberculosis Clients in the Los Angeles County Central Welfare District." Master's thesis, University of Southern California, 1936.

Reisler, Mark. *By the Sweat of Their Brow: Mexican Immigrant Labor in the United States, 1900–1940.* Westport, CT: Greenwood Press, 1976.

Roberts, Dorothy. *Killing the Black Body: Race, Reproduction, and the Meaning of Liberty.* New York: Vintage, 1997.

———. *Shattered Bonds: The Color of Child Welfare.* New York: Basic Books, 2002.

Rodgers, Daniel. "In Search of Progressivism." *Reviews in American History* 10, no. 4 (1982): 113–32.

Roediger, David. *The Wages of Whiteness: Race and the Making of the American Working Class.* London: Verso, 1991.

Romo, Ricardo. *East Los Angeles: History of a Barrio*. Austin: University of Texas Press, 1983.

Rosaldo, Renato. *Culture and Truth: The Remaking of Social Analysis*. Boston: Beacon Press, 1989.

Rosenberg, Charles. *The Cholera Years: The United States in 1832, 1849, and 1866*. Chicago: University of Chicago Press, 1962.

Rouse, Roger. "Thinking through Transnationalism: Notes on the Cultural Politics of Class Relations in the Contemporary United States." *Public Culture*, no. 7 (1995): 353–402.

Ruiz, Vicki. *Cannery Women, Cannery Lives: Mexican Women, Unionization, and the California Food Processing Industry, 1930–1950*. Albuquerque: University of New Mexico Press, 1987.

———. *From out of the Shadows: Mexican Women in Twentieth-Century America*. New York: Oxford University Press, 1998.

———. " 'We Always Tell Our Children They Are American': Méndez v. Westminster and the California Road to Brown." *College Board Review*, no. 200 (Fall 2003): 21–27.

Saito, Leland. *Race and Politics: Asian Americans, Latinos, and Whites in a Los Angeles Suburb*. Urbana: University of Illinois Press, 1998.

Saldívar-Hull, Sonia. *Feminism on the Border: Chicana Gender Politics and Literature*. Berkeley: University of California Press, 2000.

Sánchez, George. *Becoming Mexican American: Ethnicity, Culture, and Identity in Chicano Los Angeles, 1900–1945*. New York: Oxford University Press, 1993.

———. "Face the Nation: Race, Immigration, and the Rise of Nativism in Late Twentieth Century America." *International Migration Review* 31, no. 4 (1997): 1009–30.

———. " 'Go after the Women': Americanization and the Mexican Immigrant Woman, 1915–1929." In *A Multi-Cultural Reader in U.S. Women's History*, edited by Ellen DuBois and Vicki Ruiz, 284–97. New York: Routledge, 1990.

———. "Race and Immigration History." *American Behaviorial Scientist* 42, no. 9 (1999): 1271–75.

———. "Race, Nation, and Culture in Recent Immigration Studies." *Journal of American Ethnic History* 18, no. 4 (1999): 66–84.

Sánchez, Rosaura. *Telling Identities: The Californio Testimonios*. Minneapolis: University of Minnesota Press, 1995.

Saxton, Alexander. *The Indispensable Enemy: Labor and the Anti-Chinese Movement in California*. Berkeley: University of California Press, 1970.

Schlesinger, Arthur, Jr. *The Disuniting of America: Reflections on a Multicultural Society*. New York: Norton, 1998.

Scott, Joan Wallach. *Gender and the Politics of History*. New York: Columbia University Press, 1988.

Shaffer, Ralph E. "Letters from the People: *Los Angeles Times*, 1881–1889." 1999. Retrieved May 3, 2005, from www.intranet.csupomona.edu/~reshaffer/contents.htm.

Shah, Nayan. *Contagious Divides: Epidemics and Race in San Francisco's Chinatown*. Berkeley: University of California Press, 2001.

Sides, Josh. *L.A. City Limits: African American Los Angeles from the Great Depression to the Present*. Berkeley: University of California Press, 2003.

Skocpol, Theda. *Protecting Soldiers and Mothers: The Political Origins of Social Policy in the United States*. Cambridge, MA: Harvard University Press, 1992.

Solinger, Rickie. *Beggars and Choosers: How the Politics of Choice Shapes Adoption, Abortion, and Welfare in the United States*. New York: Hill and Wang, 2001.

———. *Wake up Little Susie: Single Pregnancy and Race before Roe v. Wade*. New York: Routledge, 1992.

Spalding, Sophie. "The Myth of the Classic Slum: Contradictory Perceptions of Boyle Heights Flats, 1900–1991." *Journal of Architectural Education* 45, no. 2 (February 1992): 107–19.

Stallybrass, Peter, and Allon White. *The Politics and Poetics of Transgression*. Ithaca, NY: Cornell University Press, 1986.

Starr, Kevin. *Americans and the California Dream, 1850–1915*. New York: Oxford University Press, 1973.

———. *Inventing the Dream: California through the Progressive Era*. New York: Oxford University Press, 1985.

Stepan, Nancy. *The Hour of Eugenics: Race, Gender, and Nation in Latin America*. Ithaca, NY: Cornell University Press, 1991.

Stern, Alexandra. "Buildings, Boundaries, and Blood: Medicalization and Nation-Building on the U.S.-Mexican Border, 1910–1930." *Hispanic American Historical Review* 79, no. 1 (1999): 41–81.

———. *Eugenic Nation: Faults and Frontiers of Better Breeding in Modern America*. Berkeley: University of California Press, 2005.

———. "Eugenics beyond Borders: Science and Medicalization in Mexico and the U.S. West, 1900–1950." PhD diss., University of Chicago, 1999.

———. "Sterilized in the Name of Public Health and Population Policy: Race, Immigration, and Reproductive Control in Modern California." *American Journal of Public Health* 95 (July 2005).

Sugrue, Thomas. *The Origins of the Urban Crisis: Race and Inequality in Postwar Detroit*. Princeton, NJ: Princeton University Press, 1996.

Sun-Hee Park, Lisa. "Perpetuation of Poverty through Public Charge." *Denver University Law Review* 78 (2001): 1161–77.

Tagg, John. *The Burden of Representation: Essays on Photographies and Histories*. Amherst: University of Massachusetts Press, 1988. .

Takaki, Ronald. *Strangers from a Different Shore: A History of Asian Americans*. Boston: Little Brown, 1991.

Tomes, Nancy. *The Gospel of Germs: Men, Women, and the Microbe in American Life*. Cambridge, MA: Harvard University Press, 1998.

———. "The Private Side of Public Health: Sanitary Science, Domestic Hygiene, and the Germ Theory, 1870–1900." *Bulletin of the History of Medicine* 64, no. 4 (1990): 509–39.

Underwood, Katherine. "Process and Politics: Multiracial Electoral Coalition Building and Representation in Los Angeles' Ninth District, 1949–1962." PhD diss., University of California, San Diego, 1992.

Vélez-Ibáñez, Carlos G. " 'Se Me Acabó La Canción': An Ethnography of Non-Consenting Sterilizations among Mexican Women in Los Angeles." In *Mexican Women in the United States: Struggles Past and Present,* edited by Magdalena Mora and Adelaida Del Castillo, 71–91. Los Angeles: Chicano Studies Research Center, University of California, Los Angeles, 1980.

Villa, Raúl. *Barrio-Logos: Space and Place in Urban Chicano Literature and Culture.* Austin: University of Texas Press, 2000.

Viramontes, Helena Maria. *The Moths and Other Stories.* Houston, TX: Arte Público Press, 1985.

Wailoo, Keith. *Drawing Blood: Technology and Disease Identity in Twentieth-Century America.* Baltimore: Johns Hopkins University Press, 1999.

——— . *Dying in the City of the Blues: Sickle Cell Anemia and the Politics of Race and Health.* Chapel Hill: University of North Carolina Press, 2001.

Walkowitz, Judith. *City of Dreadful Delight: Narratives of Sexual Danger in Late-Victorian London.* Chicago: University of Chicago Press, 1992.

Weber, Devra. *Dark Sweat, White Gold: California Farm Workers, Cotton, and the New Deal.* Berkeley: University of California Press, 1994.

Weindling, Paul Julian. *Epidemics and Genocide in Eastern Europe.* New York: Oxford University Press, 2000.

Weiss, Marc. *The Rise of the Community Builders: The American Real Estate Industry and Urban Land Planning.* New York: Columbia University Press, 1987.

Wellborn, Mildred. "The Events Leading to the Chinese Exclusion Acts." *Southern California Quarterly* 9 (1912–13): 49–58.

Whalen, Carmen. *From Puerto Rico to Philadelphia: Puerto Rican Workers and Postwar Economies.* Philadelphia: Temple University Press, 2001.

White, Deborah Gray. *Ar'n't I A Woman? Female Slaves in the Plantation South.* New York: Norton, 1985.

White, Richard. *"It's Your Misfortune and None of My Own": A History of the American West.* Norman: University of Oklahoma Press, 1991.

Whorton, James C. *Crusaders for Fitness: The History of the American Health Reformers.* Princeton, NJ: Princeton University Press, 1982.

Wiebe, Robert. *The Search for Order, 1877–1920.* New York: Hill and Wang, 1967.

Wu, Judy Tzu-Chun. "Mom Chung of the Fair-Haired Bastards: A Thematic Biography of Doctor Margaret Chung, 1889–1959." PhD diss., Stanford University, 1998.

Yoo, David. *Growing up Nisei: Race, Generation, and Culture among Japanese Americans of California, 1924–49.* Urbana: University of Illinois Press, 2000.

Yu, Henry. *Thinking Orientals: Migration, Contact, and Exoticism in Modern America.* Oxford and New York: Oxford University Press, 2001.

Yu, Renqiu. *To Save China, to Save Ourselves: The Chinese Hand Laundry Alliance of New York.* Philadelphia: Temple University Press, 1992.

Index

Page numbers in *italics* indicate figures and maps.

Text:	10/13 Sabon
Display:	Sabon
Indexer:	Andrew Christenson
Cartographer:	Bill Nelson
Compositor, printer, and binder:	Sheridan Books, Inc.